ILLUSTRATED
CABINETMAKING

ILLUSTRATED CABINETMAKING

How to Design and Construct Furniture That Works

Bill Hylton
Illustrations by Frank Rohrbach
and Glenn Hughes

Reader's Digest

Pleasantville, New York/Montreal

Editor: Bill Hylton
Contributing Writers: Bob Moran, Tony O'Malley, and Robert A. Yoder
Cover and Interior Book Designer: Diane Ness Shaw
Layout Designer: Jerry O'Brien
Interior Illustrators: Frank Rohrbach and Glenn Hughes
Cover Illustrator: Frank Rohrbach
Copy Editors: Barbara McIntosh Webb and Sara Cox
Indexer: Nan N. Badgett

Library of Congress Cataloging-in-Publication Data

Hylton, Bill.
  Illustrated cabinetmaking : how to design and construct furniture that works / Bill Hylton ; illustrations by Frank Rohrbach with Glenn Hughes.
      p.   cm.
  Includes bibliographical references and index.
    ISBN 0-7621-0183-0 (hardcover)
    1. Furniture making—Amateurs' manuals.
  2. Cabinetwork—Amateurs' manuals.
  I. Reader's Digest Association   II. Title.
  TT195.H92   1998
  684.I'6—dc21   98-9725

Printed in the United States of America

4 6 8 10 9 7 5 3 (hardcover)

CONTENTS

OCCASIONAL TABLES

DESKS

CHESTS

CABINETS

BUILT-IN CABINETS

BEDS

INTRODUCTION

When it comes to furniture, we woodworkers like to put our own stamp on the things we make. At the least, we adapt published plans to suit our needs, changing the size or proportions a little, rearranging drawers, or changing the style of the doors. The plans may be excellent, but we've just got to put a personal touch on the piece.

More often than not, though, we like to go even further. Disdaining published plans altogether, we like to cook up our own. The inspiration for a project might be a photo in a magazine or catalog. It might be a special piece of furniture we need—bookshelves for all those woodworking books we've bought, a stand for the new television, a bed for the child who's outgrown a crib. And how often has your spouse asked you to make a table or chest like the one they've seen in a store or at a neighbor's house? Happens to me every now and then.

The inspiration is there. The desire is real. You've got the tools and materials. You've got the woodworking know-how.

But the tough part—always!—is figuring out how to construct the piece. Even when you have a picture of what you want to build, the picture isn't likely to reveal how it's put together. So you start off with a list of questions. What joints should you use? What's the best way to attach the top? Hang the drawers? How long should the legs be? How do you deal with wood movement?

Enter *Illustrated Cabinetmaking,* unarguably the most comprehensive visual guide to furniture construction and design ever published.

In hundreds of drawings, *Illustrated Cabinetmaking* takes you inside furniture and shows you classic solutions to age-old construction problems. You'll see five or six ways to hang a drawer, four ways to attach a tabletop, the best way to peg a mortise. Everything you need to know to construct beautiful—and sound—furniture is here.

The "Joints" section of the book is an illustrated encyclopedia of joints, showing how every joint imaginable—more than 100 of them—goes together. You'll find the best joints for your applications here (or you won't find them at all).

In the "Subassemblies" section, you'll see how to use those joints to assemble tabletops, doors, drawers, and feet. You'll see how drawers are installed in cases and in tables. You'll see how complex moldings are built up and installed.

And in the paramount section, "Furniture," you'll discover how to combine joints and subassemblies in constructing the final product: a beautiful, functional, durable piece of furniture. In this exhaustive section, you'll see more than 100 exploded drawings, showing every type of furniture imaginable—gateleg table, huntboard, rolltop desk, dresser, bureau, trestle table, high-post bed, step-back cupboard, bookshelves, kitchen cabinets, tall-case clock, and over 90 more. Most of these exploded drawings are supplemented by one or two close-up details that home in on particularly complex or tricky parts of the construction, making it all the more clear. Every construction drawing is clearly labelled. Cross-references direct you to other furniture pieces or other sections that depict alternative joints or alternative approaches to constructing a subassembly.

With each furniture archetype presented, you'll see a drawing of the assembled piece with its overall dimensions called out. You'll find tips on altering the appearance of the piece. And for all but a couple, there's even a short list of good published plans for similar pieces.

In addition, the book shows rule-of-thumb design standards. For example, How high should a dining table be? And how much space should each person sitting at it have? How deep are kitchen cabinets? Are there standards for setting up a desk for a computer? It's all here.

So with all this visual information and an easy-to-read, to-the-point text at your instant disposal, you can't help but have the confidence to tackle any project you want and modify it to suit your taste, your level of woodworking skill, or your equipment.

Bill Hylton

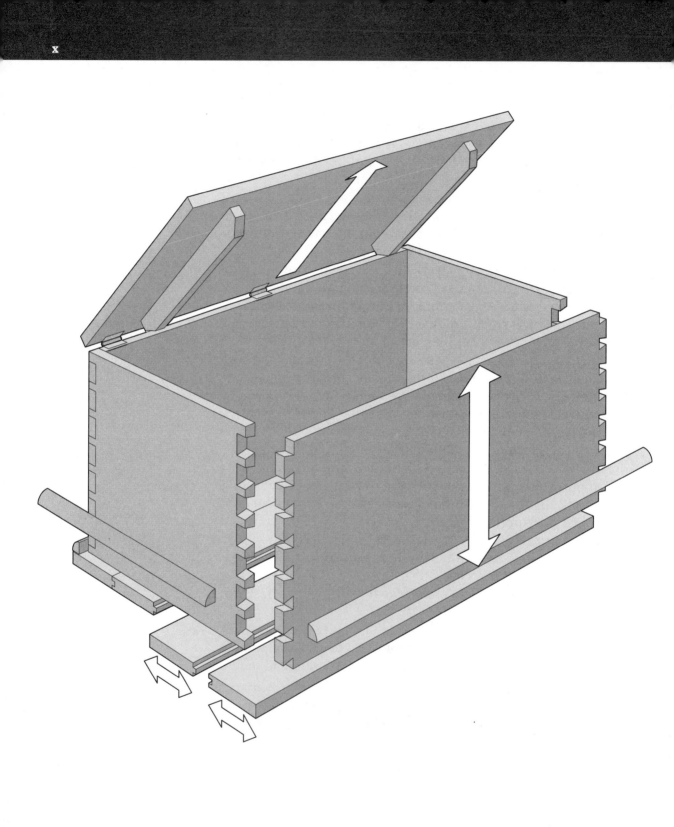

FUNDAMENTALS

FURNITURE
ANATOMY

H ere is a small dictionary of terms that are used to describe furniture parts. There are good reasons to be familiar with this nomenclature. It'll be easier to follow plans. You may find it easier to conceptualize a piece and how its components work together. And by getting to know all those parts, you'll become more aware of furniture styles and how they evolved. In other words, learning the terms can help you develop a sharper eye for identifying styles and appreciating good design and craftsmanship. If there is any truth to the saying that God is in the details, then it pays to get on a first-name basis with the details.

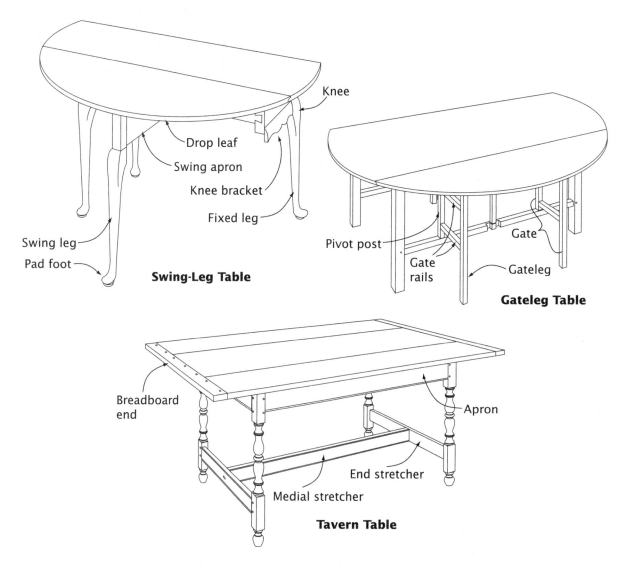

Knee

Drop leaf

Swing apron

Knee bracket

Fixed leg

Swing leg

Pad foot

Swing-Leg Table

Pivot post

Gate

Gate rails

Gateleg

Gateleg Table

Breadboard end

Apron

End stretcher

Medial stretcher

Tavern Table

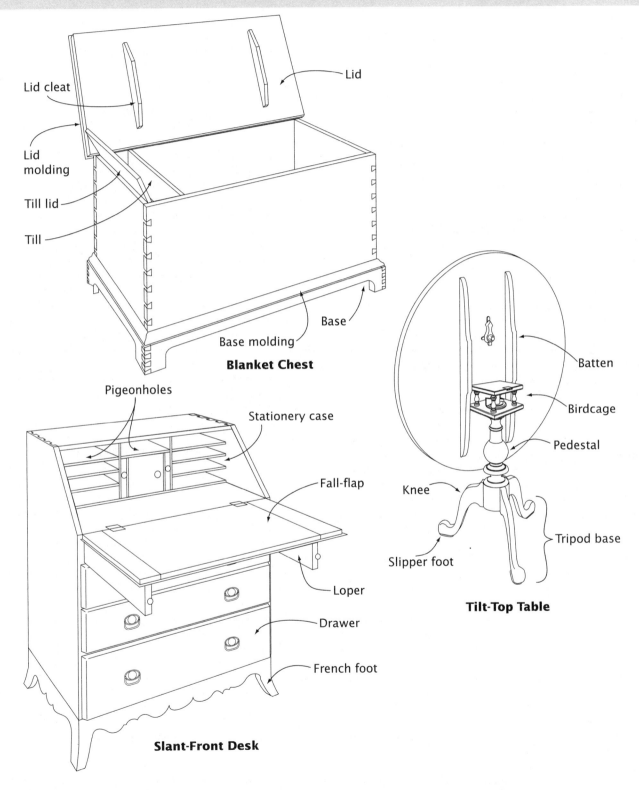

Blanket Chest

Lid cleat

Lid

Lid molding

Till lid

Till

Base

Base molding

Pigeonholes

Stationery case

Fall-flap

Loper

Drawer

French foot

Slant-Front Desk

Batten

Birdcage

Pedestal

Knee

Tripod base

Slipper foot

Tilt-Top Table

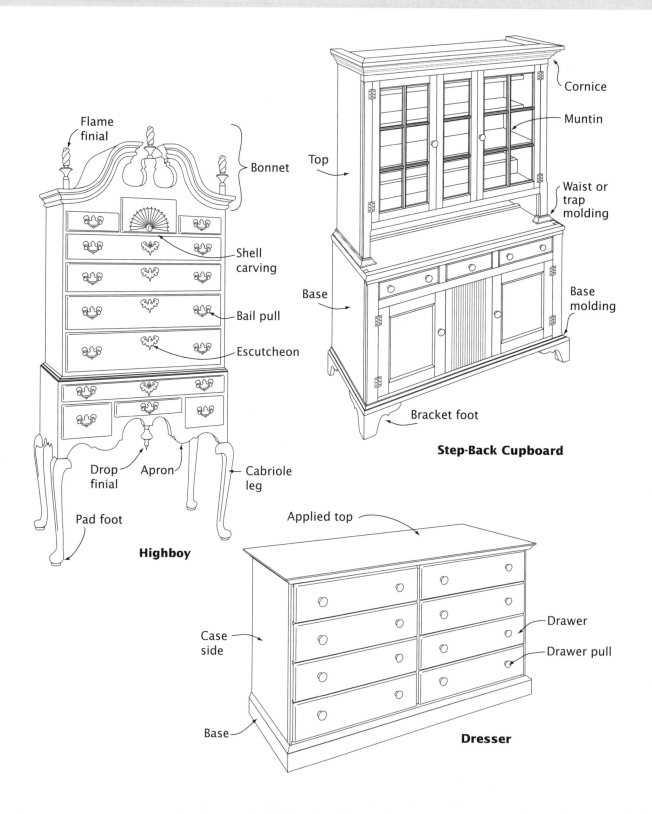

Flame finial

Bonnet

Shell carving

Bail pull

Escutcheon

Drop finial

Apron

Cabriole leg

Pad foot

Highboy

Cornice

Muntin

Top

Waist or trap molding

Base

Base molding

Bracket foot

Step-Back Cupboard

Applied top

Case side

Drawer

Drawer pull

Base

Dresser

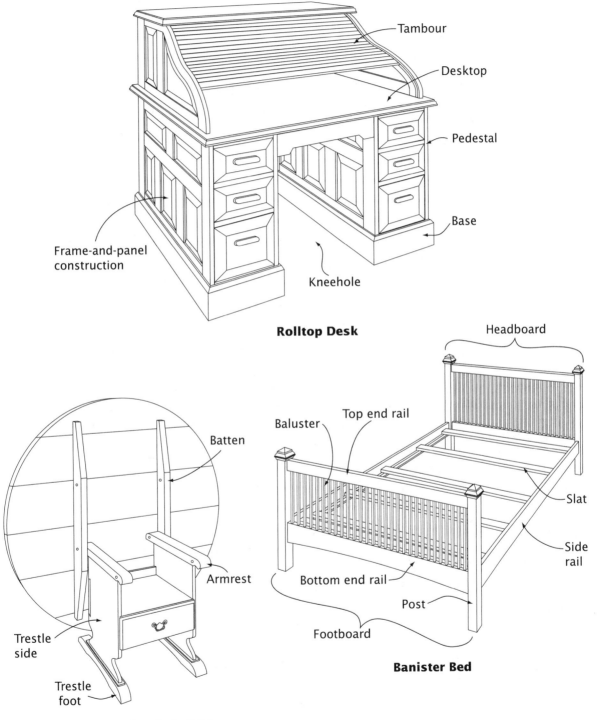

Rolltop Desk

Tambour

Desktop

Pedestal

Base

Kneehole

Frame-and-panel
construction

Settle Chair-Table

Batten

Armrest

Trestle
side

Trestle
foot

Banister Bed

Headboard

Baluster

Top end rail

Slat

Side
rail

Bottom end rail

Post

Footboard

FURNITURE
STYLES

For reasons both good and trivial, furniture weathers trends in popularity. Within just a few years, a chair that had been in vogue may look stale, even in poor taste. But it's a curiosity of furniture design—and human nature—that today's castoffs are destined to become tomorrow's treasures.

Recycling retro styles is nothing new. The Victorians revived classical, Gothic, renaissance, and colonial themes in a period of a few decades. Old styles continue to fascinate us.

You may have noticed that the terms for styles are somewhat tidier than history itself. These names were rarely in use when the furniture was produced, but were coined years later. A result is that there may be a couple of terms for the same style. Baroque and Queen Anne have been used interchangeably. So have rococo and Chippendale. Adding to the confusion, periods of style often overlap; in fact, a given piece of furniture may itself be a hybrid of two periods. Finally, it's impossible to nail down the birth-and-death dates for any style. Trends typically hatched abroad, migrated to our urban areas, then wended their way into the countryside.

The names of styles may be confusing, but they do serve as reminders of the historic lineage of the furniture we design and build. And within each style, we can learn to look for regional variations that are the pulse of the long-departed woodworkers themselves.

➤ PILGRIM: 1640 TO 1700

A colonial style based on medieval, Renaissance, and English designs, pilgrim furniture is also called Jacobean, from the Latin for James I of England. The furniture is sturdy but heavy, made of solid wood with mortise-and-tenon joinery. Characteristic features include:
- Heavy, simple turnings
- Split-spindle decorations
- Extensive carving
- Bulky perimeter stretchers

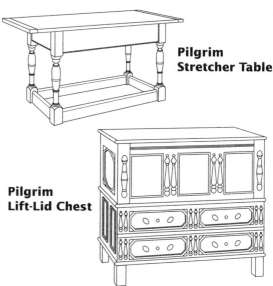

Pilgrim Stretcher Table

Pilgrim Lift-Lid Chest

➤ WILLIAM AND MARY: 1700 TO 1730

Named for the Dutch rulers who assumed the English throne and brought with them Dutch and French Huguenot influences, this style is also referred to as baroque. The furniture tends to be dark, using either walnut or lighter woods under an ebony finish. Characteristically, it has straight, angular lines and multiple turnings. Typical are:
- Sculptural carvings
- Vase, trumpet, and ball turnings
- Spanish (paintbrush) feet
- Teardrop pulls
- Decorative veneers

William and Mary Gateleg Table

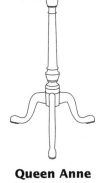

**William and Mary
Slant-Front Desk**

**William and Mary
Chest-on-Frame**

**Queen Anne
Tripod Table**

**Queen Anne
Tea Table**

➤ QUEEN ANNE: 1725 TO 1755

The gracefully curved lines of Queen Anne furniture contrast markedly with the angular lines of William and Mary designs. This style introduced the elegant, S-shaped cabriole leg to America, and indeed the cabriole leg is a prime style marker of the furniture. Makers of Queen Anne furniture favored walnut, as well as cherry, maple, and late in the period, mahogany.

Confusingly, this style was not influenced by England's Queen Anne, who died before the period. It overlaps both the earlier William and Mary and later Chippendale styles. Queen Anne style markers include:

- Fluid, curving lines
- Cabriole legs, pad feet
- Chinese ornamentation
- Delicately carved shells, rosettes, and leaves
- Finials on pediments
- Veneering on drawer fronts and chair splats
- Butterfly drawer pulls

**Queen Anne
Desk-on-Frame**

**Queen Anne
Handkerchief
Table**

**Queen Anne
Highboy**

**Queen Anne
Chest of Drawers**

▶ CHIPPENDALE: 1750 TO 1780

Named for the widely published London cabinetmaker Thomas Chippendale, and incorporating Chinese, Gothic, and rococo influences, Chippendale furniture represented a change in ornamentation more than form. Carving and fretwork decorated legs, aprons, and stretchers. The straight line was revived as a design element, and tables often had straight, untapered legs.

Mahogany was commonly used in this period, while favored domestic woods included walnut, maple, and cherry.

**Chippendale
Pembroke Table**

**Philadelphia
Chippendale Highboy**

**Chippendale
Bombé Chest**

**New York
Chippendale
Game Table**

Among the style markers of Chippendale furniture are:

- Serpentine and bombé case forms
- Piecrust tabletops
- Ornamental stretchers
- Ball-and-claw feet
- Chinese or Gothic fretwork
- Carved rococo shells
- Quarter columns on casework

▶ FEDERAL: 1780 TO 1820

Federal is the name used to delineate the early phase in America of the Neoclassical style, a style so-called because it looked back at ancient Rome and Greece. (Empire is the late phase of the style.) Federal was a reaction to the rococo flourishes of earlier furniture.

Curiously, the names of two English designers, Sheraton and Hepplewhite, are inextricably linked to Federal furniture. Each published a book of neoclassical designs that became popular in the United States. Based on their books, it is difficult to distinguish the designs of one from the other.

Although Europe and England embraced neoclassicism as passionately as America did, Federal has been called America's first home-grown style because its interpretation of neoclassicism is purely American. Characteristics of the style include:

- Thin, tapered legs
- Spade or arrow feet
- Tambour fronts
- Low-relief carving
- Use of veneer
- Delicate inlay

**Federal Swing-Leg
Card Table**

**Federal
Tripod Table**

Federal Secretary

Federal Serpentine-Front Chest

Federal Sideboard

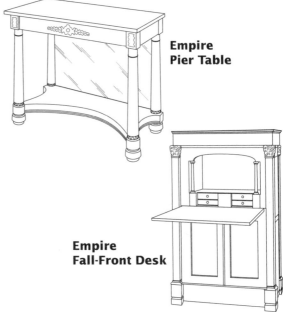

Empire Pier Table

Empire Fall-Front Desk

▶ COUNTRY: 1690 TO 1850

This is the catchall term for furniture produced outside the urban centers. As a type, this furniture is often regarded as being simplified—albeit uninhibited—versions of the rigidly styled forms produced in the cities. Country pieces put more emphasis on function than frills, and joinery is often practical and

▶ EMPIRE: 1815 TO 1840

The second phase of neoclassicism swept into America from Napoleonic France. Still inspired by classical Greek and Roman motifs, Empire furniture became heavier and far more ornate, with flamboyant decorative elements. Pieces are typically of mahogany, rosewood, and other exotic veneers. Common design motifs include:
- Turned half columns
- Saber legs
- Center pedestals
- Paw and C-scroll feet
- Bold carving
- Reeding
- Stenciling, painting, gilding

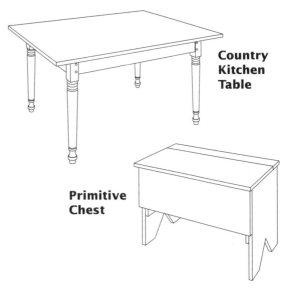

Country Kitchen Table

Primitive Chest

unsophisticated. Pine, poplar, cherry, walnut, and other native species are among the woods most often used. They frequently are painted to make up for their lack of fancy grain. Typically, the forms display:
- Simple moldings
- Simple scroll cuts
- Broad face frames
- Wooden pulls or latch closures
- Exposed hinges

**Country
Jelly Cupboard**

Country Tall Chest

► PENNSYLVANIA DUTCH: 1690 TO 1850

The tradition-loving Pennsylvania Dutch kept alive many characteristics of Old World furniture. Stolid construction harks back to medieval times, as does colorful folk painting. This furniture typically has:
- Simple bracket feet
- Straightforward pulls
- Drawers in base (of chest)

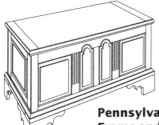

**Pennsylvania Dutch
Frame-and-Panel Chest**

**Pennsylvania Dutch
Wall Shelf**

**Pennsylvania
Dutch Hutch**

► SHAKER: 1820 TO 1870

The simple lines of this style were an expression of the values of the Shakers, a religious sect with celibate communities in several states. The woods most commonly used are pine and maple, and these blond species are often painted. In the main, Shaker furnishings have:
- No ornamental moldings
- Slender turnings
- Turned wooden knobs
- Plain feet

Shaker Sewing Desk

**Shaker
Sewing Table**

➤ VICTORIAN DESIGN REVIVALS

The Victorian era brought Gothic, rococo, and Renaissance revival styles, each producing more ornate designs than the last.

Gothic Revival

It's not known for certain just how this fascination with things medieval came about, but an interest in reading romantic Gothic novels may have been an inspiration—no doubt the only furniture style to have sprung from fiction. The heavy, brooding forms are constructed of rosewood, walnut, and dark-finished oak.

Rococo Revival

A French-inspired style, rococo revival is also known as French Antique or Louis XIV. The richness of the design is underscored by the use of rosewood veneer, walnut, and mahogany.

Renaissance Revival

A highly decorative Victorian style that draws on Renaissance and neoclassical motifs is the Renaissance revival. It was often built in walnut and ornamented with carved doodads and intriguing inlays, but lighter woods also found favor.

➤ DESIGN REFORM

By the mid–19th century, reformers heavily criticized the tasteless designs, misuse of ornamentation, and dominance of the machine. They urged an end to ornamentation and a return to handcrafted furniture.

Eastlake

Charles Locke Eastlake, one such British reformer, pared away the clutter of the preceding revival styles and published designs of straightforward oaken furniture with simple incised decoration. American examples evolved into elaborate offshoots. Characteristics include:
- Turned stiles and spindles
- Scroll-cut brackets
- Low-relief carving
- Inset decorative panels
- Light-colored finishes

Eastlake Dresser

Arts and Crafts/Mission

Arts and Crafts wasn't just a style, it was a movement. As an antidote to the industrial revolution, English designers John Ruskin and William Morris preached the value of restoring handicraft to making furniture. In America, the movement sparked the mission style, taking its name from the furniture of Franciscan missions in California. Oak was most frequently used. The grain may be emphasized with quarter-sawn stock and a fumed finish. Other characteristics include:
- Squarish components
- Exposed joinery
- Simple slat back
- Leather upholstery

Arts-and-Crafts Dresser

Arts-and-Crafts Wardrobe

WOOD
MOVEMENT

Long after it is harvested from the tree, wood continues to change in dimension. This presents a challenge to the woodworker, whose job it is to compose a sturdy, weight-bearing object. So, woodworking involves a repertoire of techniques for constraining wood while allowing some margin for its waywardness.

Wood begins life wet. On the stump, it is saturated with moisture. Fresh-cut "green" lumber oozes sap, and the bulk of this water must go before the wood is suitable for furniture making. There is a long tradition of using air-dried lumber, which is allowed to slowly give up its moisture to the atmosphere. But standard practice today is to dry it in a special kiln, using heat to drive down the wood's moisture level. Construction lumber may be ready to nail when reduced to 10 to 20 percent moisture, but wood for indoor furniture should be dried to half that range.

Of course, a board's moisture content doesn't stay put after drying. Wood will gain or lose moisture, depending upon the moisture content of the air surrounding it. When the wood arrives at a moisture content in balance with the air, we call it equilibrium moisture content, or EMC. When the humidity changes, wood moves to a new EMC, in balance with the new average humidity.

Moreover, a board doesn't always keep its tidy shape as it dries initially, or as it expands and contracts with the passage of time. Woodworkers know that the movement is primarily across the width of a board rather than along the board's length; that hardly changes at all. They also know that boards are prone to cup, bow, twist, diamond, and kink as their moisture content comes and goes. Many of these changes are a function of what part of the tree it came from and how it was sawn. The drawing *How Wood Moves* sums up most of this.

But there's more. Different species of wood have different rates of shrinkage. Some, like mahogany (a favorite of cabinetmakers for centuries), teak, redwood, catalpa, and northern white cedar, have reputations for stability; their dimensions change very little with humidity change. Others, like certain oaks, change rather dramatically and thus have reputations for being troublesome.

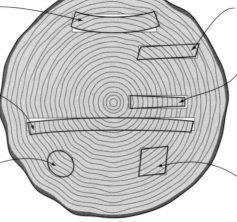

FLAT-SAWN: Cups away from heart of tree; shrinks much more in width than in thickness

THROUGH-AND-THROUGH: Boards follow above shrinkage patterns according to annual ring orientation

POST OR DOWEL: Shrinks to oval shape

RIFT-SAWN: Combines radial and tangential patterns

QUARTER-SAWN: Shrinks slightly in width and thickness; bark edge of board shrinks more in thickness than heartwood edge.

SQUARE BLOCK: Shrinks to diamond shape

How Wood Moves

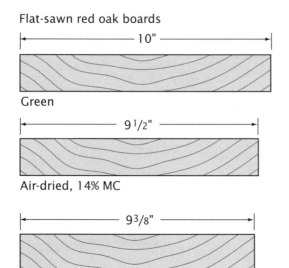

Flat-sawn red oak boards

|← 10" →|

Green

|← 9 1/2" →|

Air-dried, 14% MC

|← 9 3/8" →|

Kiln-dried, 7% MC

Range of Movement

A red oak board that was flat-sawn to a 10-inch width is shown in the drawing *Range of Movement*. Red oak is one of those troublesome woods. The 10-inch-wide board will shrink to a width of (approximately) 9 1/2 inches if air dried (to about a 14 percent moisture content). Kiln dry it to a 7 percent MC and its width will shrink to approximately 9 3/8 inches.

▶ DEALING WITH MOVEMENT

A cabinetmaker combines four of those red oak boards in a tabletop. In summer, when it is humid for a protracted period, the tabletop will be 38 inches wide. In winter, when central heat dries the air, the tabletop will shrink to a 37 1/2-inch width. That's a lot of movement! The cabinetmaker has to attach that tabletop to a leg-and-apron frame in a way that will accommodate that movement. (One way is shown in the drawing *Solid Panel Construction;* others, in "Tabletops" on page 78.)

But wood movement is a problem with almost any solid-wood panel—a lid, a door, a case side. It is going to move, so you've got to accommodate that movement.

Very early on, cabinetmakers came to grips with the issue of wood movement. A 2-foot-wide panel for a cabinet side might move 1/16 to 3/8 inch between summer and winter, depending upon the species of wood used. A case side can't be attached the way a tabletop can, so what to do?

Frame-and-panel construction: This approach developed early on. It is so effective that it is still widely used. The wide panel, which will move the most, is set into a frame in such a way that it can expand and contract

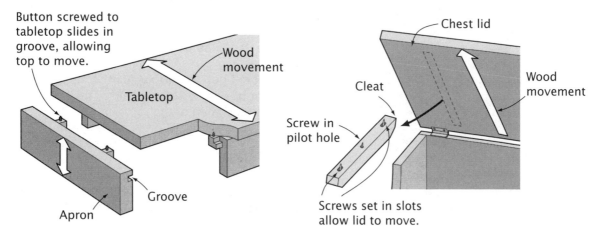

Button screwed to tabletop slides in groove, allowing top to move.

Wood movement

Tabletop

Groove

Apron

Chest lid

Cleat

Screw in pilot hole

Wood movement

Screws set in slots allow lid to move.

Solid Panel Construction

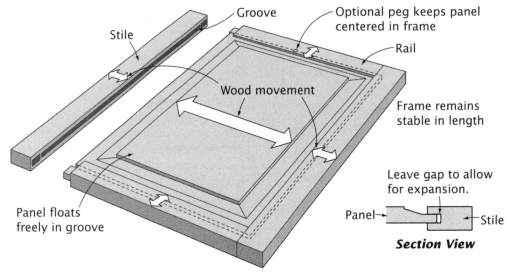

Groove

Optional peg keeps panel centered in frame

Stile

Rail

Wood movement

Frame remains stable in length

Leave gap to allow for expansion.

Panel→ ←Stile

Section View

Panel floats freely in groove

Frame-and-Panel Construction

without bursting the frame. Because it is made up of narrow members, the frame doesn't change much.

To make the typical frame, two rails are trapped between two stiles. The frame's length

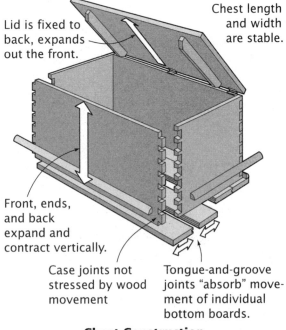

Lid is fixed to back, expands out the front.

Chest length and width are stable.

Front, ends, and back expand and contract vertically.

Case joints not stressed by wood movement

Tongue-and-groove joints "absorb" movement of individual bottom boards.

Chest Construction

is set by the stile length. And because normal wood doesn't move longitudinally, the frame's length won't change. Where the change in dimension comes is across the frame: The stiles will expand and contract. But the stiles are only, say, 2 inches wide, so even that red oak will move only about $1/32$ inch across each stile. Maxed out, that 24-inch-wide frame-and-panel assembly will expand only $1/16$ inch. A lot more manageable than $3/8$ inch.

The panel, being about $20 1/2$ inches wide, will expand and contract about $5/16$ to $3/8$ inch if it is red oak. And set in grooves in the frame, it can do that without damaging the frame.

Chest construction: Another approach to dealing with wood movement involves getting the grain of the parts uniformly oriented. A six-board chest, for example, properly has the grain of the front, sides (or ends), and back extending horizontally. These parts are joined end-grain to end-grain. As the wood expands, the chest gets a little taller. But the joinery is unaffected. When a bottom is attached, the cabinetmaker has to deal only with the movement of the bottom itself, not the chest.

Case construction: Stand a chest on end, and it becomes a case. Having all the boards uniformly oriented ensures that the parts will move in tandem. The problems arise when cross-grain elements like drawer runners and moldings are introduced. Now the parts are moving in two different, conflicting directions. The tensions that result can crack case sides and pop moldings off.

Many solutions to these cross-grain construction problems have been developed. Just one is shown in the drawing *Case Construction*. Others are shown in "Casework" (page 84) and "Moldings" (page 119).

With a chest of drawers, the cabinetmaker has an additional challenge. Because a drawer is like a chest, it will get taller in high humidity. But because of how the case is constructed, the drawer opening height is stable. The size of the opening must account for this wood movement, or the drawer will stick.

▶ NOT QUITE WOOD

The spunky variability of solid wood can be tamed by converting it to plywood or medium-density fiberboard (MDF). Plywood is composed of thin plies of real wood, of course; but each is positioned at right angles to its neighboring layers, helping to neutralize the effects of movement. MDF is made up of wood particles that are too small and scattered to influence the board.

You wouldn't want to feature sheets of these materials on the face of a traditional piece, of course, but they serve dependably as backs and other seldom-seen components.

▶ FINISHING

Finishes can't prevent wood's natural moisture exchange—nothing can stop it entirely—but many modern furniture finishes will slow it (oil finishes are less effective). Make sure to apply finish over all surfaces of a piece, and not just to visible areas; uneven moisture exchange is an invitation to warping. A project built of kiln-dried wood and finished on all sides will rarely succumb to extreme wood movement. This is because the finish allows the wood to absorb only a limited quantity of water before seasonal changes cause it to lose water again, thus limiting the overall range of movement.

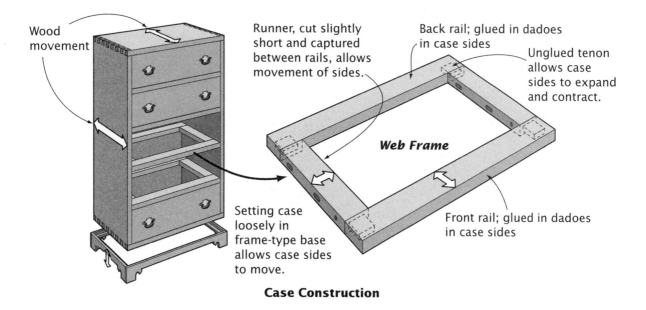

Wood movement

Runner, cut slightly short and captured between rails, allows movement of sides.

Back rail; glued in dadoes in case sides

Unglued tenon allows case sides to expand and contract.

Web Frame

Setting case loosely in frame-type base allows case sides to move.

Front rail; glued in dadoes in case sides

Case Construction

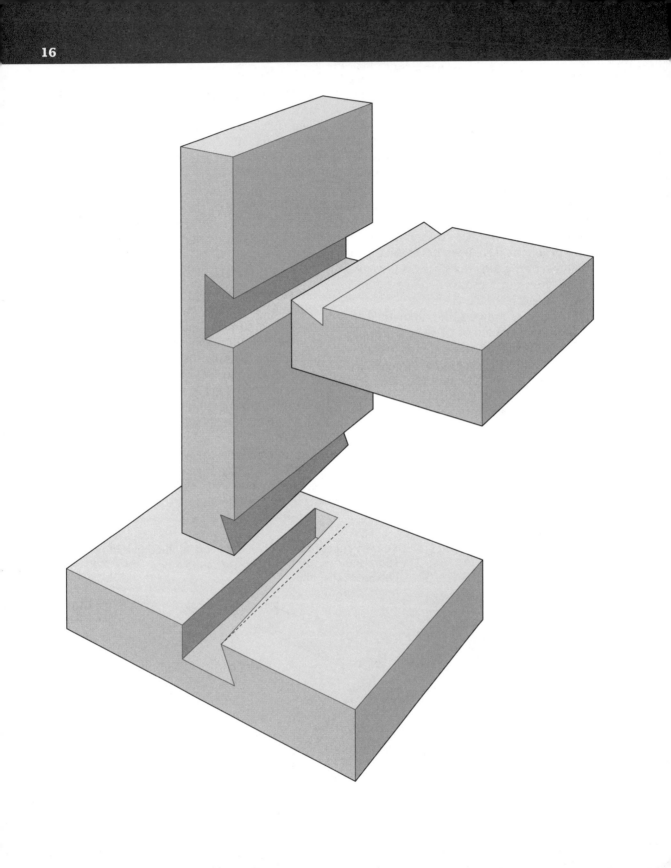

JOINTS

EDGE JOINTS

Two hundred years ago, a six-board chest was built with, literally, six boards, each 2 or more feet wide. The mammoth trees that yielded such boards are long gone. Nowadays, trees are slender and yield mostly narrow boards. To create a 2-foot-wide panel, several narrow boards must be assembled edge-to-edge with edge joints. To build a six-board chest today might require as many as two dozen boards.

A reasonable question: Will that glued-up panel be as strong as a single board?

The answer is yes. Glued edge joints are very strong. The long grain in the surfaces that are being joined glues well. And because you are gluing one long-grain surface to another long-grain surface, you aren't going to introduce a conflict due to wood movement.

The edge-to-edge joint is only one of the three common types of edge joints. The other two are edge-to-face and face-to-face.

Edge-to-edge is a joint in which flat, narrow boards are set out side by side and pulled together in interlocking and/or glued joints, forming wider boards.

Edge-to-face is a joint in which the narrow surface, or edge, of one board is joined to the broad surface, or face, of another. Sometimes collectively called corner edge joints, they form the vertical corners of cabinets and columns.

Face-to-face is a joint in which the face of one board is joined to the face of another. When you need a leg blank that is 3 inches square in section, you may have to glue up this blank from thinner boards. You can do the same thing when you need a massive section, wide and thick, as for a sturdy bench seat, a beam, or the top of a workbench.

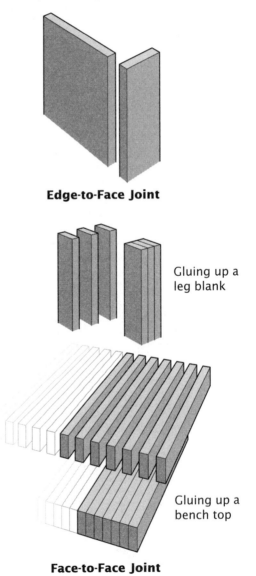

Edge-to-Face Joint

Gluing up a leg blank

Gluing up a bench top

Face-to-Face Joint

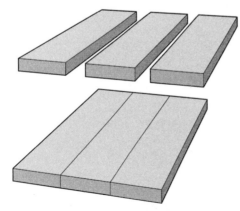

Edge-to-Edge Joint

➤ BUTT JOINTS

In edge joinery, where the joints are long-grain to long-grain, the simple butt joint is most effective, especially when the stock is well machined and you are using a modern glue. Splines, biscuits, or dowels don't make the joint stronger.

Edge-to-Edge

Despite the strength of the glued edge-to-edge joint, many woodworkers also use biscuits, splines, or dowels. Machining the stock for them is extra work that usually doesn't pay. For a complex assembly, however, or with wood that's mildly bowed, these alignment devices can help a great deal.

Biscuited edge-to-edge joint: Biscuit joinery can ensure close alignment at the surface of a joint, while permitting a surprising amount of end-to-end movement—as much as 1/4 inch. Biscuits come in three standard sizes. Always use the largest that will fit.

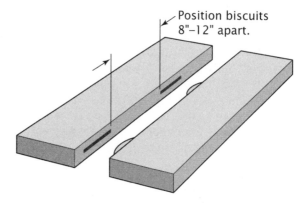

Position biscuits 8"–12" apart.

Biscuited Edge-to-Edge Joint

Splined edge-to-edge joint: One of the best edge-joint alignment tools is the spline. Grooves (either through or stopped) are cut in the adjoining edges. A strip of plywood or hardboard is fit into the grooves as you glue up the joint, making alignment easier. Fit the spline carefully so it won't push the boards apart if the wood shrinks.

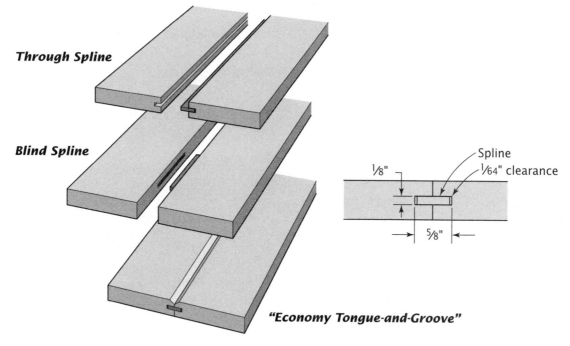

Through Spline

Blind Spline

Spline
1/64" clearance
1/8"
5/8"

"Economy Tongue-and-Groove"

Splined Edge-to-Edge Joints

Doweled edge-to-edge joint: Dowels are not a good alignment option. It is extremely difficult, first of all, to drill precisely matching holes in the mating boards; and it's equally difficult to get all the holes parallel to the face of the wood. Even if you succeed in this, dowels make a good edge joint bad by introducing a cross-grain element to a long-grain joint. If the wood shrinks, the dowels can push the joint apart.

Butterfly key: A traditional fastener used for edge-to-edge joints in Japan is the butterfly key. It is often used in contemporary furniture as a decorative element, as well as a functional one. The key can be used to join boards without glue, especially where they might later need to be disassembled.

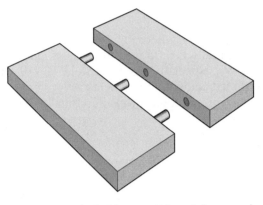

Doweled Edge-to-Edge Joint

Edge-to-Face

The vertical corners of cabinets and furniture present a problem in combining strength and ease of assembly. Since the mating surfaces of the two parts consist entirely of long grain, the simple butt joint has all the strength it will ever need. No additional reinforcement is necessary. There is no cross-grain instability to worry about, since the parts are parallel to one another.

Glued edge-to-face joint: The easiest corner joint to cut is a simple butted corner joint. The parts will glue up into a very strong assembly. The appearance can suffer if there's a contrast between the grain of the two parts. The seam between the two parts can be concealed by cutting a V-groove on it.

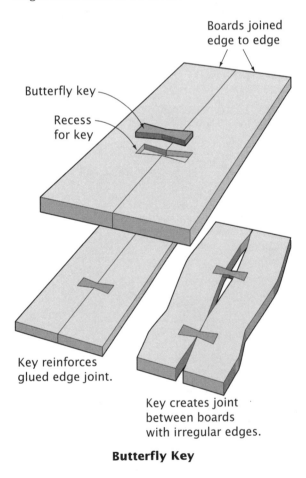

Boards joined edge to edge

Butterfly key

Recess for key

Key reinforces glued edge joint.

Key creates joint between boards with irregular edges.

Butterfly Key

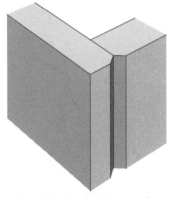

Glued Edge-to-Face Joint

Fastened edge-to-face joint: Fasteners can be used in an edge-to-face joint instead of, or in addition to, glue. While the fasteners won't strengthen a glued joint, they can eliminate the need to clamp the joint until the glue cures.

Biscuited edge-to-face joint: Keeping a butted corner joint aligned during assembly is the perfect job for biscuits. Use one every 8 inches to maintain alignment. But don't expect them to strengthen the joint.

Splined edge-to-face joint: Another joint alignment approach is the full-length spline. The mating parts are grooved (either through or stopped) for a plywood or hardboard spline.

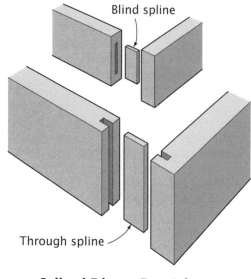

Splined Edge-to-Face Joint

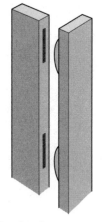

Finishing nail

Screw, set flush

Screw, countersunk and concealed by plug

Fastened Edge-to-Face Joint

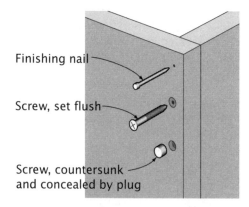

Biscuited Edge-to-Face Joint

▶ TONGUE-AND-GROOVE JOINTS

The tongue-and-groove joint is the older brother of the splined-edge joint. Instead of being separate, the spline is an integral part of the board. In furniture, it is found in case backs, tabletops, and other panels. It's the joint traditionally used in breadboard constructions.

It is probably most common in applications where it is not glued. It provides a mechanical lock between boards that are fastened to another surface or a frame rather than to each other. This allows the boards to expand and contract without adverse effect. It also provides a rudimentary aesthetic—the wood can shrink without opening the joint enough to expose whatever is behind it.

Tongue-and-groove joints are usually made with a tongue that's about one-third the thickness of the stock. Thus, the tongue and the two walls of the groove are all about the same strength.

The length of the tongue (and the depth of the groove) is less important than its thickness. If the boards are less than 3 inches wide, and therefore unlikely to expand and contract very much, make the tongues as long as they are thick and cut the grooves to match. If the boards are wider, make the tongues as long as half the stock thickness and the grooves about 1/16 inch deeper.

The bead or V-groove commonly seen on the face of a tongue-and-groove joint is camouflage. It's there to disguise an opening that varies in width due to the seasonal expansion and shrinkage of the boards.

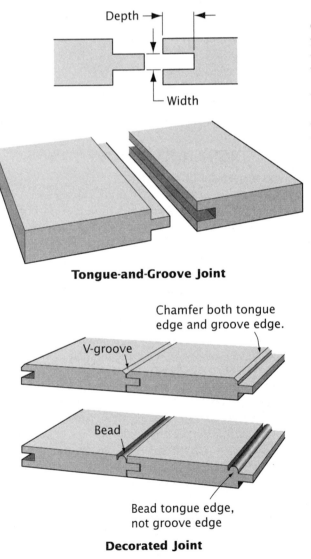

Tongue-and-Groove Joint

Chamfer both tongue edge and groove edge.

V-groove

Bead

Bead tongue edge, not groove edge

Decorated Joint

➤ RABBET JOINTS

A rabbet is an L-shaped cut made into the edge of a board. When a second board is set into the cut, it creates a rabbet joint. This is a right-angle joint, used in joining edge grain to face grain. There are a few variations.

Single-rabbet joint: This is a joint formed when only one of the mating parts is rabbeted. Typically, the rabbet is proportioned so its width matches the thickness of the mating board. This proportion yields a flush fit.

A useful variation puts a chamfer on the edge of the rabbet. The chamfer separates the face grain of one part from the edge grain of the other. Since the chamfer is at an angle to both faces, it will look good regardless of grain pattern differences.

A secondary variation produces a very attractive reversed corner detail, which can be emphasized with paint or a decorative molding

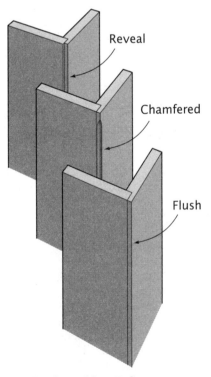

Reveal

Chamfered

Flush

Single-Rabbet Joint

and then glued in place after assembly. To produce this reveal, the rabbet's width is cut slightly less than the mating part's thickness.

Double-rabbet joint: A bit of an interlock can be created by rabbeting both of the mating boards.

Rabbet-and-groove joint: This is a good rack-resistant joint that assembles easily because both boards are positively located. The groove doesn't have to be big; often it's a single saw kerf, no deeper than one-third the board's thickness. Into it fits an offset tongue created on the mating board by the rabbet.

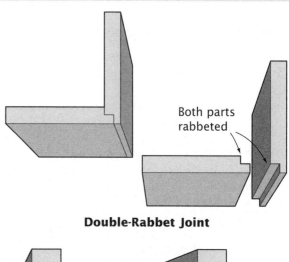

Both parts rabbeted

Double-Rabbet Joint

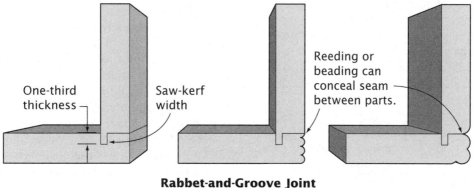

One-third thickness

Saw-kerf width

Reeding or beading can conceal seam between parts.

Rabbet-and-Groove Joint

> **SHIPLAP JOINT**

A substitute for the tongue-and-groove joint is the shiplap. It is formed by cutting identical rabbets cut into opposite faces of the adjoining boards. The rabbeted edges are then overlapped, preventing visible gaps from opening between the boards.

The joint can't keep the surfaces of the boards flush, however. This difference makes the tongue-and-groove clearly superior. Nevertheless, the shiplap is adequate if the wood is stable and the design allows you to fasten the parts at frequent intervals, as you can when attaching a back to every shelf of a bookcase or hutch.

This joint's advantage is that it can be cut much more quickly than a tongue-and-groove and with simpler tools.

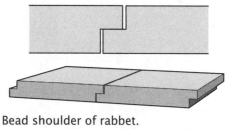

Bead shoulder of rabbet.

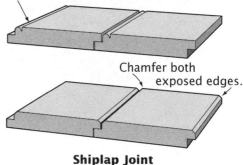

Chamfer both exposed edges.

Shiplap Joint

➤ EDGE MITER JOINTS

Tightly crafted, the miter joint is almost totally hidden: There's a barely discernible seam, and *right there,* the wood changes direction sharply. You don't see any end grain.

The worst thing about the joint is that it is vexing to assemble. Because of the angles involved, a mitered corner always wants to slide out of line when you apply clamping pressure to it.

Glued edge miter: As with all of the other long-grain edge joints, glue alone is enough to hold an edge miter together. The advantage of the miter is that it has *more* gluing surface than a butt joint.

Nevertheless, glue blocks, either a continuous strip or short blocks spaced along the joint, can be used to reinforce the miter. A plus here is that the grain of the glue blocks parallels that of the joining boards, so wood movement isn't a problem.

Fastened edge miter: The need for clamping a glued joint can be eliminated if fasteners are used. Position nails or screws as shown.

Biscuited edge miter: Biscuits in a miter joint prevent the beveled edges from slipping sideways as you apply clamping pressure. How well they function depends on how snugly the biscuits fit and how closely you space them. You have no control over the fit of manufactured biscuits, but you can improve things by spacing them closely, say every 3 or 4 inches.

Splined edge miter: Adding a long-grain, solid-wood spline is a good way to keep an edge miter joint aligned as you're gluing up. Keep in mind that the spline doesn't make the joint appreciably stronger; in fact, if the spline isn't placed properly, it may actually weaken the joint.

Make the width of the groove equal to the thickness of the saw blade, locate it as shown in the drawing, and don't go deeper than a third of the way through the wood.

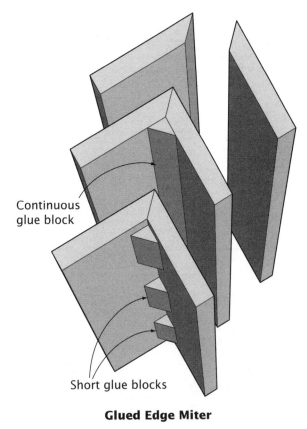

Continuous glue block

Short glue blocks

Glued Edge Miter

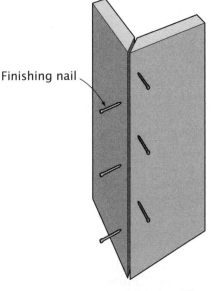

Finishing nail

Fastened Edge Miter

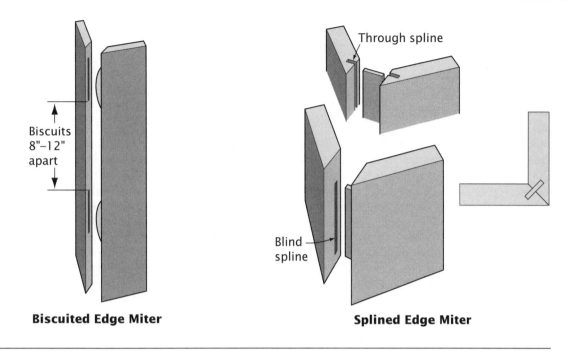

Biscuited Edge Miter

Biscuits
8"–12"
apart

Through spline

Blind
spline

Splined Edge Miter

➤ ROUTED EDGE JOINTS

Woodworkers are constantly seeking the perfect edge joint, one that provides a maximum of glue surface as well as some form of mechanical interlock to force the boards into perfect alignment during assembly.

Router bit manufacturers have come up with a variety of special bits for edge joinery. All the bits are for router table use only, and each requires but a single setup. The edge configurations they produce offer all the characteristics of the perfect joint.

Glue Joint: The simplest of the bits produces a sort of tongue-and-rabbet profile.

The idea is that one board in a joint is routed face up, the other face down. If the boards are flat and the height of the bit is just right, the two boards will fall together with their faces flush.

Because of the interlock, the boards can't shift up or down. It's important to mark the boards clearly so you orient each one correctly when making the cuts.

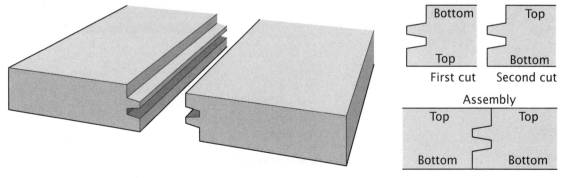

Bottom		Top
Top		Bottom
First cut		Second cut

Assembly

Top		Top
Bottom		Bottom

Glue Joint

Finger joint: This joint is a positive-negative interlock, in which tapered projections (the fingers) on one piece fit into tapered grooves in the other. The profile expands the glue area threefold. You can use it to join boards edge-to-edge and, with some trepidation, end-to-end.

The cutting sequence is the same as with the previously described specialty bits. You rout one workpiece's edge with the stock face up and the other piece with the stock face down. When the bit height is correct, the two pieces should slide together with their faces perfectly flush.

Lock miter joint: This joint can be used for edge-to-edge joinery as well as edge-to-face. Both joints are easy to assemble, and in either arrangment, the routed joint's glue area is significantly larger than that of a plain glue joint.

One setup suffices for cuts on both pieces to be joined. To use the joint in an edge-to-face arrangement, one panel is machined while it's flat on the router table, the other while on edge against the fence. To produce an edge-to-edge arrangement, one board is machined with its face down, the other with its face up.

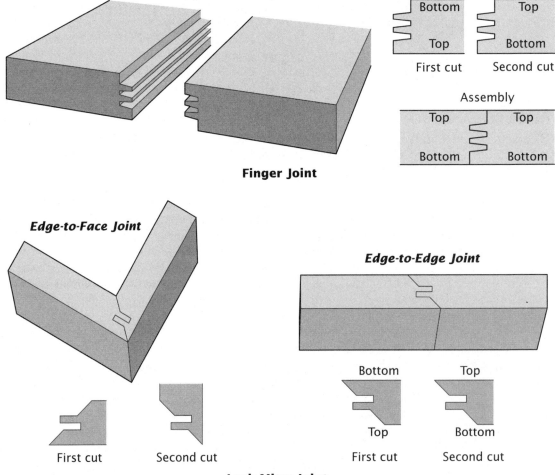

Finger Joint

Lock Miter Joint

CASE JOINTS

In case construction, boards are joined end-to-end to create a box. In the corner joints used in case construction, strength comes from two potential sources: the mechanical interlocking of the pieces and the glue and/or fasteners used to hold them together.

Fortunately, with case joints, strength usually is not the main issue: Case furniture typically stands, unmoving, supporting itself and whatever is stored inside. The common corner joints shown below have more than enough interlocking wood and gluing area to resist these static loads. While racking stress can be a problem in large cases, interior dividers add stiffness, as does a frame-and-panel or plywood back.

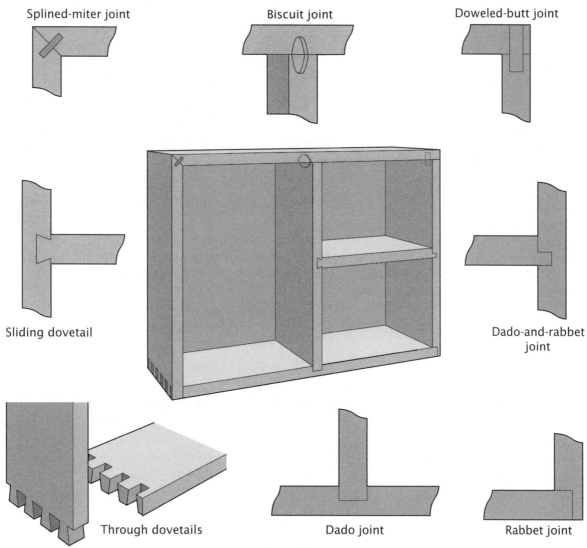

Splined-miter joint

Biscuit joint

Doweled-butt joint

Sliding dovetail

Dado-and-rabbet joint

Through dovetails

Dado joint

Rabbet joint

Case Joints

➤ BUTT JOINTS

Butt joints need help if they are to be good case joints. They present a poor situation for gluing, and they lack any sort of mechanical interlock. To make a sturdy butt joint, you need to reinforce the joint.

Glued butt joint: The butt joint gets its name from the fact that one board is butted against the other. In case joinery, this places the end grain of one board against the face grain of its mate. Because end grain glues poorly to face grain, this is not a sturdy joint.

Butt joint with glue block: Glue blocks are triangular or square pieces of wood used to strengthen and support two adjoining surfaces. They can be continuous or intermittent. In case joinery, glue blocks generally are a cross-grain construction.

Butt joint with fasteners: A faster, and less problematic, way to reinforce a butt joint is with fasteners. For additional strength, drive nails at an angle into the wood as shown.

Doweled butt: Dowels, used like nails, can reinforce a butt joint. While this joint is often shown with blind dowels, constructing it that way is extremely difficult. Instead, assemble the joint, then drill holes and drive dowels. You'll have a strong joint, and the exposed dowel ends can be a decorative element.

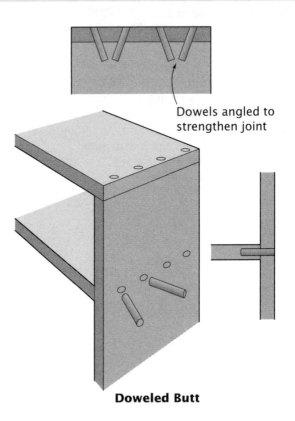

Dowels angled to strengthen joint

Doweled Butt

Biscuited butt: A popular way to reinforce a butt joint is with biscuits. Matching slots are cut into the end grain of one piece and into the face grain of the other. At assembly, a football-shaped wooden wafer,

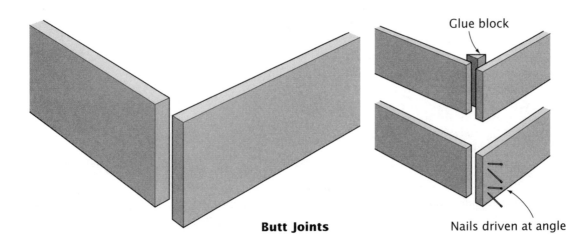

Glue block

Butt Joints

Nails driven at angle

or biscuit, is glued into each pair of adjoining slots, as shown.

Where a horizontal board tops an upright, the biscuits should be offset. Likewise, biscuits used in joining a shelf to an upright should be located below center to increase the shelf's resistance to toploading.

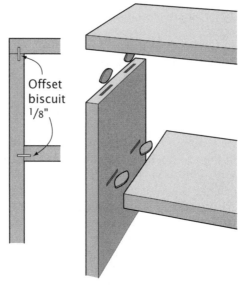

Biscuited Butt

➤ DOVETAIL JOINTS

The dovetail joint was developed (before reliable glues and cheap fasteners were available) as a very utilitarian means of holding pieces of wood together. It has some major advantages. The dovetail allows expansion and contraction of the wood without losing any of its structural integrity. This is extremely desirable when joining large pieces of wood, such as cases. It can be

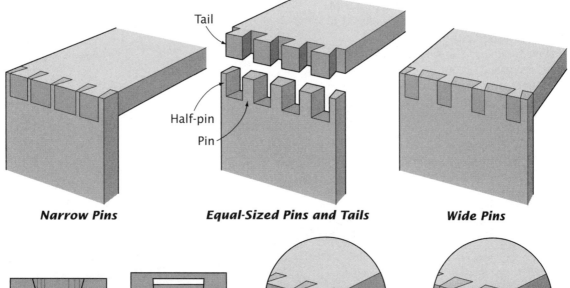

| Narrow Pins | Equal-Sized Pins and Tails | Wide Pins |

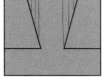 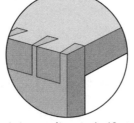 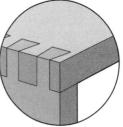

Too much slope   Too little slope   Joint ending in half-pin   Joint ending in half-tail

Dovetail Particulars

used to good advantage in "natural wood" projects.

The dovetail consists of "pins," which fit into triangular sockets between the "tails." The pin at the edge of the board is called a half-pin, not because it is half as wide as the others but because it slopes on only one face. Likewise, the tail at the end of the joint is called a half-tail.

The strength of the joint derives from two things: the interlocking pins and tails and an expansive glue area. The more pins and tails, the stronger the joint will be.

The traditional dovetail joint has broad tails and small pins, with the tails cut in the horizontal piece of wood. Layouts, however, vary widely. Two design factors must be considered in laying out the joint:

Dovetail spacing: There's no need to space dovetails uniformly. On a wide joint, they often have close pins and small tails near the edges, which has the effect of putting three or four glue lines in the first inch of width, helping to resist cupping.

Dovetail angle: The slope, or gradient, should not vary. If your dovetails have too little slope, they surrender part of their mechanical strength and begin to look like the fingers of a box joint. If they have too much slope, the short grain at the tips of the tails will be weakened and may break off during assembly.

Through dovetails: This is the basic dovetail joint. Both pieces go completely through each other, and the joint is visible on the outside surfaces of both pieces.

Decorative dovetails: A standard through dovetail is attractive enough, but try varying the size, spacing, and shapes of the pins and tails. Shown are just three of the (probably) endless possibilities—all hand-cut.

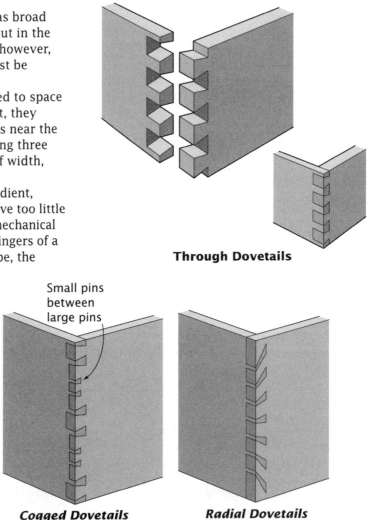

Through Dovetails

Extra pins at edges keep wood flat.

Small pins between large pins

Varied Spacing of Pins and Tails

Cogged Dovetails

Radial Dovetails

Decorative Dovetails

Dovetails with mitered shoulders:
Viewed from the edge, an assembled through dovetail looks like a butt joint. If the appearance of a mitered corner is your desire, it can be fulfilled. Normally, a dovetail joint begins and ends with a half-pin, but here you should start (and end) with a half-tail.

Half-blind dovetails: Though it is THE traditional means of joining drawer fronts to sides, the half-blind dovetail bears the stigma of being the machine-cut dovetail.

Unlike a through dovetail, which is visible from both the front and side, the half-blind dovetail can be seen only from the side.

Full-blind dovetails: Here is the dovetail joint that looks like a miter joint. It is used where the strength of dovetails—but not their appearance—is needed. When the joint is closed, both pins and tails are concealed. The joint is sometimes called the secret mitered dovetail.

Full-Blind Dovetails

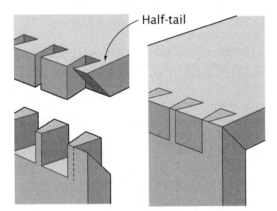

Dovetail with Mitered Shoulder

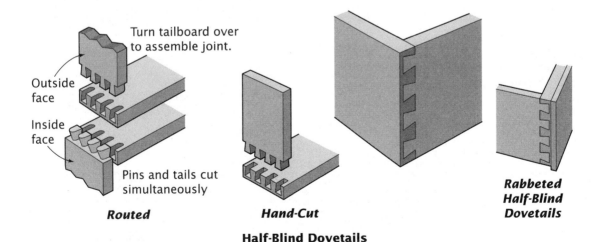

Half-Blind Dovetails

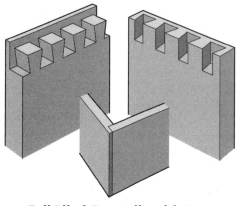

Full-Blind Dovetails with Lap

Full-blind dovetails with lap: This dovetail joint could easily be taken for a rabbet joint. The pinboard is worked as if for a half-blind dovetail. Like the pins, the tails are formed using stopped cuts. Thus both pins and tails are concealed within the joint.

Sliding dovetail: This joint is a hybrid of the dado and the dovetail. One of the mating pieces has a groove plowed in it, the other has a tongue formed on it; the tongue fits in the groove. Because both the groove walls and the tongue sides are angled like dovetail slots or pins, the joint has to be assembled by sliding the tongue into the groove.

One advantage of the joint is its mechanical strength. Even without glue, the mating pieces will stay linked together.

Another advantage is that the joint allows the parts to move without coming apart. A good example of this is a tabletop's breadboard end, as shown in *Sliding Half-Dovetail.*

Tapered sliding dovetail: The tapered sliding dovetail—if cut with precision—allows especially easy assembly but closes extremely tightly. Both the pin and the groove are tapered. The narrow end of the pin enters the wide end of the groove and slides effortlessly through the groove. But as the groove closes down on the pin, the joint gets tight.

Sliding half-dovetail: This joint has an angled side and a straight side, as shown in the drawing, and can be made in both uniform and tapered versions.

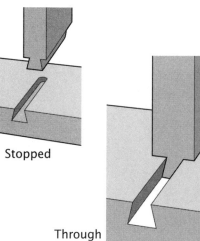

Stopped

Through

Sliding Dovetail

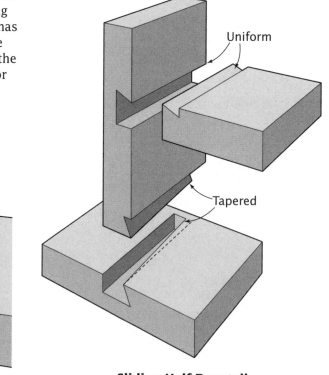

Uniform

Tapered

Sliding Half-Dovetail

➤ BOX JOINTS

The box joint is a sort of square-pinned, machine-cut through dovetail. It doesn't benefit from the wedging effect of dovetails, but it nevertheless does have good mechanical strength. Its many fingers create a great deal of long grain–to–long grain gluing area (the sort of glue area that yields the strongest bonding). Thus, it's hard to beat it for strength.

Typically, each of the joining pieces has an alternating pattern of equally sized fingers and slots. The fingers of one piece line up with the slots on the other piece. Usually, the width of the fingers is equal to stock thickness. Thin fingers, with a width less than the stock thickness, are more work to cut, but they yield a stronger joint.

The box joint's one major limitation is its checkerboard appearance.

Decorative box joint: A box joint with equally spaced fingers has a certain spare elegance. You can soften the joint's severity by varying proportions and spacing. The joint is much more difficult to cut, of course.

Angled box joint: With the proper setup, box joints can be cut for parts that join at something other than a 90-degree angle.

Half-blind box joint: Like the half-blind dovetail, this joint can be seen only from one side. It is a reasonable alternative to the half-blind dovetail.

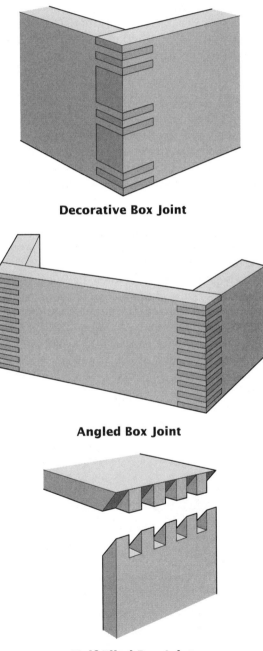

Decorative Box Joint

Angled Box Joint

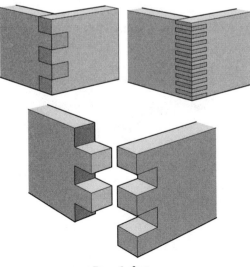

Box Joint

Half-Blind Box Joint

▶ END MITER JOINTS

A miter joint hides the end grain of both of its components. In its most basic form, it is made by mitering the ends of both components at 45 degrees, then butting these ends together.

A significant problem is that seasonal expansion and contraction of wood opens up even the best-fitting miter joint. Few stay tight over their lifetime. Nevertheless, the miter joint is tremendously useful.

End miter: This joint is weak for two reasons: The components don't interlock, and the glue surfaces are essentially end grain.

A simple way to strengthen the joint is with nails. Driving nails into both sides of a miter locks it together. Keep the nails toward the inside of the joint, and drill pilot holes for them to avoid splitting the stock.

Diagonally splined end miter: Though not as strong as the dovetail or the box joint, the splined miter is a workable case joint.

The spline can run either the full length of the joint or only partway. The latter is called a *blind-splined miter.* The spline should be placed close to the inner corner. This way, the slot can be as deep as possible without weakening the case sides.

Biscuited end miter: The biscuit is an alternative to the spline. Unlike the through slots for splines, the cuts for biscuits are intermittent and won't introduce the weaknesses. Thus, they can be anywhere between the middle and the inside edge.

Box-jointed loose tenons: This joint offers the strength of a box joint and the clean appearance of a miter joint; but while its combination of features is appealing, the joint is neither quick nor easy to make. The boards or panels to be joined must be mitered, then

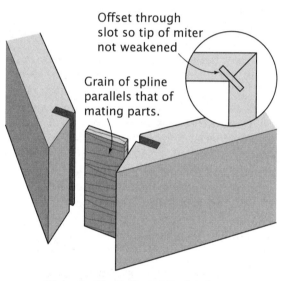

Offset through slot so tip of miter not weakened

Grain of spline parallels that of mating parts.

Diagonally Splined End Miter

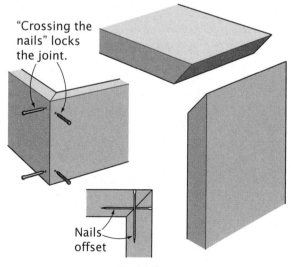

"Crossing the nails" locks the joint.

Nails offset

End Miter

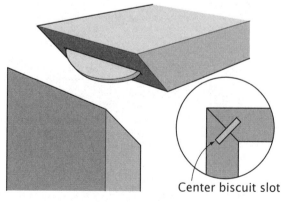

Center biscuit slot

Biscuited End Miter

mortised. Pairs of loose tenons must be joined with box joints. Then the two case parts must be assembled with the box-jointed tenons.

End miter with spline keys: This joint is made by cutting slots through the outside corner of a miter joint, then gluing splines into the slots and trimming them flush. The joint has great strength, and it looks good, too. At first glance it may look like a box joint, and it is often called a mock box joint.

End miter with dovetail keys: This joint is a decorative variation on the end miter with

spline keys, made with a dovetail bit instead of a straight bit or saw blade. If you like the look of the dovetail shape, these mock dovetails will give it to you on two surfaces. If desired, the keys can be a contrasting wood.

End miter with feather keys: A feather key is a thin slip of wood glued into a saw kerf. The spacing of the keys impacts the joint's strength and appearance. The more you use, the stronger the joint. The cuts can be straight or angled, the keys matching or contrasting.

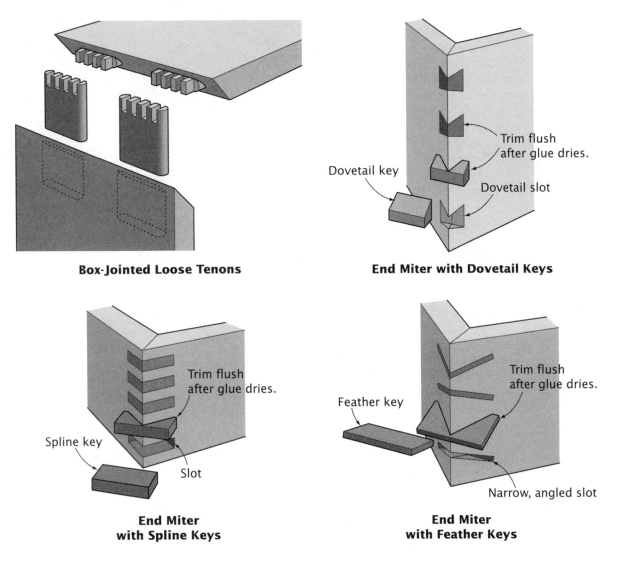

Box-Jointed Loose Tenons

End Miter with Dovetail Keys

Trim flush after glue dries.

Dovetail key

Dovetail slot

End Miter with Spline Keys

Trim flush after glue dries.

Spline key

Slot

End Miter with Feather Keys

Trim flush after glue dries.

Feather key

Narrow, angled slot

➤ MULTIPLE TENON JOINTS

Mortise-and-tenon joints are generally regarded as frame joints, but they have a place in case construction, too. They are strong and attractive joints for using to join mid-section structural elements like shelves and partitions to the sides, top, and bottom of the case.

The joints can be through or blind. If they are through, it is customary to secure them with hardwood wedges driven into saw cuts made across the end grain of each tenon.

In contrast to any of the dado joints, multiple tenon joints provide plenty of long-grain gluing surface on both faces of each tenon. This means that the joint can be used where the shelf must pull in the case sides. They also eliminate the need to make continuous cuts through the face of sheet materials, cuts that can seriously erode the strength of the material.

A row of evenly spaced, small mortises and tenons makes an excellent joint. The tenons should be the full thickness of the stock. The wider the piece, the more mortises and tenons you should use.

Twin-tenon case joint: An interesting variation is a joint that uses pairs of mortises and tenons. A pair of tenons is located near the edges of the shelf or partition, often with a web or tongue between the tenon pairs. The tongue is housed in a shallow dado cut between the mortises. This construction helps the case resist racking and the shelf resist the downward loading.

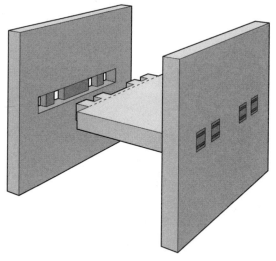

Twin-Tenon Case Joint

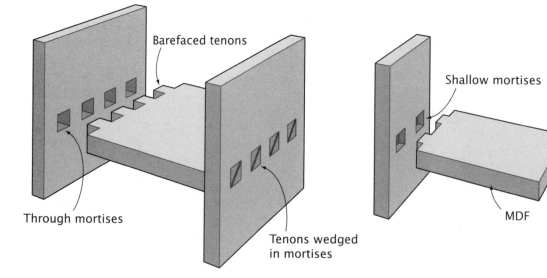

Barefaced tenons

Through mortises

Tenons wedged
in mortises

Shallow mortises

MDF

Multiple-Tenon Case Joint

➤ LOCK JOINTS

Locking joints are variations on the simple rabbet-and-dado. They are used primarily for attaching drawer fronts to sides.

Of the two lock joints shown, the "simple" joint is more common, and easier to cut, than the "complex" joint. Precision cuts are required to produce either version.

Lock miter joint: The lock miter is excellent because it combines the appearance of a miter corner with the strength of a dado. Because of its built-in locking action, it needs to be clamped only in one direction.

Routed drawer lock joint: This joint is cut with a special router bit or shaper knives. Only one setup is needed. The first piece is run through standing on end against the fence, the second flat on the table.

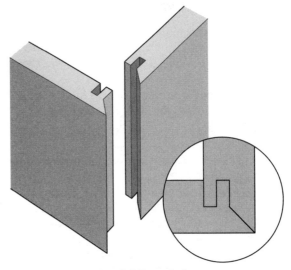

Lock Miter Joint

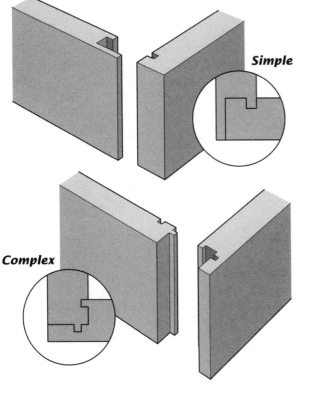

Simple

Complex

Lock Joints

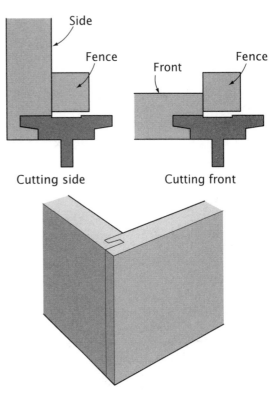

Cutting side   Cutting front

Routed Drawer Lock Joint

➤ DADO JOINTS

A dado is a rectangular groove cut across the grain of a board. All of the dado joints center on that cut. One board has the dado, the other board fits into the dado.

A dado cut in a case side provides a ledge to support the weight of a shelf and everything loaded on it. The dado also prevents the shelf from cupping. But it does nothing to prevent the shelf from pulling out of the side. Only glue or fasteners can do that. Because all of the gluing surfaces involve end grain, the glue strength is limited.

The dado does not have to be deep to create a strong through dado joint. One-eighth inch is deep enough in solid wood, 1/4 inch in plywood, MDF, or particleboard.

Through dado: When the dado extends from edge to edge, it is a through dado. The most common objection to the through dado joint is that it shows on the front edges of side panels. But a face frame or trim covering the case edges conceals the joint.

Stopped dado: A dado or groove doesn't have to be through. It can begin at one edge and end before it reaches the other (stopped), or it can begin and end shy of either edge (blind).

To make this joint, the corner(s) of the mating board must be notched, and the projecting edge should be just a tad shorter than the dado. You want a little play from end to end, so you can be sure the front edge of the divider is flush with the edge of the case side.

Dado-and-spline: This joint is perfect for MDF and particleboard, which have no grain and thus none of its strength. The spline should penetrate about one-third of the side's thickness, and about twice that distance into the horizontal piece. Too deep a cut into the side will weaken it. Too shallow a cut into the horizontal piece will not add enough strength. A spline located below center can support a heavier load without breaking.

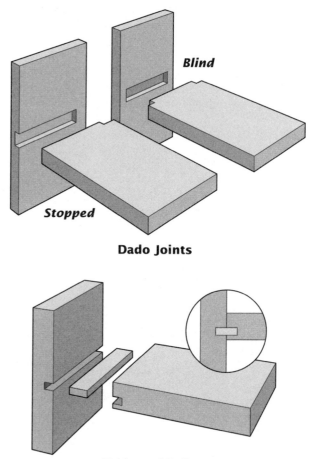

Dado Joints

Blind

Stopped

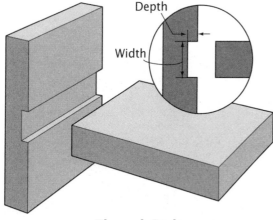

Through Dado

Depth

Width

Dado-and-Spline

Dado-and-rabbet: As its name says, this joint combines a dado and a rabbet. The rabbet cut forms a tongue (or barefaced tenon) that fits into the dado. In terms of theoretical gluing strength, this joint is all end grain to long grain (which isn't good); but in practice, it will glue well if the tongue is properly fitted to the dado. To do this, you match the thickness of the tongue to the dado.

The orientation of the joint is important.

The shelf can carry more weight if the rabbet is in the top surface. Otherwise, you risk the board's splitting below the tongue.

Tongue-and-dado: Beyond the dado-and-rabbet is the tongue-and-dado, which can be made in both through and stopped forms. The latter hides shrinkage and gaps. An advantage of this joint over a dado-and-rabbet is the increased stability that comes with the extra shoulder.

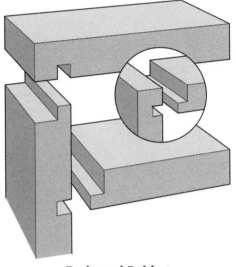

Dado-and-Rabbet

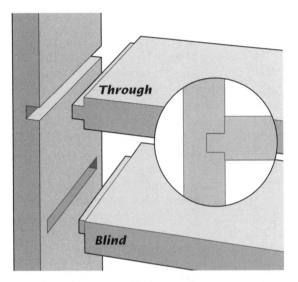

Tongue-and-Dado

▶ RABBET JOINTS

An open-sided channel or recess cut along the edge or across the end of a board or panel, the rabbet is used in several case joints.

The most common use in casework is in joining the back to the case. But it is also used to join the top and bottom to the sides, and to join the sides of a drawer to the front.

There are only end grain–to–long grain gluing surfaces in the rabbet joints. Typically, rabbet joints are joined together with fasteners instead of with glue.

Single-rabbet joint: This is a joint formed when only one of the mating parts is rabbeted.

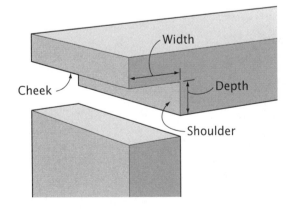

Single-Rabbet Joint

Typically, the rabbet is proportioned so that its width matches the thickness of the mating board. This proportion yields a flush fit.

The depth of the rabbet for this joint should be one-half to two-thirds its width. The deeper the rabbet, the less end grain that will be exposed in the assembled joint. When assembled, the rabbet conceals the end grain of the mating board.

Double-rabbet joint: In this joint, both of the mating pieces are rabbeted. The rabbets don't have to be the same, but typically they are.

Mitered rabbet: This joint, sometimes called the "miter-with-rabbet" or the "offset miter," combines elements of both rabbet joints and miter joints. Assembled, it looks like a miter joint; but structurally, the rabbet adds resistance to shear and racking stresses.

The joint is made by rabbeting both parts. One rabbet is twice the width of the other. Then the tips of the rabbets are mitered.

Mitered rabbet with dowels: One way to reinforce the mitered rabbet joint (without changing its outward appearance) is with hidden dowels. Assuming the holes for the dowels are accurately aligned across the joint, assembly is simple. Achieving that alignment is easier said than done.

Dovetailed rabbet: An alternative to more familiar case corner joints (such as rabbets and lock miters) is this corner joint. It is more resistant to racking than a conventional rabbet joint.

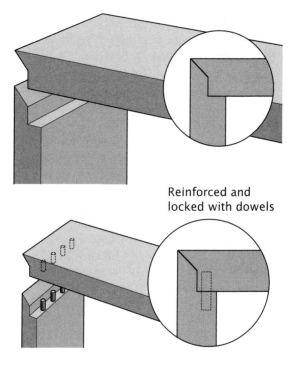

Reinforced and locked with dowels

Mitered Rabbet

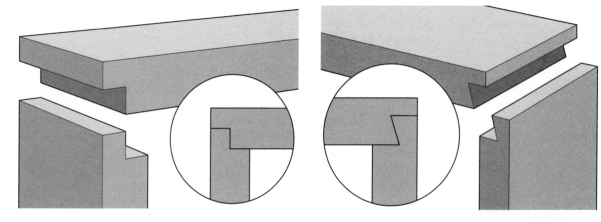

Double-Rabbet Joint

Dovetailed Rabbet

CORNER BLOCK JOINTS

A corner block is an intermediary. Instead of joining a case side directly to the top, for example, the two parts are joined to a corner block. It can be done with solid wood or man-made sheet materials.

Using solid wood corner blocks gives you a lot of design choices and detailing opportunities. For example, you can make the corner block of a contrasting wood. It can be thicker than the adjoining panels so it stands proud, creating a shadow detail. It can be molded or shaped.

There are a variety of ways to join a corner block to panels; but regardless of the joinery, proper orientation of the corner block's grain is vital. When joining the block to plywood, its grain must run parallel to the edge of the plywood (not necessarily parallel to the grain of the plywood's face veneer). When joining the block to a solid-wood panel, the block's grain must be oriented to run in the same direction as the grain of the sides.

Corner block with tongue-and-groove: The demands of cutting tongues on the corner block make this the most difficult of the corner block joints. For the strongest construction, the block should be roughed out with the grain running diagonally from tongue to tongue.

Corner block with splines: Substituting splines for the tongues makes this an easier joint to make.

Corner block with biscuits: A solid-wood corner block, joined with biscuits and glue, is an excellent way to join man-made sheet materials in building a case. All that's necessary is to cut the plywood or MDF perfectly straight and square. Space the biscuits about a hand's breadth apart, and be sure to spread glue on the full edge of the plywood.

MULTIPLE-SPLINE JOINTS

Just as you can make a mortise-and-tenon joint using a separate spline as the tenon, you can make a box joint using separate splines as the joint's fingers. To make a mortise and loose-tenon, you mortise both of the boards to be joined. To make a multiple-spline joint, you cut matching slots in both pieces, then glue up the joint with separate splines inserted in the

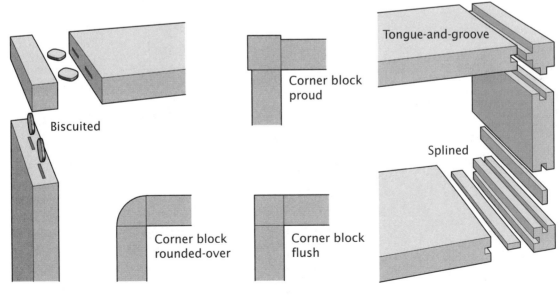

Biscuited

Corner block proud

Corner block rounded-over

Corner block flush

Tongue-and-groove

Splined

Corner Block Joints

slots. This loose-spline joint is strong because it involves lots of long grain–to–long grain gluing surfaces. Moreover, you can make it on the table saw.

The design possibilities of the joint are extensive. You can vary the length, thickness, and spacing of the splines. You can make the spline uniform in length and placement, or you can be random. The splines can be made of the same wood as the case, or they can be a contrasting color.

Half-blind multiple-spline joint: This joint is a variant of the router-cut dovetail joint. It is labeled half-blind because, as in the half-blind dovetail, the joinery is not visible from the front, only from the side.

To make the half-blind version of the multiple-spline joint, matching stopped slots are cut in both components. Carefully fitted splines are glued into the slots in one piece, then the second piece is added.

Because of the great amount of long grain–to–long grain gluing surface created, a multiple-spline joint is stronger than a comparable dovetail joint.

Full-blind multiple-spline joint: This is a strongly reinforced miter joint.

The miter is weak because the gluing surfaces are end grain to end grain. The splines used in this particular joint are small, but there are enough of them to dramatically increase the long grain–to–long grain gluing surface. Equally important, the splines are completely invisible. The joint looks like a miter.

Each spline is like a loose tenon. You cut a recess in both mating surfaces, and link the mating pieces together with the spline that fits into one recess and extends into the other. If the joint is to line up perfectly, the sockets for the splines have to line up.

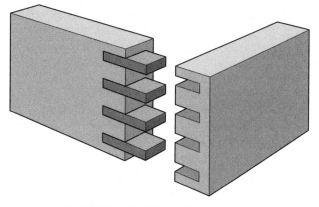

Half-Blind Multiple-Spline Joint

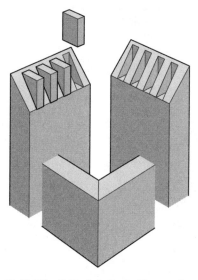

Multiple-Spline Joint

Full-Blind Multiple-Spline Joint

FRAME JOINTS

Frames are constructed, typically, by joining boards end to edge. While a simple butt joint glues poorly because it is all end grain to edge grain, there are many other frame joints that do the job excellently.

And it's a good thing, for the world of furniture would be much diminished without frames. Consider their many uses.

Web frames tie a case together and support and separate drawers.

A face frame finishes the front of a case, stiffening it and setting off areas for doors and drawers.

Frame-and-panel constructions serve as case elements—sides, back, top—and doors.

Frames are a time-honored way of dealing with wood movement. They predate plywood and the other relatively stable man-made sheet goods that replace solid-wood frames in many contemporary cabinets.

The frame-and-panel construction system was the early woodworker's way of dealing with wood's "come and go." The rails and stiles forming the frame are relatively narrow, and the dimensional changes in it that accompany humidity changes are correspondingly modest. While the panel is much wider than the stiles, it's set into a groove or rabbet such that dimensional changes are "absorbed" without damaging the structure, even cosmetically. So the frame contributes dimensional stability, and the panel (usually) contributes good looks.

A minimal frame, such as a simple face frame, consists of two stiles and two rails. When the frame is displayed vertically, as in a face frame, the stiles are the vertical elements and the rails are the horizontal elements. The rails invariably fit between the stiles. The edges are unembellished.

In a web frame, the stiles are usually called runners, and they fit between the rails.

A more elaborate frame can have three or more rails, as well as intermediate vertical members called mullions or muntins. The edges are embellished with beads, ogees, coves, or combinations of these shapes.

A number of different joints can be used to assemble the frame: miters, laps, dowels, biscuits, and the traditional mortise-and-tenon.

➤ BUTT JOINTS

In a butt joint, the end of one of the pieces forming the joint is literally butted against the edge of the other. There's no interlocking of the parts, and the gluing surfaces are entirely end grain to long grain. The result is an unsatisfactory joint.

Reinforcement is what a butted frame joint needs. If the frame members are narrow, nails or screws can be driven through the edge of one member into the end of the other. In a frame with wide members, nails or screws can be toenailed into the joint.

Doweled butt: A dowel is, in effect, a loose tenon. When it is glued into a hole drilled in the butt end of a rail, the gluing

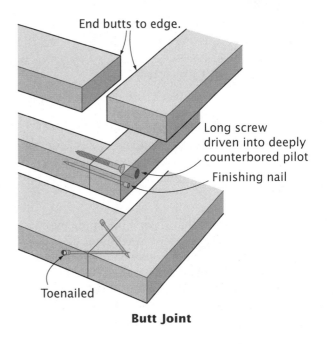

End butts to edge.

Long screw driven into deeply counterbored pilot

Finishing nail

Toenailed

Butt Joint

surfaces are long grain to long grain, which is excellent. But when glued into a hole drilled into the edge of a stile, the gluing surfaces are largely long grain (the dowel) to end grain (the stile), which is bad.

Though furniture manufacturers swear by dowels for frame joints, most woodworkers swear at them. At minimum, a joint should have two dowels. The biggest problem for the woodworker is getting the dowel holes precisely aligned across the joint. Even a small misalignment can prevent the joint from being closed.

Manufacturers get away with dowel joints because they have systems to control the moisture content of the dowels and the wood, as well as hi-tech machinery to bore holes that are precisely sized and positioned.

Biscuited butt: An excellent way to reinforce a butted frame joint is with biscuits. Many woodworkers regard this joint as a good alternative to the conventional mortise-and-tenon for joining rails and stiles in cabinet doors and for face frames and the like.

Always use the largest biscuit you can fit across the width of the parts.

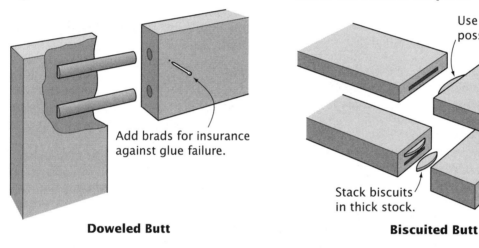

Add brads for insurance against glue failure.

Doweled Butt

Use widest biscuit possible.

Stack biscuits in thick stock.

Biscuited Butt

➤ FLAT MITER JOINTS

The miter joint represents the best and worst in joinery. It makes a neat right-angle corner without leaving end grain exposed.

Tightly crafted, it is almost totally hidden: There's a barely discernible seam, and *right there,* the figure of the wood changes direction sharply. You don't see any end grain. That's the best of it.

The worst is that the simple miter joint is—structurally—a pretty weak joint. If you glue it, you're trying to glue one tangentially cut end grain surface to another. It's a less than optimal glue joint. Run some fasteners into it, and you're running them into end grain, where they won't hold very well.

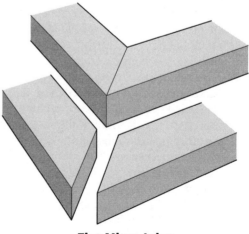

Flat Miter Joint

Moreover, the joint is vexing to assemble. Because of the angles involved, a mitered corner always wants to slide out of line when you apply clamping pressure to it.

Like a butt joint, the miter needs some form of reinforcement.

Nailed flat miter: A practical, light-duty frame can be constructed with miter joints, if nails are used to reinforce the joints. Drive finishing nails into each joint, two from each direction, as shown.

Doweled flat miter: In theory, the dowels aid in alignment, but this is true only if the holes for the dowels match perfectly across the joint line. This joint is easy to draw but difficult to execute in wood.

Biscuited flat miter: An alternative to nailing or doweling a miter joint is to use biscuits to secure the joint. A joint in a

cabinet face frame doesn't need to be as strong as that in a cabinet door, so a single small biscuit will be enough.

Flat miter with spline key: This is a miter joint that is reinforced with a spline *after* it is assembled. The spline should penetrate quite deeply into the miter joint, as indicated in the drawing. If the spline is to strengthen the joint, its grain direction must be perpendicular to the miter.

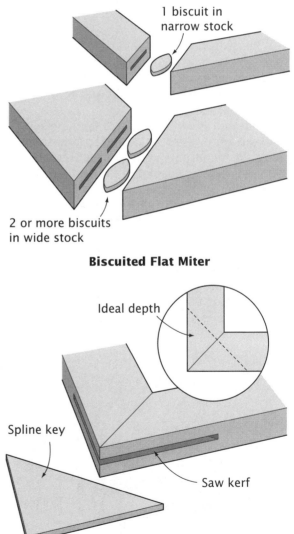

1 biscuit in narrow stock

2 or more biscuits in wide stock

Biscuited Flat Miter

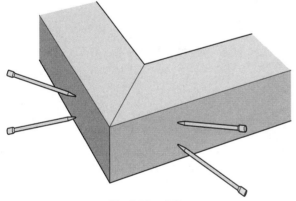

Nailed Flat Miter

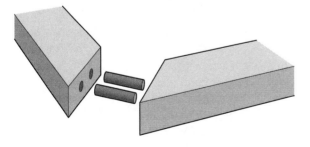

Doweled Flat Miter

Ideal depth

Spline key

Saw kerf

Flat Miter with Spline Key

The cut for the spline is made after the glue in the miter joint has cured. It is the width of a single saw kerf. The spline is glued into the kerf and then trimmed flush with the surfaces of the frame.

The spline can be made of a matching or a contrasting wood.

Flat miter with dovetail key: The difference between this joint and the previous one is the shape and size of the key. Here the slot for the key is cut with a dovetail bit. The key is a short piece of wood shaped like a dovetail.

Regardless of the size of the frame members, the key makes only a shallow penetration of the frame's outside corner. What limits the depth of the penetration is the size of the bit used to cut the slot.

The slot is cut in the glued-up miter joint, and the key is glued into it. The protruding ends are then trimmed flush. The finished joint has a dovetail-shaped bit of end grain on either side of the corner.

Flat miter with feather keys: A feather key is thinner by far than a spline key. Often bits of veneer are used as feather keys. A thin-bladed hand saw is used to kerf the glued-up miter joint for the keys.

Flat miter with butterfly key: This miter joint is reinforced with a key inlaid in the surface of the frame, spanning the joint line between the two frame members. The key strengthens the joint and, at the same time, provides a visual accent.

The key looks, impressionistically, like a butterfly. It's a little rectangle that's been pinched in the middle. The grain must run from end to end.

Of course, the key is installed after the joint has been glued up. A recess that is the exact size of the key is routed or chiseled into the frame. The narrow waist lies directly on the joint line. The key is then glued into the recess and trimmed flush.

The key is an excellent fastener. It holds the joint together effectively, but it cannot withstand bending or twisting.

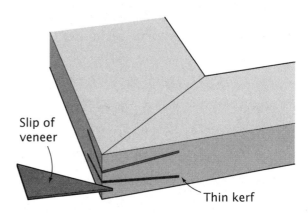

Slip of veneer

Thin kerf

Flat Miter with Feather Keys

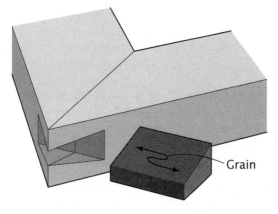

Grain

Flat Miter with Dovetail Key

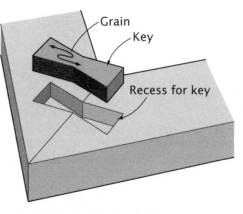

Grain

Key

Recess for key

Flat Miter with Butterfly Key

Splined flat miter: A spline is a good solution to the structural shortcomings of the butted flat miter joint. It doesn't have to affect the pure, pristine appearance of the miter in any way.

A spline is a separate piece of wood, often plywood, that reinforces the joint. The spline is set into slots in the mating surfaces in such a way that the grain of the spline will run across the main joint to resist splitting along that joint. This placement just happens to be ideal for holding the pieces in place for gluing, too.

The easiest joint of this sort to make is one with a through spline. The slots in the ends of mating parts can be cut from edge to edge. The joint is strong, but the spline is visible in both the inside and outside corners.

The most difficult to make is one with a full blind spline. Here the slots must be stopped short of both edges of the mating pieces. The spline is shorter, but it is concealed inside the joint.

Splined four-way flat miter joint: Sometimes you want a joint that makes the crossing parts appear to merge. This one connects four separate pieces sturdily. Each piece is twice mitered and slotted. During assembly, a spline is inserted.

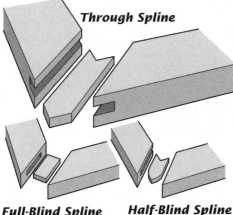

Through Spline

Full-Blind Spline   *Half-Blind Spline*

Splined Flat Miter

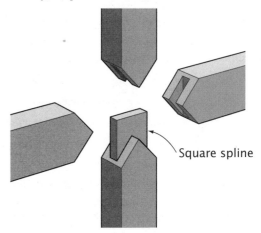

Square spline

Splined 4-Way Flat Miter Joint

➤ LAP JOINTS

A joint in which one member is notched to accept the other member is a lap joint. These joints—the variations abound—are a simple way of joining two pieces that cross or meet, forming an X, L, or T.

Despite their simplicity, these joints can be extraordinarily strong if they are properly made. This strength stems from the strength of modern glues, of course, but equally from the mechanics of the joint. Regardless of the glue used, it is relatively easy to twist apart two boards that have been crossed at right angles and glued face-to-face. But the joint

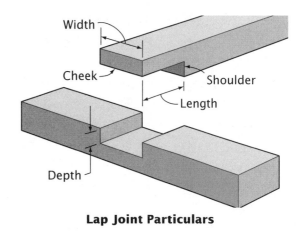

Width

Cheek

Shoulder

Length

Depth

Lap Joint Particulars

can be greatly strengthened by introducing a mechanical interlock, however modest.

In the lap joints, one or both of the mating surfaces are cut to create a square-sided recess (like a dado or rabbet) that is just wide enough for the other board. When the joint is assembled, the side of the recess, called the *shoulder,* prevents one board from twisting on the other.

In a full-lap joint, only one piece is notched; the other's full dimension is set into the notch.

In any of the half-lap joints, both members are notched, usually with half the total material to be removed coming from each piece. The British call these *halved joints,* which is sensible.

End lap: This is a corner joint made by cutting a rabbet at the ends of both pieces, giving each a *cheek* and a *shoulder.* In the assembled joint, a rectangle of end grain is exposed on each edge, which can be regarded as unsightly.

The mating surfaces must be flat and the shoulders must be square to the cheeks. Glue is applied, and the joint is assembled cheek to cheek. The shoulder of each piece should be tight up against the edge of the mating piece. The joint must be clamped up in every direction while the glue sets.

T-lap: The end of one member joins the middle of the other in this joint. To make it, a dado is cut on one piece and a rabbet on the other.

Cross-lap: The cross-lap joint is one that makes a crossing intersection, usually of equal-sized parts. The pieces may cross at any angle.

The joint is made by cutting dadoes of equal width and depth on the two pieces so

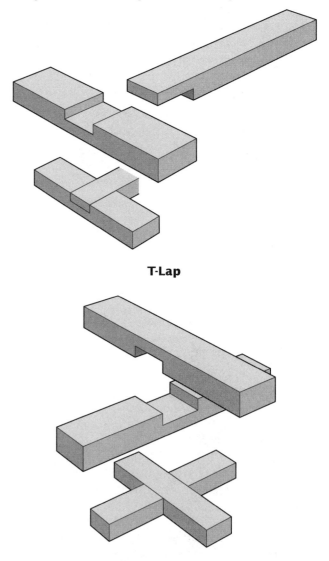

T-Lap

Cross-Lap

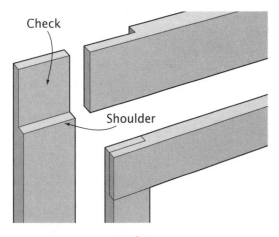

Check

Shoulder

End Lap

that the face surfaces are flush when assembled. Because each piece is trapped between the shoulders of the other, this is a can't-fail joint: The wood will break first.

Glazing-bar cross-lap: This is the joint to use when building a gridwork of *muntins* (or *glazing bars,* as British woodworkers call them) for a window or glazed door. The advantage of the joint is that it allows the muntins to be continuous from side to side and from top to bottom. This yields a more rigid gridwork.

The joint is fundamentally a cross-lap; but because a muntin is complex in section, the cutting of this joint is more demanding than an ordinary cross-lap.

Pocket lap: A stopped lap, a lap that doesn't cut all the way across the face of the workpiece, is known as a pocket lap. You might use pocket laps in a face frame where you didn't want end grain showing on the sides. The lap joint between rail and stile would be hidden on the inside of the cabinet.

Mitered half-lap: The mitered half-lap combines the strength of the half-lap with the neat appearance of the miter. It is a sound choice for cabinet doors.

The mitered half-lap makes it easy to incorporate a sticking profile on the inside edges of the frame. You simply cut a profile on the inside edge of each joining piece before assembly. After assembly, the profile will meet, fair and square, at the miter, regardless of the profile's shape.

To make the joint, you can't simply miter two pieces that have already been half-lapped. One part of the joint could be done this way, since on the rails, the shoulder cut is square while the butt end is mitered. But on the stiles, the shoulder cut is mitered while the butt end is square. The joint must be laid out and cut from the start as a mitered half-lap joint.

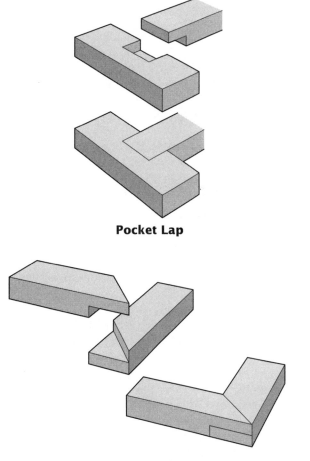

Pocket Lap

Glazing-Bar Cross-Lap

Mitered Half-Lap

Dovetailed half-lap: An additional mechanical lock is offered by the dovetail half-lap. The end lap can't just slip out of the cross-lap; it's got to be lifted. So it is a stronger joint than the standard half-lap. To boot, it has that dovetail look, so it imparts a touch of class to your frame.

To get these benefits, you have to do only a little extra work, since it is only marginally more difficult to make than the standard square-shouldered joint.

Dovetail-keyed half-lap: This is an unusual variation on the T-lap joint. What's distinctive about it is the angled shoulders and edges on the joining parts. To assemble the joint, the end lap has to be slid into the recess. Once assembled, the joint looks like a T-lap with shoulders on the stem of the T.

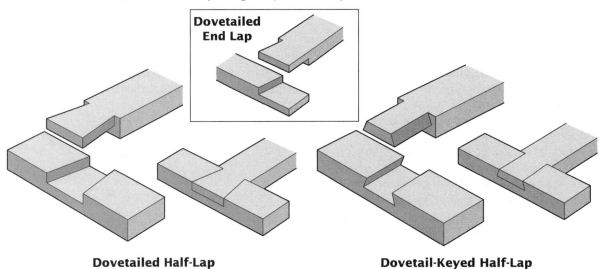

Dovetailed End Lap

Dovetailed Half-Lap

Dovetail-Keyed Half-Lap

➤ MORTISE-AND-TENON JOINTS

The mortise-and-tenon is woodworking's essential frame joint. Examples of the joint that date back 5,000 years exist in museums. Even today, it's used in everything from furniture frames to post-and-beam building frames.

Mortise-and-tenon joints take many different forms. The basic elements are the mortise, which is a hole—round, square, or rectangular—and the tenon, which is a tongue cut on the end of the joining member to fit the mortise.

The names of the joint's parts are derived from human physiology. The opening of the mortise is called the *mouth.* The interior faces, as well as the wood alongside the mortise, are called the *cheeks.* The tenon also has cheeks, which is the name given to its broad, flat sides. The plane adjacent to the cheek at the tenon's base is called the *shoulder.* The narrow shoulder at the tenon's edge, which doesn't contribute to the strength of the joint, is sometimes called the *cosmetic shoulder.*

A mortise-and-tenon joint should be scaled to give the maximum long grain–to–long grain gluing surface. But at the same time, the tenon can't be too long or wide, and it shouldn't be too narrow.

Consider the tenon's length. The joint *is* a cross-grain construction. Moisture-induced movement actually may make a joint with a longer tenon weaker than one with a shorter tenon—unless you take the tenon all the way through the stile and wedge it from the other side.

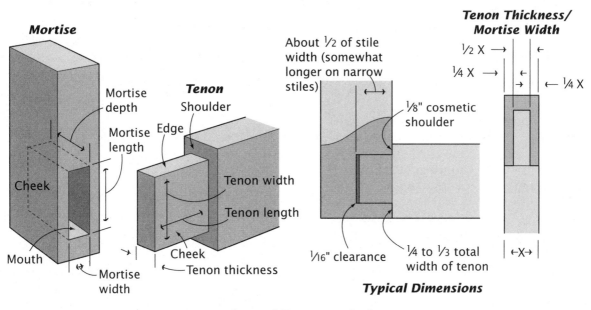

Mortise

Mortise depth

Mortise length

Cheek

Mouth

Mortise width

Tenon

Shoulder

Edge

Tenon width

Tenon length

Cheek

Tenon thickness

About ½ of stile width (somewhat longer on narrow stiles)

⅛" cosmetic shoulder

1/16" clearance

¼ to ⅓ total width of tenon

Tenon Thickness/ Mortise Width

½ X →

¼ X →

← ¼ X

← X →

Typical Dimensions

Mortise-and-Tenon Particulars

The best compromise is to mortise about halfway into the stile. In narrow stock, go a bit more than halfway. Thus, if the stile is 3 inches wide, make the tenon 1½ inches long. But if the stile is only 1½ inches wide, make the tenon about 1 inch long.

Consider the tenon's width. Generally, the tenon should be as wide as possible. But remember that wood moves considerably across the grain and very little along it. The wider a tenon is, the more it will move in relation to the mortised piece, which isn't moving at all. The resulting stress can cause the joint to fail and/or the pieces to crack. If you need a very wide tenon, divide it into two or more even tenons, which helps distribute the cross-grain stress.

Consider the tenon's thickness. The width of a mortise, by tradition, is no more than one-third the thickness of the stock. When all mortises were chopped out with chisels, this "rule" ensured that the surrounding stock was strong enough to resist splitting. A well-fitted and glued mortise-and-tenon joint will

be stronger, however, if the tenon is one-half the thickness of the stock. With today's machining techniques, you can cut a wide mortise with far less risk of splitting.

Through mortise-and-tenon: When the mortise penetrates the stile from edge to edge, it's a through mortise—one that's open at both ends. The tenon, of course, is sized to fill the mortise, and its end grain is exposed.

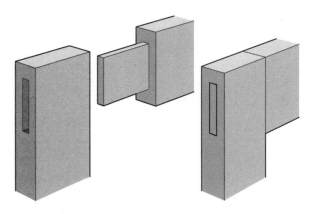

Through Mortise-and-Tenon

Blind mortise-and-tenon: If a mortise is cut only partway through the frame member, so that it has a bottom, it is called a stopped or blind mortise. Once the tenon is glued into the mortise, there is no obvious sign of the joint. This is the mortise-and-tenon used in most furniture these days.

Haunched tenon: A haunch is a tongue that projects from a tenon's shoulder between the tenon's edge and the rail's edge. The most common use of the haunched tenon today is in frame-and-panel construction, where the haunch fills a through panel groove. A haunch is always present on old work because you couldn't make a stopped groove with a hand plow plane.

A haunch is sometimes used in leg-and-apron construction, and when it is, a groove especially for the haunch must be cut in the leg. An alternative is to miter the haunch.

Long-and-short-shouldered tenon: If you are making a glazed frame or door, the glass is usually set into rabbets, then retained by a molding tacked into the rabbet. The easiest way to make the frame is to rabbet the rails and stiles first.

Because the rabbets are through, the mortise-and-tenon joints need to have longer shoulders at the back than at the front. The back of the stile is cut away, hence the necessity for the back shoulder of the rail to be longer than the front one.

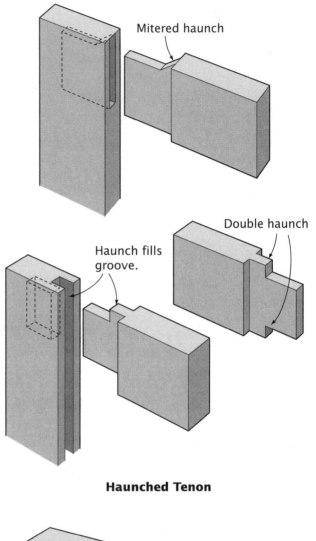

Mitered haunch

Haunch fills groove.

Double haunch

Haunched Tenon

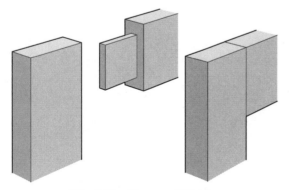

Blind Mortise-and-Tenon

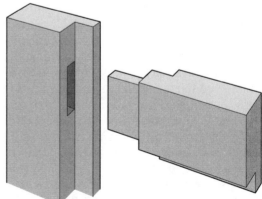

Long-and-Short-Shouldered Tenon

Loose tenon: In this joint, both pieces are mortised, and the tenon is a separate piece of wood. When the tenon has been glued into the end of the rail, it behaves exactly as if it had grown there.

Mortise-and-tenon with stuck molding: Stuck molding is a profile cut directly on the rails and stiles of a frame. The trick in joining the frame parts is to have the profile on the rail meet the profile on the stile in a neat miter.

To do this, you cut the decorative profile directly on the inside edge of each frame part, then pare the molding back to a miter in the area of the mortise. Cut a matching miter on the tenon piece.

Mortise-and-tenon with mitered shoulders: If your design calls for a curved shape between rail and stile, or leg and rail, the curved part should be mitered at the shoulder. Otherwise, the end grain is likely to break or split off. Glue matching blocks of wood to the rail and stile. Miter the parts where they meet, then shape the curve.

Double mortise-and-tenon: As a rule of thumb, the double mortise-and-tenon should be used whenever the width of a single large

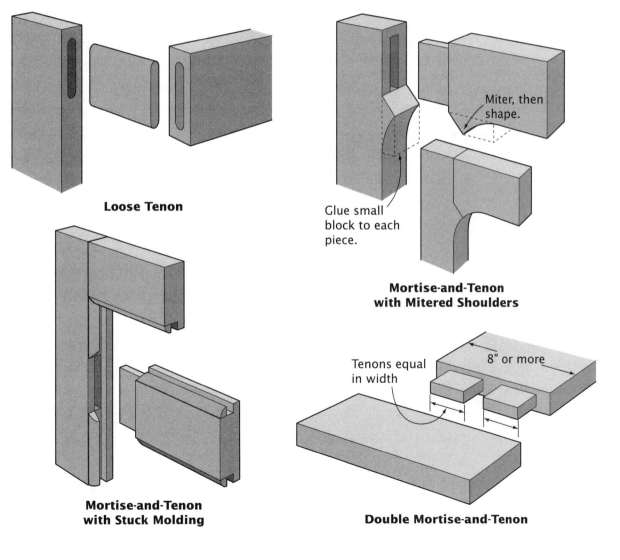

Loose Tenon

Miter, then shape.

Glue small block to each piece.

Mortise-and-Tenon with Mitered Shoulders

Tenons equal in width

8" or more

Mortise-and-Tenon with Stuck Molding

Double Mortise-and-Tenon

tenon is more than ten times its thickness. That tenon should be divided roughly into thirds—tenon, space, tenon. The divided mortise is better able to accommodate the stresses of wood movement. To keep the rail from warping, leave a short stub of wood, known as a haunch, between the tenons.

Wedged mortise-and-tenon: Wedges will hold mortise-and-tenon joints together so securely that glue is quite unnecessary. In addition to the mechanical strength that wedges contribute, they can provide a nice decorative touch.

Wedges are most effective when the mortise is tapered and the wedges spread the end of the tenon into a dovetail shape.

It's *possible* to wedge a blind tenon; this is called a "fox-wedged tenon." The joint must be crafted with precision. As the tenon enters the mortise, the wedges will hit the bottom of the mortise and be driven into the kerfs. As long as you get everything perfect, you'll have a strong joint. But if the assembled joint isn't right, there is no way to disassemble the joint to make adjustments.

Pegged mortise-and-tenon: Don't trust the holding power of glue? Peg the joint. If the glue fails, the peg will hold the joint together.

Before pegging (or pinning) the joint, first glue and clamp it. Drill a hole through the joint and drive in a dowel or peg. You can turn

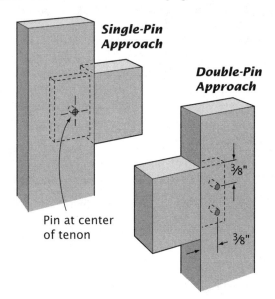

Single-Pin Approach

Double-Pin Approach

3/8"

3/8"

Pin at center of tenon

Pegged Mortise-and-Tenon

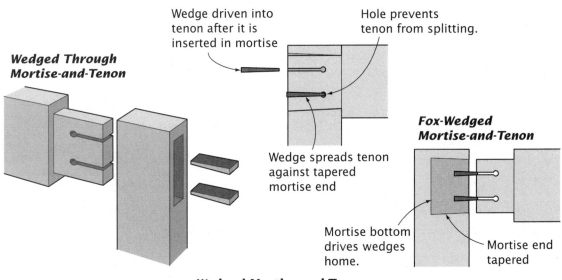

Wedge driven into tenon after it is inserted in mortise

Hole prevents tenon from splitting.

Wedged Through Mortise-and-Tenon

Wedge spreads tenon against tapered mortise end

Fox-Wedged Mortise-and-Tenon

Mortise bottom drives wedges home.

Mortise end tapered

Wedged Mortise-and-Tenon

pegs from a contrasting wood, you can turn them with decorative heads, or you can whittle square heads on round pegs.

Groove-and-stub-tenon: A stub tenon is really an oversized tongue, a tongue just big enough to fit the typical panel groove. The tongue provides a little bit of long grain–to–long grain gluing surface. This is a light-duty joint to use in building frames that are anchored to a case.

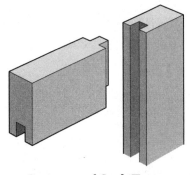

Groove-and-Stub-Tenon

➤ COPE-AND-STICK JOINT

One of the big challenges in frame-and-panel construction is finding practical, economical ways to meld strength and utility with beauty. The joinery has to be strong, especially if the unit is to be a door. The mortise-and-tenon is the traditional framing joint, but it can be time-consuming to make, especially if you are assembling a couple dozen cabinet doors. Attractive appearance is often as important as the joinery. But adding a series of operations to embellish a workpiece adds to the project's cost.

In relatively recent years, more and more of these frames—for cabinet doors in particular—have been assembled with what's known as the cope-and-stick joint (sometimes it's called a cope-and-pattern joint).

Two cuts are required to complete the frame parts. The first cut, made on both rails and stiles, forms a decorative profile on the edge of the frame member and at the same time cuts the groove for the panel. The second cut is made only on the ends of the rails. It forms a tongue and a reverse of the decorative profile. When the cuts are properly aligned on the workpieces, the tongue fits into the groove and the rail end conforms perfectly to the profile. Bonded with a modern glue, it is a strong joint.

Some Available Profiles

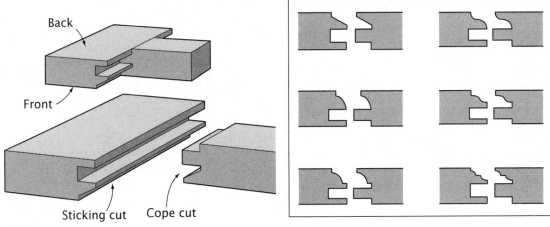

Cope-and-Stick Joint

▶ SLIP JOINTS

Slip joints are often called open mortise-and-tenon joints, and with good reason. The rails have a tenon, and the stiles have a mortise with an open top, open bottom, and open edge.

There are two basic kinds of slip joints. The joint that joins the end of one piece to the end of another is the slip joint or open mortise-and-tenon. The joint that joins the end of one piece to the middle of the other is called a bridle joint. Functionally they are very similar to a regular mortise-and-tenon and can be as strong or stronger.

A very big advantage of the slip joint is the ease with which it is made. It can be cut on the table saw using a tenoning jig.

The slip joint's disadvantage is that you have to clamp the tenon shoulder tightly against the mortise (as you do in all mortise-and-tenon glue-ups), but you must also clamp the mortise sides to guarantee that they are glued to the mortise sides.

Tapered slip joint: This form of the slip joint has a specialized application, and that is for frames that will be veneered.

If veneer is applied over the face of a regular slip joint, differences in expansion and contraction of the rail and the stile will, over time, produce a distinct line in the veneer.

The tapered slip joint is designed to eliminate that line. It does it by making the tenon shoulder immediately under the veneer very narrow. Because the mortise cheek is so thin where it meets the tenon shoulder, it doesn't move much, and thus it stays virtually flush.

Mitered slip joint: The mitered slip joint combines the appearance of the miter joint with the strength of the slip joint.

There are two versions. In the through joint, the end grain of the tenon is exposed. In the blind version, the slot is not through, so the tenon's end grain is hidden.

Both versions have about the same strength. The through version is a bit easier to make, but the blind joint offers a better appearance.

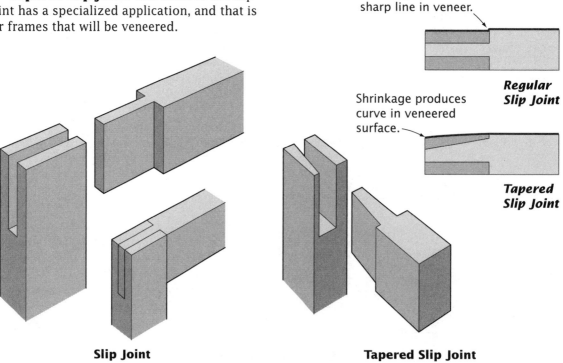

Shrinkage produces sharp line in veneer.

Regular Slip Joint

Shrinkage produces curve in veneered surface.

Tapered Slip Joint

Slip Joint

Tapered Slip Joint

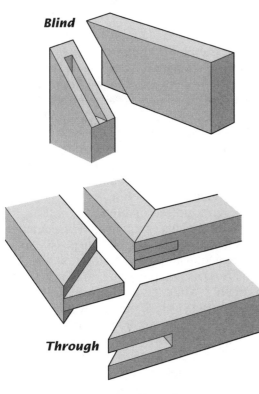

Blind

Through

Mitered Slip Joint

Bridle joint: This is an open mortise-and-tenon that joins the end of one part to the middle of another. It is most often used in table construction, to join a leg to the middle of a long apron. The leg post is slotted (the open mortise), and laps are cut into both faces of the apron.

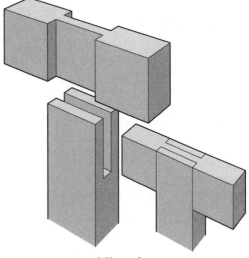

Bridle Joint

➤ MITERED SHOWCASE JOINT

This elegant showcase joint is a traditional means of joining the frame for a glass-front showcase. While it is quite strong, the joint isn't as robust as a regular mortise-and-tenon, and it should be reserved for more delicate assemblies, such as a freestanding curio cabinet or a wall-hung display case.

The key to making this joint is the loose tenon. Making the pieces with traditional integral tenons is very difficult because one shoulder must be pared to a precise miter around the tenon and the other shoulder must be carefully mortised. However, with loose tenons, mitering the shoulders and mortising the pieces are very straightforward operations.

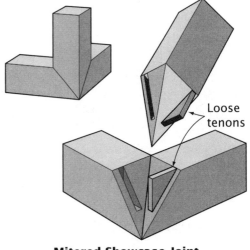

Loose tenons

Mitered Showcase Joint

RAIL JOINTS

Rail joints, such as the mortise-and-tenon, are used in leg-and-apron and post-and-rail constructions. These are constructions in which, as in frames, end grain is to be joined to long grain.

This is, of course, the poorest of situations to be in, for end grain glues poorly. But there is a catalog of joints that have proven sound and durable for these constructions.

The secret of most of these rail joints is that they contrive to present long grain–to–long grain gluing surfaces. In most of these constructions, one piece is cross-grain to the other, and moisture-induced conflict is inevitable. But this is a far better fix to be in than trying to joint long grain to end grain.

► MORTISE-AND-TENON JOINTS

The main goal in designing a mortise-and-tenon is to maximize the glue area, especially the long grain–to–long grain gluing surface. Choose the joint and its proportions according to the job it must do.

Here are rules of thumb for establishing the width and length of your tenons. The size of the mortise obviously follows from the size of the tenon. (It's much easier to match the tenon to the mortise; so when making the joint, you nearly always make the mortise first.)

The bigger the tenon, the stronger it will be, but at the possible expense of the piece with the mortise in it. You don't want the mortise walls to be too thin.

You have to keep in mind what will be required of the pieces involved. For example, aprons mortised into the table legs will be under tension-compression stress, so the tenons need as much height and length as you can provide. While the tenons won't get much shear or torque stress, the legs will be heavily leveraged, so you don't want to weaken them. The upshot: Make the tenons fairly thin.

The mortise-and-tenon forms most common to rail joinery are shown in the drawing *Mortise-and-Tenon Options.*

Full-height tenon: This joint responds to the rule of thumb that says you should

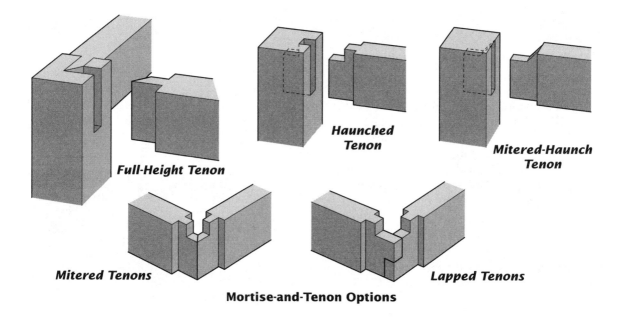

Full-Height Tenon

Haunched Tenon

Mitered-Haunch Tenon

Mitered Tenons

Lapped Tenons

Mortise-and-Tenon Options

provide as much height as possible to the tenon. As shown the tenon is the full height of the apron, with shoulders on only the sides, not the edges.

Haunched tenon: More common in frame joinery, the mortise-and-haunched-tenon does have a place in rail joinery. It provides a compromise between joint concealment and tenon height. For example, the version with a mitered haunch is invisible, once assembled, so it would be a good choice for a stand that will support a plate-glass tabletop.

Mitered or lapped tenon: Tenon length is usually limited by the girth of the member it penetrates, especially when two tenons join the same member at right angles. This, of course, is typical in leg-and-apron constructions.

The usual practice is to miter the ends of the tenons, which allows one cheek of each tenon to be slightly longer than it would be if the tenons were square-cut. (Every little bit of glue surface helps.) The British sometimes lap the ends of the tenons.

Barefaced tenon: The idea in a barefaced tenon is that at least one cheek is flush with the face of the tenoned part. The genuine article presumably has no shoulders at all. The width and length of the mortise matches the thickness and width of the joining part.

But there are other variations. The barefaced tenon can have a single shoulder across one end or across both ends. It can have a shoulder across a face, or a shoulder across both ends and the face. In any of these variations, it is still a barefaced tenon. The advantage of the genuine barefaced tenon is that it is as strong as the member. The offset barefaced tenon—which has the three shoulders—allows the woodworker to keep the mortise walls reasonably thick, maintain a stout tenon, and still have the apron's face flush with the face of the leg.

Offset tenon: The offset tenon provides all the benefits of the barefaced tenon, but it also has a fourth shoulder, which some craftsmen contend is an additional benefit.

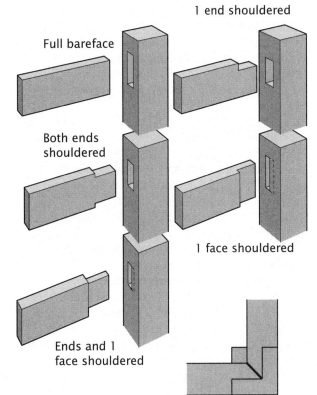

Barefaced Tenons

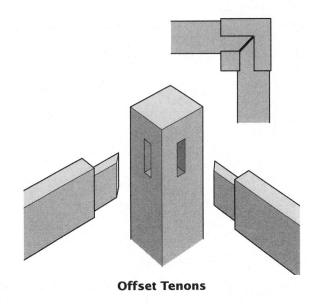

Offset Tenons

The section view detail in the drawing *Offset Tenons* makes clear both the offset of each tenon and its benefits.

Angled mortise-and-tenons: This is more a chair joint than a cabinetry joint, but it may come up if you are doing very contemporary things.

There are two approaches. In the first, the tenon juts off the rail at an angle, whilst the mortise is cut perpendicular. But sometimes the resulting tenon is weakened because it doesn't have enough long grain extending from its end all the way into the rail.

Better is the second approach, which is to cut the mortise at an angle and have the tenon parallel to the plane of the rail (although with angled shoulders).

Mortise in a round: In some contemporary table designs, the rails are sometimes joined to round legs. Because it is so difficult to cut concave shoulders on the tenons, the usual practice is to cut a flat on the round, as shown in the drawing, then cut the mortise into it. Typically, the tenon is offset to the bottom edge, and the top edge is coved to mate with the leg's curve.

Round mortise-and-tenon: A round mortise-and-tenon can be used on rectilinear stock or on round stock, as shown in the drawing on the opposite page.

Twin mortise-and-tenon: This joint is used to join a drawer rail to a leg. The temptation, when designing a joint for this application, is to orient the tenon across the width of the rail. This approach yields major long grain–to–end grain gluing surfaces, which is no good.

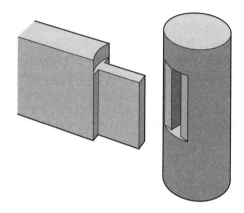

Mortise in a Round

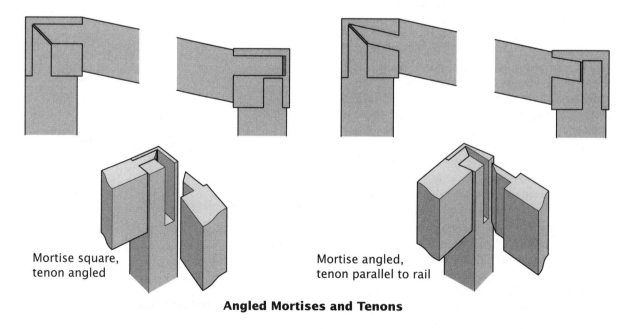

Mortise square, tenon angled

Mortise angled, tenon parallel to rail

Angled Mortises and Tenons

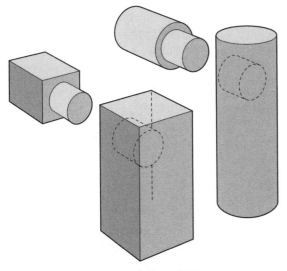

Round Mortise-and-Tenon

The tusk tenon is long enough to extend through the mortise and stick out on the other side. It has a mortise through it, taking one or more removable wedges that lock the joint together.

In designing and constructing a tusk tenon joint, you must heed the shear stress that the locking wedge exerts toward the tenon's end. Not only must the tusk be large enough to be mortised, it must have enough wood beyond the mortise to resist the wedge's pressure.

Ideally, the joint is constructed with the wedge (or tusk) oriented vertically. With seasonal swelling and shrinking of the wood and the racking of the joint during heavy use, a well-designed tusk with a bit of side

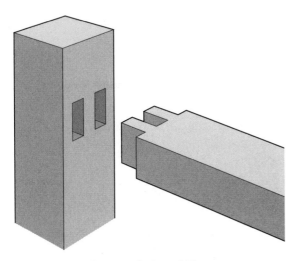

Twin Mortise-and-Tenon

Instead, divide the rail into two (or more) tenons oriented with the rail's thickness, as shown. This maximizes the long-grain gluing surfaces and yields a strong joint.

Tusk tenon: This joint is very functional if the furniture needs to be disassembled from time to time. It's a knockdown joint commonly used in table trestles, beds, and looms.

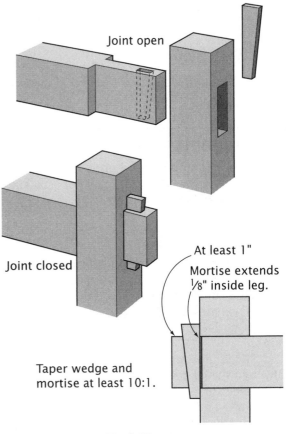

Joint open

Joint closed

At least 1"

Mortise extends 1/8" inside leg.

Taper wedge and mortise at least 10:1.

Tusk Tenon

clearance will drop farther into its mortise, tightening the joint. A horizontal tusk will just wiggle looser. When making this joint, be sure to angle the second mortise—the one through the tenon—to match the angle on the tusk. Also, be sure to give the tusk enough side clearance that you can drop it into the mortise before giving it a final tap.

Variations abound. Shown are just three of these varations.

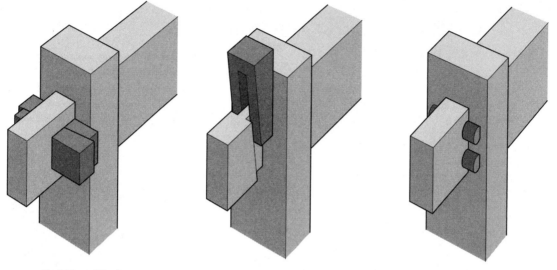

Folding Wedges   **Forked Wedge**   **Twin Round Wedges**

➤ SLIP JOINTS

Though slip joints are used primarily in frame construction, there are a couple of special slip joint variants that are especially good in rail joinery.

Bridle joint: This type of slip joint comes into play primarily in tables with curved aprons. It is easiest to create the apron as a continuous piece with glue lamination or bricklaid construction. If you need to add a leg anywhere along the curve, it's best to use a joint that doesn't break the continuity of the apron.

The joint is formed by cutting a slot through the leg post. The apron is lapped on both faces to reduce its thickness to match the slot's width. The recesses have shoulders to strengthen the assembled joint, resisting shear and racking forces.

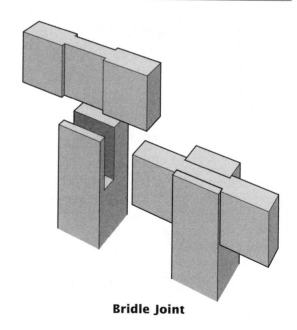

Bridle Joint

Table-leg joint: This is an unusual version of the bridle joint, seen most often on British-made tables. It is used in the same applications as the bridle joint.

Instead of both faces of the apron being lapped, only the front is. In place of the second lap, a mortise is cut. The leg typically is both slotted and rabbeted. The rear extension created by the slot is shortened and becomes the tenon. The face of the leg can be flush with the apron, or it can stand slightly proud.

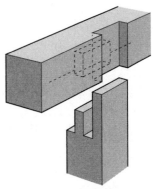

Table-Leg Joint

➤ LAP JOINTS

In rail joinery, laps are most likely to be used on a workbench or some other heavy-duty post-and-rail structure. It isn't really a handsome joint; rather it is a sturdy, hardworking joint.

Full-lap: The definition of a full-lap joint is: a joint in which one part is lapped or recessed to receive the full dimension of the other.

The drawing shows two types of full-lap joints that might be used in a workbench. In the post-and-rail situation, the heavy post has been lapped to receive both the rails. Since the long grain–to–long grain gluing area is clearly quite small, this joint should be reinforced with fasteners. In the brace-and-apron situation, the apron has been notched to take the brace, an acceptable approach in a table built for utility more than appearance.

Edge-lap: In terms of post-and-rail joinery, the edge lap is used primarily to link stretchers that cross. A notch is cut into the edge of each of the joining members so that they can be interlocked, egg-crate style. The parts can join at any angle if the shoulders are cut at the proper angle. One danger with this joint is that the material beside the notch can split away along the grain. Fit it carefully so it can be assembled without force, which can break the wood.

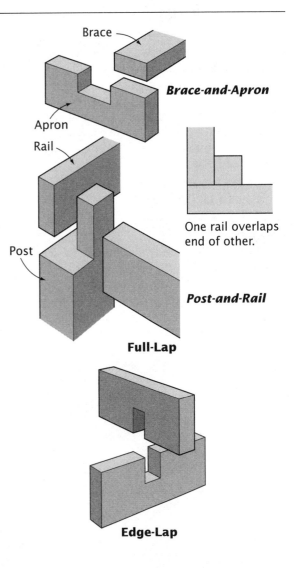

Brace

Brace-and-Apron

Apron

Rail

One rail overlaps end of other.

Post

Post-and-Rail

Full-Lap

Edge-Lap

➤ DOVETAIL JOINT

The classic way to join a top drawer rail to table legs is the dovetail. A single large tail is cut on the rail's end, and it drops into a socket cut into the leg top. (The socket cut can be said to form two half-pins.)

Even without being glued, the dovetail joint resists all four stresses extremely well. With the lower drawer rail serving as a fulcrum, the leg levers in and out, putting a lot of stress on that dovetail.

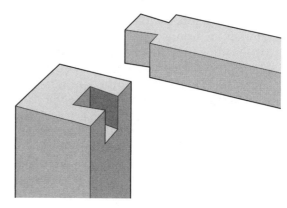

Dovetail Joint

➤ DOWEL JOINT

Dowels alone don't make particularly great rail joints. The gluing surfaces in the apron are long grain to long grain; but in the leg, they are strictly long grain to end grain.

One fix is to reinforce the joint with a simple corner block that is glued and screwed to the aprons, as shown in the drawing. It makes the joint very similar to the corner plate joint shown below.

➤ BOLTED JOINTS

Specialized hardware can be used to produce rail joints.

Bolted rail: Beds frequently are bolted together. Special bolts, called bed bolts, are typically used. The nut is trapped (and sometimes concealed) in a pocket in the side rail. The bolt is fed through a hole in the leg and

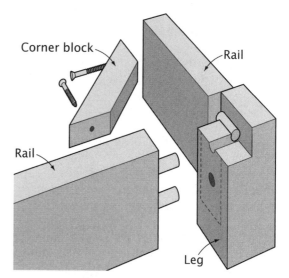

Corner block

Rail

Rail

Leg

Dowel Joint with Corner Block

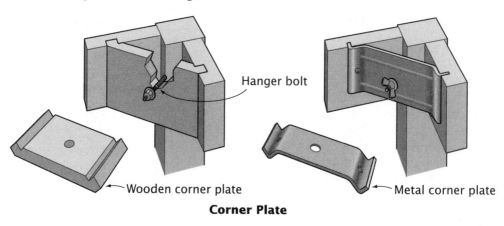

Hanger bolt

Wooden corner plate

Metal corner plate

Corner Plate

side rail to the nut. The long bolt has a tapered tip to make it easy to get it started in the nut. When the bolt has been tightened, its head is hidden by a decorative cover.

The same concept can be used with regular bolts to join heavy legs and aprons or stretchers. It is a knock-down joint.

Corner plate: Here is a way of assembling aprons to a leg with butt joints. The secret is a plate with tongues or flanges that catch in dadoes or kerfs cut in the aprons, as shown in the drawing. A hanger bolt, which has tapered threads on one end and machine threads on the other, is screwed into the arris of the leg and extends through a hole in the plate. A nut turned onto the bolt cinches the plate and pulls the aprons tight to the leg.

The wooden corner plate is a shop-made version of the plate, constructed from scrap wood. Dadoes must be cut in the aprons to house the ends of the plate.

The metal corner plate needs only a saw kerf across each apron. Typically the hanger bolt needed to pull the joint together is supplied with the plate.

Bolt and barrel nut: A hardware joint for relatively lightweight leg-and-apron pieces. Barrel nuts (or cross dowels, as they are often called) are metal and have a 1/4-inch threaded hole through the side. Drill a hole through the rail's face for the barrel nut. Then drill a pilot for the bolt, intersecting the first at right angles. Drill a pilot through the mating piece also. Fit the parts together, and insert and tighten the bolt—hex-head bolt, cap-head bolt, round-head or flat-head stove bolt, or whatever.

➤ DADO JOINT

This joint is used to install a shelf between the legs of a table. A dado is cut along the edge of a leg, and a corner is cut from the shelf. The shelf's corner fits into the dado.

A dowel is often incorporated in the joint as an alignment aid during assembly. The dowel contributes little to the joint's strength.

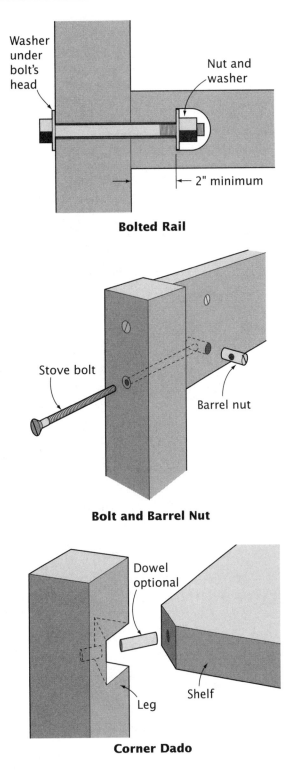

Bolted Rail

Bolt and Barrel Nut

Corner Dado

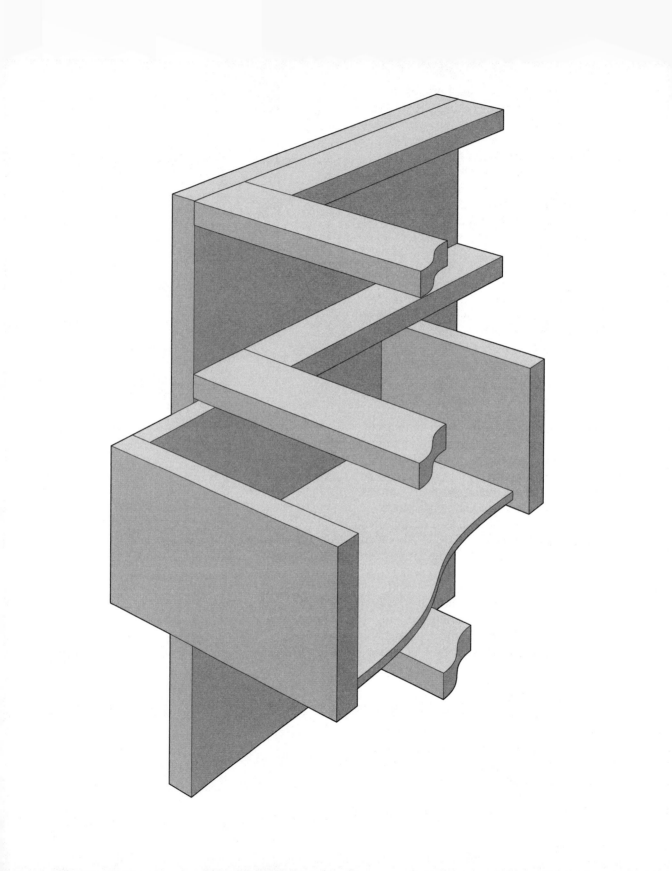

SUBASSEMBLIES

POST-AND-RAIL
CONSTRUCTION

Vertical posts joined by horizontal rails form one of the strongest structures in woodworking. Most post-and-rail structures (and leg-and-apron ones, too) form four-legged pieces of furniture: We're talking about beds, benches, and tables—even some desk forms and stands for chests.

Think of a post-and-rail structure as a bridge. A bridge carries its load successfully as a result of careful engineering. A post-and-rail structure requires a similar concern with the proportion and strength of its parts and joinery. One constant to keep in mind is that the wider the rails are, the more sturdy the post-

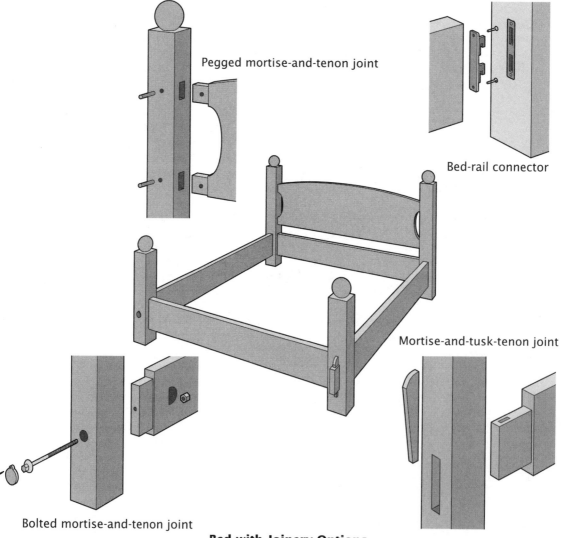

Pegged mortise-and-tenon joint

Bed-rail connector

Mortise-and-tusk-tenon joint

Bolted mortise-and-tenon joint

Bed with Joinery Options

and-rail construction will be. When designing furniture, you must balance this factor against the look and function of the piece.

➤ BEDS

A bed frame is kin to any table or workbench. The immediately obvious differences among them are the girths of the parts and the fact that the bed's rails are not flush with the ends of its posts. Another is that, due to its size, an assembled bed frame is not exactly easy to pick up and move to another room, let alone out the front door. So at least some of the joints in a bed frame are of the knockdown variety.

The drawing *Bed with Joinery Options* shows several joints commonly used in bed construction. Typically a bed consists of two end frames, which are post-and-rail assemblies, and two side rails. In the bed shown, there's a head end and a foot end. The end assemblies are joined with permanent joinery, while the side rails are connected to the end frames with knockdown joinery.

One good way to permanently attach a headboard panel and a rail between two posts is with pegged mortise-and-tenon joints.

Knockdown techniques for connecting a bed's side rails to the headboard and foot-board include using mortise-and-tusk-tenon joints, bed bolts, and bed-rail connectors.

The mortise-and-tusk-tenon joint displays itself prominently. Of course it looks pretty neat, and it shows craftsmanship. It's an exacting joint to cut, especially the two through mortises. But if made properly, with the tusk vertical (as shown in the drawing), the joint is quite likely to stay tight, despite the stresses of everyday usage and even the wood's come and go. If it shrinks a bit, the tusk will simply drop deeper into its mortise.

Bed bolts are used in conjunction with a mortise-and-tenon joint, so this joint is a hybrid. It combines the strong mechanical attributes of a mortise-and-tenon joint with the knockdown convenience of a nut and bolt. The bolt head is typically concealed under a decorative metal plate or a removable wood plug.

The bed-connector approach bypasses any wood-to-wood joinery and uses interlocking steel components, one mortised into the end of the rail and the other mortised into the face of the post. This hardware is very strong and reliable, and completely invisible, too.

➤ BENCHES

A workbench is a beefy table. It just sounds right to call it a "post-and-rail structure" instead of a "leg-and-apron stand." Its joinery need not be quite as elegant as a table's. Consequently, workbench rails are often just

Full-lap joint   Half-lap joint

Workbench with Joinery Options

bolted to the posts. A slightly improved approach, visually and structurally speaking, is to use a lap joint to connect the rails to the posts.

Two ways to use lap joints in a bench are shown in the drawing *Workbench with Joinery Options* on page 69. The easiest method is to lap the entire thickness of a rail into the post. Or you can lap the rails and the posts so that they form the same neat corner, the rails ending up flush with the posts. In either case note that the posts need to be large enough so that when you create the shoulders, there's still some stock left to attach the rails to.

Finally, though gluing the lap joint will provide some strength, it would be wise to add screws or bolts to reinforce the connection. To add plenty of strength to a bench, add stretchers, which are just rails located lower on the posts.

▶ TABLES

Leg-and-apron construction (the light-duty version of post-and-rail construction) is the workhorse of table making. The leg-and-apron framework is commonly called a "stand," and it needs to be structurally sound without relying on the tabletop. A tabletop made of solid wood is attached to its base in a way that allows for expansion and contraction. (See "Tabletops" on page 78.) It's the table's understructure, the stand, that has to stand up to the stress and strains of everyday use. There are many good ways to join table legs to aprons, and several are shown in the drawing *Leg-and-Apron Stand with Joinery Options.*

Mortise-and-Tenon Joints

The tried-and-true joint for leg-and-apron construction is the mortise-and-tenon, which has innumerable variations. It is the old standby because it is one of the strongest joints that can be used to connect apron to leg. It provides mechanical strength as well as good gluing surfaces. An added benefit is that an assembly made with accurately cut mortises

and tenons is more likely to go together square than one made using other joints.

Surely the full-height mortise-and-tenon is most common in dining and occasional tables of all kinds. Easy to make, strong, traditional. One shortcoming, if you are being picky, is that the mortise is open at the top of the leg, and conceivably, severe shear stress could lever it loose. (If it has been glued properly, the tenon should break first.)

The mortise-and-haunched tenon, used in a leg-and-apron assembly, responds to that concern. You get the full height possible at the haunch to resist racking, but you also get some of the leg's stock over top of the extended tenon.

Barefaced tenons are used when the alignment of the apron vis-à-vis the leg surfaces is important to the design yet you don't want to compromise the joinery. The tenon might, as shown in the drawing, be cut half the apron's thickness and flush with its inside face. That gives it strength yet sets the mortise in the center of the leg so *it* will be strong. Having but a single shoulder isn't ideal, but it does offer some racking resistance.

In all leg-and-apron assemblies, note how the rail tenons compete for the same mortise space within the leg. If the mortises are offset, it makes the joinery more complicated and may even weaken it. One solution is to miter the ends of the tenons. Then they're both the same length and as long as possible. A more complicated solution is to interlock the tenons with mating notches and shoulders, as shown. Puzzling, yes. But exceptionally strong.

Doweled Joints

Doweled leg-and-apron joints are a product of the industrial revolution and mass production. When done with machines, dowel joints can be precise and strong. Done by hand, they tend to be less strong and more troublesome. And the dowels have to be offset so they don't hit each other inside the leg.

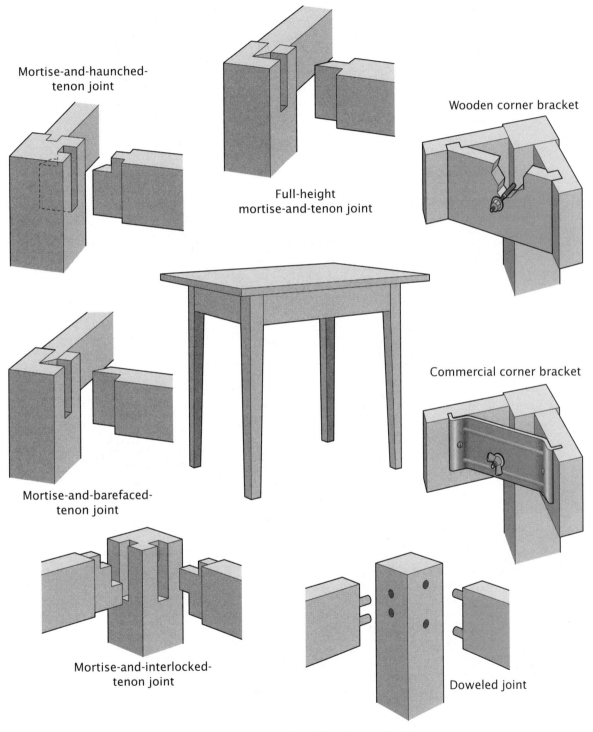

Mortise-and-haunched-tenon joint

Full-height mortise-and-tenon joint

Wooden corner bracket

Mortise-and-barefaced-tenon joint

Commercial corner bracket

Mortise-and-interlocked-tenon joint

Doweled joint

Leg-and-Apron Stand with Joinery Options

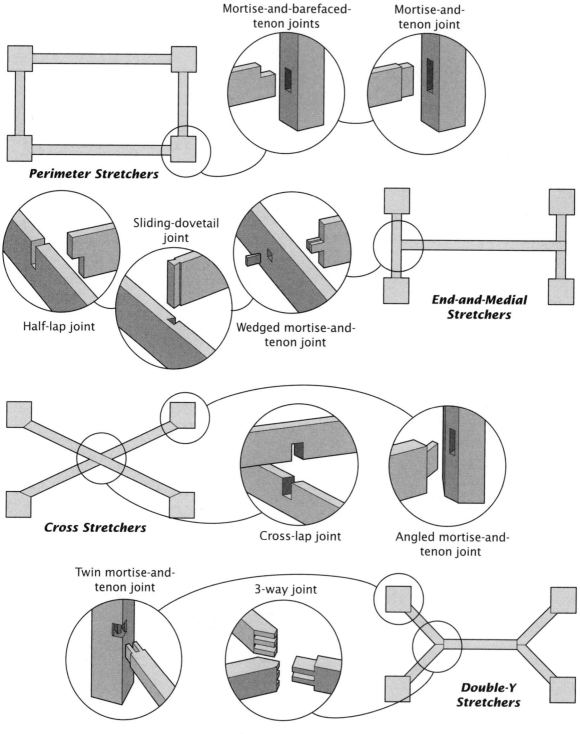

Mortise-and-barefaced-tenon joints

Mortise-and-tenon joint

Perimeter Stretchers

Sliding-dovetail joint

Half-lap joint

Wedged mortise-and-tenon joint

End-and-Medial Stretchers

Cross Stretchers

Cross-lap joint

Angled mortise-and-tenon joint

Twin mortise-and-tenon joint

3-way joint

Double-Y Stretchers

Stretcher Joinery Options

Corner Brackets

A century ago, the corner block, angled across the inside corners of a leg-and-apron stand and screwed to the aprons, provided insurance against weak joinery and helped square the frame during assembly. In some cases, it provided a means of attaching the tabletop.

Today its offspring, the corner bracket, is used to assemble the stand. The bracket is a wooden or metal plate dadoed into the aprons and bolted to the leg with a hanger bolt. The hanger bolt has tapered threads on one end and machine threads on the other; no head. One end is screwed into the wooden leg, the other passes through the bracket, and a nut is turned on and tightened. The bolt pulls the leg tight against the ends of the aprons, and *that's* the joint.

▶ TABLES WITH STRETCHERS

A stretcher is a rail that reinforces a leg-and-apron assembly at or near the foot. In the 17th century, almost every table had stout stretchers, like duplicate aprons located at floor level. They aren't ubiquitous today, but many tables do have stretchers, and they can make an important contribution to the strength and rigidity of a leg-and-apron structure.

The drawing *Stretcher Joinery Options* shows four likely stretcher configurations, along with appropriate joinery for each.

Perimeter stretchers connect the legs one to the next, which adds lots of strength. But the stretchers may get in the way of the user's feet and legs. The end-and-medial stretcher arrangement addresses the foot-room problem by moving a long stretcher to the stand's middle, where it extends between the end

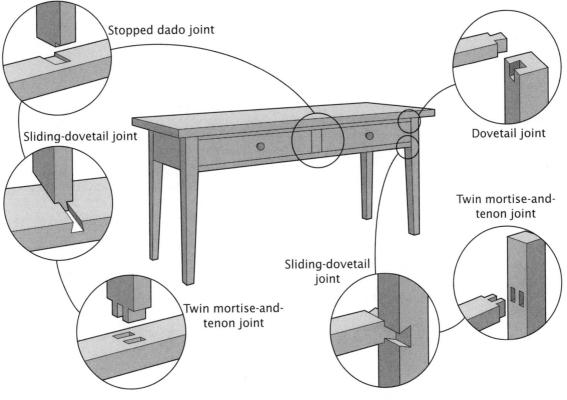

Stopped dado joint

Sliding-dovetail joint

Twin mortise-and-tenon joint

Dovetail joint

Twin mortise-and-tenon joint

Sliding-dovetail joint

Stand with Drawers between Rails

stretchers. Cross stretchers and double-Y stretchers address the same practical problem, but these present solutions that require fairly demanding joinery.

➤ TABLES WITH DRAWERS

Adding a drawer or two to a table makes it more useful. In the kitchen, it becomes a worktable, the drawer holding utensils. In the den, the same table becomes a desk, with the drawer holding writing paper and pens.

Tables with drawers are more challenging to engineer because the drawer occupies space where a solid apron would otherwise be. A design variable that's critical to the construction design is the drawer's width. If the drawer (or drawers) spans the space from leg to leg, then a double-rail construction is appropriate.

This may be the most common approach. In it, the legs are connected with two rails, laid flat, so the drawer or drawers can fit between them. The top rail is almost always let into the top of the legs with a dovetail joint. The bottom rail is joined to the legs with either a sliding-dovetail or a twin mortise-and-tenon joint. A number of different support setups are possible; see "Drawer Construction" on page 104 for more details.

Two drawers fitted side by side under a tabletop are always separated by a vertical divider, which is joined to the horizontal drawer rails with a stopped dado, a twin mortise-and-tenon, or a sliding-dovetail joint. The latter

offers the best structural support because it locks the parts together mechanically in a way the other two joints do not.

Another approach comes into play when a small drawer is located in a much larger apron. In some cases, the drawer opening can be cut right into the apron, with the cutout then used as the drawer front. The benefit is improved appearance: With the drawer closed, the grain on the apron looks unbroken.

Making such a cut is easier said than done, of course. An alternative (and easier) means to the same end is shown in the drawing *Apron with Drawer Opening.* The apron is ripped into three strips. After the drawer front is crosscut from the center strip, the wood is reglued to form an apron with a drawer opening.

A couple of cautions are in order here. Remember, when planning a table with drawers, that the wider the span, the more likely it is that the drawer-rail assembly will sag. Remember, too, that the total height of the drawer-rail assembly should be no more than 6 inches if you expect to sit with your legs under the table.

➤ TABLE LEG FORMS

While the post or leg is a fundamental structural component, it is also, intrinsically, a design element. Over the centuries an incredible range of forms have been used in the effort to make legs attractive. Just a few of the ways legs have been shaped, sculpted, carved, and turned are shown on the opposite page.

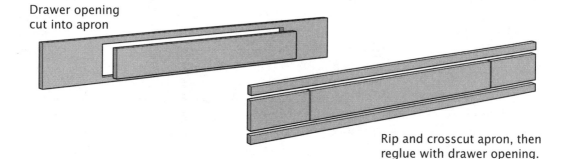

Drawer opening cut into apron

Rip and crosscut apron, then reglue with drawer opening.

Apron with Drawer Opening

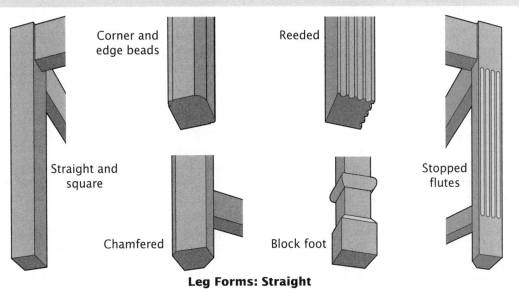

Corner and
edge beads

Reeded

Straight and
square

Stopped
flutes

Chamfered

Block foot

Leg Forms: Straight

Straight Legs

We may think of a straight and square leg as suitable only for benches and utility tables, but in Chippendale's day, it was a favorite for high-style furniture. The square leg was hardly plain, as these examples make clear. Chamfering the inside corner tends to lighten the appearance of the leg, while fluting, reeding, and other profiling make it more interesting.

Tapered Legs

Tapering a table leg solves a fundamental design problem: how to make it look proportionate and attractive and yet still have enough girth at the top for a spacious mortise to house the apron's tenon.

A standard taper typically starts at the apron and runs to the foot. It may be slight or extreme, on the inside faces only, or on all

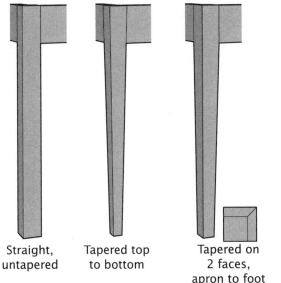

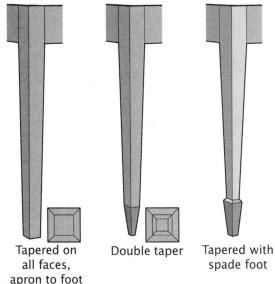

Straight,
untapered

Tapered top
to bottom

Tapered on
2 faces,
apron to foot

Tapered on
all faces,
apron to foot

Double taper

Tapered with
spade foot

Leg Forms: Tapered

four faces. A double taper forms a sort of pointed foot. A spade foot is formed by tapering all four faces first, then tapering more deeply (at a sharper angle) from the top end of the leg to the top of the foot, as shown.

Tapers are used widely in Federal, Shaker, and country styles.

Turned Legs

Turning a table leg on a lathe allows a wide range of shape and ornamentation. A turned leg may be tapered along its length or only part of its length. It may have a combination of shapes like bulbs, spools, rings, coves, cups, and vases. Or it may have reeds or flutes cut into it after being turned. In any event, the joinery should be cut before the leg is turned.

Turned legs are one of the most stylized features found in furniture, as shown in the symmetrical vase and bead shapes of a William and Mary–style leg or the reeded taper and distinctive foot pattern of a Federal-style leg.

Cabriole Legs

Of all the furniture legs ever designed, the cabriole leg is probably the most distinctive,

graceful, and versatile. Though associated primarily with the Queen Anne and (to a lesser extent) Chippendale styles, the cabriole leg has been adapted and modified (often badly) by furniture designers, makers, and manufacturers to fit most major furniture forms.

Originally, the cabriole leg, like everything else, was handmade—sawed to shape out of a blank of wood, then hand carved. Skilled craftsmen continue this tradition, though manufacturers produce thousands a day on large machines. A less curvaceous version of the leg can also be turned on the lathe.

Cabriole legs vary in curvature, contour, girth, and many other subtle details. Queen Anne–era craftsmen shaped slender, graceful, but frail cabriole legs, while relatively few years later, Chippendale-era woodworkers were producing squat, stocky cabriole legs.

Variety can be found even in the foot, as shown on the opposite page. Conservators and collectors of authentic 18th-century furniture look at subtle differences in the feet to distinguish between different makers. Most cabriole feet patterns, especially the ball-and-claw foot, require exceptional skill to create.

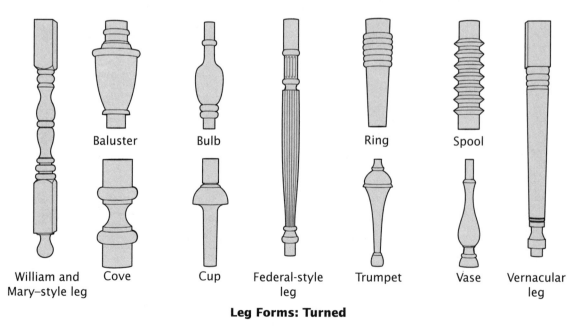

Baluster   Bulb   Ring   Spool

William and   Cove   Cup   Federal-style   Trumpet   Vase   Vernacular
Mary–style leg   leg   leg

Leg Forms: Turned

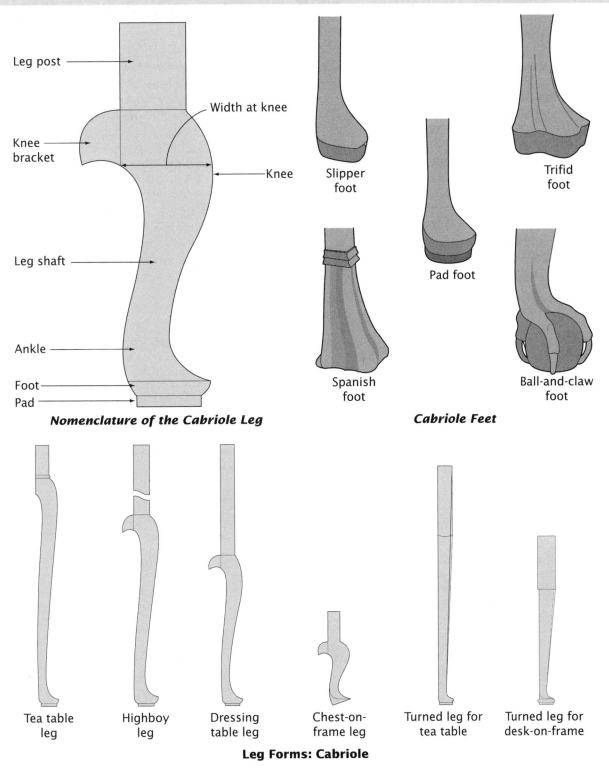

Leg post

Width at knee

Knee bracket

Knee

Leg shaft

Ankle

Foot

Pad

Nomenclature of the Cabriole Leg

Slipper foot

Trifid foot

Pad foot

Spanish foot

Ball-and-claw foot

Cabriole Feet

Tea table leg

Highboy leg

Dressing table leg

Chest-on-frame leg

Turned leg for tea table

Turned leg for desk-on-frame

Leg Forms: Cabriole

TABLETOPS

The width of the single board he once used for a tabletop is the woodworker's version of the big fish story.

While the fisherman will exaggerate the number of people fed by his huge catch, the woodworker will brag about how easy it was to complete the tabletop. No glue-up. No clamps. Just screwed it down.

But if you read the chapter "Wood Movement" on page 12, you know that every single board, even a wide one, is prone to expand and contract with the seasons; when they do, they are prone to cup and bow and twist. So even a single-board tabletop has to be dealt with carefully.

➤ WOOD MOVEMENT

In response to changes in the moisture content in the air, wood expands and contracts *across* the grain but minimally along the grain. So a tabletop, whether made of a single board or formed by gluing several edge-to-edge, will have a range of movement of as much as 3/8 inch, depending upon the species of wood and the width of the tabletop.

Wood movement has both cosmetic and structural consequences. The cosmetic effect is that a tabletop, over the course of a year, will change in size and sometimes in shape. In prolonged periods of low humidity, for example, a round tabletop will shrink across the grain and become elliptical. The change may go unnoticed in a large table, but in a small table it could be quite evident.

A large rectangular tabletop, especially one with a substantial overhang, may cup or bow slightly or get wavy along the end. The traditional preventive measure is the "breadboard end," a strip joined across the end of the tabletop.

This does help to maintain flatness, but it has a cosmetic problem of its own: The joint between the edge of the breadboard end and the edge of the table will vary with wood movement. When humidity is highest, the tabletop will expand and extend beyond the ends of the breadboard. When humidity is lowest, the tabletop will shrink and the ends of the breadboard will be proud.

The structural impact of a tabletop's

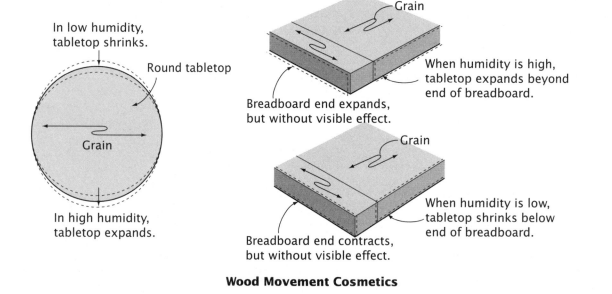

Wood Movement Cosmetics

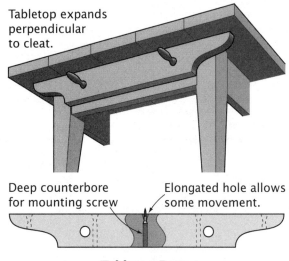

In high humidity, tabletop expands.

Expanding tabletop tends to lever joints open.

Tension stress on apron-to-leg joinery

Tabletop expands perpendicular to cleat.

Deep counterbore for mounting screw

Elongated hole allows some movement.

Tabletop Batten

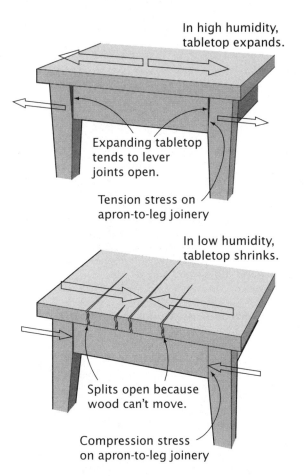

In low humidity, tabletop shrinks.

Splits open because wood can't move.

Compression stress on apron-to-leg joinery

Structural Impact of Wood Movement

expansion and contraction is considerable, as shown in *Wood Movement Cosmetics*. If the tabletop is firmly fixed to the leg-and-apron assembly, several things can happen. The tabletop can buckle as it expands, or crack and split as it shrinks. It can also promote joint failure in the framework.

▶ KEEPING THE TOP FLAT

The first order in making a tabletop, then, is to keep it flat in a way that doesn't cause it to damage itself.

With trestle tables and tavern tables, the tabletop is often kept flat by screwing a batten or cleat to the underside. The batten

might even double as a connection between the tabletop and the trestle or leg structure. In any event, to allow the wood to expand and contract, the mounting screws must be run through slots in the cleat rather than through tight pilot holes.

Breadboard Ends

Another way to keep a tabletop (or other panel, like a desk flap) flat is with breadboard ends. The breadboards first must be dead-flat and then carefully fitted to the ends of the panel in a way that permits expansion and contraction. At the same time, breadboard ends do reduce expansion and contraction by covering the tabletop's end grain. Reducing exposed end grain can also be viewed as a cosmetic improvement, since end grain looks different than face grain when finished.

Joinery options abound. A primitive breadboard is simply nailed to the end of the tabletop. The nails are surprisingly good fasteners, offering a little give without completely surrendering their grip.

More sophisticated is the tongue-and-groove. Glued at the center only, it may be the most common joint for a breadboard end. It can run through the end or be blind. It even

Glue at center only.

**Through
Tongue-and-Groove**

Glue at center only.

**Blind
Tongue-and-Groove**

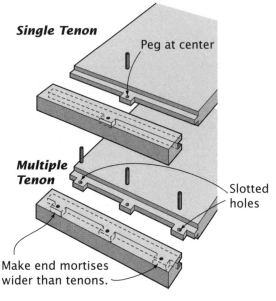

Single Tenon

Peg at center

*Multiple
Tenon*

Slotted
holes

Make end mortises
wider than tenons.

Mortise-and-Tenon Breadboard

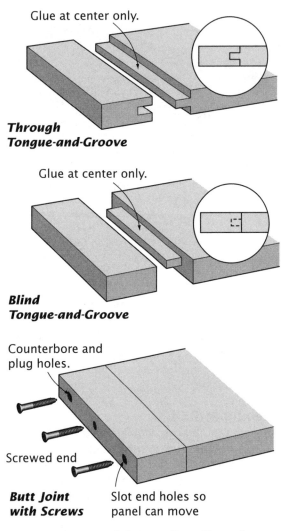

Counterbore and
plug holes.

Screwed end

**Butt Joint
with Screws**

Slot end holes so
panel can move

Tongue-and-Groove Breadboard

can be attached with screws driven through slotted holes, as shown above.

Centuries ago, cabinetmakers sometimes took a more elaborate approach, adding mortises and tenons to the simple tongue-and-groove. They made the end mortises wider than the tenons to allow for movement. Again, a center peg, or a peg through each tenon, locks the breadboard end to the tabletop.

A sliding dovetail locks the breadboard on the end of the tabletop, with nary a spot of

glue, but still allows movement. A single peg through the center of the joint will keep the breadboard end from being slid completely off.

The mitered breadboard is used on desk flaps and some small and formal tables. It has the advantage of concealing *all* the end grain.

Two versions, one good, the other not so good, are used. A breadboard end that's mitered on one end only, and properly attached (as described below), leaves the

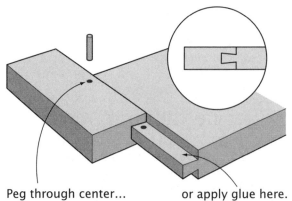

Peg through center...   or apply glue here.

Sliding Dovetail Breadboard

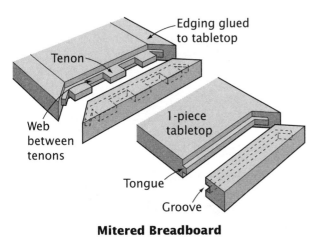

Edging glued to tabletop

Tenon

1-piece tabletop

Web between tenons

Tongue

Groove

Mitered Breadboard

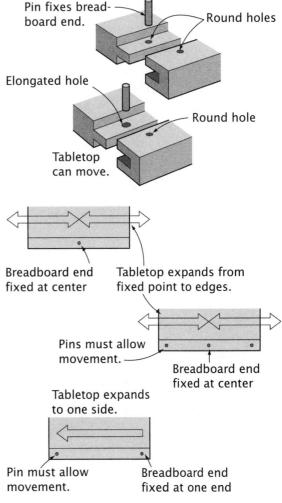

Pin fixes bread-board end.

Round holes

Elongated hole

Round hole

Tabletop can move.

Breadboard end fixed at center

Tabletop expands from fixed point to edges.

Pins must allow movement.

Breadboard end fixed at center

Tabletop expands to one side.

Pin must allow movement.

Breadboard end fixed at one end

Pinning Breadboard Ends

tabletop free to move at the back. This works fine. But adding mitered pieces around a solid table produces a tabletop that looks good initially but that will eventually have broken or opened the miters. When the tabletop shrinks, the breadboard end will be too long, and it will put enormous compression stress on the mitered edges of the tabletop.

When pinning a breadboard end, the goal is to lock it to the tabletop so it can't pop off, but still allow the top to expand and contract. A single peg in a round hole at the center allows expansion at both ends of the breadboard strip, as shown in the drawing *Pinning Breadboard Ends*. If pegs are added at the ends of the strip, they must be in elongated holes to allow movement, as shown. A pin in a round hole at one end and a pin in an elongated hole at the other is a sound option when you want one end of the breadboard to always be flush with the tabletop edge.

▶ ATTACHING TABLETOPS

A couple hundred years ago, cabinetmakers sometimes would attach a tabletop to its stand with blocks glued securely to both the aprons and the tabletop. Of course, this didn't allow the tabletop to expand and contract

freely, and such tables would eventually split or buckle from the resulting stresses. We should chalk that up to their experience.

A fairly similar approach that's still presented today in books is to screw blocks or ledger strips to the aprons, then drive screws through them into the tabletop. Not a good approach, either, unless slotted pilots are used. The slots must be perpendicular to the tabletop's grain.

Screw or glue the blocks securely to the aprons. Then drive screws through the slots

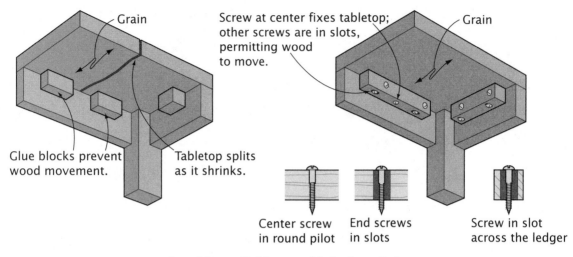

Grain

Screw at center fixes tabletop; other screws are in slots, permitting wood to move.

Grain

Glue blocks prevent wood movement.

Tabletop splits as it shrinks.

Center screw in round pilot

End screws in slots

Screw in slot across the ledger

Attaching a Tabletop with Ledger Strips

With either approach, elongate pilots across tabletop's grain.

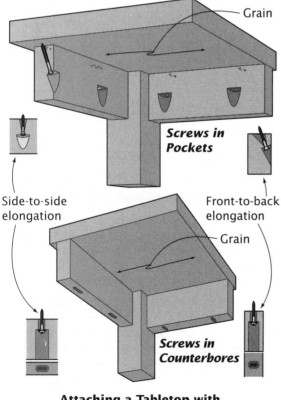

Grain

Screws in Pockets

Side-to-side elongation

Front-to-back elongation

Grain

Screws in Counterbores

Attaching a Tabletop with Screws through Aprons

into the underside of the tabletop. At the center of the cross-grain ledger is a "fixed pilot," which has a pilot hole matched to the diameter of the screw. This anchors the tabletop; all the movement occurs on either side of this point.

You can use a similar technique when mounting a tabletop directly to the aprons with screws. Instead of slotting the apron, however, you can simply drill an oversized or elongated counterbore for the screw head to move within, as shown in the drawing *Attaching a Tabletop with Screws through Aprons*. Depending on the width of the aprons, the pilot holes can be drilled either straight through or at an angle, forming screw pockets.

And there's yet another solution, and this one doesn't require slotted holes. Wood "buttons," often called cabinetmaker's buttons, are simple blocks cut from a length of stock with a rabbeted end. The tongue on the button moves along, or in and out of, a groove cut along the inside face of all the aprons, as shown in the drawing *Attaching a Tabletop with Buttons*. There's also a metal version of this simple tabletop fastener.

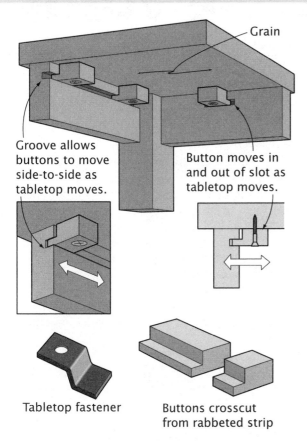

Grain

Groove allows buttons to move side-to-side as tabletop moves.

Button moves in and out of slot as tabletop moves.

Tabletop fastener

Buttons crosscut from rabbeted strip

Attaching a Tabletop with Buttons

➤ RULE JOINT

A drop-leaf table is where the rule joint is used. It's an oddity, as joinery goes, because it isn't a fixed joint—it's a hinged joint. It gets its name from its resemblance to the joint on a traditional cabinetmaker's folding rule.

In the rule joint, a roundover profile is cut along the tabletop edge. A matching cove profile is cut along the bottom edge of the leaf. Special hinges, each with one long leaf and one short leaf, are set into mortises in the underside of the tabletop and table leaf.

When the leaf is open, the cove fits over the roundover. Lower the leaf, and the tip of the cove sticks up enough to hide the gap between the leaf and the tabletop.

With the leaf opened, there is a tight seam between the leaf and the tabletop. If properly fitted, the tip of the cove actually rests on top of the roundover at the quirk, relieving the stress on the hinges. When folded down, the leaf still overlaps the edge of the top slightly, so there is never an open gap between the two. To prevent binding when the leaf is raised and lowered, the roundover needs to be exaggerated a tad along the bottom edge of the tabletop.

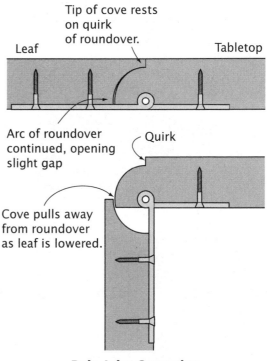

Tip of cove rests on quirk of roundover.

Leaf

Tabletop

Arc of roundover continued, opening slight gap

Quirk

Cove pulls away from roundover as leaf is lowered.

Rule Joint Operation

CASEWORK

Case construction is the art and science of building boxes. To a woodworker, any enclosed structure—a chest with or without a lid, a cabinet with drawers or doors, even a bookcase that's open front and back—is casework. Sure, we are more likely to think of big pieces like kitchen cabinets, a big chest of drawers, or a hutch as casework; but even individual drawers are cases.

How is a case built? There are many forms and approaches, as the drawing *Casework Construction Types* demonstrates. In choosing one over another, the cabinetmaker has to consider ease of construction, appearance, cost, weight, strength, and durability.

Until plywood (and other man-made sheet goods like particleboard and medium-density fiberboard) came along, a case would be built of solid wood, and *the* key construction consideration was how to accommodate that wood's movement.

Solid-wood panel construction may be most aesthetically pleasing, but it is also the most problematic in wood movement terms. The biggest mistake you can make in solid-wood case construction is to join components with their grain directions perpendicular to each other. The drawing *Cross-Grain Construction Problems* shows three examples, and in each one, the cross-grain orientation has resulted in cracks in a wide panel.

Historically, the best structural answer has been frame-and-panel construction, which produces the most stable solid-wood case. But

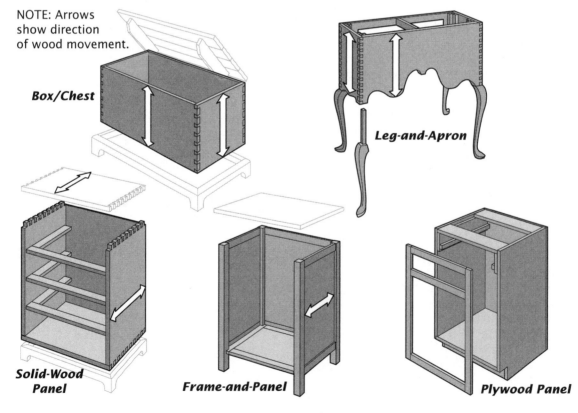

NOTE: Arrows show direction of wood movement.

Box/Chest

Leg-and-Apron

Solid-Wood Panel

Frame-and-Panel

Plywood Panel

Casework Construction Types

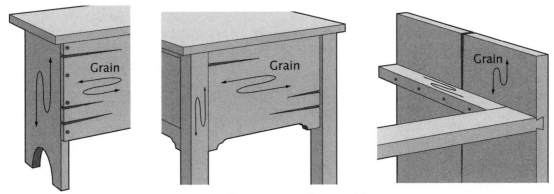

Cross-Grain Construction Problems

plywood has changed all that because it is like solid wood in aesthetics, and like frame-and-panel in terms of stability.

➤ BUILDING A BOX

Cases have been built in so many variations that it is difficult to delineate one basic, archetypal approach. How the case will be used, what it is to be made of, what it is supposed to look like, and even the abilities of the maker all enter into "case construction."

The most elemental case is a simple open-topped box. All that's needed are four sides and a bottom. These parts are assembled with appropriate joints (see "Case Joints," beginning on page 27) to form the box.

The drawing *Box/Chest Construction* shows a basic box assembled with through dovetails, the quintessential case joint. Several good alternative joints are also shown. The box could be a small drawer, a large chest, or even a traditionally leg-and-apron structure like a dressing table. The essentials

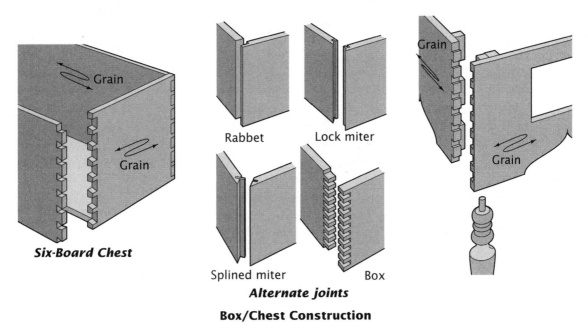

Six-Board Chest

Rabbet   Lock miter

Splined miter   Box

Alternate joints

Box/Chest Construction

are the same, regardless: Orient the grain of all sides the same so the parts are joined end-to-end and so they will move in tandem.

Case Construction

A cupboard or chest of drawers introduces new aspects to case construction. The box now is standing on end, with the front and back open. It looks like the Basic Case shown in the drawing *Case Construction*. Add a back, a door, and a base, and you have a cabinet.

Joining solid boards to form a case is surely one of the oldest construction techniques around. Depending on the width of the case and the available material, the case parts may be a single board, or several

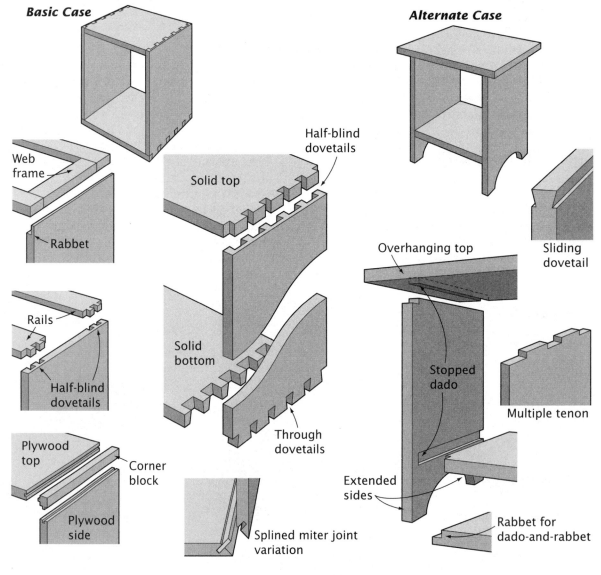

Case Construction

boards glued edge-to-edge into a wider panel. (It's important to remember that a glued-up panel expands and contracts just as much as a single board of equal width.)

In a solid-wood case, the grain direction of the sides, top, and bottom must be parallel, with the parts joined end-to-end. The ideal case joint requires a combination of good mechanical strength and ample gluing surfaces. Dovetails, cut quickly by an experienced cabinetmaker, are strong, and they circumvent cross-grain constructions that are problematic in solid wood. But other case joints can be used, of course.

Today's cabinetmaker is likely to use plywood or MDF for a case. Compared to solid wood, manufactured panels are dimensionally stable. But that doesn't really change the way the basic case is built. What it *does* change is how you can install components like drawer runners and moldings. The drawing shows a couple of joints—miters and corner blocks—that conceal the edges of manufactured panels; but many others will work, too.

Case construction is flexible enough to permit less boxlike configurations, as the Alternative Case shown in the drawing demonstrates. The sides can extend beyond the bottom (or a similar top, for that matter). The top (or the bottom) can overhang the sides. Some of the most likely joints to use for these constructions are shown, but also check the "Case Joints" chapter. In the Alternative Case, the top is both structural and visual.

Where a solid top isn't needed (or wanted), rails or a web frame can be substituted, as the drawing shows. Either can be joined to the case sides using dovetails, rabbet joints, or dado-and-rabbet joints.

Frame-and-Panel Case Construction

Frame-and-panel is an excellent construction approach that produces a very stable case, even when solid wood is used exclusively.

As with other approaches, there are trade-offs. The system makes good use of relatively narrow boards. For a large surface—the side of a wardrobe, for instance—a frame-and-panel

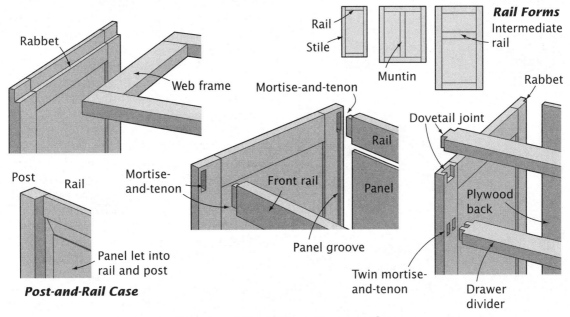

Frame-and-Panel Case Construction

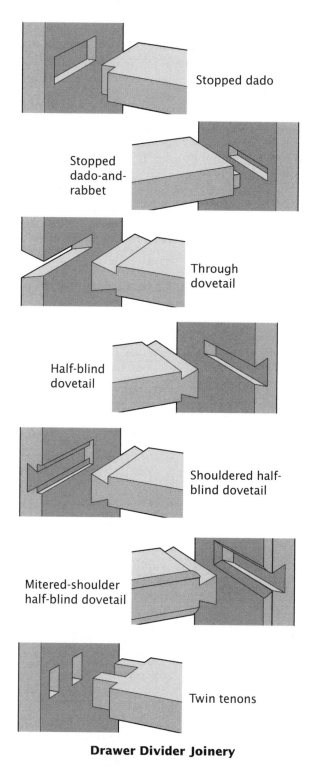

Stopped dado

Stopped dado-and-rabbet

Through dovetail

Half-blind dovetail

Shouldered half-blind dovetail

Mitered-shoulder half-blind dovetail

Twin tenons

Drawer Divider Joinery

assembly adds visual interest by breaking up what would otherwise be a large flat plane into smaller areas.

But frame-and-panel construction is time-consuming, and the completed case is likely to be heavier than a comparable solid-wood or plywood case.

The basics of constructing a frame-and-panel assembly can be found in "Door Construction" on pages 94–103. The drawing *Frame-and-Panel Case Construction* on page 87 shows how frame-and-panel units are combined to create a case.

▶ DIVIDING THE BOX

Seldom is an open, undivided case considered a finished product. It needs doors, shelves, or perhaps drawers to complete it. A face frame may be added to define and complete the facade of the piece.

Fixed shelves typically are dadoed into the case sides, though other case joints will do as well. Adjustable shelves have been used in cabinets and cupboards for centuries, but contemporary hardware makes it easier than ever to do. Two simple approaches are shown in the detail drawing *Adjustable Shelf Support Options* on page 295.

The many different ways that doors can be constructed and fitted to a case are shown in "Door Construction," beginning on page 94.

Likewise, the methods of making and hanging drawers is covered in "Drawer Construction," beginning on page 104. Many of the subassemblies that hang drawers in a case must be incorporated as the case itself is constructed. Modern hardware makes it easy, albeit fairly expensive, to hang drawers in an open, undifferentiated case; but this approach is largely limited to kitchen cabinetry and similar built-ins. Most of the cabinets and cupboards that we consider to be "furniture" are still built using traditional approaches. The traditional approach is to

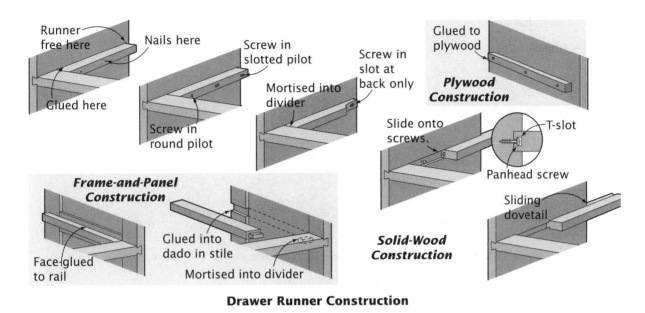

Drawer Runner Construction

divide the case, using drawer dividers or web frames, thus creating a separate compartment for each drawer.

Drawer dividers: These do more than separate one drawer opening from another. They also keep the case sides straight and parallel. As such, they need to be integral to the overall design and construction of the case.

There are various ways drawer dividers can be joined to the sides, all shown in the drawing *Drawer Divider Joinery* on the opposite page.

Both the dado and the dado-and-rabbet joints are easy to do and work for all constructions (solid-wood, plywood, and frame-and-panel). The dado can be through (exposed on the front edge), but most often, it is stopped. The divider itself needs to be notched at the front corner. These joints present little resistance to tension stress; in theory, the case side could bow outward and pull the joint apart.

The various dovetail variants *do* present good resistance to tension stress, presenting a mechanical resistance to any tendency of the side to bow out.

A modern approach that is well suited to plywood cases with solid-wood drawer dividers is the *twin tenon*. The mortises for the joint are intermittent and do less damage to the structural integrity of the sheet's face veneer. If the design calls for it, the mortises can be through and the tenons wedged.

Drawer runners: To support the drawer, you need runners. They are inevitably installed cross-grain; and if not mounted so that the case side can expand and contract, they can prompt splitting and buckling of the side.

In building a solid-wood case, use one of the appropriate methods shown in the drawing *Drawer Runner Construction*. In each approach (except the top right one), the runner is housed in a shallow dado. The dado joint takes the weight of the drawer, and the fastening options all are intended simply to hold the runner in the dado.

When the runner is being joined to a frame-and-panel assembly, wood movement is moot. The runner can be edge-glued to a rail in the side assembly, or it can be set into dadoes in the side assembly's stiles and glued, so long as it isn't glued to the panel. The

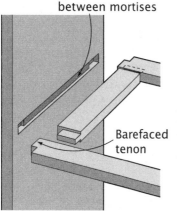

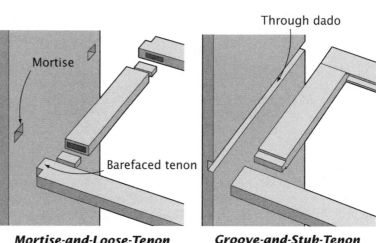

Mortise-and-Tenon   **Mortise-and-Loose-Tenon**   **Groove-and-Stub-Tenon**

Web Frame Construction

runner could also be mortised into a drawer divider and glued to the back stile.

In plywood construction, a runner can be glued into a shallow dado or simply glued and screwed directly to the plywood side.

Web frames: In many situations, the system of drawer dividers and runners is turned into a complete frame, with rails front and back and two runners (or stiles). The resulting frames, usually called web frames, can be constructed and installed in a variety of ways.

The drawing *Web Frame Construction* shows three workable ways of constructing

and installing a web frame. Typically, the parts of the web frame are not glued together, though the frame is glued to the case.

In most cases, the runner should be slightly—about 1/8 inch—short at the back so that the side can shrink, closing this gap between the runner and the back rail without pushing the rail out.

Dust panels: To keep the contents of the drawers clean, dust panels are often fitted into web frames. The drawing *Dust Panel* shows several ways to do it. Before plywood was invented, a solid-wood panel would be

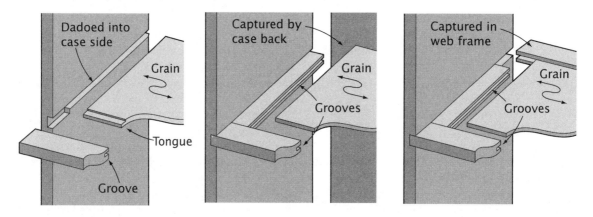

Dust Panel

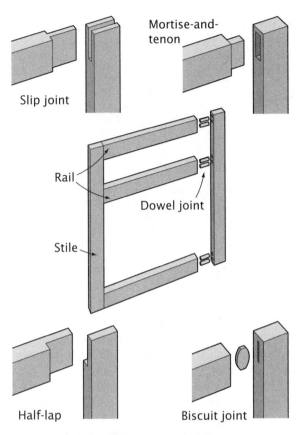

Face Frame Construction

The drawing *Face Frame Construction* shows a basic unit, with an array of joints that can be used. Because a face frame is attached permanently to the case, the stresses on its joints are minimal. Typically, then, the joinery is selected for ease of construction rather than strength. The face frame can be glued to the case edges, though biscuits are often used to help align it.

Quarter Columns

Quarter columns are used to give a case more presence. The idea is to make a turning blank that can be split cleanly into quarters. You turn and reed (or flute) the blank, then split it. A quarter-round strip is set into a niche where the case side meets the face frame or drawer dividers. The side then looks thicker and more interesting because of the column.

The niche is created, as you can see in the drawing *Quarter Column Construction,* by rabbeting a strip of wood, then gluing it edge-to-face to the case side. The column is glued into the rabbet thus formed. You need to use drawer guides, and the joinery between drawer divider and side is a little more demanding.

incorporated to double as a runner. Nowadays, plywood or hardboard panels are fitted to the web frames.

Face Frame Construction

A face frame is an assembly of rails and stiles that's attached to the front of a case. It beautifies the case and defines the spaces into which it is divided.

Not every case has a face frame, of course, but it is quite common on kitchen cabinetry. In this type of cabinet, it is as much visual as structural. The frame does help stiffen case sides, and doors are hinged to it. But drawers are hung on slides that are mounted to the case sides and operate independent of the face frame. The frame's main function is to create a facade for the cabinet.

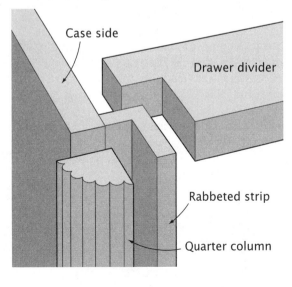

Quarter Column Construction

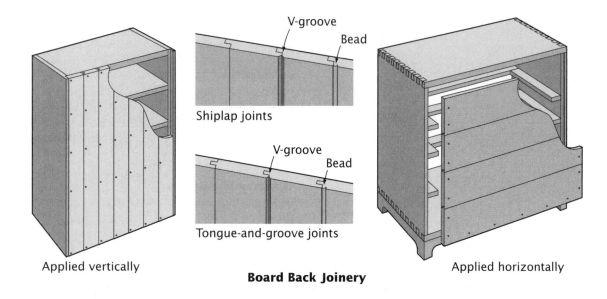

V-groove

Bead

Shiplap joints

V-groove

Bead

Tongue-and-groove joints

Applied vertically

Board Back Joinery

Applied horizontally

►BACK CONSTRUCTION

Without a back, a case is incomplete. A back closes in the case and provides bracing to keep it from racking. Occasionally, the back helps support drawer runners or shelves.

Aesthetic demands vary. In an enclosed cupboard, the back may be strictly functional, and looks are of little or no consequence. In a bookcase or display cabinet, the inner face will be visible, so it needs to be attractive, too. Occasionally, a back has to present an attractive appearance both inside and outside of the case, and this can be done.

Several construction approaches are possible.

Board back: Boards can be nailed to the case, oriented either horizontally or vertically. In a rustic construction, the boards may simply be butted edge-to-edge. In a more sophisticated piece, they'll be joined— unglued—with shiplap or tongue-and-groove joints to allow for movement. A board back almost always is set into rabbets in the sides, if not the top and bottom. If the back is exposed inside the case—as in a hutch or corner cupboard—the boards might have beads or chamfers cut on the edges.

Frame-and-panel back: Stronger and certainly more finished in appearance is the frame-and-panel back. Because it is more work

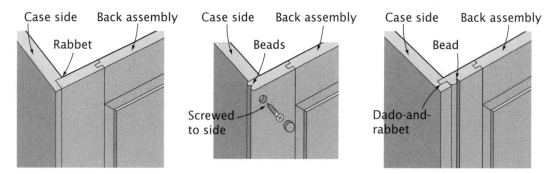

Case side   Back assembly

Rabbet

Case side   Back assembly

Beads

Screwed to side

Case side   Back assembly

Bead

Dado-and-rabbet

Installing a Frame-and-Panel Back

to make, it would be used primarily where the back of the cabinet will be exposed (where the completed piece will be used in the center of a room, for example).

Construction of frame-and-panel assemblies is depicted in "Door Construction," beginning on page 94, while the several options for attaching one to a case are shown in the drawing *Installing a Frame-and-Panel Back*.

Plywood back: Today's solution is the plywood back. Strong, stable, fast to make, economical, light in weight, it is ideal, functionally. A hardwood-plywood back can even be attractive if it is installed carefully.

The drawing *Installing a Plywood Back* shows two flexible constructions.

➤ ATTACHING A TOP

If the top is not an integral part of the case, it has to be attached. An attached top often overhangs the case in front and on the sides. It may have profiled edges. And often, the wood used will have very showy figure.

In most situations, the top is mounted to the case just the way a top is attached to a

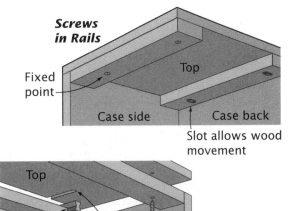

Screws in Rails

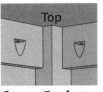

Butterfly Key

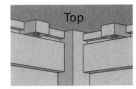

Screw Pockets   *Cabinetmaker's Buttons*

Attaching a Case Top

table. The drawing *Attaching a Case Top* shows four good ways to do it.

If the top is secured to top rails with screws, round pilots are used at the front to fix the top there so that it will always look the same in relation to the case's facade. Movement is allowed to happen in relation to the case's back, where it will be obscured, by using slotted pilots in the back rail.

A traditional construction, invented by an 18th-century cabinetmaker, accomplishes the same thing using butterfly keys at the back. Keys would be glued into slots in the back top rail, and matching slots would be cut into the underside of the top. The top would then be slid onto the keys—without glue—and then attached to the front rail with screws.

Screws can also be driven through pockets in the sides, front, and back. Cabinetmaker's buttons are another option.

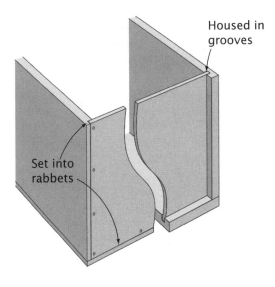

Installing a Plywood Back

DOOR
CONSTRUCTION

For as simple as a door is, we ask—and expect—a lot of it. It is required to look nice, of course. We want it to open and close easily at all times of the year. It should stay flat, naturally, and stay square and rigid, and not get all loosey-goosey. We don't want to hear that panel rattle or those hinges creak.

Typically, doors do do all of this. (We remember best the few that don't.) Nevertheless, doors are pretty easy to make. The styles are relatively few, the materials required are minimal, and the suitable joinery is limited.

The style of a piece of furniture usually determines the design and construction used for the doors. A traditional country piece, for example, probably will look better with frame-and-panel doors, while a lean and hungry contemporary piece may call out for flush plywood doors.

There is no one path to follow in designing and engineering doors for your project. But as you do start designing a piece, don't go too far before you determine the way the door will relate to its cabinet.

➤ DOOR FUNDAMENTALS

How it will open and close is a more practical starting point for choosing door construction than fretting about materials and joinery. Those choices will confront you in due time.

Door configurations: There are many ways to mount a door to a cabinet. The best way depends on the size of the door and how the cabinet will be used. The standard side-hinged door does the job in the widest range of circumstances. Certainly, it is the configuration that comes to mind first.

The other configurations are useful in particular circumstances when that standard won't work. On a wide cabinet without a center muntin, for example, folding doors may be a better approach than side-hinging extremely wide (and thus relatively heavy) doors to the case. Sliding doors solve the problem of limited

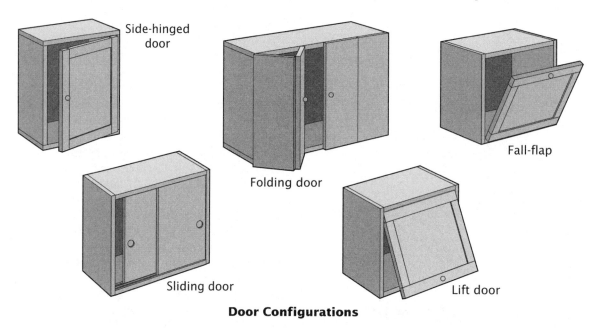

Side-hinged door

Folding door

Fall-flap

Sliding door

Lift door

Door Configurations

space in front of a cabinet. A fall-flap can give a door a secondary function, as a writing surface or counter. A lift door may be the best solution where a door used for security on a wall cabinet needs to stand open to allow ready access throughout a work session.

Door placements: Doors also vary in the way they engage the case. As shown, a door can be flush (or inset), overlay, or lipped. This fundamental detail affects how the piece will look, what the dimensions are, and what hardware options are available.

Door stability: This is what door construction is all about. To make us happy about a door—to *not* remember it, in other words—it needs to be easy to open yet easy to close and to keep closed. So it needs to stay flat and undergo minimal change due to wood movement. If a door is unstable, it will be loose in winter's drying central heat, tight and binding in summer's high humidity. It will warp or perhaps knock itself apart.

A door made from solid, glued-up boards (or even a single board) is subject to a lot of across-the-grain expansion and contraction. Thanks to the battens, a board-and-batten

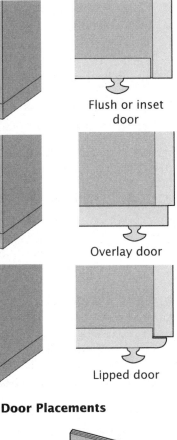

Flush or inset door

Overlay door

Lipped door

Door Placements

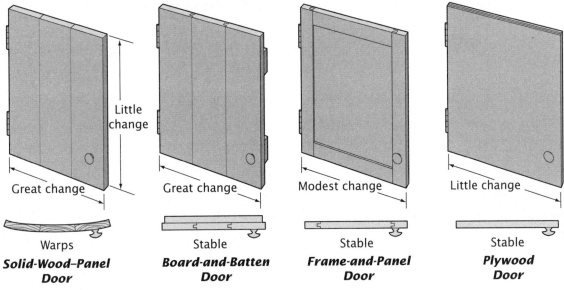

Little change

Great change

Warps

Solid-Wood–Panel Door

Great change

Stable

Board-and-Batten Door

Modest change

Stable

Frame-and-Panel Door

Little change

Stable

Plywood Door

Door Types and Their Stability

door will suffer less warp than a solid-panel door, but it will still be dimensionally unstable across its width.

The two most stable constructions are the frame-and-panel door and the plywood door. In the former, most of the wood movement is confined to the panel, which is held in a relatively stable frame. (See the drawing *Frame-and-Panel Construction* on page 14.) In the plywood door, the stability stems from the nature of the material.

▶ DOOR CONSTRUCTION

The fact is, there is not a whole lot of variation in how doors are constructed. Doors with very different appearances can turn out to be very similar in construction.

Board-and-Batten Door

A primitive door is constructed by butting boards edge to edge, then nailing a pair of battens across them. Adding a tongue-and-groove joint between boards helps prevent a gap from opening when the boards contract. If the joint's shoulder is beaded or chamfered, that dresses up its appearance.

To lengthen the door's life, the battens should be screwed in place as shown. A diagonal brace will triangulate the assembled door, preventing the assembly from sagging.

Solid-Wood–Panel Door

Solid wood alone, whether a single wide board or a panel glued up from narrow boards, does not make a stable door. And unless stiffened somehow, it is prone to warp.

One way to stiffen it is to screw a batten across the panel near each end. Another is to add breadboard ends (see "Breadboard Ends," pages 79–81). In either case, allowance must be made for wood movement across the grain.

Flush Door

Flush doors are made from flat manufactured panels, like plywood, particleboard or medium-density fiberboard (better known by its initials, MDF). These materials are dimensionally stable, though they can warp if used

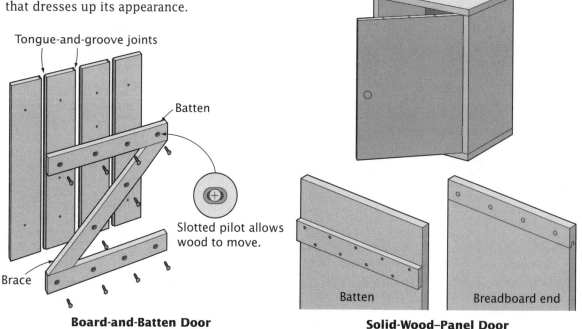

Tongue-and-groove joints

Batten

Slotted pilot allows wood to move.

Brace

Board-and-Batten Door

Batten

Breadboard end

Solid-Wood–Panel Door

Plywood with
taped edges

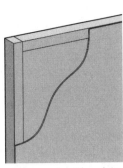
Plywood with edge
bands, veneer over
assembly

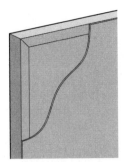
Plywood with mitered
edge bands, veneer
over assembly

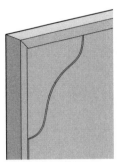
Plywood with veneer
butted to mitered
edge bands

Flush Door

incorrectly. For example, if veneer (or plastic laminate) is applied to only one face, the panel can warp due to uneven exchange of moisture across its faces.

Plywood is especially good for flush doors; it's lighter in weight and it holds screws much better than other panel products. The raw plywood edges need to be banded, and several ways to do this are shown.

Frame-and-Panel Door

A frame-and-panel assembly makes a great door. It is dimensionally stable, as noted earlier. Joinery options abound; there are many different ways to join the frame and install the panel. Moreover, different appearances can be achieved because the frame can easily be molded (or molding can be attached). The panel, too, can be varied.

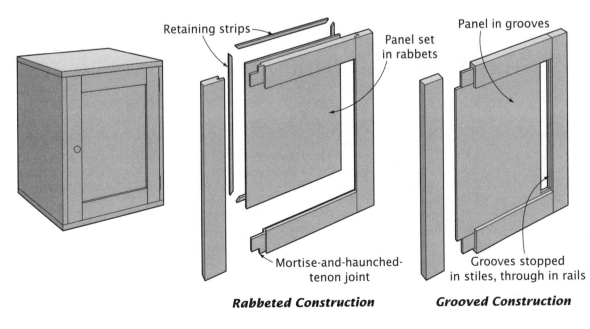

Retaining strips

Panel set
in rabbets

Panel in grooves

Mortise-and-haunched-
tenon joint

Grooves stopped
in stiles, through in rails

Rabbeted Construction   *Grooved Construction*

Basic Frame-and-Panel Door

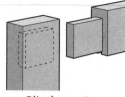

Blind mortise-and-tenon joint

Mortise-and-haunched-tenon joint

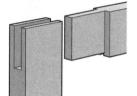

Slip joint

Groove-and-stub-tenon joint

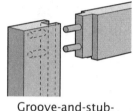

Groove-and-stub-tenon with dowels

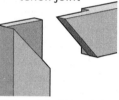

Mitered half-lap joint

Frame-and-Panel Joinery

Basic Frame-and-Panel Door shows that frames are typically joined with mortise-and-tenon joints for the greatest strength, while the panels can be either held in a rabbet with a retaining strip or locked in a groove. These are the basic ingredients.

But they are strictly basics. *Frame-and-Panel Joinery* shows some of the many variations on the basic mortise-and-tenon joint, as well as the mitered half-lap, which is a surprisingly strong joint.

Cope-and-Stick: This is a widely used, modern joint that incorporates a molded edge into the joinery. It is produced with a table-mounted router or a shaper using matched cutters. One cutter forms a profile and a groove (the sticking cut); each frame member is machined end to end with it. The other cutter forms a counterprofile (the cope cut) and simultaneously produces a stub tenon that fits into the groove; the rail ends are machined with this cutter. Cut correctly, the parts fit together like a hand in a glove.

The same appearance can be achieved by making a sticking cut on all the frame parts

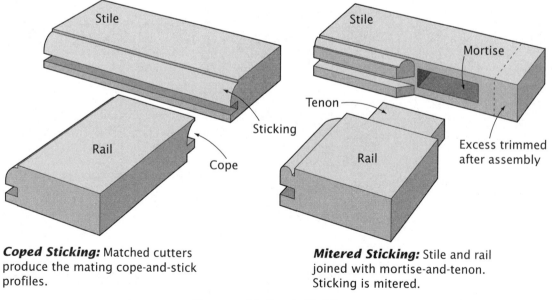

Coped Sticking: Matched cutters produce the mating cope-and-stick profiles.

Mitered Sticking: Stile and rail joined with mortise-and-tenon. Sticking is mitered.

Frame with Stuck Molding

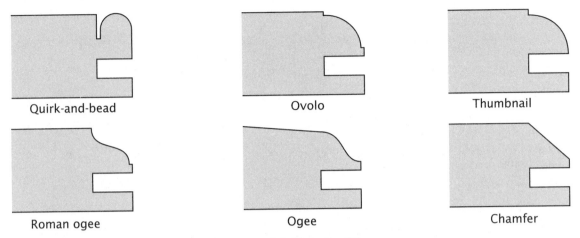

Common Sticking Profiles

Quirk-and-bead
Ovolo
Thumbnail
Roman ogee
Ogee
Chamfer

using profile router bits or even hand tools—no special cutters needed. After mortise-and-tenon joints are cut, the sticking profile is mitered where it intersects as the frame is assembled.

The drawing *Common Sticking Profiles* shows sticking profiles that are commonly used. Not every profile shown can be produced using cope-and-stick cutters. The quirk-and-bead, for example, has to be produced by mitering the sticking.

Applied molding: There's one more method for getting a mitered profile on a frame edge: Join the parts with square edges, then attach separate molding strips, mitering the pieces together at the inside corners. With this approach, a rabbet is sometimes cut into the frame for the panel, which is captured by applied molding.

Alternatively, the molding can be rabbeted to fit over the edge of the frame. This is referred to as a bolection molding.

One big advantage of applied molding is that it allows the panels to be finished before assembly. It's also a good method for making a glazed door with only a single pane of glass.

Types of door panels: There are many ways of producing a panel for a frame. You must balance materials choices with construction alternatives with appearance desires. As the drawing *Basic Frame-and-Panel*

Door (page 97) shows, the simplest is a thin, plain panel. Using a 1/4-inch-thick plywood panel set in grooves in a 3/4-inch-thick frame is a common way to build simple cabinet doors.

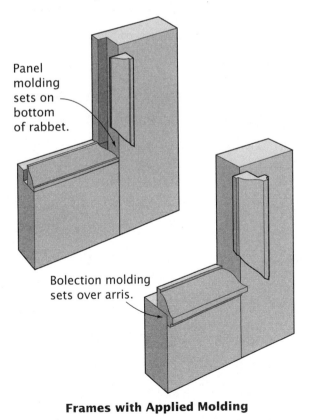

Panel molding sets on bottom of rabbet.

Bolection molding sets over arris.

Frames with Applied Molding

When the panel material chosen is thicker or is solid wood (or both), the groove can be made wider to accommodate it; but it's more likely you will rabbet or raise it to reduce its thickness at the edge. Here again, materials choice has an impact.

A plywood panel would be rabbeted and can be left flush or elevated (with a molding masking its edge plies). It would not be raised unless it will be painted, and probably not even then.

A solid-wood panel can be rabbeted or raised, on one side or on both. What is not shown here is the range of raised-panel profiles; for that you need to consult some router-bit or shaper-cutter catalogs.

All of these possibilities offer subtle aesthetic differences in the look of a door. They don't affect the strength of the door (except when a plywood panel is glued in place) because the panels "float" inside the frame.

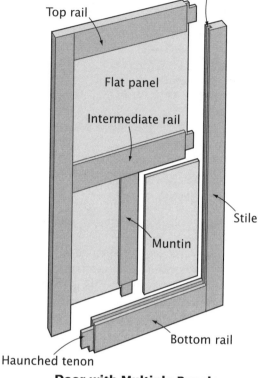

Door with Multiple Panels

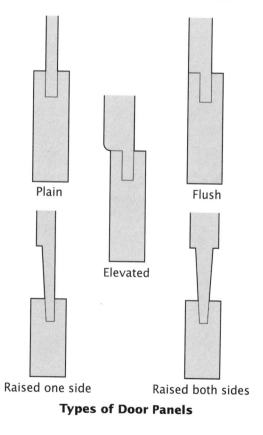

Types of Door Panels

Multiple-panel doors: Large doors are often divided into smaller segments. There are aesthetic reasons to do this—large unbroken planes tend to look ill-proportioned or staid. And there are structural reasons—a large door may need intermediate members to help hold the outer frame together. Finally, wide panels expand and contract more than narrower ones, and that can lead to problems in very wide panels.

To divide a door horizontally requires adding an intermediate horizontal rail, as shown in *Door with Multiple Panels*. This rail is made just like the bottom and top rails, joined to the stiles with mortise-and-tenon joints, though it will have a panel groove (or rabbet) in both edges. So adding another rail is not difficult.

But dividing the door, or a portion of the door, with a vertical member can be more challenging, if only because it begins to make assembly a puzzle. Intermediate vertical frame pieces, called muntins, have to be joined to two rails. They can use the same mortise-and-tenon joinery used elsewhere in the assembly, or they can be given a stub tenon that merely fits the panel groove.

To build a complex door, the best approach is to lay out and construct all the frame parts, assemble the door frame dry, and then determine the exact sizes of all the panels.

Glazed Doors

Cupboards, secretary-bookcases, and display cases commonly have glazed doors, which keep the dust out while showing off the contents. Glazed doors have a standard door frame and a network of intersecting muntins dividing the framed area into a grid for panes.

There are two distinct approaches to building glazed doors. In a traditional, hand-tool approach, the muntins are built up from a spine and a molding. The spines are rectangular bars, cross-lapped at the intersections and fitted into slots in the frame. The moldings are grooved to fit over the spines, mitered where they intersect, and fit into a rabbet along the frame, as shown.

Machine-cut joinery for glazed doors looks like its traditional predecessor in the end, but it is put together differently. Each muntin is a single piece of wood (not two), shaped with a special cutter. The ends of the

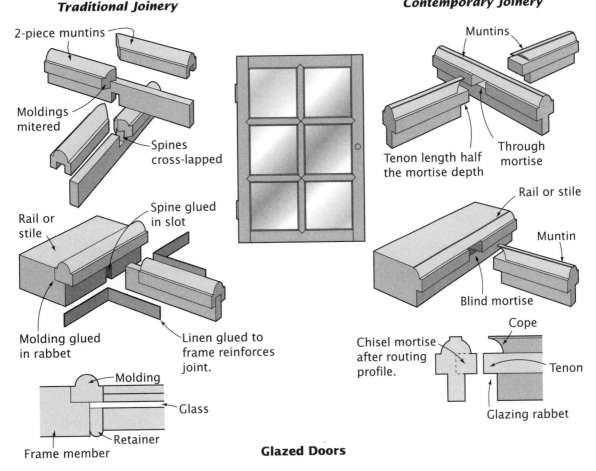

Traditional Joinery

2-piece muntins

Moldings mitered

Spines cross-lapped

Rail or stile

Spine glued in slot

Molding glued in rabbet

Linen glued to frame reinforces joint.

Molding

Glass

Retainer

Frame member

Contemporary Joinery

Muntins

Tenon length half the mortise depth

Through mortise

Rail or stile

Muntin

Blind mortise

Chisel mortise after routing profile.

Cope

Tenon

Glazing rabbet

Glazed Doors

muntins are shaped with a counterprofile—
including a stub tenon—with a matched
cutter. Where muntins intersect, a through
mortise is cut by hand for the tenon. (See also
"Cope-and-Stick" on page 98.)

▶ INSTALLING DOORS

Hanging a door correctly is almost as important as building it well. The hinge that binds,
the misalignment that jams the door in the
case—these things will wear the door over
time, leading to failure.

Hinges

Different hinges call for different fitting
allowances and mounting procedures, so
you'll want to choose the hinge type, if not
the actual hinges, early on.

Butt hinges are the traditional workhorses
and continue to represent the most simple
and elegant way to hang doors. They can be
mortised in or surface mounted, as shown.

Knife hinges are an alternative, though
they work only on inset doors. Mortised into
the top and bottom edges of a door, they're
nearly invisible—the flat pivot on each hinge
is all that can be seen when the door is closed.

Hidden hinges are completely concealed
when the door is closed. They're designed to
be mounted into the edges of an inset door, as
shown. Many cabinetmakers know hidden
hinges only as Soss hinges, a common brand.

Hanging doors has been an unforgiving
part of cabinetmaking because most hinges
can't be adjusted once screwed into place. The
Euro-style cup hinge has changed that. One

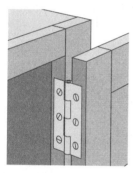

Butt hinge

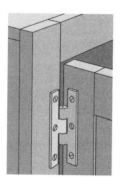

Surface-mounted
hinge

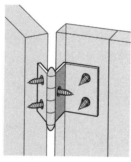

Concealed
offset hinge

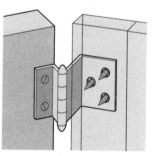

Semiconcealed
offset hinge

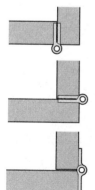

Butt-hinge
mounting options

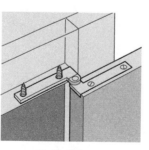

Knife hinge

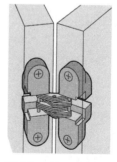

Hidden (Soss) hinge

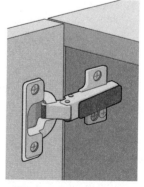

Euro-style cup hinge

Hinges

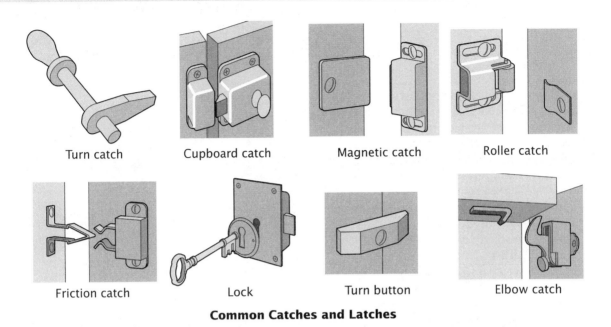

Turn catch   Cupboard catch   Magnetic catch   Roller catch

Friction catch   Lock   Turn button   Elbow catch

Common Catches and Latches

part of the hinge is attached to the inside face of the door, the other to the inside face of the cabinet side. Once installed, the hinge can be adjusted three ways: up or down, side to side, and in and out. Designed originally for "frameless" cabinets, there are now models for traditional face frame–style cabinets.

Catches and Latches

Selecting a way to keep a door closed is often an afterthought, which rarely is a problem, since so many simple devices will do the job. You'll find a mechanical catch for any door configuration or mounting scenario, most of which require use of a separate pull. Turn catches and cupboard catches double as door pulls, as can the key of a lock.

Double Door Treatments

The one unfinished piece of work here is contriving how a pair of doors will meet. Obviously, this is a decision that must be made early in the design process. Sizing of the doors and the choice of catches are contingent upon such choices. Three options are shown.

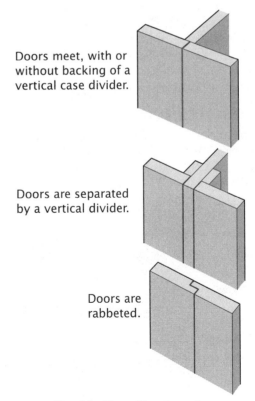

Doors meet, with or without backing of a vertical case divider.

Doors are separated by a vertical divider.

Doors are rabbeted.

Double Door Treatments

DRAWER
CONSTRUCTION

A drawer receives more punishment than any other component in furniture. It's jerked open. It's slammed shut. Open. Bang! shut. Open. Bang! shut.

So a strong and lasting drawer results not just from good drawer joinery but also from the methods used to mount it in a cabinet or under a table and to guide its movement as it is opened and closed.

Traditionally, drawers were constructed and fitted with a lot of handwork. But contemporary woodworkers favor machine-cut joinery and easy fits. There is, it turns out, no one way to build a drawer.

Drawer construction is often distinguished by how the front relates to the case it resides in. As shown in the drawing *Drawer Front Options,* it can be set flush within the case, it can fully overlay the case, or it can have a lip cut into it so that it partly overlays the case. Specific drawer constructions will work better with one of these arrangements than with another.

► DRAWER JOINERY

Furniture lovers are fond of opening a drawer to determine what joinery is used. It's a good gauge of quality, as long as you know what you're looking at.

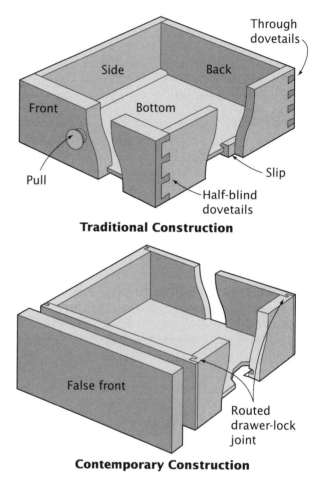

Traditional Construction

Contemporary Construction

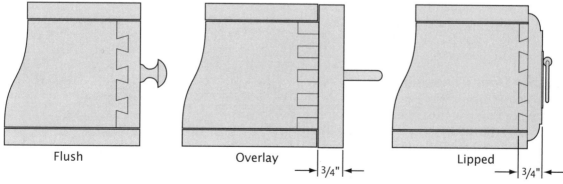

Flush   Overlay   Lipped

Drawer Front Options

Front-to-Side Joinery

The front-to-side joints take the bulk of the strain on a drawer; and with a badly built drawer, you can come away with just the drawer front in your hand.

Dovetails generally indicate a well-made drawer. The half-blind dovetail is *the* traditional joint for this application. It can be used to produce all three types of drawers, although you need to use a false front to get an overlay

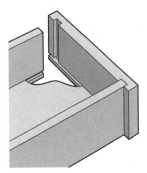

Dado joint

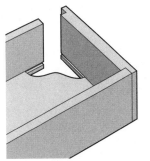

Rabbet joint

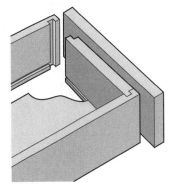

Dado-and-rabbet joint

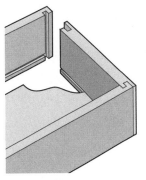

Lock joint

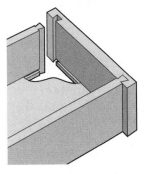

Sliding-dovetail joint

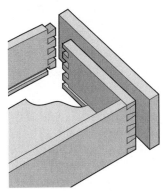

Through-dovetail joint

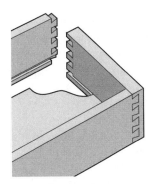

Half-blind dovetail joint

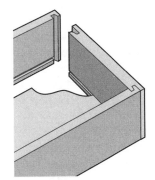

Routed drawer-lock joint

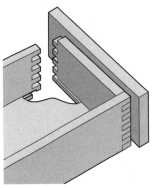

Box joint

Front-to-Side Joinery

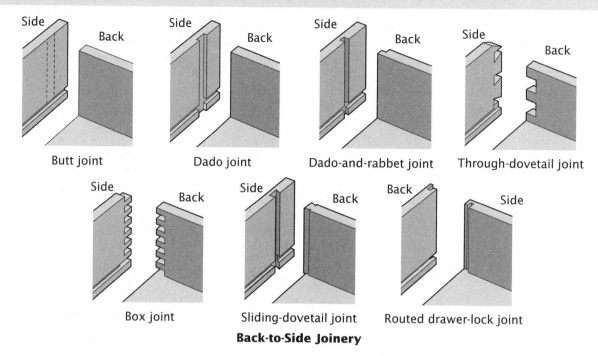

Butt joint   Dado joint   Dado-and-rabbet joint   Through-dovetail joint

Box joint   Sliding-dovetail joint   Routed drawer-lock joint

Back-to-Side Joinery

drawer. Through dovetails are strong, but they show. If exposed joinery is part of the design, that's good. Otherwise, a false front is needed to conceal them. The sliding dovetail is strong and easy to make, but it demands some extra stock on either side. Thus, it will work only on an overlay drawer (or a flush drawer on commercial side-mounted slides).

A box joint looks akin to a dovetail, but it's strictly a machine-made joint (with a router or table saw). It doesn't lock the parts together like a dovetail but makes up for that with plenty of gluing surfaces. It shares the through dovetail's applications.

Lock joints, including the routed drawer-lock joint, are strong and simple; they work equally well on overlay and inset drawers.

The advantage of the drawer with a plain rabbet or dado joint joining the front to the sides is ease of construction. Neither has any locking mechanism that's integral to the joint; and there's no good gluing surfaces, so you shouldn't expect the drawer to survive for generations. A dado-and-rabbet joint does lock the parts together and is easy to make.

Back-to-Side Joinery

Historically, through dovetails were used at the back of a drawer. But the back joints of a drawer receive less stress and strain than the fronts do. So it's common these days to join the backs and sides with less fuss—a dado, dado-and-rabbet, even a nailed butt joint may be suitable. If you're making the front joints with a machine setup, however, it's practical to make the back joints the same way.

Fitting Bottoms

A drawer bottom can be tacked right to the bottom edges of the other parts. Drawers were commonly built this way until the 18th century, and occasionally they still are. The drawback is that the weight of the contents may separate the bottom from the drawer over time.

Drawer bottoms can also be fitted into grooves in the sides, front, and back, as though it were a freestanding box, in an approach known as fully enclosed construction. This bottom must be installed during assembly.

Surely the most common approach is to cut the back less wide than the sides so the

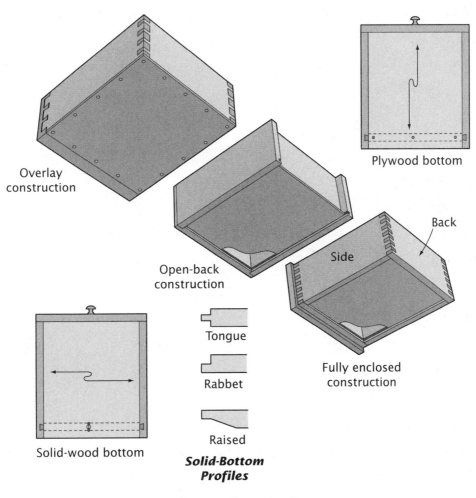

Overlay construction

Plywood bottom

Open-back construction

Back

Side

Tongue

Rabbet

Raised

Fully enclosed construction

Solid-wood bottom

Solid-Bottom Profiles

Bottom Construction

bottom can be slid underneath it, into grooves in the sides and front. This is usually called open-back construction. It allows the bottom to be finished separately and slipped into the drawer afterward.

Plywood drawer bottoms (typically 1/4 inch thick) make things really simple—just cut the groove so the bottom slides in easily.

Solid-wood drawer bottoms, unless they're very small, need to be thicker than 1/4 inch (thin wood being more prone to crack than plywood). To reduce the thickness where it enters the grooves, the edges of such a bottom will get a tongue or a rabbet, or it will

be raised. Solid bottoms should be used only on open-back construction, with the grain direction parallel to the back. To ensure that the bottom can expand and contract, use a screw in a slotted hole to secure the back edge of the bottom.

On very wide drawers, a large, one-piece bottom is likely to sag and later break. By adding a center muntin, two smaller panels can be used to form the bottom. This muntin must be grooved like the sides, and it must be securely anchored to the front and back. A tongue or dovetail is used at the front, while a rabbet forms a simple lap joint at the back.

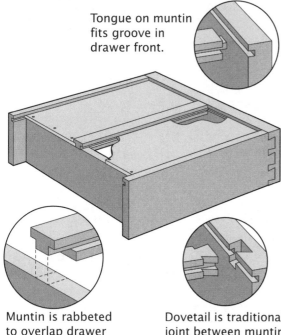

Tongue on muntin fits groove in drawer front.

Muntin is rabbeted to overlap drawer back.

Dovetail is traditional joint between muntin and front.

Center Muntin

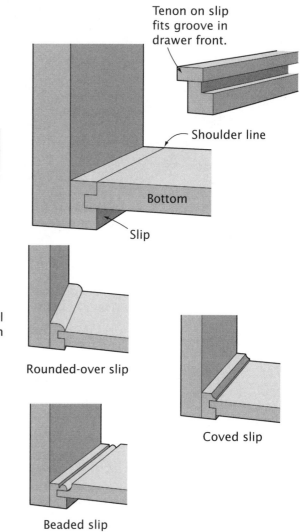

Tenon on slip fits groove in drawer front.

Shoulder line

Bottom

Slip

Rounded-over slip

Coved slip

Beaded slip

Drawer Slips

Drawer Slips

If a drawer's sides are made from thin stock, grooves for the bottom will seriously weaken them, and they'll be prone to crack. Moreover, thin drawer sides that slide on runners will gradually wear down over the years, diminishing a good fit. Drawer slips are a traditional solution to these problems.

Drawer slips run front to back and are glued to the sides at their bottom edges, increasing the bearing surface there. The slips are grooved for the bottom, which is rabbeted to fit the groove. The front of the bottom fits into a groove in the drawer front in the conventional way.

► MOUNTING DRAWERS

Movement of a drawer into and out of the case can be controlled in several ways. Some mounting systems are integral to the case, while others are add-ons. Regardless, the mounting system should be carefully planned along with the case and drawer design.

Runners, Guides, and Kickers

The most common approach to supporting a drawer is with an arrangement of runners, as shown in the drawing *Drawer Runners and Guides.*

Most simple is to attach runners directly to the case sides. The big caveat here is that the runners cannot be glued to solid-wood sides, because they'll restrict the sides from expanding and contracting. Instead, the runners are set into dadoes and glued at one end only, attached

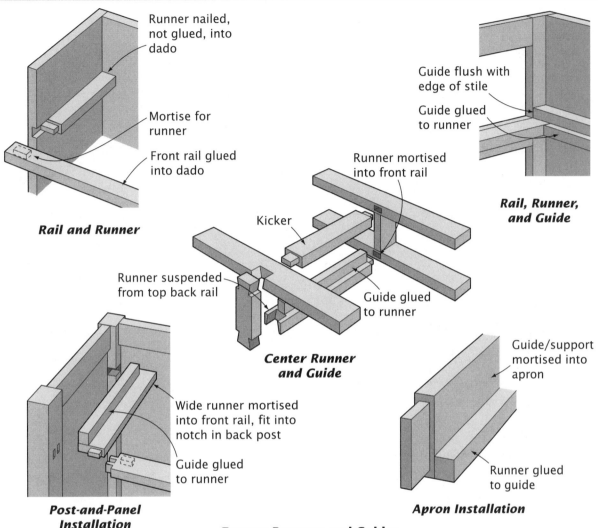

Runner nailed, not glued, into dado

Mortise for runner

Front rail glued into dado

Rail and Runner

Guide flush with edge of stile

Guide glued to runner

Runner mortised into front rail

Rail, Runner, and Guide

Kicker

Runner suspended from top back rail

Guide glued to runner

Center Runner and Guide

Wide runner mortised into front rail, fit into notch in back post

Guide glued to runner

Post-and-Panel Installation

Guide/support mortised into apron

Runner glued to guide

Apron Installation

Drawer Runners and Guides

with screws in slots, or housed (unglued) in dovetail slots. A long-standing practice is to capture the (slightly short) runners (unglued) between front and back rails that are glued in place. (See "Casework" on page 84.)

A case with a face frame requires an addition—the drawer guide—to limit side-to-side movement.

Other drawer installations shown are used for side-by-side drawers, for post-and-panel and frame-and-panel case construction, and for drawers in tables with aprons.

An important element in most drawer-mounting systems is the kicker. A kicker prevents the drawer from tipping down as it is opened. It is just like a runner, but generally, it's mounted above the drawer side. A single center kicker may be used for a top drawer.

Side Mounts

Some furniture designs, especially contemporary styles, make it difficult to use runners. Consider, for example, a case that has no rails separating the drawers. In this

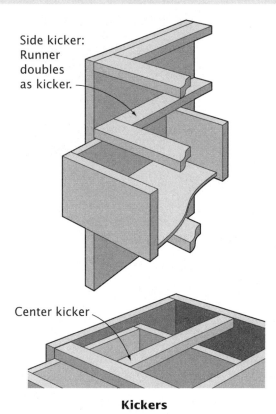

Side kicker: Runner doubles as kicker.

Center kicker

Kickers

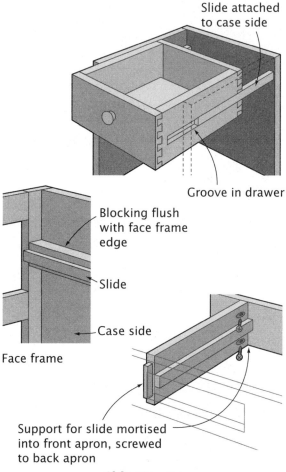

Slide attached to case side

Groove in drawer

Blocking flush with face frame edge

Slide

Case side

Face frame

Support for slide mortised into front apron, screwed to back apron

Side Mounts

situation, you can use side-mounted slides. The slide is a strip of wood attached to the case side. Grooves for the slides must be cut in the drawer sides.

Center Runners

Wide drawers supported by side runners have a tendency to cock slightly and bind as they are moved. The wider the drawer, the more likely this is to happen.

A single center-mounted runner and guide is the solution. The runner, which is attached to the underside of the drawer, has a channel in it that rides over a guide that's attached to the apron or web frame, as shown.

Drawer-Mounting Hardware

Metal slides with ball-bearing wheels are another drawer-mounting technique. These slides are either surface-mounted in pairs to the case and drawer, or singly under the

center of the drawer. They offer a smooth opening-and-closing action that's not affected by wood movement. They can be used in most furniture applications. Full-extension slides allow the full depth of the drawer to be exposed, something you can't get with the other drawer-mounting techniques shown. And there are slides made for file drawers and similar heavy-duty applications.

Top Mounts

A unique drawer-mounting situation is where there is neither an apron nor case sides to work with. Trestle tables and workbenches are good examples of this challenge.

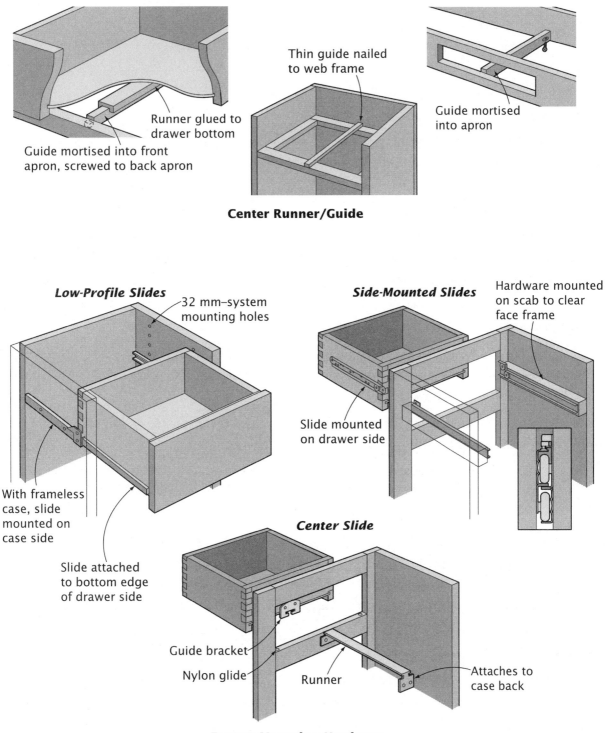

Center Runner/Guide

Runner glued to drawer bottom

Guide mortised into front apron, screwed to back apron

Thin guide nailed to web frame

Guide mortised into apron

Low-Profile Slides

32 mm–system mounting holes

With frameless case, slide mounted on case side

Slide attached to bottom edge of drawer side

Side-Mounted Slides

Hardware mounted on scab to clear face frame

Slide mounted on drawer side

Center Slide

Guide bracket

Nylon glide

Runner

Attaches to case back

Drawer-Mounting Hardware

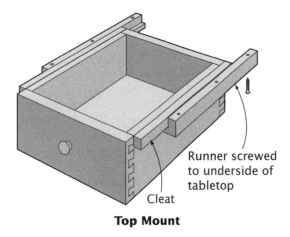

Top Mount

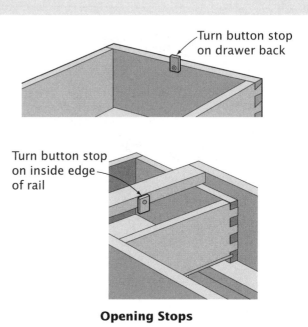

Opening Stops

The solution is an L-shaped runner that's screwed to the underside of the top, as shown in *Top Mount.* Cleats attached to the top edges of the drawer sides ride in the runner.

Drawer Stops

Drawer stops keep all styles of drawers from falling out of their cases (opening stops) and flush drawers from sliding too far into their cases (closing stops).

A turn button is the simplest opening stop. It can be mounted on the inside of the drawer back or on the back edge of the front rail. Pivoting it out of the way allows the drawer to be inserted or removed.

A small block of wood tacked or glued to the back of the runner is the easiest way to make a closing stop. With the back removed and each drawer inserted so it's perfectly flush with the cabinet face, apply the closing stops with a dab of glue. Then add a couple of brads or a small screw. You can also mount the closing stops onto the front rail, as shown, so they will catch against the back of the drawer front. They're definitely harder to locate and attach here, but such a stop could work for both opening and closing.

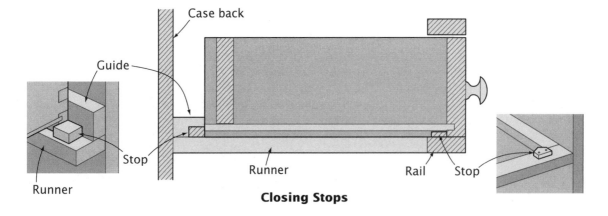

Closing Stops

CABINET BASES

It's a rare and unusual chest or cabinet that rests directly on the floor. Rather, it is customary to fit a case with feet or a base, which lifts it off the floor both visually and literally.

Whether you choose some sort of feet or a base depends as much upon the style and design of a piece as upon its construction. As you might expect, there is more than one way to achieve a given appearance. For example, that baseboard extending around a cabinet might be applied over extended case sides, but it might also be a separate frame attached to the case bottom.

Moreover, most constructions can be adapted to suit a style. The bracket foot, for

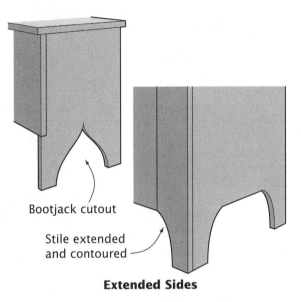

Bootjack cutout

Stile extended and contoured

Extended Sides

example, has been used on different styles of furniture from the 17th century right on up to the present day. The bracket foot can be styled to be rustic, country, traditional, or contemporary.

Integral Feet

The most obvious way to get a cabinet or chest up off the floor is to extend the sides past the bottom so the structure rests on their bottom edges, as shown above. To minimize the area in actual contact with the floor, the side can be cut out to form feet. The cutouts provide four points for the chest to rest on. That's better for bridging high and low spots in uneven floors.

Historically, some of the cutouts used resembled the cutout used on a bootjack, and these foot-forming cutouts became known as bootjack cutouts.

This approach may seem primitive and may bring to mind primitive examples, like lidded chests and water benches. But many country case pieces continue to be built this way—hutches, jelly cupboards, bookshelves,

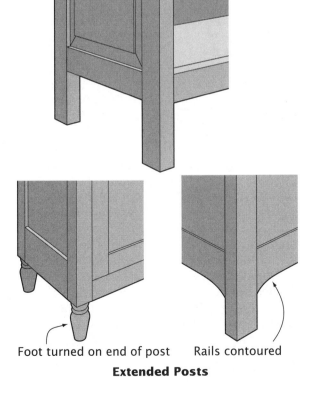

Foot turned on end of post   Rails contoured

Extended Posts

Straight Baseboard   **Inset Baseboard**   **Cutout Baseboard**

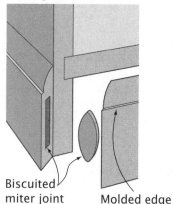

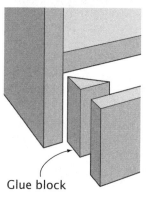

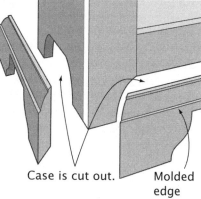

Biscuited
miter joint   Molded edge

Glue block

Case is cut out.   Molded
edge

Applied Bases

dry sinks, and the like. On the latter pieces, the cutout is often quite decorative, and the face frame stiles, if there are any, carry the theme across the front of the case.

If the case is post-and-panel construction, as shown at bottom left on page 113, then simply extending the posts several inches past the bottom produces feet. This has been a common practice from the Jacobean period right up to the present day. These feet can be set off visually by turning them or contouring the rails.

Applied Bases

The applied base is used to finish off the bottom of a case piece that is self-supporting; that is, that already has a structural base, such as sides that extend past the bottom to the floor. What it needs is something to buff the appearance.

Straight baseboard: Shelves or cabinets that are built-in may simply have the room's baseboard run along the sides and front, tying the piece into the room visually. A case piece

that is *not* built-in may still have baseboard-like trim on the sides and front. These are applied bases.

Usually, the base is a few inches high, solid, topped with a molding, and mitered at the front corners. If the case piece is free-standing and will be viewed from all sides, the base will extend all the way around.

Cutout baseboard: A base with a cutout in the front creates the illusion that the case has feet. Occasionally, the base will have cutouts on the sides as well; here the case sides must be relieved so they don't show. Sometimes the baseboard is applied only to the front. It can be applied to the front with the bottom shelf overlapping it.

Inset baseboard: A baseboard might be applied but inset. Visualize a bookcase with bootjack sides. The space between the bottom and the floor is filled by a plain board that's inset $1/8$ inch to create a shadow line. This plinth, as it is sometimes called, can be straight and solid, or it can be cut out in some way.

➤ ATTACHED FEET

Sometimes the sides can't (or shouldn't) be extended. How, for example, does a lidded chest that's dovetailed together in proper chest construction fashion get feet? There are several ways, it turns out, all flexible in design terms, all reasonably sturdy in construction terms.

Two movement problems typically must be dealt with in any of the following constructions. The first is the familiar *wood*-movement one. The other is *case* movement. A foot can easily break off if—when—the piece is pushed or dragged across a floor.

Trestle Foot

One seldom-seen option is the trestle foot. Some Pennsylvania Dutch chests rest on trestle feet. It is a pretty primitive construction, as the drawing shows, but it works.

Shaped Foot

More common is the turned or otherwise shaped foot (the C-scroll, block, or molded foot, for example). This kind of foot has been used under lidded chests, chests of drawers, even kitchen furniture.

In the past, a round tenon would be used to attach the foot to the underside of the case, sometimes with a filler block used to thicken the area housing the mortise. Some contemporary methods are shown in the drawing *Shaped Foot*.

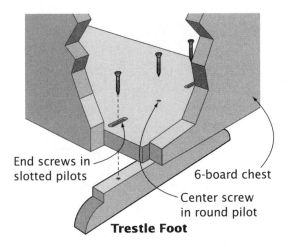

End screws in slotted pilots

6-board chest

Center screw in round pilot

Trestle Foot

Ball-and-Claw Foot

This foot, on the right piece of furniture, looks great; but attaching it is a major headache. The drawing below shows that the

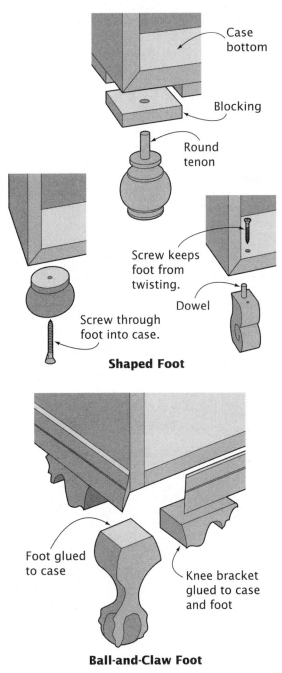

Case bottom

Blocking

Round tenon

Screw keeps foot from twisting.

Dowel

Screw through foot into case.

Shaped Foot

Foot glued to case

Knee bracket glued to case and foot

Ball-and-Claw Foot

Chippendale cabinetmaker's solution was simply to glue it to the case bottom and use the knee brackets to reinforce the joint. Of course, the joint between the foot and the bottom is end grain to long grain, which glues poorly. The knee brackets present some similar grain mismatches that glue poorly. Remarkably, many of these feet are still attached to their cases.

Bracket Foot

The bracket foot can be a little confusing to the uninitiated. With a base molding tying everything together, a set of bracket feet has a baselike appearance. So why call this construction "feet"? Because there is, in fact, a separate foot assembly at each corner of the case.

Typically—traditionally—a bracket foot is made by joining two short pieces of wood end-to-end at right angles. This bracket is mounted under a corner of a case with glue blocks and a vertical post, as shown in the drawing *Bracket Foot*. In most applications, the case's weight is borne by the post, which

is cut a skosh longer than the bracket is high. While the bracket assembly is positioned so it does actually extend under the case, most of the top edge protrudes as a seat for the base molding.

As old and as common as the bracket foot is, this traditional construction is problematic, and it is a common failure point in old pieces. The problem? All the cross-grain glue surfaces. One glue block will always be cross-grain to the case bottom. The post is always cross-grain to the bracket. Years of wood movement, as minimal as it might be in such narrow pieces, will weaken the glue joints; and when the foot is stressed by dragging the case across a floor, it breaks off.

A better way to construct the foot is also shown in the drawing. Here the post is built up so its grain parallels that of the bracket pieces. The support is glued into rabbets in the bracket, and it can be attached to the case bottom with screws driven through slots, which will allow the bottom to move without dislodging the foot.

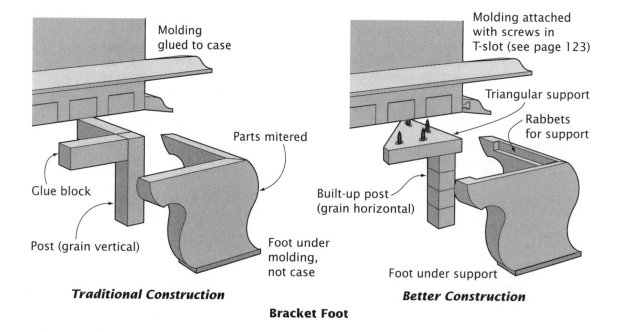

Molding glued to case

Parts mitered

Glue block

Post (grain vertical)

Foot under molding, not case

Traditional Construction

Molding attached with screws in T-slot (see page 123)

Triangular support

Rabbets for support

Built-up post (grain horizontal)

Foot under support

Better Construction

Bracket Foot

➤ SEPARATE BASES

The last option is to make a separate frame to set the cabinet or chest on. The frame can be well braced so that it is strong. It is easy to attach it to a case in a way that accommodates wood movement. It can be attractive as well.

Plinth Base

The lowest element in an architectural base, a plinth is straight, flat, and unembellished.

Traditionally, it is a little wider and deeper than the case it supports, with a molding easing the visual transition from base to cabinet. A more contemporary approach is to make the plinth base smaller than the cabinet, thus using negative space to separate the case from the floor.

Regardless of style, a plinth base is little more than a box frame, reinforced with one or more cross members and stiffened with corner blocks. Screws driven through corner blocks, pockets, or cleats attach the base to the case.

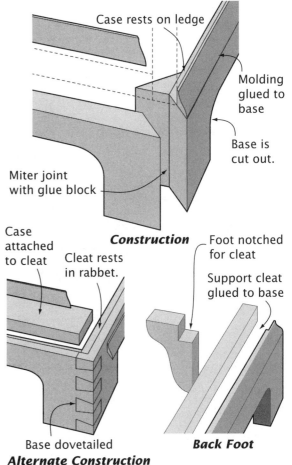

Case rests on ledge

Molding glued to base

Base is cut out.

Miter joint with glue block

Construction

Case attached to cleat

Cleat rests in rabbet.

Foot notched for cleat

Support cleat glued to base

Base dovetailed

Alternate Construction

Back Foot

Bracket Base

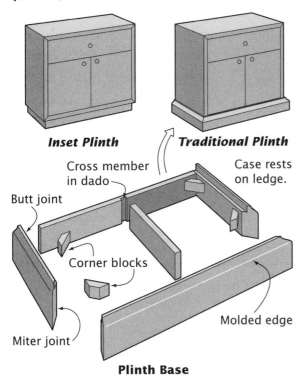

Inset Plinth   **Traditional Plinth**

Cross member in dado

Case rests on ledge.

Butt joint

Corner blocks

Molded edge

Miter joint

Plinth Base

Bracket Base

Making cutouts to form "feet" transforms a traditional plinth base into a bracket base.

The drawing *Bracket Base* shows two of many constructions possible. Note that the case and a base molding generally share the base's top edge, but cleats can be added to widen that surface. Occasionally, a foot is used instead of a full-length back member.

Bracket-Foot Base

This construction is unusual but effective. Frame rails are dovetailed into squat posts to form a structural base. Brackets are joined and attached to the base, as is a base molding, which conceals the rails and simultaneously creates a modest lip that masks the seam between case and base.

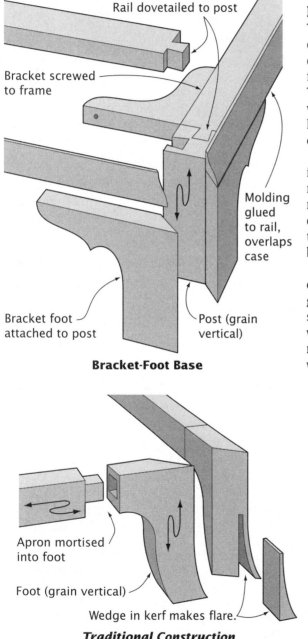

Bracket-Foot Base

Rail dovetailed to post

Bracket screwed to frame

Bracket foot attached to post

Molding glued to rail, overlaps case

Post (grain vertical)

The completed assembly can be screwed to the bottom of the case. Running the screws through slots will allow the case bottom to expand and contract.

French Foot

This is a sophisticated base that was popular on Federal furniture. The "foot" is typically quite tall and slender (as compared to a bracket foot, for example) and flares out at the bottom. The drawing *French Foot* shows two different ways of constructing this base, and each has at least one inherent weakness. (Note in each construction how the flare is produced.)

In the traditional construction, the base is created by joining legs and aprons with mortises and tenons, then assembling the resulting subframes, usually with miter joints of one sort of another, into the base. A potential problem is the cross-grain orientation between foot and apron.

An alternative is to cut each leg-and-apron element from a single board to keep all the grain going the same direction. The resulting skirts are glued to the edges of a flat frame, with miters at the corners. Here a problem may be the relative weakness of the feet, which results from the grain orientation.

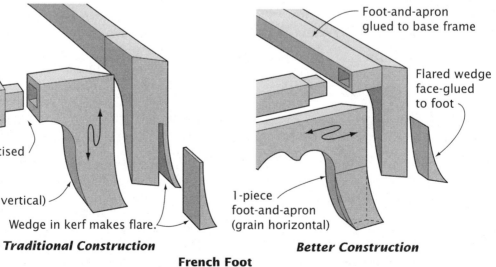

Apron mortised into foot

Foot (grain vertical)

Wedge in kerf makes flare.

Traditional Construction

Foot-and-apron glued to base frame

Flared wedge face-glued to foot

1-piece foot-and-apron (grain horizontal)

Better Construction

French Foot

MOLDINGS

M oldings are style setters. Undeniably, these concave and convex surfaces, collectively called profiles, have enormous impact on furniture appearance.

They please the eye by easing transitions between parts and surfaces, by dividing up large open areas, and by refining edges, corners, and other borders. The size and shape of a molding can enhance (or upset) the visual balance or scale of a piece, or even create an illusion of motion.

More than occasionally, a molding serves a functional role in the construction: hiding joinery, fasteners, or end grain, masking gaps, providing a physical connection between two separate parts of the construction.

The drawing below, *Where Moldings Are Used,* depicts the most common locations for moldings on a large case piece.

Most obvious are the moldings used across the top and bottom. These moldings provide a decisive termination of the piece at

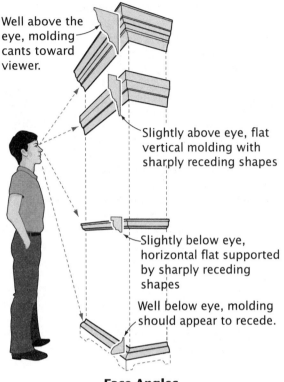

Well above the eye, molding cants toward viewer.

Slightly above eye, flat vertical molding with sharply receding shapes

Slightly below eye, horizontal flat supported by sharply receding shapes

Well below eye, molding should appear to recede.

Face Angles

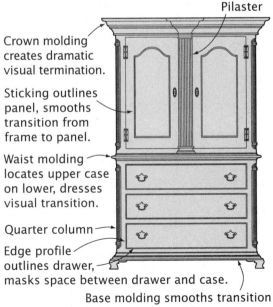

Pilaster

Crown molding creates dramatic visual termination.

Sticking outlines panel, smooths transition from frame to panel.

Waist molding locates upper case on lower, dresses visual transition.

Quarter column

Edge profile outlines drawer, masks space between drawer and case.

Base molding smooths transition between base and lower case.

Where Moldings Are Used

top and bottom. They separate it visually from the room. Often they are the most prominent moldings on the piece.

Where the piece consists of two cases, another molding, often called the waist molding, provides a visual transition from one to the other. At the same time, it provides a mechanism to link the two cases structurally. (The molding generally is attached to the lower case in such a way that it creates a lip inside of which the upper case just fits. The molding traps and aligns the upper case, and gravity holds it in place.)

Additional moldings can be used around drawers and doors and along the vertical edges of the case.

Face Angles: When designing moldings for a cabinet, you need to structure them properly to look right. The cumulative experience of designers—*and viewers*—suggests that for best appearance, the face of the molding should be angled toward the eye. The shapes used should be selected according to location—above or below eye level—and the scale of those shapes should be proportional to the distance from the eye.

A molding well above eye level, for example, should cant toward the viewer. Its profile should be composed of deep coves, reverse ogees, and wide vertical flats with narrow horizontal ones. Near eye level, moldings should be flat surfaces supported by sharply receding profiles. The orientation of the flat depends upon whether the molding is slightly above or slightly below eye level. Above eye level and the flat is vertical, below and it is horizontal. Moldings well below eye level—those at the base, in other words— should appear to recede, and be topped with ogees and coves.

▶ PROFILES

There are two sorts of moldings: simple and complex. A simple molding is composed of a single basic shape. A complex molding combines two or more of the basic shapes.

What this means is that, regardless of their size and complexity, all moldings are composed of just a few basic geometric shapes. You can vary the size of the basic shapes, and you can vary the way they are arranged, but you won't have much luck trying to invent new ones. There aren't any.

The basic shapes are shown in the drawing *Simple Molding Profiles.* Some common combinations are shown in the drawing *Complex Molding Shapes.*

This, of course, is old stuff. The fundamental shapes of straight and angled planes and of concave and convex curves were

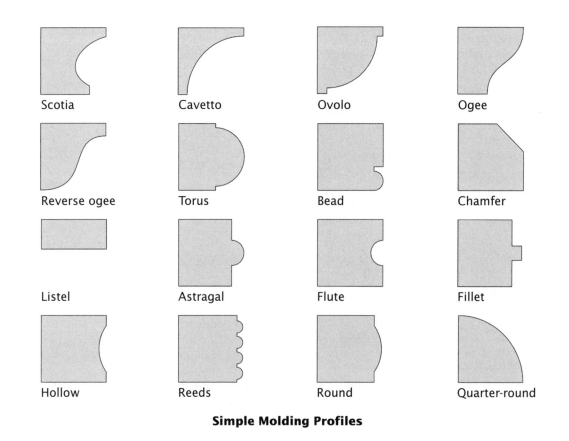

Scotia	Cavetto	Ovolo	Ogee
Reverse ogee	Torus	Bead	Chamfer
Listel	Astragal	Flute	Fillet
Hollow	Reeds	Round	Quarter-round

Simple Molding Profiles

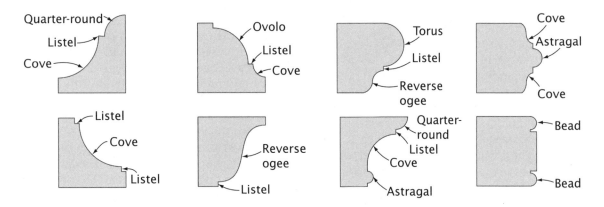

Complex Molding Shapes

identified and categorized by the ancient Greeks and Romans. The Greeks based any of the curved shapes on the ellipse, the Romans on the circle. As a practical matter, most of the stock moldings and cutters used today are Roman.

As you devise a molding, remember first that a molding need not be a separate strip of wood in all situations. Quite often, a profile is cut directly on a furniture component—a tabletop or countertop, a drawer front, a case edge, a table leg, a base. The basic shapes can usually be produced with a single cutter, and there are cutters available to produce many complex shapes.

A molding with just one of the simple shapes can be very effective. Starting with a square edge, for example, you can knock off the corner, or arris, to create a chamfer. You can round the edge to make a quarter-round or, going a bit further, make an ovolo, which is a quarter-round with a flat at each end of the arc.

On the other hand, a molding sometimes needs to be so big and have so many elements that it can't be cut on a single piece of wood. In this situation, it is created from several separate strips that are joined together. Some examples of these constructions are shown in the drawing *Built-Up Moldings.*

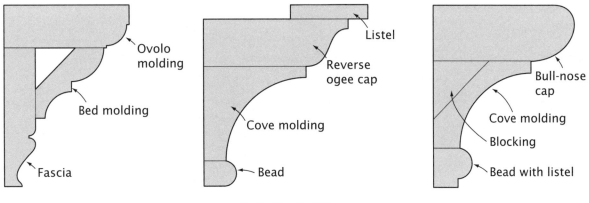

Built-Up Moldings

➤ ATTACHING MOLDINGS

Good case construction allows sides, top, and bottom to move in tandem. Across the case front, the grain in the molding parallels the grain of the case, so the molding can simply be glued (and/or fastened) in place. But when you apply moldings to the sides of a cabinet, they are crossing the grain of the sides. Depending upon how they are attached, they can restrict the movement of the wood. The resulting tensions have been known to crack case sides, break bases, and pop off moldings.

Over time, cabinetmakers have developed several ways of attaching moldings that don't restrict wood movement.

In the simplest, the mitered front end is glued and fixed firmly to the case, while the back end is tacked on with wire brads, but not glued. The brads do flex as the case side moves, so the molding stays in place. If the molding is a substantial one—like a built-up cornice molding—nails can be used instead of the brads. A nail will enlarge its hole at the point where it passes out of the molding and into the case side, allowing movement, while the point of the nail will remain relatively fixed and secure.

Two of the more sophisticated solutions are shown in the drawing *Cross-Grain Molding*

Joinery. You can fix the back end of the molding with a screw driven from inside the case. The screw passes through a slotted pilot in the case side, so the side can move.

Another approach is to mount the back part of the molding on a short runner. The runner, because it is short, can be screwed tightly to the side. It can be as simple as a panhead or roundhead screw. It can be a dovetail key or a T-shaped key. The back of the molding is slotted from end to end to accommodate the key. It is driven onto the key, then glued to the case and the adjoining molding at the miter.

Base Moldings

One molding that tends to differ in construction from cornice and waist moldings is the base molding. That's because it can often be integrated into the base. When it is a separate element, it can sometimes be glued to the base, circumventing wood movement problems.

Here are three slightly different approaches to dealing with a base molding.

Case-Mounted Base Molding: In this first approach, the molding is attached directly to the case, with the separate strips being joined at the corners with miter joints. The strip on the front of the case is glued

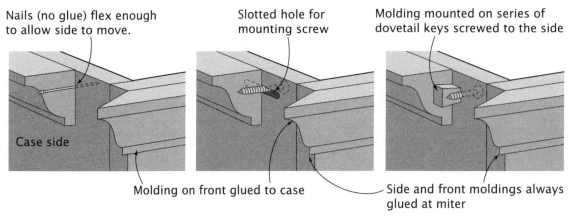

Nails (no glue) flex enough to allow side to move.

Case side

Slotted hole for mounting screw

Molding on front glued to case

Molding mounted on series of dovetail keys screwed to the side

Side and front moldings always glued at miter

Cross-Grain Molding Joinery

there; it is a straightforward edge-to-edge joint. At the sides, the attachment is, of course, problematic from a wood movement standpoint. Any of the approaches outlined above will work.

Shown here at top right is a method of mounting the molding on screws, so the case side can expand and contract, while the front end of the molding remains glued securely at the miter joint. A T-slot is plowed in the back of the molding. Panhead or roundhead screws are driven into the case along a line, but with the heads left protruding. The molding is pushed onto the screws and glued at the miter. The glue joint keeps the molding fixed in relation to the case front, the screws keep the molding tight to the case side, but the side is free to expand and contract.

Molded Base: With a bracket base or a traditional plinth base, the base molding can be incorporated into the base instead of being separate. The desired profile can be cut directly on the base.

The center drawing at right shows a bracket base that is assembled around a separate frame. The frame is constructed with mortise-and-tenon joints. The base members, already molded and scroll-cut, are glued to the frame and are joined to each other with miters. The miters are reinforced with glue blocks. The frame is slightly recessed in the base, so the molded edge overlays the case slightly.

The assembly is screwed to the bottom of the case. In the front, the screws pass through round pilots; on the sides, the pilots are elongated, allowing some movement of the screws as the case expands and contracts. There are not screws through the back frame member.

Molded Frame: When the case is mounted on bracket feet, it's best to attach the feet to a base frame, then screw the frame to the case. If the frame is assembled with miter joints, as shown at bottom right, the molding profile can be cut directly on it.

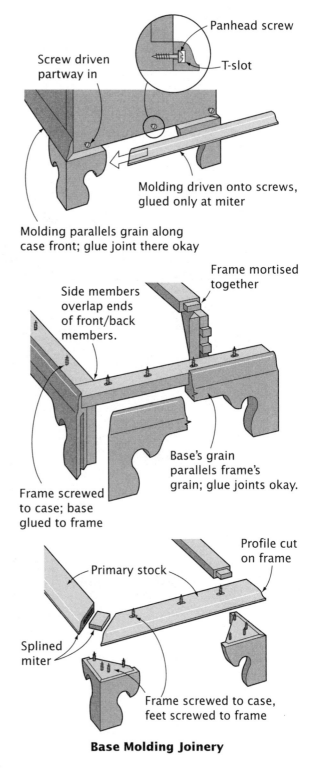

Screw driven partway in

Panhead screw

T-slot

Molding driven onto screws, glued only at miter

Molding parallels grain along case front; glue joint there okay

Side members overlap ends of front/back members.

Frame mortised together

Base's grain parallels frame's grain; glue joints okay.

Frame screwed to case; base glued to frame

Primary stock

Profile cut on frame

Splined miter

Frame screwed to case, feet screwed to frame

Base Molding Joinery

FURNITURE

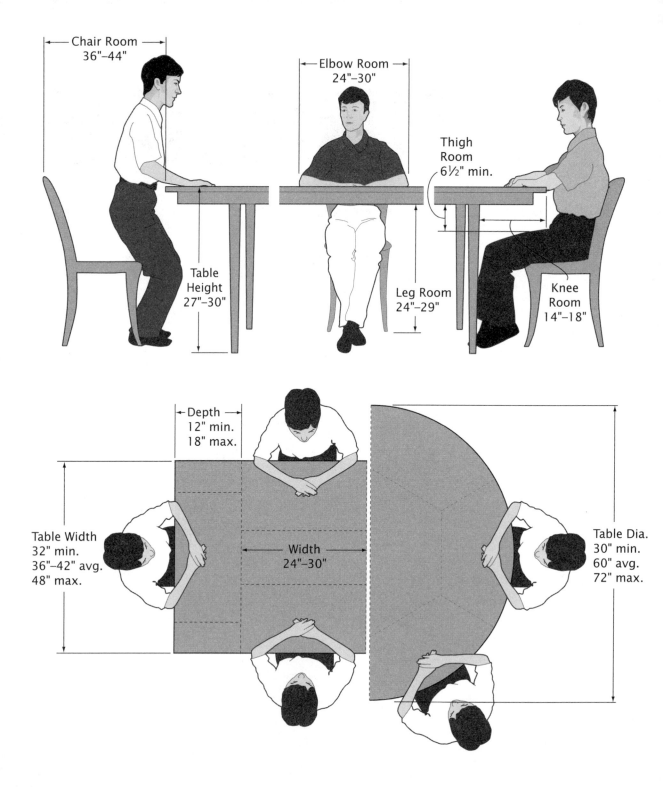

Chair Room
36"–44"

Elbow Room
24"–30"

Thigh
Room
6½" min.

Table
Height
27"–30"

Leg Room
24"–29"

Knee
Room
14"–18"

Depth
12" min.
18" max.

Table Width
32" min.
36"–42" avg.
48" max.

Width
24"–30"

Table Dia.
30" min.
60" avg.
72" max.

DINING TABLES

It's a perverse truism: The dining table that you remember best is typically the poorly designed one. The one that was too low or too high, the one that cramped your feet and legs, the one that wasn't roomy enough. To help you design a table you'll remember only for its appearance, here are basic standards.

TABLE HEIGHT: Distance from floor to top surface of the tabletop. Typically, this is 28 to 30 inches.

LEG ROOM: Distance from floor to lower edge of apron; a measure of the vertical space for your legs. The minimum space would be about 24 inches.

KNEE ROOM: Distance from table's edge to a leg; a measure of the clearance provided for your knees when your chair is drawn up to the table. Minimums range from 10 to 16 inches; a good range would be 14 to 18 inches.

THIGH ROOM: Distance from chair seat to bottom edge of apron; a measure of the vertical space available for your thighs if you sit in a given chair, drawn up to the table. Minimum is $6\frac{1}{2}$ inches.

ELBOW ROOM: Space allowance for each diner. The minimum seems to be 24 inches, but 30 inches is far better.

REACH: Depth allowance for each place setting. Less than 12 inches is too little; more than 18 inches is too much.

CHAIR ROOM: Space allowance between the tabletop's edge and the wall for you to push your chair away from the table and stand up. The architects say 36 inches is the minimum; 44 inches is the optimum.

LEG-AND-APRON
TABLE

60"

37½"

29½"

Kitchen Table, Worktable

PLANS

Becksvoort, Chris. "Leg-and-Apron Table," *The Best of Fine Woodworking: Traditional Furniture Projects.* Newtown, CT: The Taunton Press, 1991. A round-topped expanding table presented in tightly conceived drawings and how-I-built-it text.

•

Lynch, Carlyle. "Country Breakfast Table," *American Woodworker,* Vol. IV, No. 2 (May/June 1988), pp. 46–49. A splendid Lynch measured drawing of a round-topped table, together with construction guidelines.

When you think *table,* don't you think of a flat board supported on four legs? Don't you think of a table like that shown above? That table is an archetype among archetypes.

In its most simple form, a table—the archetypal table—is formed of just three kinds of parts: the legs, the aprons, and the tabletop. The legs and aprons are joined to form a sturdy, but nonetheless open, support structure. Structurally speaking, many tables are leg-and-apron tables, though we very seldom call them that. We're more likely to name them for the use we put them to or the place we keep them: kitchen table, bedside table, coffee table.

As you page on, you'll see archetypes of all sorts of other tables, and many of them will refer back to this fundamental table.

This table is just the sort that would be found in a kitchen. Its bulk conveys a sense of sturdiness. While the legs are heavy, the turned profile reduces their bulk visually. Moreover, the generous dimensions of the leg posts make them ideal for strong joints.

DESIGN VARIATIONS

Despite the simplicity of the leg-and-apron table, endless varieties are possible. The table can be round, square, oval, or rectangular. Its legs can be square, turned, tapered, or sculpted. Even the aprons can alter the appearance of a table.

The round table, for example, has the same turned legs as the archetype table yet looks completely different. The square leg-and-apron assembly and the round tabletop give it that different look. Despite its elegant turned cabriole legs, the Queen Anne table, with its deep aprons, is clearly a worktable. The relieved aprons of the third table produce big visual and practical differences, making the table appear lighter and taller and at the same time offering increased thigh room.

Round-Topped Table

Queen Anne Worktable

Table with Relieved Aprons

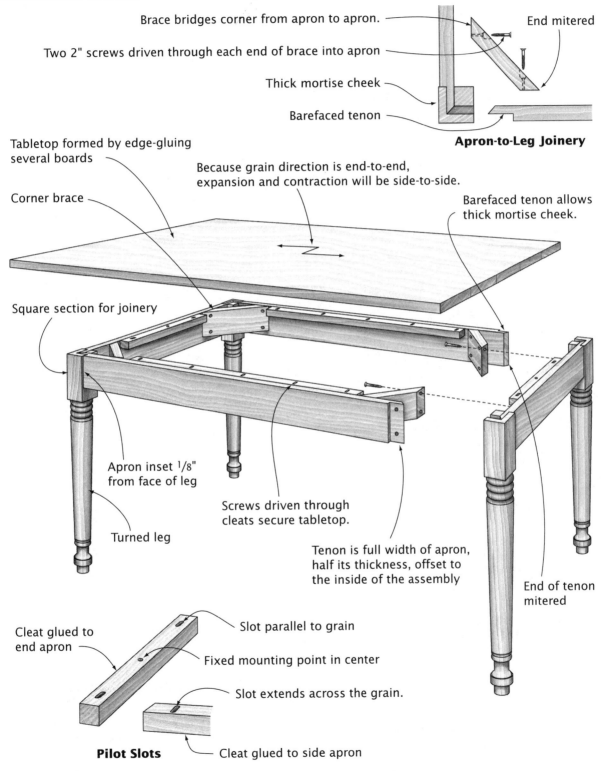

Brace bridges corner from apron to apron.

Two 2" screws driven through each end of brace into apron

Thick mortise cheek

Barefaced tenon

End mitered

Apron-to-Leg Joinery

Tabletop formed by edge-gluing several boards

Because grain direction is end-to-end, expansion and contraction will be side-to-side.

Corner brace

Barefaced tenon allows thick mortise cheek.

Square section for joinery

Apron inset 1/8" from face of leg

Turned leg

Screws driven through cleats secure tabletop.

Tenon is full width of apron, half its thickness, offset to the inside of the assembly

End of tenon mitered

Cleat glued to end apron

Slot parallel to grain

Fixed mounting point in center

Slot extends across the grain.

Cleat glued to side apron

Pilot Slots

TAVERN
TABLE

76"

36"

29¾"

PLANS

Bentzley, Craig. "Tavern Table," *American Woodworker*, No. 19 (March/April 1991), pp. 29–35. Plans for a 42" × 72" table with 2 drawers and a removable top.

•

Lyons, Richard A. "Tavern Table," *Making Country Furniture*. Englewood Cliffs, NJ: Prentice-Hall, 1987. A different turn on the tavern table theme: a table for 1.

Everyone has a slightly different vision of a tavern table. Furniture scholars usually describe it as a plain, low, oblong table on sturdy framework of turned or square legs and stretchers. That pretty much covers it: It's a leg-and-apron table with stretchers.

Stretchers, particularly stout ones like those on the table shown, add a great deal of strength and rigidity to a table. When it is subjected to aggressive daily use, those stretchers can add years to its useful life. The name "tavern table" surely derives from the use of such tables in inns and taverns in the 17th and 18th centuries. The surviving examples of such tables generally do have stout stretchers, though they're worn from the scuffings of thousands of feet.

The table shown has a medial stretcher rather than side stretchers, in deference to the people sitting at the table. Many very early tables of this sort did have side stretchers, though.

Construction is straightforward. The aprons and stretchers are mortised into the legs and pinned. The tabletop is a broad panel with breadboard ends.

DESIGN VARIATIONS The easiest way to alter the design of a table is to change the leg. The archetype table has a turned leg, and you can vary the turning in an infinitude of ways. Just remember that you need a flat, square surface for the stretcher-to-leg joinery.

With a tavern-style table, you can also alter the stretchers—in appearance, but also in configuration, as the drawings below suggest.

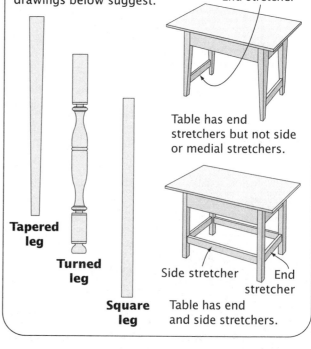

Tapered leg

Turned leg

Square leg

End stretcher

Table has end stretchers but not side or medial stretchers.

Side stretcher

End stretcher

Table has end and side stretchers.

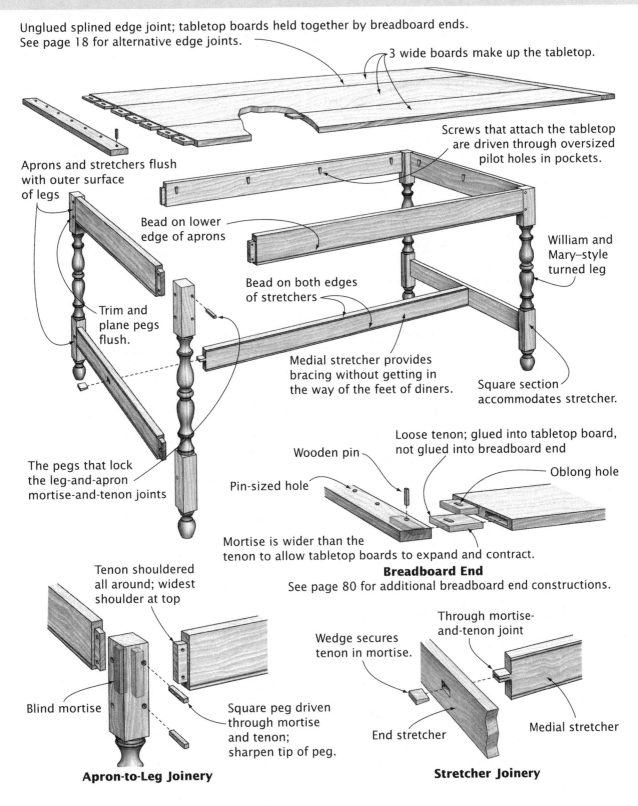

Unglued splined edge joint; tabletop boards held together by breadboard ends. See page 18 for alternative edge joints.

3 wide boards make up the tabletop.

Screws that attach the tabletop are driven through oversized pilot holes in pockets.

Aprons and stretchers flush with outer surface of legs

Bead on lower edge of aprons

William and Mary–style turned leg

Bead on both edges of stretchers

Trim and plane pegs flush.

Medial stretcher provides bracing without getting in the way of the feet of diners.

Square section accommodates stretcher.

The pegs that lock the leg-and-apron mortise-and-tenon joints

Wooden pin

Loose tenon; glued into tabletop board, not glued into breadboard end

Pin-sized hole

Oblong hole

Mortise is wider than the tenon to allow tabletop boards to expand and contract.

Breadboard End
See page 80 for additional breadboard end constructions.

Tenon shouldered all around; widest shoulder at top

Wedge secures tenon in mortise.

Through mortise-and-tenon joint

Blind mortise

Square peg driven through mortise and tenon; sharpen tip of peg.

End stretcher

Medial stretcher

Apron-to-Leg Joinery

Stretcher Joinery

LEG-AND-APRON
TABLE WITH DRAWER

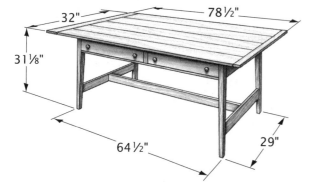

32"

78½"

31⅛"

64½"

29"

approach is simply to cut an opening in the apron. For a (relatively) small drawer in an expansive apron, this is satisfactory. If the openings become so large as to undermine the integrity of the board, it is better to substitute rails. The rails can be turned on edge so their width matches the thickness of the leg. Multiple-tenon joinery provides structural rigidity. A design that uses rails both above and below the drawer is best, since the upper rail prevents the legs from flexing and toeing in.

The leg-and-apron table isn't a stylistic form so much as a construction form. Leg-and-apron tables are the basis for kitchen tables, library tables, writing desks, and so forth. Even workbenches.

Incorporating a drawer or two enhances the utility of a table, since tools used when working at the table can be kept there. In some cases, a slender drawer will serve, but in others, the largest drawer possible is needed.

There are only a couple of ways to incorporate that drawer. A straightforward

PLANS

Abram, Norm. "Kitchen Worktable," *Classics from the New Yankee Workshop*. Boston: Little, Brown, 1990. Plans for a table very much like our archetype.

●

Margon, Lester. "Library Table," *More American Furniture Treasures*. New York: Architectural Book Publishing Co., 1971. Measured drawing of an early-18th-century Pennsylvania table with 2 deep drawers.

DESIGN VARIATIONS

Incorporating a drawer into a round table's apron is possible. But if the table's leg-and-apron assembly is square (or rectangular), you must be prepared to have only limited access to the drawer's interior. In a table with a curved apron, the drawer front needs to be of blockfront or bent-lamination construction so its contour will match that of the apron.

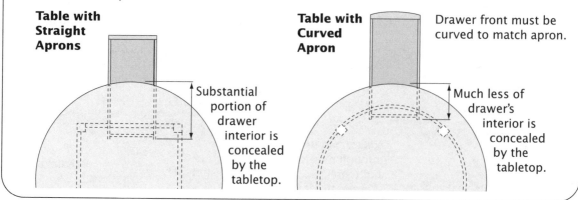

Table with Straight Aprons

Substantial portion of drawer interior is concealed by the tabletop.

Table with Curved Apron

Drawer front must be curved to match apron.

Much less of drawer's interior is concealed by the tabletop.

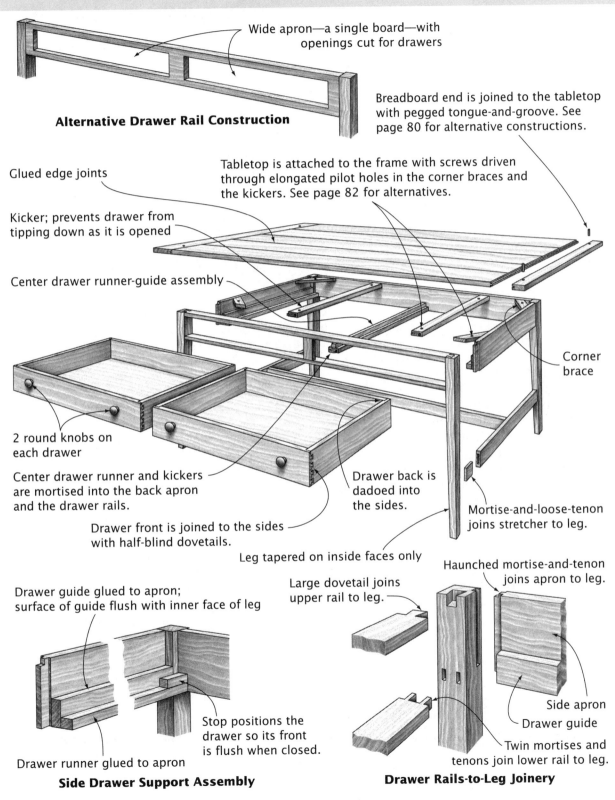

Wide apron—a single board—with openings cut for drawers

Alternative Drawer Rail Construction

Breadboard end is joined to the tabletop with pegged tongue-and-groove. See page 80 for alternative constructions.

Glued edge joints

Tabletop is attached to the frame with screws driven through elongated pilot holes in the corner braces and the kickers. See page 82 for alternatives.

Kicker; prevents drawer from tipping down as it is opened

Center drawer runner-guide assembly

Corner brace

2 round knobs on each drawer

Center drawer runner and kickers are mortised into the back apron and the drawer rails.

Drawer back is dadoed into the sides.

Drawer front is joined to the sides with half-blind dovetails.

Leg tapered on inside faces only

Mortise-and-loose-tenon joins stretcher to leg.

Drawer guide glued to apron; surface of guide flush with inner face of leg

Large dovetail joins upper rail to leg.

Haunched mortise-and-tenon joins apron to leg.

Stop positions the drawer so its front is flush when closed.

Side apron

Drawer guide

Drawer runner glued to apron

Twin mortises and tenons join lower rail to leg.

Side Drawer Support Assembly

Drawer Rails-to-Leg Joinery

PEDESTAL
TABLE

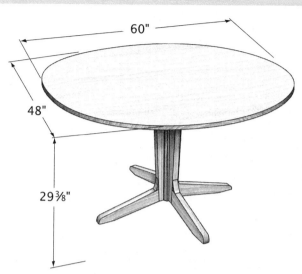

60"

48"

29⅜"

each direction. Anything markedly less, and you risk having the table tip when anyone puts weight on the table's edge.

Critical structural considerations include the strength of the central column and the joinery between it and the base or feet. The table shown here has an oval top and, to match the major and minor axes of the top, feet of two different lengths. The feet are joined to tapering uprights with twin slip joints, as are the supports to which the tabletop is attached. These assemblies are in turn glued to a square core, creating a pedestal assembly that spreads as it rises.

An alternative to the table with a leg at each corner is the pedestal table. Here the tabletop is attached to a central pillar that rises out of a base or arrangement of low but spreading feet. Aprons are structurally unnecessary, although some pedestal tables have them.

Ostensibly, a table without legs (and without aprons) is a table with unrestricted leg room. The truth is that although there usually *is* plenty of leg, knee, and thigh room, the base typically gets in the way of your feet. This is the price paid for stability: The base's footprint should be within 6 inches of the top's shadow in

PLANS

Burchett, John. "Building an Open-Pedestal Table," *The Best of Fine Woodworking: Tables and Chairs.* Newtown, CT: The Taunton Press, 1995. Magazine article collected into a book provides broad construction directions but no detailed measurements.

Watts, Simon. "Oval Table," *Building a Houseful of Furniture.* Newtown, CT: The Taunton Press, 1983. Contemporary design and joinery presented through good drawings and good text.

DESIGN VARIATIONS The pedestal form originated in the 18th century as a small table—an occasional table—with a tripod base. To make a dining-sized table, early cabinetmakers would join two pedestal tables or attach two tripod bases to a single oblong tabletop. Contemporary styles range from the utilitarian to the multicolumnar. The multicolumn pedestal's structural advantage is its increased resistance to twisting. Though its footprint might be significantly smaller than the tabletop, a large table with this base can be stable because of the pedestal's mass.

Federal-Style Pedestal Table

4-Column Pedestal Table

Simple Pedestal Table

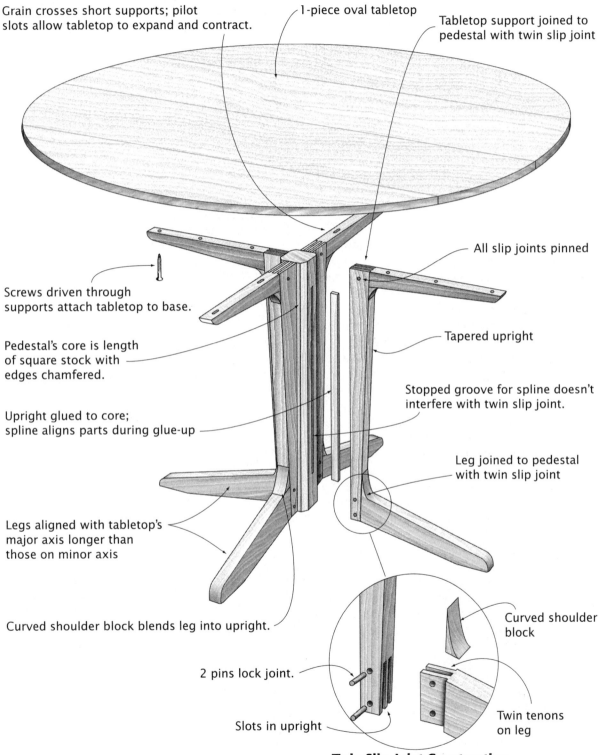

Grain crosses short supports; pilot slots allow tabletop to expand and contract.

1-piece oval tabletop

Tabletop support joined to pedestal with twin slip joint

Screws driven through supports attach tabletop to base.

All slip joints pinned

Pedestal's core is length of square stock with edges chamfered.

Tapered upright

Upright glued to core; spline aligns parts during glue-up

Stopped groove for spline doesn't interfere with twin slip joint.

Leg joined to pedestal with twin slip joint

Legs aligned with tabletop's major axis longer than those on minor axis

Curved shoulder block blends leg into upright.

2 pins lock joint.

Curved shoulder block

Slots in upright

Twin tenons on leg

Twin Slip Joint Construction

TRESTLE
TABLE

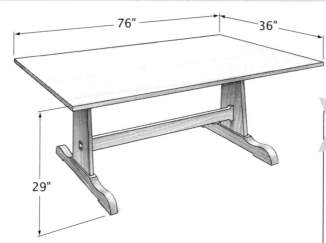

76"

36"

29"

DESIGN VARIATIONS

Noodling with the contour of the trestle and its foot is the easiest way to alter a trestle table's appearance. Several examples are shown here. Although the original trestles were similar to sawhorses, the X-shaped (or sawbuck) trestle was very common in medieval Europe. The Pennsylvania Dutch and other Germanic settlers brought this form to America, and it is still seen often on picnic tables. Most common today is the I-shaped trestle. The Shakers, who made quite a few trestle tables, generally used a slender foot with a "high instep."

Contemporary I-Section Trestle End

Scroll-Cut Sawbuck Trestle End

Shaker-Style Trestle End

L ay a wide, thick board across a couple of horses or trestles, and you have a table. This is the very genesis of the trestle table, which just may be the earliest table form. Since medieval day the form has become considerably more sophisticated, but it remains an easy-to-build, easy-to-knock-down table.

The most rudimentary form remains a board (or sheet of plywood) laid on a couple of freestanding horses or trestles. It is when the trestles are not freestanding that the assemblage becomes a table, for then they must be connected to one another, to the top, or to both.

In the table illustrated, each trestle is composed of a fairly wide post mortised into a foot on the bottom and a tabletop support on top. The wider the trestle, the better able it is to resist side-to-side racking. A long, stout stretcher is mortised into each trestle. The tabletop is screwed to the trestles, making the assembly fixed.

While there is considerable room beneath the trestle table for legs and feet, you have to keep the stretcher in mind; no one wants to bark their shins repeatedly while seated at a table. Likewise, the tabletop end must overhang the trestle by 14 to 18 inches to provide adequate leg room for a person seated at the end.

Many trestle tables are designed to knock down quickly. Common ways of constructing the table so it can easily be knocked down are shown on the opposite page.

PLANS

Frid, Tage. "Trestle," in "Tables." *Tage Frid Teaches Woodworking, Book 3: Furnituremaking.* Newtown, CT: The Taunton Press, 1985. A contemporary design with drawers under the tabletop.

●

Margon, Lester. "Sawbuck Dining Table from Pennsylvania," *Construction of American Furniture Treasures.* New York: Dover Publications, 1975. A knockdown table with scroll-cut legs and a single large drawer.

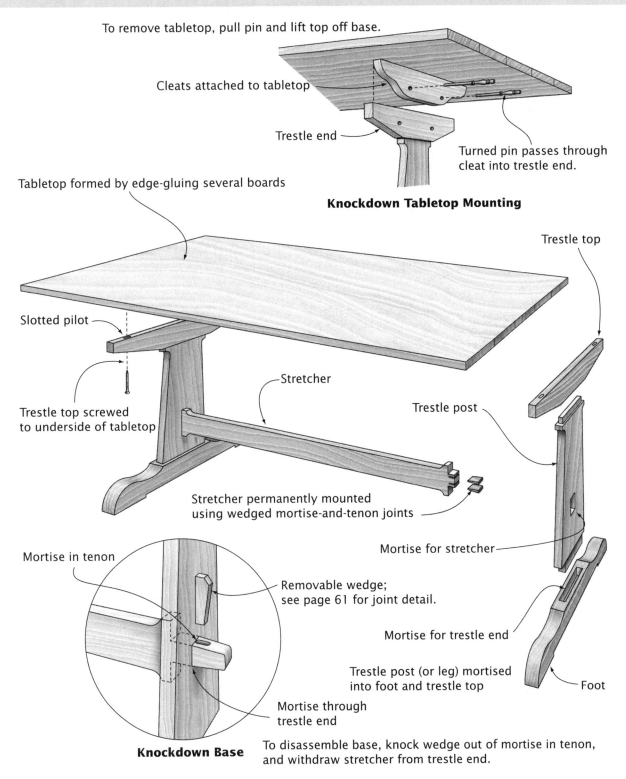

To remove tabletop, pull pin and lift top off base.

Cleats attached to tabletop

Trestle end

Turned pin passes through cleat into trestle end.

Knockdown Tabletop Mounting

Tabletop formed by edge-gluing several boards

Trestle top

Slotted pilot

Trestle top screwed to underside of tabletop

Stretcher

Trestle post

Stretcher permanently mounted using wedged mortise-and-tenon joints

Mortise for stretcher

Mortise in tenon

Removable wedge; see page 61 for joint detail.

Mortise for trestle end

Trestle post (or leg) mortised into foot and trestle top

Foot

Mortise through trestle end

Knockdown Base

To disassemble base, knock wedge out of mortise in tenon, and withdraw stretcher from trestle end.

EXTENSION
TABLE

Pull-Out Table,
English Pull-Out Table

42"

68"

44"

30"

A familiar dining table is the one that can be expanded by adding extra leaves. The table that just accommodates the immediate family for meals can easily to enlarged to seat guests as well.

What may not be immediately obvious is that the extension table is a standard leg-and-apron table that's been sawed in half, then rejoined with special slides. The slides can be purchased or constructed along with the table. Each leaf made for the table should be 24 inches wide, the optimal width for a place setting.

PLANS

Beckvoort, Chris. "Leg-and-Apron Table," *The Best of Fine Woodworking: Traditional Furniture Projects.* Newtown, CT: The Taunton Press, 1991. Concise drawings, good text on building a round extension table with square leg-and-apron assembly.

●

Frid, Tage. "English Pullout," in "Tables." *Tage Frid Teaches Woodworking, Book 3: Furnituremaking.* Newtown, CT: The Taunton Press, 1985. Construction drawings for a "plain-Jane" extension table, with very good directions for making the extension slides.

●

Moser, Thomas. "Round Extension Table," "Oval Extension Table," "Round-Ring Extension Table," and "Oval-Ring Extension Table," *Measured Shop Drawings for American Furniture.* New York: Sterling Publishing Co., 1985. In 1 book, measured drawings only (as the book title says) for 4 tables.

▶ **DESIGN VARIATIONS** The design of an extension table can be varied in all the usual ways, like altering the appearance of the legs and the aprons. The shape of the tabletop (and contour of the aprons) has little or nothing to do with the overall construction. So long as you are talking about a leg-and-apron structure, the pull-out form is dealt with in the same way. As the range of a table's expansion increases, though, an additional leg may be needed to support the center section. And don't overlook the impact of small elements, like attaching aprons to the leaf.

Leaves with Aprons

Round Pull-Out Table

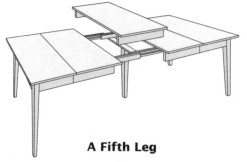

A Fifth Leg

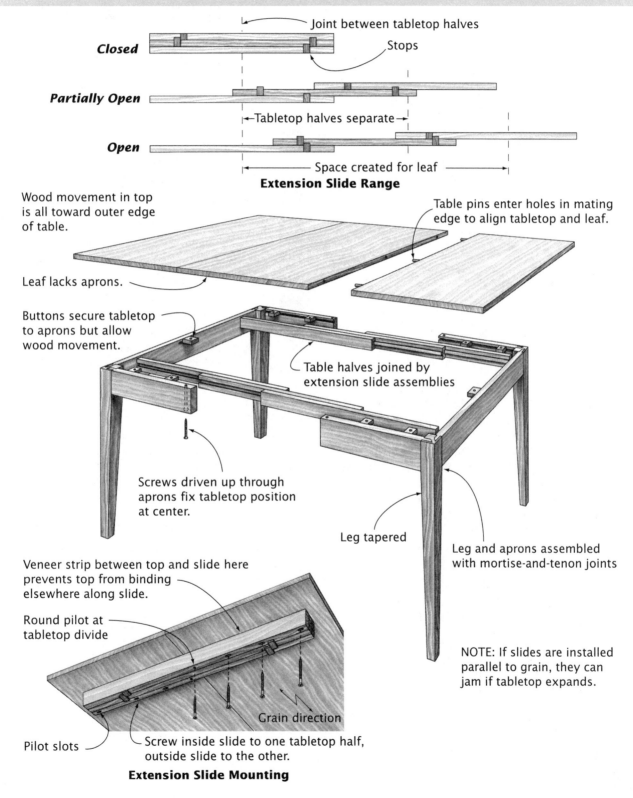

Closed

Joint between tabletop halves

Stops

Partially Open

←Tabletop halves separate→

Open

Space created for leaf

Extension Slide Range

Wood movement in top is all toward outer edge of table.

Table pins enter holes in mating edge to align tabletop and leaf.

Leaf lacks aprons.

Buttons secure tabletop to aprons but allow wood movement.

Table halves joined by extension slide assemblies

Screws driven up through aprons fix tabletop position at center.

Leg tapered

Leg and aprons assembled with mortise-and-tenon joints

Veneer strip between top and slide here prevents top from binding elsewhere along slide.

Round pilot at tabletop divide

NOTE: If slides are installed parallel to grain, they can jam if tabletop expands.

Grain direction

Pilot slots

Screw inside slide to one tabletop half, outside slide to the other.

Extension Slide Mounting

PEDESTAL
EXTENSION
TABLE

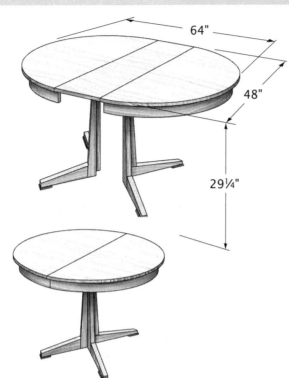

64"

48"

29¼"

PLANS

Frid, Tage. "Circular Pedestal Pullout," in "Tables." *Tage Frid Teaches Woodworking, Book 3: Furnituremaking.* Newtown, CT: The Taunton Press, 1985. Good drawings and construction notes for a contemporary expanding pedestal table.

•

"Round Dining Table," *Woodsmith*, No. 30, pp. 16–21. Illustrated construction directions for a contemporary table seating 4 to 6 people.

•

Salomonsky, Verna Cook. "Duncan Phyfe Dining Table," *Masterpieces of Furniture Design.* New York: Dover Publications, 1953. Measured drawing of a Federal-era double-pedestal table; detail enough for the advanced woodworker only.

The pedestal table is a fundamental table form, one that has some advantages over leg-and-apron types. If you need a table that can be expanded, don't fail to consider this form.

Drop leaves, draw leaves, or a folding top can be incorporated into a pedestal table, making it expandable. But the most common way to expand a pedestal table is with the pull-out extension system.

As shown opposite, the tabletop is cut in two, and the halves reconnected with special extension slides. The tabletop halves thus can be pulled apart so a leaf can be added.

What happens to the pedestal is the key question for the cabinetmaker. The size of the tabletop and the size of the pedestal's footprint must be closely matched if the table is to be stable. In the example shown, the pedestal is split vertically, with half attached to each tabletop section. When the tabletop is pulled apart, the pedestal separates.

DESIGN VARIATIONS

The archetypal table has a pedestal that splits when the table is expanded. That's not the only way it can be done. As long as a modest expansion—say 12 to 16 inches—is acceptable, an expanding table can be built on a solid pedestal. Another alternative is to construct a double-pedestal table. With a pedestal supporting each table half, you can have a large table that expands an additional 3 to 4 feet.

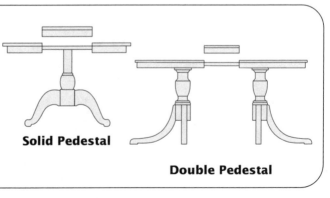

Solid Pedestal

Double Pedestal

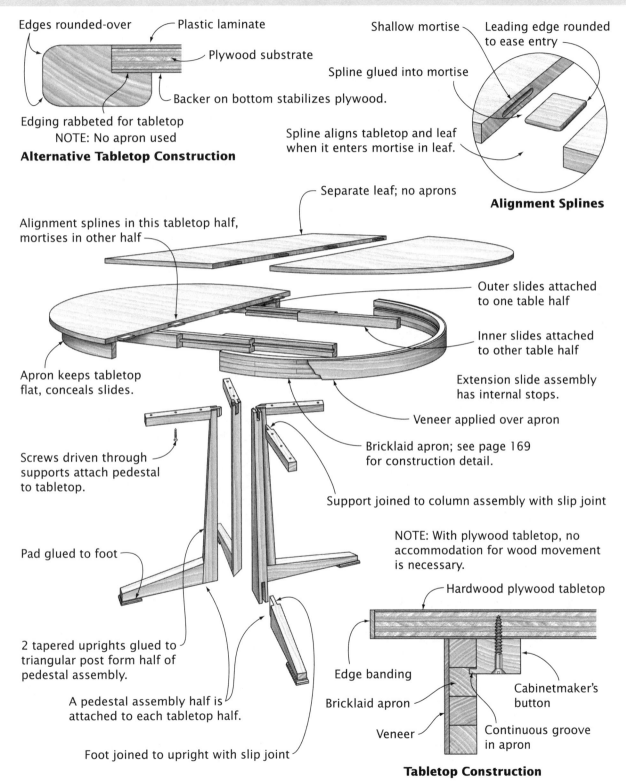

Edges rounded-over

Plastic laminate

Plywood substrate

Backer on bottom stabilizes plywood.

Edging rabbeted for tabletop
NOTE: No apron used
Alternative Tabletop Construction

Shallow mortise

Leading edge rounded
to ease entry

Spline glued into mortise

Spline aligns tabletop and leaf
when it enters mortise in leaf.

Alignment Splines

Separate leaf; no aprons

Alignment splines in this tabletop half,
mortises in other half

Outer slides attached
to one table half

Inner slides attached
to other table half

Apron keeps tabletop
flat, conceals slides.

Extension slide assembly
has internal stops.

Veneer applied over apron

Screws driven through
supports attach pedestal
to tabletop.

Bricklaid apron; see page 169
for construction detail.

Support joined to column assembly with slip joint

Pad glued to foot

NOTE: With plywood tabletop, no
accommodation for wood movement
is necessary.

Hardwood plywood tabletop

2 tapered uprights glued to
triangular post form half of
pedestal assembly.

Edge banding

Cabinetmaker's
button

A pedestal assembly half is
attached to each tabletop half.

Bricklaid apron

Veneer

Continuous groove
in apron

Foot joined to upright with slip joint

Tabletop Construction

DRAW-LEAF
TABLE

19"   50½"   32½"

30"

Dutch Pull-Out Table,
Dutch Draw-Leaf Table

PLANS

Frid, Tage. "Dutch Pullout" in "Tables." *Tage Frid Teaches Woodworking, Book 3: Furnituremaking.* Newtown, CT: The Taunton Press, 1985. Plans for a draw-leaf table of contemporary design.

•

Kriegshauser, John. "Expandable Dining Table," *Workbench,* August/September 1996, pp. 20–23, 26, 61. Plans for a double-pedestal draw-leaf table that seats 4 to 6.

When you are making an expanding table, one of the most interesting systems to consider is the draw-leaf. It is simple to make and use.

There's nothing unusual about the table's basic structure. Except for the notches in the end aprons, it could be any other leg-and-apron unit. The difference lies atop the legs and aprons.

Instead of the tabletop being attached to the leg-and-apron assembly, the leaves, which are attached to long tapered slides, are set atop the assembly. The slides fit into the notches in the aprons. A center board, which separates the leaves, is screwed to the aprons. The tabletop is placed on top of the center board and leaves, but not fastened down.

When you want to expand the table, you simply pull out the leaf from under the tabletop. The slides have stops that prevent the leaf from being pulled out too far. The tabletop will tip up as the leaf moves, but the leaf and the tabletop will end up flush.

With the leaves integral to the table, you don't need to rummage around in a closet or corner to find them when you need space for an extra place setting. You just pull out a leaf, even after the table's been set for dinner.

DESIGN VARIATIONS

The draw-leaf system can work with any type of table support setup, provided it includes aprons. Thus a trestle table or a pedestal table (like the one at right), outfitted with aprons, can have draw leaves to expand its seating capacity.

The system will not, however, work well for tabletop shapes other than rectilinear ones. When not in use, the leaf retreats beneath the tabletop, and its edges are (or should be) visible. If its shape differs from that of the tabletop, the closed-down table's appearance probably would be odd. Stowing a semicircular leaf beneath a square or rectangular top, for example, would produce a gap between the top and the aprons.

Double-Pedestal Draw-Leaf Table

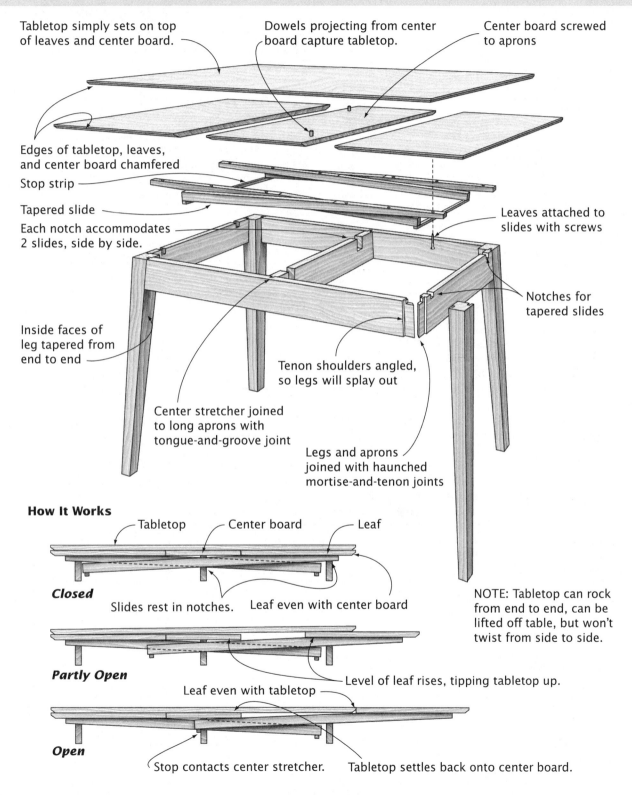

Tabletop simply sets on top of leaves and center board.

Dowels projecting from center board capture tabletop.

Center board screwed to aprons

Edges of tabletop, leaves, and center board chamfered

Stop strip

Tapered slide

Each notch accommodates 2 slides, side by side.

Leaves attached to slides with screws

Inside faces of leg tapered from end to end

Notches for tapered slides

Tenon shoulders angled, so legs will splay out

Center stretcher joined to long aprons with tongue-and-groove joint

Legs and aprons joined with haunched mortise-and-tenon joints

How It Works

Tabletop   Center board   Leaf

Closed

Slides rest in notches.   Leaf even with center board

Partly Open

Level of leaf rises, tipping tabletop up.

Leaf even with tabletop

Open

Stop contacts center stretcher.   Tabletop settles back onto center board.

NOTE: Tabletop can rock from end to end, can be lifted off table, but won't twist from side to side.

SLIDING FOLDING-TOP TABLE

60"

22"

30¾"

PLANS

Frid, Tage. "Sliding Flip-Top Table," in "Tables." *Tage Frid Teaches Woodworking, Book 3: Furnituremaking.* Newtown, CT: The Taunton Press, 1985. Excellent drawings of a contemporary folding-top table. The text focuses on the slide mechanism.

A rarely seen type of expanding table is the sliding folding-top table. Despite its rarity, the sliding folding top is an excellent system.

The table has a single leaf—a duplicate of the tabletop—hinged to the tabletop and, when not in use, folded over on it. To expand the table, you slide the tabletop as far as it will go—halfway across the table's base—then unfold the leaf. The top edges of the aprons should be covered with felt to ease the top's movement.

Constructing the slide mechanism is easy. Each block has a tongue that fits a groove in its runner. The setup's one hitch is that the tongues can bind in the grooves in periods of high humidity.

The archetypal table is configured much like a side table. The expanded tabletop's edges are well clear of the stand, providing plenty of legroom for those seated at the table. The Y-form stretcher provides legroom for the person seated at the end of the table.

DESIGN VARIATIONS

Closed, the sliding folding-top table makes an odd dining table. To limit the overhang of the top when it is opened, the base size must be closely matched to the dimensions of the closed tabletop. Consequently, the folding top is used on the kind of table that doesn't look odd with a modest tabletop overhang. Good candidates include side tables like the archetype, sofa tables like the one below, and other occasional tables. Such tables can be set against a wall when their tops are folded.

Folding tops are commonplace on traditional card tables, but the sliding system is not. Nevertheless, the sliding system is workable on them. The example shown here is otherwise the same as the "Turn-Top Card Table" shown on page 168.

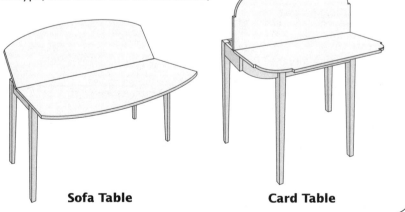

Sofa Table   **Card Table**

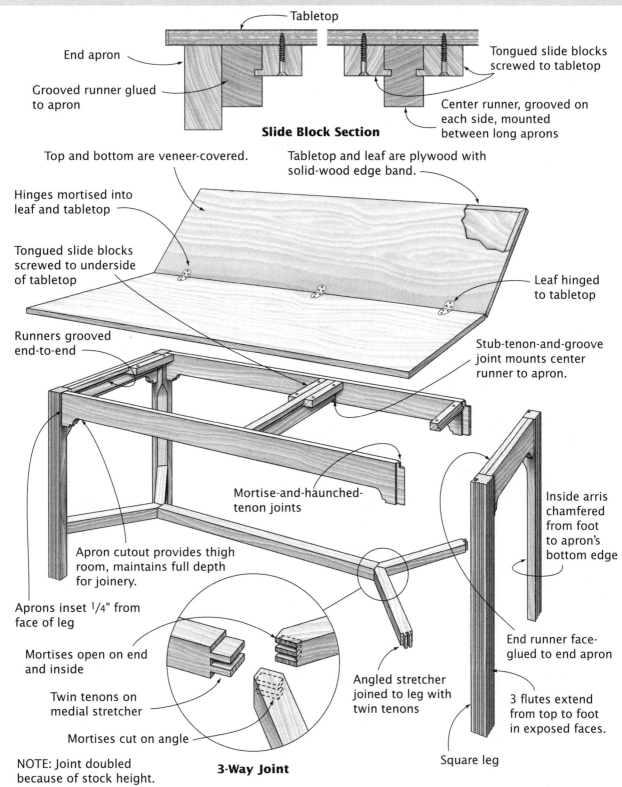

Tabletop

End apron

Grooved runner glued
to apron

Tongued slide blocks
screwed to tabletop

Center runner, grooved on
each side, mounted
between long aprons

Slide Block Section

Top and bottom are veneer-covered.

Tabletop and leaf are plywood with
solid-wood edge band.

Hinges mortised into
leaf and tabletop

Tongued slide blocks
screwed to underside
of tabletop

Leaf hinged
to tabletop

Runners grooved
end-to-end

Stub-tenon-and-groove
joint mounts center
runner to apron.

Mortise-and-haunched-
tenon joints

Inside arris
chamfered
from foot
to apron's
bottom edge

Apron cutout provides thigh
room, maintains full depth
for joinery.

Aprons inset 1/4" from
face of leg

Mortises open on end
and inside

Twin tenons on
medial stretcher

Mortises cut on angle

Angled stretcher
joined to leg with
twin tenons

End runner face-
glued to end apron

3 flutes extend
from top to foot
in exposed faces.

Square leg

NOTE: Joint doubled
because of stock height.

3-Way Joint

DROP-LEAF
TABLE

Folding Table, Harvest Table

21"

10"

29"

78"

D rop-leaf is a generic term for any table that has leaves hinged to the tabletop. It's a commonplace form and has been throughout America's history. In every furniture style from William and Mary through contemporary, you can find a drop-leaf table.

In a drop-leaf, the leaves are an integral part of the tabletop. When not in use, they can be lowered (or dropped) to hang vertically, thus reducing the space the table occupies. There are quite a few ways to support the leaves in the raised position. The table shown uses slide-out supports—you lift the leaf, reach under, and pull the slide out of the table's apron (like opening a drawer). See "Gateleg Table" on page 148, "Swing-Leg Table" on page 150, "Butterfly Table" on page 170, and the several card tables for some other leaf-support approaches.

A prime consideration in the form shown is the width of leaf that can be handled adequately by sliding or pivoting supports. Stick with relatively narrow leaves, say, no more than 15 inches. For wider leaves, see the gateleg and swing-leg forms beginning on page 148. A long leaf, as in the "harvest table" shown, needs multiple supports.

"Harvest," by the way, is a 20th-century name applied to a relatively long, informal drop-leaf. It evokes the picture of a large table, expanded as much as possible, and laden with food for a crew of hungry harvest-time field workers. Regardless of what we call it now, the folks sitting at that table in 1840 or 1880 probably called it a drop-leaf or folding table.

DESIGN VARIATIONS While the archetype table is long and relatively narrow, with a square-cornered rectangular top, a drop-leaf table can be almost any size, proportion, and shape. The top of the table could have the leaves rounded or slightly bowed. On a shorter or square leg-and-apron assembly, you could mount a square, round, or oval top. You could round the leaf corners or bow the exposed leaf edges.

Seats 4;
1 support
for each leaf

Seats 6;
2 supports
for each leaf

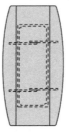

Seats 8;
2 vertical sliding
supports for each leaf

Seats 6;
2 supports
for each leaf

PLANS

Engler, Nick, and Mary Jane Favorite. "Harvest Table," *American Country Furniture*. Emmaus, PA: Rodale Press, 1990. Plans for a table similar to the archetype shown here.

•

Hylton, Bill. "Drop-Leaf Kitchen Table," *Country Pine*. Emmaus, PA: Rodale Press, 1995. An informal table for 4.

•

Mandel, Mitch. "Harvest Table," *American Woodworker*, No. 30 (January/February 1993), pp. 42–47.

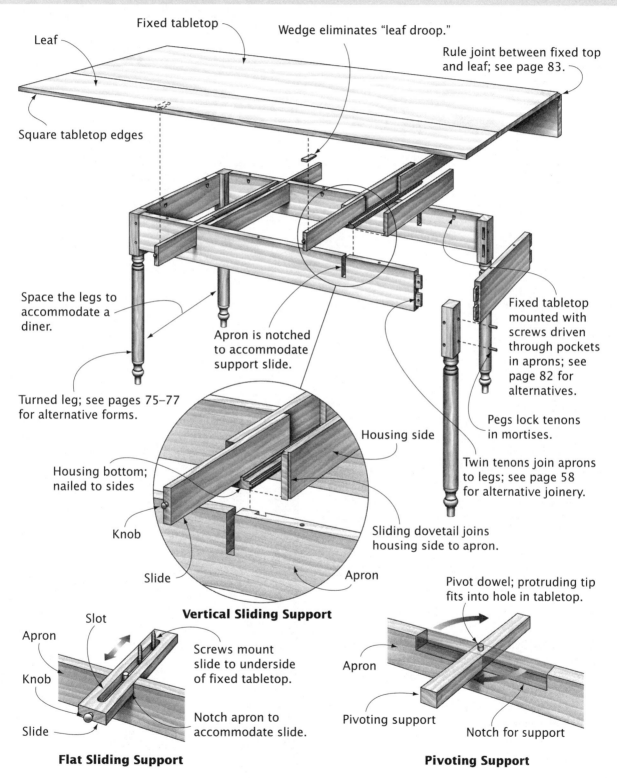

Leaf

Fixed tabletop

Wedge eliminates "leaf droop."

Rule joint between fixed top and leaf; see page 83.

Square tabletop edges

Space the legs to accommodate a diner.

Apron is notched to accommodate support slide.

Fixed tabletop mounted with screws driven through pockets in aprons; see page 82 for alternatives.

Turned leg; see pages 75–77 for alternative forms.

Pegs lock tenons in mortises.

Housing side

Housing bottom; nailed to sides

Knob

Slide

Apron

Twin tenons join aprons to legs; see page 58 for alternative joinery.

Sliding dovetail joins housing side to apron.

Vertical Sliding Support

Pivot dowel; protruding tip fits into hole in tabletop.

Apron

Slot

Screws mount slide to underside of fixed tabletop.

Knob

Slide

Notch apron to accommodate slide.

Apron

Pivoting support

Notch for support

Flat Sliding Support

Pivoting Support

GATELEG
TABLE

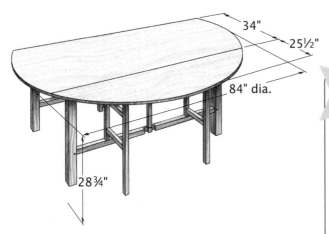

34"

25½"

84" dia.

28¾"

A gateleg is so-called because it is hinged, like a gate, to a table's leg-and-apron-and-stretcher assembly. The leg is connected to a pivot post by upper and lower rails (or stretchers). And the leg is hinged so it can be swung under a raised leaf to support it.

The gateleg is the predecessor to the swing leg. There's a lot of structure to it, reflecting the state of the cabinetmaker's art back in the 16th century, when it first appeared. But like a well-made gate, it is rigid and offers excellent support for a drop-leaf.

Though early gateleg tables typically had 2 gate legs, 1 for each leaf, tables with a single leaf and gate were not uncommon, and a few mammoths had as many as 12 gates. When closed, the tables were usually quite narrow and thus saved space.

A large table with two gates for each leaf can be designed so the gates pivot either toward or away from each other. If they pivot toward each other, the gatelegs will nestle next to the main legs when the leaves are down, visually increasing their bulk. By having the gates pivot away from each other, the legs will stand side by side, giving the table the appearance of having six legs.

Early tables were usually produced in the Baroque styles, with elaborately turned legs. The example shown, however, is thoroughly contemporary.

DESIGN VARIATIONS A significant benefit of the gateleg configuration is its ability to support a very wide leaf. You can get a leg under the leaf, so the table, even with only one leaf raised, is very stable and won't tip. Thus, you can make a very narrow table with wide leaves. Closed, the table takes up very little space. Open, it provides a vast tabletop.

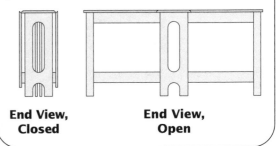

End View, Closed

End View, Open

PLANS

"Gate-Leg Table," *Making Antique Furniture*. Hertfordshire, UK: Argus Books, 1988. A small, round table with turned legs.

Margon, Lester. "Gate-Leg Dining Table with Oval Top from the Brooklyn Museum," *Construction of American Furniture Treasures*. New York: Dover Publications, 1975. A large 17th-century table.

Rogowski, Gary. "Gate-Leg Table Is Light But Sturdy," *The Best of Fine Woodworking: Tables and Chairs*. Newtown, CT: The Taunton Press, 1995. A large contemporary table with an oval top.

Taylor, V. J. "Jacobean Oval Gate-Leg Table," *How to Build Period Country Furniture*. New York: Stein and Day, 1978. A mid-sized, oval-topped table.

Watts, Simon. *Building a Houseful of Furniture*. Newtown, CT: The Taunton Press, 1983. A large, contemporary table with a rectangular top.

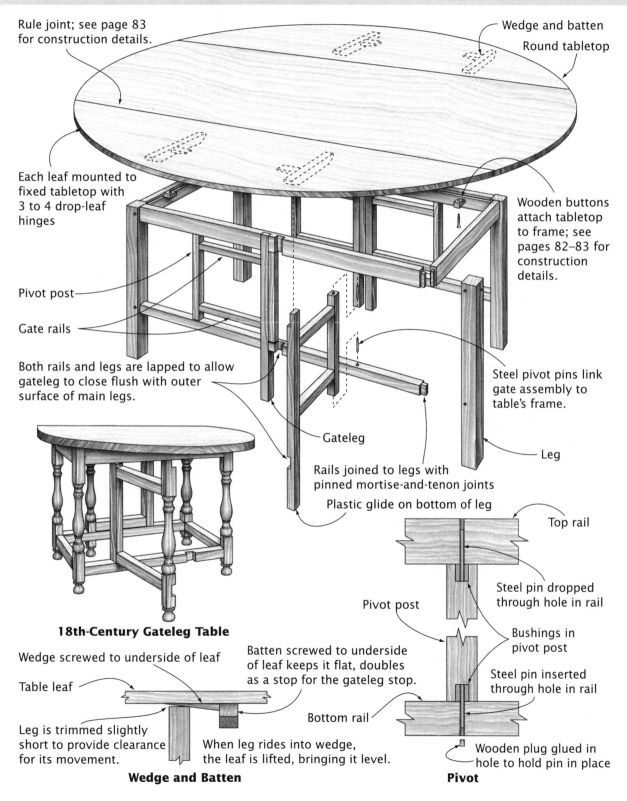

Rule joint; see page 83 for construction details.

Wedge and batten

Round tabletop

Each leaf mounted to fixed tabletop with 3 to 4 drop-leaf hinges

Wooden buttons attach tabletop to frame; see pages 82–83 for construction details.

Pivot post

Gate rails

Both rails and legs are lapped to allow gateleg to close flush with outer surface of main legs.

Gateleg

Steel pivot pins link gate assembly to table's frame.

Leg

Rails joined to legs with pinned mortise-and-tenon joints

Plastic glide on bottom of leg

18th-Century Gateleg Table

Wedge screwed to underside of leaf

Table leaf

Leg is trimmed slightly short to provide clearance for its movement.

Batten screwed to underside of leaf keeps it flat, doubles as a stop for the gateleg stop.

When leg rides into wedge, the leaf is lifted, bringing it level.

Wedge and Batten

Top rail

Steel pin dropped through hole in rail

Pivot post

Bushings in pivot post

Steel pin inserted through hole in rail

Bottom rail

Wooden plug glued in hole to hold pin in place

Pivot

SWING-LEG
TABLE

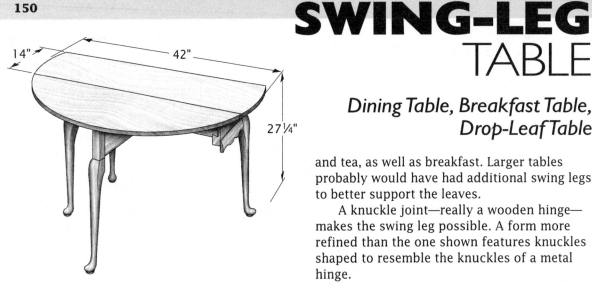

Dining Table, Breakfast Table,
Drop-Leaf Table

and tea, as well as breakfast. Larger tables probably would have had additional swing legs to better support the leaves.

A knuckle joint—really a wooden hinge—makes the swing leg possible. A form more refined than the one shown features knuckles shaped to resemble the knuckles of a metal hinge.

Although this table might legitimately be called a drop-leaf table, the swing leg is what sets it apart from other drop-leaf tables. The swing leg is a descendent of the gateleg. (See "Gateleg Table" on page 148.) While the gateleg has a gatelike apron-and-stretcher connection to the table's frame, the swing leg is attached only to the apron. A lighter appearance is the result.

Size, rather than the swing-leg construction, makes this a dining table. The 42-inch-diameter tabletop will comfortably accommodate four. The swing-leg feature has been used on card tables, which usually have smaller, folding tops. During the Queen Anne period, a small version of the table shown was known as a breakfast table, and it would have been used for games

DESIGN VARIATIONS

The swing-leg design for drop-leaf tables originated in the first half of the 18th century. While we chose a table in the Queen Anne style as archetypal, the swing leg has been used on tables of many styles. The leg form usually is the hallmark of a style.

Chippendale swing-leg tables often have cabriole legs, but always with ball-and-claw feet. Square, molded legs are also used on Chippendale tables. In the Federal era, Hepplewhite tables had tapered legs, as shown below, while Sheraton tables used turned, often reeded, legs.

Lifting leaves transforms rectangular tabletop into a square.

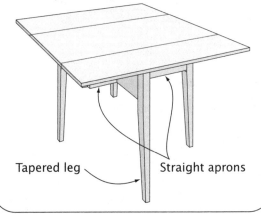

Tapered leg

Straight aprons

PLANS

Dunbar, Michael. "Gateleg Table," *Federal Furniture.* Newtown, CT: The Taunton Press, 1986. An informal table for 4.

•

Treanor, Robert. "Drop-Leaf Breakfast Table," *The Best of Fine Woodworking: Tables and Chairs.* Newtown, CT: The Taunton Press, 1995. A small Queen Anne table.

•

Vandal, Norman. "Circular Drop-Leaf Table," *Queen Anne Furniture.* Newtown, CT: The Taunton Press, 1990. Plans for reproducing an exquisite round Queen Anne table.

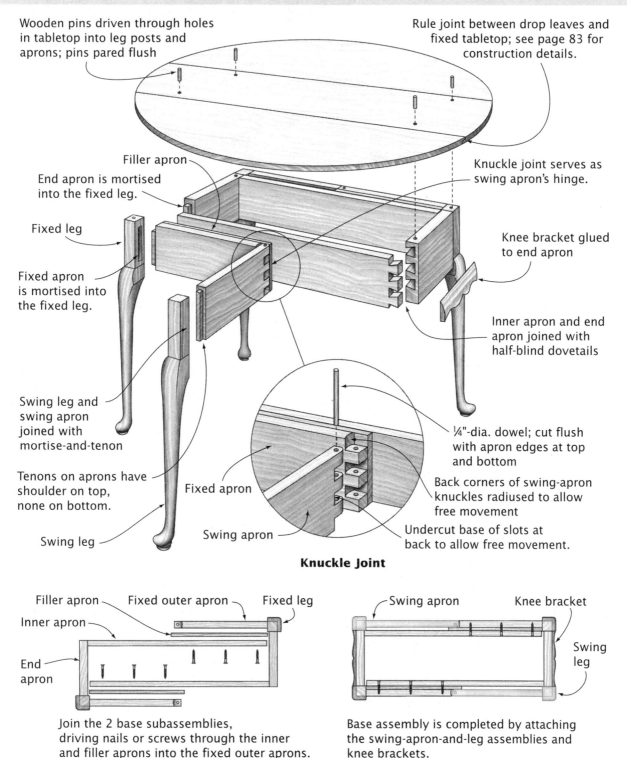

Wooden pins driven through holes in tabletop into leg posts and aprons; pins pared flush

Rule joint between drop leaves and fixed tabletop; see page 83 for construction details.

Filler apron

End apron is mortised into the fixed leg.

Knuckle joint serves as swing apron's hinge.

Fixed leg

Knee bracket glued to end apron

Fixed apron is mortised into the fixed leg.

Inner apron and end apron joined with half-blind dovetails

Swing leg and swing apron joined with mortise-and-tenon

¼"-dia. dowel; cut flush with apron edges at top and bottom

Tenons on aprons have shoulder on top, none on bottom.

Fixed apron

Back corners of swing-apron knuckles radiused to allow free movement

Swing leg

Swing apron

Undercut base of slots at back to allow free movement.

Knuckle Joint

Filler apron   Fixed outer apron   Fixed leg

Swing apron   Knee bracket

Inner apron

Swing leg

End apron

Join the 2 base subassemblies, driving nails or screws through the inner and filler aprons into the fixed outer aprons.

Base assembly is completed by attaching the swing-apron-and-leg assemblies and knee brackets.

Base Assembly

SLIDING-LEG
TABLE

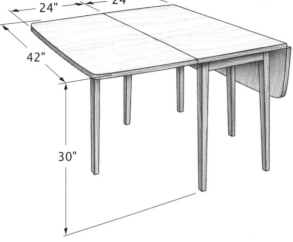

24"   24"

42"

30"

The advantage the gate-leg table has over the swing-leg table is the stability created by its extra legs. When its leaves are raised, those extra two legs are deployed to support them. The sliding-leg table shares that advantage over the swing-leg, but it has one over the gate-leg as well.

Like the gate-leg, this table has an extra leg to support each leaf. But only a narrow stretcher connects each extra leg to the table. The stretchers are housed between two cross members that are mounted between the side aprons, and one projects through a slot in each apron. The leg is joined to the stretcher.

Lift the leaf, pull the extra leg out, and lower the leaf into it. You have a leg to support the leaf, but you still have four legs under the fixed tabletop. The setup can support very wide leaves.

PLANS

Frid, Tage. "Drop-Leaf," in "Tables." *Tage Frid Teaches Woodworking, Book 3: Furnituremaking.* Newtown, CT: The Taunton Press, 1985. Excellent drawings and good construction notes for a frill-free contemporary drop-leaf with sliding leg supports.

●

"Italian-Style Card Table of the 18th Century," *Making Antique Furniture.* Hertfordshire, UK: Argus Books, 1988. Drawings, construction directions, and cutting list for a triangular-topped card table; very demanding project.

DESIGN VARIATIONS

Here are two very different sliding-leg tables, each of which benefits from the stability the extra leg (or legs) provides when the table is expanded.

When the card table is folded and set at a wall, the extra leg is unobtrusive. Set up the table for entertaining, with the extra leg supporting the leaf, and you will find there's a leg under each corner of the tabletop. Perfect.

Sliding legs are likewise the perfect complement to a long drop-leaf table. With two legs under such long leaf, the table won't tip when someone's elbows lean on the table.

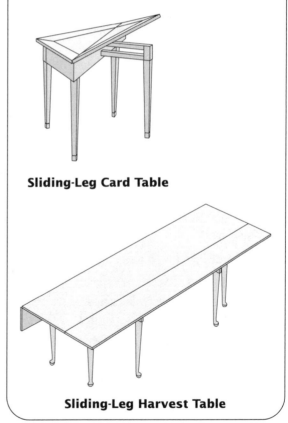

Sliding-Leg Card Table

Sliding-Leg Harvest Table

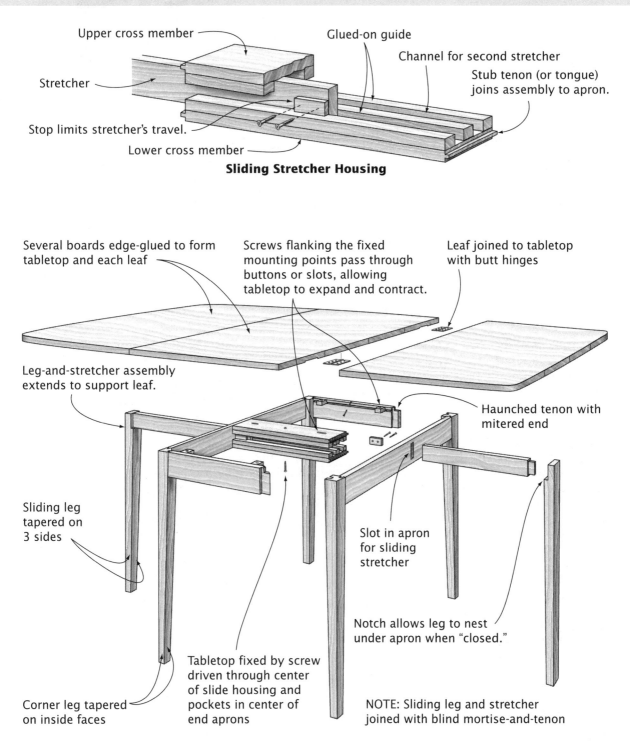

Upper cross member

Glued-on guide

Channel for second stretcher

Stretcher

Stub tenon (or tongue) joins assembly to apron.

Stop limits stretcher's travel.

Lower cross member

Sliding Stretcher Housing

Several boards edge-glued to form tabletop and each leaf

Screws flanking the fixed mounting points pass through buttons or slots, allowing tabletop to expand and contract.

Leaf joined to tabletop with butt hinges

Leg-and-stretcher assembly extends to support leaf.

Haunched tenon with mitered end

Sliding leg tapered on 3 sides

Slot in apron for sliding stretcher

Notch allows leg to nest under apron when "closed."

Corner leg tapered on inside faces

Tabletop fixed by screw driven through center of slide housing and pockets in center of end aprons

NOTE: Sliding leg and stretcher joined with blind mortise-and-tenon

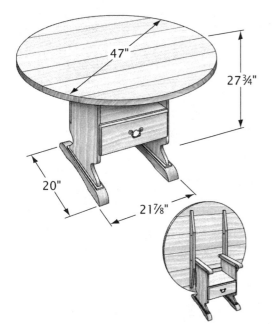

47"

27¾"

20"

21⅞"

SETTLE
CHAIR-TABLE

Bench Table, Table Chair, Settle Table

shoe-shaped feet make the chair more stable; the wide, shaped armrests make it more comfortable. The chair even includes a drawer under the seat, a more refined storage approach than a lidded bin. The tabletop is joined with sliding dovetails.

The roots of the chair table are grounded in medieval practicality. Shelters were small and drafty back in the Middle Ages. Every piece of furniture was dear; each was made by hand with human-powered tools. If a piece of furniture could serve more than one purpose, so much the better.

The chair table clearly is multipurpose. With the tabletop lowered, it's a table. With the tabletop raised, it's a seat. As with most multipurpose stuff, though, its functionality is less than ideal.

As furniture evolved, the chair table became more refined in appearance and construction. The version shown has feet and armrests joined to the chair sides with mortise-and-tenon joints. The distinctive

PLANS

Engler, Nick, and Mary Jane Favorite. "Shoe-Foot Settle Table," *American Country Furniture.* Emmaus, PA: Rodale Press, 1990. Round table with a storage hopper under the seat.

•

Hylton, Bill. "Bench Table," *Country Pine.* Emmaus, PA: Rodale Press, 1995. A rectangular tabletop on a bench.

DESIGN VARIATIONS Early American chair tables date from the 1600s. The earliest American examples have ornate turnings. The pieces continued to be made over the next couple of centuries, especially in rural areas, and they lost most of their embellishments along the way.

The two primitives shown below demonstrate just how easily a five-board bench can be transformed into a table. The legs are simply extended beyond the seat. The appearance is strictly functional, but the effect is nevertheless appealing. Moreover, these are pieces that can be constructed quickly using only the most basic of tools.

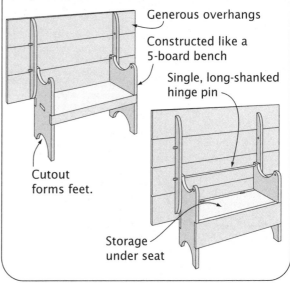

Generous overhangs

Constructed like a 5-board bench

Single, long-shanked hinge pin

Cutout forms feet.

Storage under seat

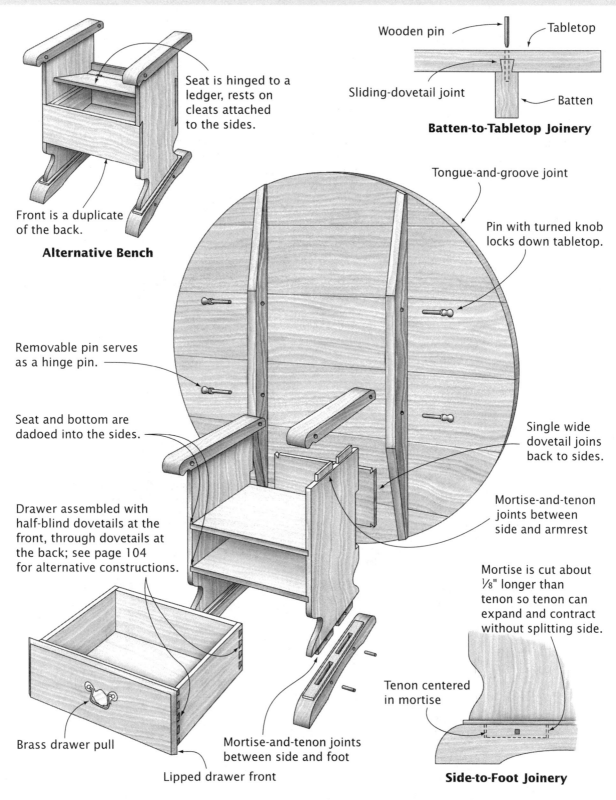

Alternative Bench

Seat is hinged to a ledger, rests on cleats attached to the sides.

Front is a duplicate of the back.

Wooden pin

Tabletop

Sliding-dovetail joint

Batten

Batten-to-Tabletop Joinery

Tongue-and-groove joint

Pin with turned knob locks down tabletop.

Removable pin serves as a hinge pin.

Seat and bottom are dadoed into the sides.

Single wide dovetail joins back to sides.

Drawer assembled with half-blind dovetails at the front, through dovetails at the back; see page 104 for alternative constructions.

Mortise-and-tenon joints between side and armrest

Mortise is cut about ⅛" longer than tenon so tenon can expand and contract without splitting side.

Brass drawer pull

Mortise-and-tenon joints between side and foot

Tenon centered in mortise

Lipped drawer front

Side-to-Foot Joinery

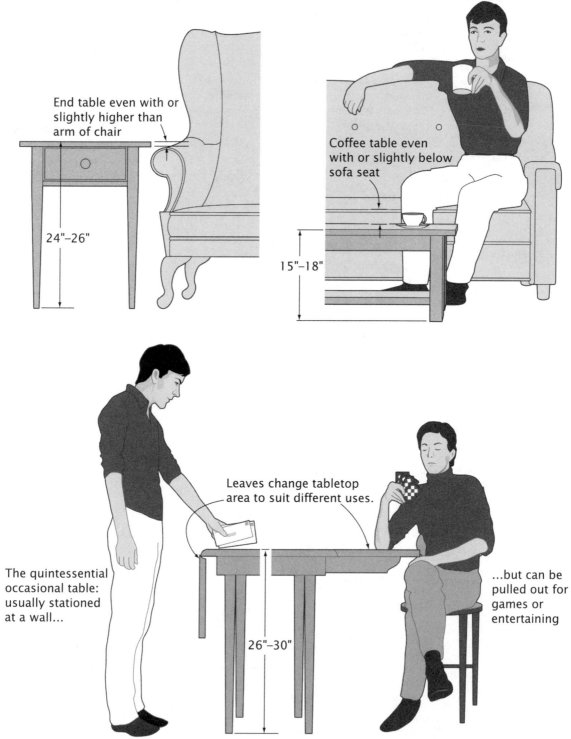

End table even with or slightly higher than arm of chair

24"–26"

Coffee table even with or slightly below sofa seat

15"–18"

Leaves change tabletop area to suit different uses.

The quintessential occasional table: usually stationed at a wall...

...but can be pulled out for games or entertaining

26"–30"

OCCASIONAL TABLES

Occasional tables fill special needs. They are important partners to sofas, easy chairs, beds, hallway niches, and "occasional" activities. Their dimensions should be tailored to the furniture or activity that they accompany.

END TABLE: Slightly higher than the arm of the sofa or easy chair, large enough to hold a lamp, the TV remote, and a beverage and snack. Thus, the front-to-back dimension is usually greater than the width. Typically, end tables are about 24 inches high, 14 to 16 inches wide, and 20 to 23 inches deep.

Traditionally an occasional table was small, but equipped with leaves. With them dropped or folded, it was used as a side table or hall table; with them open, the table became large enough to accommodate informal dining or a game board and moved sitters far enough apart to be comfortable.

COFFEE TABLE: A table designed to be in front of a relatively long, low sofa also needs to be long and low so neither the table nor the things on it obstruct interaction between sofa sitters and others in the room. The tabletop height and depth should make it easy for a seated person to reach to the outer edge of the table. Dimensions range from 15 to 18 inches high and 22 to 30 inches wide, with a length between 3 and 5 feet.

BEDSIDE TABLE: Height generally is even with or just a bit lower than the top of the mattress. At one time, the top was small—18 to 20 inches square—because of the limited reach of a person in bed. As the number of objects we *need* at the bedside increases—lamp, alarm clock, telephone, TV remote, beverage and snack, eyeglasses, tissue box—bedside table proportions likely will increase.

HALL TABLE: Long and narrow, to fit its specialized location; relatively high, both because it is a stand-alone piece and to allow sorting through mail or looking at tabletop knicknacks.

SIDE TABLE: Up to 30 inches high and usually somewhat wider than an end table—maybe 20 to 24 inches.

DEMILUNE
TABLE

26"

26¾"

13"

Pier Table, Semicircular Table, Half-Round Table, Bow-Front Table, D-Shaped Table

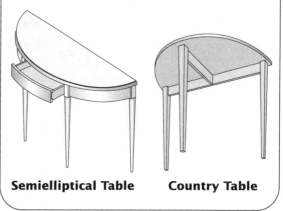
This table takes its name from the half-moon shape of its top. It's an inclusive name for a table, and consequently, you'll find a wide variety of tables that could legitimately be called half-round or demilune tables.

Perhaps the first examples were massive three-legged side tables made in Europe and England in the early 17th century. In the 17th century, four-legged versions with folding tops were popular for use as card tables (see "Turn-Top Card Table" on page 168). Later tables more closely resembling the example shown became fashionable to use in pairs, in alcoves, or between windows. Even smaller demilune tables were used in the hallway, and, oddly enough, these became known as hall tables.

In building a demilune table, the most problematic part is the curved apron. It can be made as one continuous piece, as in the model shown, with the front legs joining it with bridle joints. A one-piece apron with as pronounced a curve as this can be bricklaid (see *Bricklaid Construction* on page 169) and veneered, or glue-laminated from thin plies bent around a curved form. Alternatively, the curved apron could be made up of three separate pieces, each of which extends from one leg to the next. Each piece would be cut from a piece of thick stock.

PLANS

Clinton, Bill. "A Semielliptical Table," *The Best of Fine Woodworking: Tables and Chairs.* Newtown, CT: The Taunton Press, 1995. A well-designed, well-made table you can duplicate.

●

Hill, Jack. "Half-Round Hall Table," *Making Family Heirlooms.* New York: St. Martin's Press, 1985. A British-made demilune.

●

Hylton, Bill. "Half-Round Table," *Country Pine.* Emmaus, PA: Rodale Press, 1995. Very detailed, easy-to-follow instructions; for country furniture buffs.

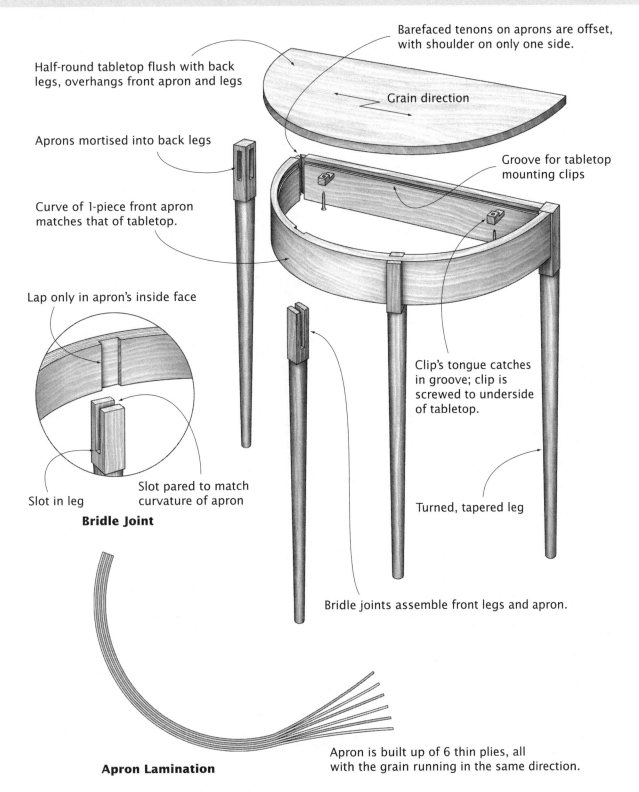

Barefaced tenons on aprons are offset, with shoulder on only one side.

Half-round tabletop flush with back legs, overhangs front apron and legs

Grain direction

Aprons mortised into back legs

Groove for tabletop mounting clips

Curve of 1-piece front apron matches that of tabletop.

Lap only in apron's inside face

Slot in leg

Slot pared to match curvature of apron

Bridle Joint

Clip's tongue catches in groove; clip is screwed to underside of tabletop.

Turned, tapered leg

Bridle joints assemble front legs and apron.

Apron Lamination

Apron is built up of 6 thin plies, all with the grain running in the same direction.

TEA TABLE

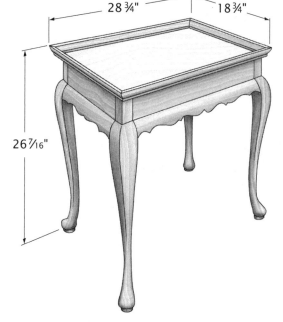

28 ¾" 18 ¾"

26 ⁷⁄₁₆"

Tray-Top Tea Table

Tea tables like the Queen Anne example shown were part of the ceremonial trappings. Initially, they were simple occasional tables, but they became more elaborate as the ceremonial stakes were raised.

The joinery shown represents an improvement over that of the 19th century, when it was common to nail tops directly to bases. In this reproduction table, the top is fastened to the aprons with cabinetmaker's buttons. Old-time cabinetmakers didn't *always* get it right.

PLANS

Bird, Lonnie. "Connecticut Tea Table," *American Woodworker,* No. 49 (December 1995), pp. 46–51. A graceful old form reproduced using contemporary tools and techniques.

●

Vandal, Norman. "Tray-Top Tea Table" and "Porringer-Top Tea Table," *Queen Anne Furniture. History,* Newtown, CT: The Taunton Press, 1990. Two different tea tables in one book! Thorough, excellent plans and directions for each table.

During the late 16th century, the British took up tea drinking. Teapots and teacups, teaspoons and tea caddies, even strainers were invented or introduced from the Orient. By the early 18th century, tea drinking—even in the colonies—had become an elaborate ceremony in which manners, wit, and equipage proved one's gentility and wealth.

DESIGN VARIATIONS

While the tray-top form was archetypal of Queen Anne tea tables, it wasn't the only tea table built during that period. The porringer-top table, here with turned cabriole legs, apparently derived its name from the porridge-bowl–like turrets at the corners of the top. While it is a more flexible form of occasional table, it is less sophisticated. But the tray-top form didn't disappear with the waning of the Queen Anne period.

As shown here, tray-top tea tables were built in the Chippendale and Federal periods. The serpentine-form table, with its showy stretchers, was directly inspired by Chippendale's pattern book. Sharing the serpentine form was the Federal urn stand, smaller because it was intended to hold only the large teapot, not all the tea-ceremony trappings.

Porringer-Top Queen Anne Tea Table

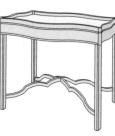

Philadelphia Chippendale Tea Table

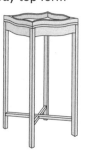

Southern Hepplewhite Urn Stand

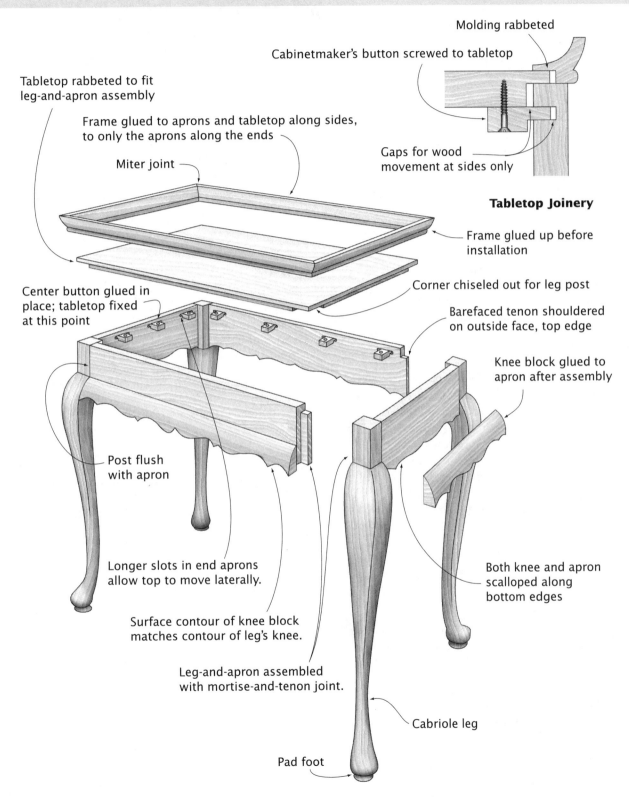

Molding rabbeted

Cabinetmaker's button screwed to tabletop

Tabletop rabbeted to fit
leg-and-apron assembly

Frame glued to aprons and tabletop along sides,
to only the aprons along the ends

Miter joint

Gaps for wood
movement at sides only

Tabletop Joinery

Frame glued up before
installation

Center button glued in
place; tabletop fixed
at this point

Corner chiseled out for leg post

Barefaced tenon shouldered
on outside face, top edge

Knee block glued to
apron after assembly

Post flush
with apron

Longer slots in end aprons
allow top to move laterally.

Both knee and apron
scalloped along
bottom edges

Surface contour of knee block
matches contour of leg's knee.

Leg-and-apron assembled
with mortise-and-tenon joint.

Cabriole leg

Pad foot

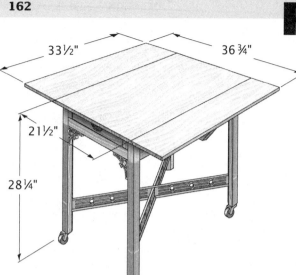

33½"   36¾"

21½"

28¼"

PEMBROKE
TABLE

Breakfast Table

square in section but range from an almost chunky, untapered shape to delicate tapers.

No authoritative source exists for the name. The lore is that it was named after the Earl of Pembroke or for Lady Pembroke.

A Pembroke table is, quite simply, a small drop-leaf table with a drawer. It was often used at breakfast and consequently was often called a breakfast table.

In spite of the leaves generally being narrow, the length of most Pembrokes with their leaves down becomes the width with their leaves up. Invariably, the leaves are supported by a swing-out section of the apron called a "fly." Beyond these similarities, however, the tops vary widely. Common shapes include rectangular, oval, and generally rectangular but with curves in the edges.

There is also considerable variation in the leg structures. Many have stretchers, but many don't. Those that do usually have crossing diagonal stretchers that provide foot room for someone seated at the table. The legs are usually

DESIGN VARIATIONS

Pembroke tables were made in wonderful variety, and usually with exemplary craftsmanship. The archetype shown here is in the Chippendale style. The square legs are densely fluted, and the stretchers are pierced to the point of frailty. The casters are a practical touch for a breakfast table.

A different Chippendale-style table shown below retains the square legs but eschews the surface ornamentation. Its distinctions are its serpentine top and shaped cross stretchers.

The other Pembrokes shown are country tables. The Piedmont table has shaped leaves and a bit of inlay. The New England version has distinctive cross stretchers.

Chippendale Table

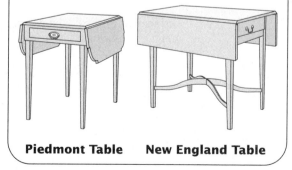

Piedmont Table   **New England Table**

PLANS

Dunbar, Michael. "Pembroke Table," *Federal Furniture*. Newtown, CT: The Taunton Press, 1986. Complete drawings and adequate instructions for elegant Federal Pembroke with clean lines.

●

Margon, Lester. "Pembroke Table," *Construction of American Furniture Treasures*. New York: Dover Publications, 1975. Complete drawings with many details, adequate instructions for a Chippendale table.

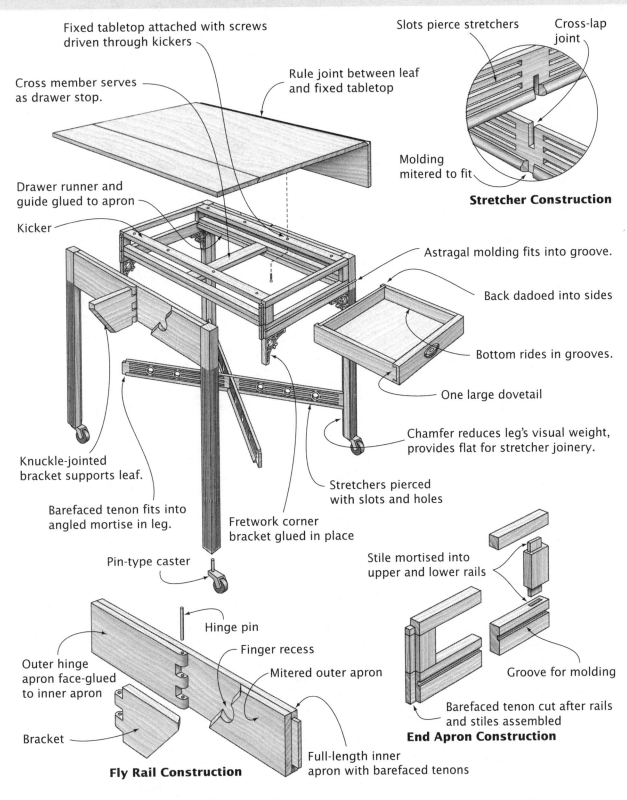

Fixed tabletop attached with screws driven through kickers

Cross member serves as drawer stop.

Rule joint between leaf and fixed tabletop

Slots pierce stretchers

Cross-lap joint

Molding mitered to fit.

Stretcher Construction

Drawer runner and guide glued to apron

Kicker

Astragal molding fits into groove.

Back dadoed into sides

Bottom rides in grooves.

One large dovetail

Knuckle-jointed bracket supports leaf.

Barefaced tenon fits into angled mortise in leg.

Fretwork corner bracket glued in place

Chamfer reduces leg's visual weight, provides flat for stretcher joinery.

Stretchers pierced with slots and holes

Pin-type caster

Stile mortised into upper and lower rails

Outer hinge apron face-glued to inner apron

Hinge pin

Finger recess

Mitered outer apron

Groove for molding

Bracket

Barefaced tenon cut after rails and stiles assembled

End Apron Construction

Fly Rail Construction

Full-length inner apron with barefaced tenons

SWING-LEG
CARD TABLE

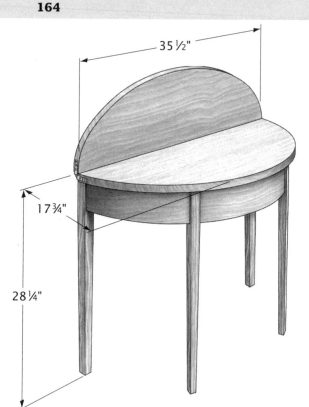

35 ½"

17 ¾"

28 ¼"

DESIGN VARIATIONS

Many swing-leg card tables antedated the Federal era. Queen Anne versions were light and elegant, typically with a drawer in the apron. Chippendale tables were far more ornate. Some of these had five legs, which made the open table more stable. Many had recesses for chips or markers and places for candlesticks. In rural areas, more rectilinear styles were common.

Queen Anne Card Table

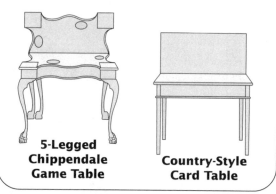

5-Legged Chippendale Game Table

Country-Style Card Table

Did a lack of closets 200 years ago lead to the creation of attractive card tables like the one shown? Contemporary card tables are chintzy affairs: flimsy metal folding legs supporting a pasteboard top. When a card table isn't in active use, it's in a closet. Out of sight.

But when the example shown was built, the card table was always on display. When friends and neighbors came to socialize, often by playing cards or other popular games, the table would be opened up, doubling its size.

The rest of the time, the table would be placed against a wall, out of the way but still a visible and attractive part of the decor.

The linchpin of this genre of card table is the two-part top. The leaf is hinged so that it folds over top of the fixed section when not in use. Shown is a demilune, swing-leg table. One back leg is attached to a hinged apron that can be swung 45 to 60 degrees, providing support for the unfolded leaf. The arrangement is not very stable; leaning on the open tabletop between the back legs can easily upset it.

PLANS

Dunbar, Michael. "Card Table," *Federal Furniture.* Newtown, CT: The Taunton Press, 1986. Construction drawings of a demilune card table.

•

Landon, Eugene E. "Making a Hepplewhite Card Table," *The Best of Fine Woodworking: Traditional Furniture Projects.* Newtown, CT: The Taunton Press, 1991. Reproducing a fine antique, complete with dimensioned drawings.

•

Pittman, Frank M. "Building a Gate-Leg Card Table," *The Best of Fine Woodworking: Tables and Chairs.* Newtown, CT: The Taunton Press, 1995. Make a card table with serpentine-curved aprons and tabletop.

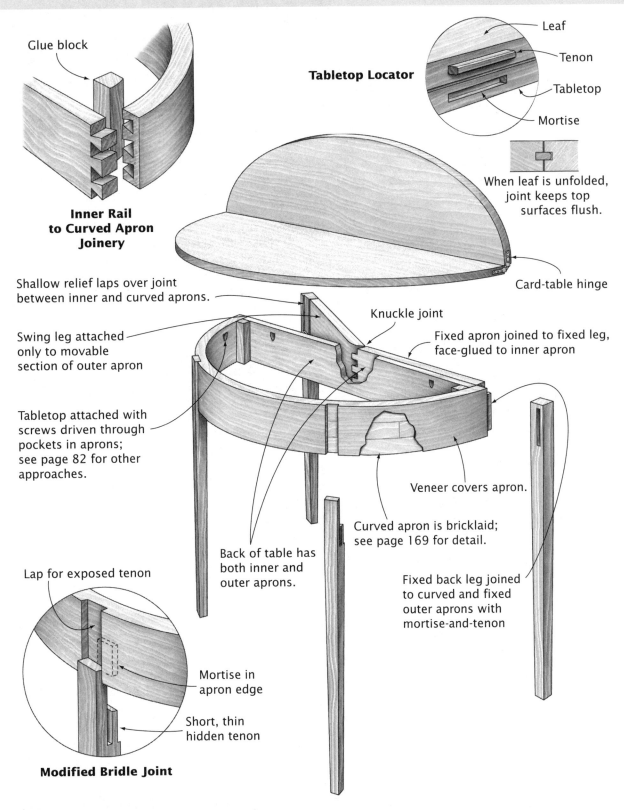

Glue block

**Inner Rail
to Curved Apron
Joinery**

Tabletop Locator

Leaf

Tenon

Tabletop

Mortise

When leaf is unfolded,
joint keeps top
surfaces flush.

Card-table hinge

Knuckle joint

Fixed apron joined to fixed leg,
face-glued to inner apron

Shallow relief laps over joint
between inner and curved aprons.

Swing leg attached
only to movable
section of outer apron

Tabletop attached with
screws driven through
pockets in aprons;
see page 82 for other
approaches.

Veneer covers apron.

Curved apron is bricklaid;
see page 169 for detail.

Back of table has
both inner and
outer aprons.

Fixed back leg joined
to curved and fixed
outer aprons with
mortise-and-tenon

Lap for exposed tenon

Mortise in
apron edge

Short, thin
hidden tenon

Modified Bridle Joint

EXPANDING-FRAME CARD TABLE

35⅝"

35⅛"

27"

Stability is the advantage this card table form has over the swing-leg form. Instead of a single, off-center leg supporting the unfolded leaf—half the tabletop—two legs, one under each outside corner, support it. Enhancing both the rigidity and the appearance of the opened table are the side aprons, which look and function like full-length aprons when they unfold as the frame is expanded.

The price of the improvement is a more sophisticated and demanding-to-construct framework. A dozen hinges are needed simply to assemble the expanding frame. As with the swing-leg version, you need extra bracing for the frame, despite the structure's small size.

Shown is an elaborate Queen Anne table, with cabriole legs, turrets at the front corners, and a drawer. The center of the tabletop is covered with a baize cloth. This somewhat delicate feature is protected when the leaf is folded over the fixed tabletop.

While the table shown is representative of 18th-century high-style, the expanding frame feature is not exclusive to that style of table.

PLANS

Monteith, Edward R. "Convertible Furniture," *The Best of Fine Woodworking: Tables and Chairs.* Newtown, CT: The Taunton Press, 1995. Reproducing a 200-year-old Dutch table; only the expanding frame feature is shown in detailed, dimensioned drawings.

DESIGN VARIATIONS While examples of expanding-frame tables are not common, the feature is relatively easy to incorporate into a modest-sized folding-top table. The frame of the table must be rectangular, rather than demilune or otherwise shaped. Shown below are two examples of the form: a period table with moldings and fretwork, and a very straightforward table with straight aprons and simply turned legs.

As frame expands, corner bracket stays with leg and astragal molding divides.

Chinese Chippendale Card Table

Turned-Leg Card Table

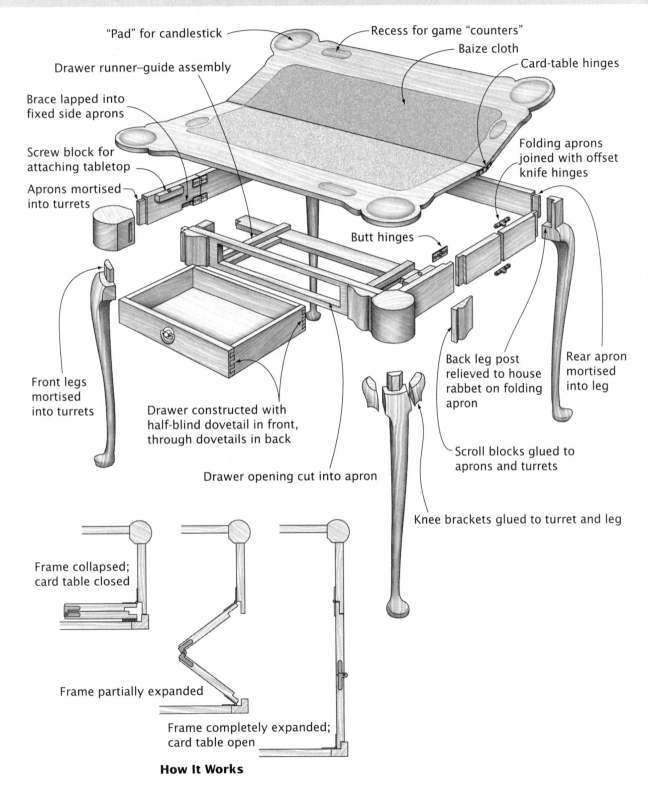

"Pad" for candlestick

Recess for game "counters"

Drawer runner–guide assembly

Baize cloth

Card-table hinges

Brace lapped into fixed side aprons

Screw block for attaching tabletop

Folding aprons joined with offset knife hinges

Aprons mortised into turrets

Butt hinges

Rear apron mortised into leg

Front legs mortised into turrets

Drawer constructed with half-blind dovetail in front, through dovetails in back

Back leg post relieved to house rabbet on folding apron

Drawer opening cut into apron

Scroll blocks glued to aprons and turrets

Knee brackets glued to turret and leg

Frame collapsed; card table closed

Frame partially expanded

Frame completely expanded; card table open

How It Works

TURN-TOP
CARD TABLE

18⅛"

36¼"

28¾"

hang is evenly distributed around the table. The only trick is in positioning the pivot.

The tabletop is attached to the frame only through the pivot. Expansion and contraction of the tabletop thus isn't a problem, although the mounting offers no resistance to cupping.

The particular table shown is called a D-shaped table. This configuration was common during the Federal era, a time when folding-top card tables were particularly popular. Curved aprons are traditionally made using bricklaid construction, as shown on the opposite page. Though the stance of the legs may not be *ideal,* the additional bracing required to accommodate the curved aprons and the leg positioning certainly stiffens and strengthens the table's framework.

This "turn" on the card-table form offers the stability of the expanding-frame structure without its complications.

The framework of the turn-top table is not compromised by swinging legs and accordioned aprons; it is a rigid construction of legs and aprons and braces. To expand the tabletop, you turn its "fixed" section 90 degrees, then unfold the leaf. The joint between the two tabletop halves falls across the center of the frame, and the over-

PLANS

Frid, Tage. "Turning Flip-Top," in "Tables." *Tage Frid Teaches Woodworking. Book 3: Furnituremaking.* Newtown, CT: The Taunton Press, 1985. While not for a card table, this plan for a turn-top table explains the technique for locating the pivot for the tabletop. And the table project is a pleasant, well-designed contemporary piece.

DESIGN VARIATIONS
Turn-top construction makes possible a variety of folding-top tables that would not otherwise be workable. Two are shown here.

Lurking behind that shaped perimeter apron of the pedestal table is bracing and a pivot, so the tabletop can be turned and unfolded. Neither leg-swing nor expanding-frame construction would work with a pedestal table. While you *could* build the spare, contemporary design shown in either of the other constructions, it looks and works best when built using the turn-top construction.

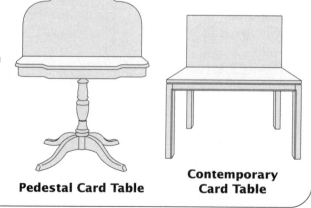

Pedestal Card Table

Contemporary Card Table

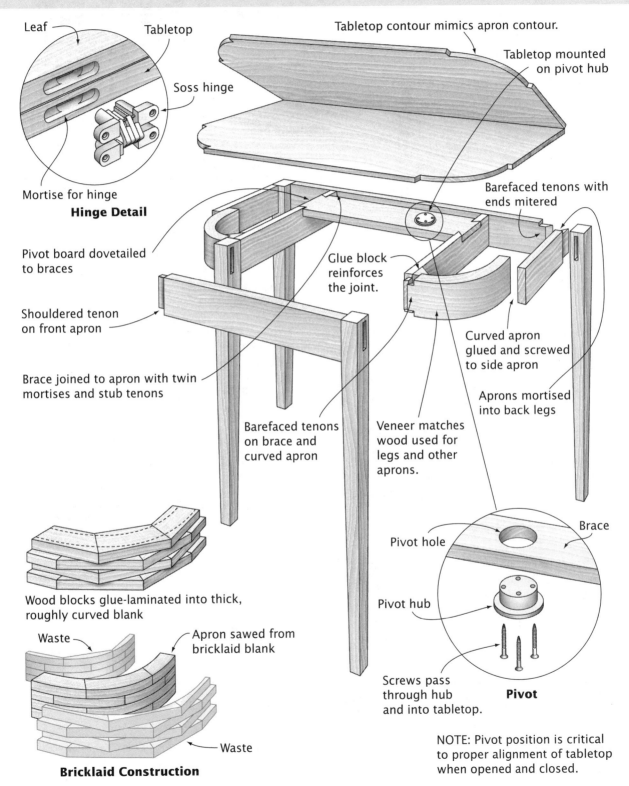

Leaf

Tabletop

Tabletop contour mimics apron contour.

Tabletop mounted on pivot hub

Soss hinge

Mortise for hinge

Hinge Detail

Pivot board dovetailed to braces

Barefaced tenons with ends mitered

Glue block reinforces the joint.

Shouldered tenon on front apron

Curved apron glued and screwed to side apron

Brace joined to apron with twin mortises and stub tenons

Aprons mortised into back legs

Barefaced tenons on brace and curved apron

Veneer matches wood used for legs and other aprons.

Pivot hole

Brace

Wood blocks glue-laminated into thick, roughly curved blank

Pivot hub

Waste

Apron sawed from bricklaid blank

Screws pass through hub and into tabletop.

Pivot

Waste

Bricklaid Construction

NOTE: Pivot position is critical to proper alignment of tabletop when opened and closed.

BUTTERFLY
TABLE

12"

14"

29½"

26"

17"

tabletops were recut at some point in their long lives, making them round.

To broaden the base and make the table more stable, the legs are splayed. But without a leg that can swing under the leaf to support it fully, the table nevertheless is somewhat unstable and tippy when the leaves are raised. Thus, these tables are usually smaller than the more common gateleg tables.

T he supports for this small drop-leaf table open like the wings of a butterfly. And thus it was named: the butterfly table.

The table is rare, and until English versions of it were discovered relatively recently, it was thought to be a strictly American form. It was most prominent in the William and Mary period.

Butterfly tables generally have two wide leaves and a narrow tabletop. The surviving examples generally have round or oval tops, though the experts believe many square

DESIGN VARIATIONS The butterfly table is distinctly a form of Pilgrim furniture. The example shown in the archetype is the form's zenith. Common variations are tables with turned stretchers as well as turned legs. The support wings sometimes were rudderlike, other times scalloped. Tabletops were round and oval.

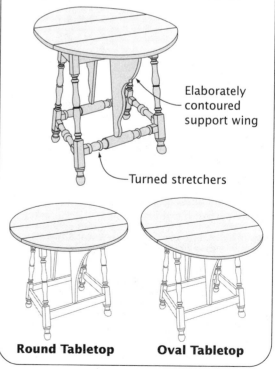

Elaborately contoured support wing

Turned stretchers

Round Tabletop   **Oval Tabletop**

PLANS

Kettell, Russell Hawes. "Drawing 34: Maple and Pine Butterfly Table," *The Pine Furniture of Early New England.* New York: Dover Publications, 1956. A measured drawing, but no directions.

•

Margon, Lester. "Butterfly Table from the Berkshire Museum," *Construction of American Furniture Treasures.* New York: Dover Publications, 1975.

•

Salomonsky, Verna Cook. "Butterfly Table," *Masterpieces of Furniture Design.* New York: Dover Publications, 1953. This is not a project per se but does have a measured drawing with details.

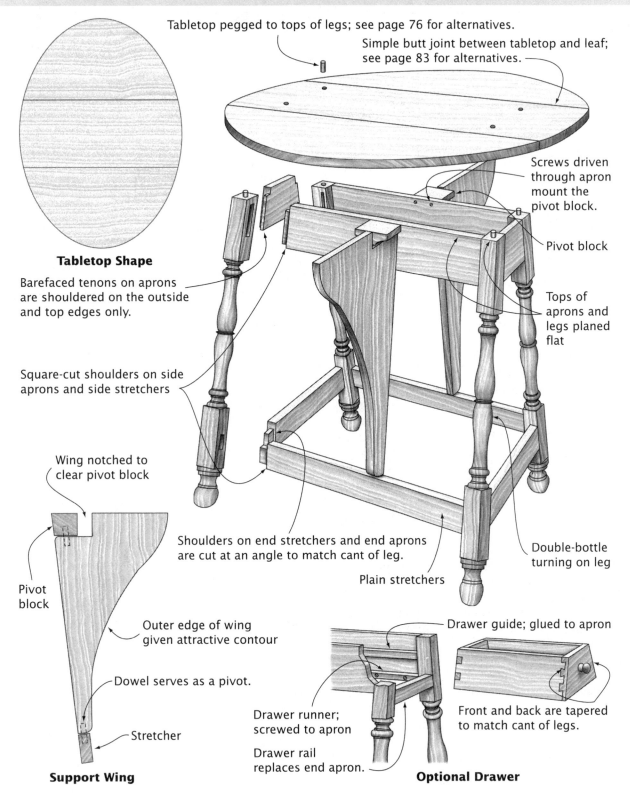

Tabletop pegged to tops of legs; see page 76 for alternatives.

Simple butt joint between tabletop and leaf; see page 83 for alternatives.

Screws driven through apron mount the pivot block.

Pivot block

Tops of aprons and legs planed flat

Barefaced tenons on aprons are shouldered on the outside and top edges only.

Square-cut shoulders on side aprons and side stretchers

Double-bottle turning on leg

Tabletop Shape

Wing notched to clear pivot block

Shoulders on end stretchers and end aprons are cut at an angle to match cant of leg.

Plain stretchers

Pivot block

Outer edge of wing given attractive contour

Dowel serves as a pivot.

Stretcher

Support Wing

Drawer guide; glued to apron

Drawer runner; screwed to apron

Drawer rail replaces end apron.

Front and back are tapered to match cant of legs.

Optional Drawer

HANDKERCHIEF
TABLE

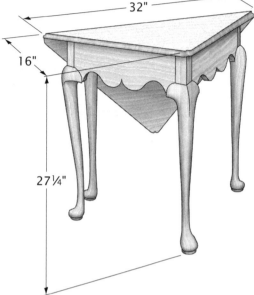

32"

16"

27¼"

Folding Corner Table

cutting only one rule joint, because there's only one leaf. (Note that the archetype table has an unusual form of this joint.)

The reward for the work, however, is in having an unusual and attractive piece of furniture.

A very special, unusual, and rare swing-leg drop-leaf table is the handkerchief table. The table is square with a leg at each corner when the leaf is raised. But swing the leg and drop the leaf, and the table becomes triangular.

The table was first built in this country during the Queen Anne period, and fewer than two dozen examples have survived. If you admire the airy grace of Queen Anne furniture, you'll love this table. If you like the form but favor more contemporary designs, it is certainly adaptable.

As a small, occasional table, it was used for games, tea, and light meals. Between such uses, the leaf would be lowered and the table placed against a wall or, more likely, in a corner (hence the name folding corner table). Set in a corner, the dropped leaf would be on display, while set against a wall, the scroll-cut aprons would be exhibited. In either setting, it could be used as a small display or side table.

While the table is small, it isn't any less work to construct than a full-sized drop-leaf table. Only two of the four legs are the same, so extra time and care must go into the making of them. Crafting the joinery for the two acutely angled corners is a challenge. The saving is in

DESIGN VARIATIONS Two other period examples of the handkerchief table may feed your creativity. Instead of a swing leg, the New England table has a pull-out leg (see also "Sliding-Leg Table" on page 152), so the leg is centered on the long apron. This table also has a small drawer. The Virginia table has lathe-turned cabriole legs, sometimes called country cabriole legs.

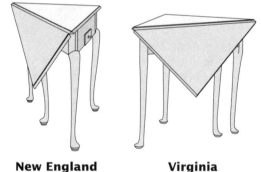

New England Handkerchief Table   **Virginia Handkerchief Table**

PLANS

Landon, Eugene. "Queen Anne Handkerchief Table," *Fine Woodworking*, No. 52 (May/June 1985), pp. 38–41. Excellent drawings and construction story.

•

Vandal, Norman. "Corner Table," *Queen Anne Furniture.* Newtown, CT: The Taunton Press, 1990. A slightly different approach to building a handkerchief table.

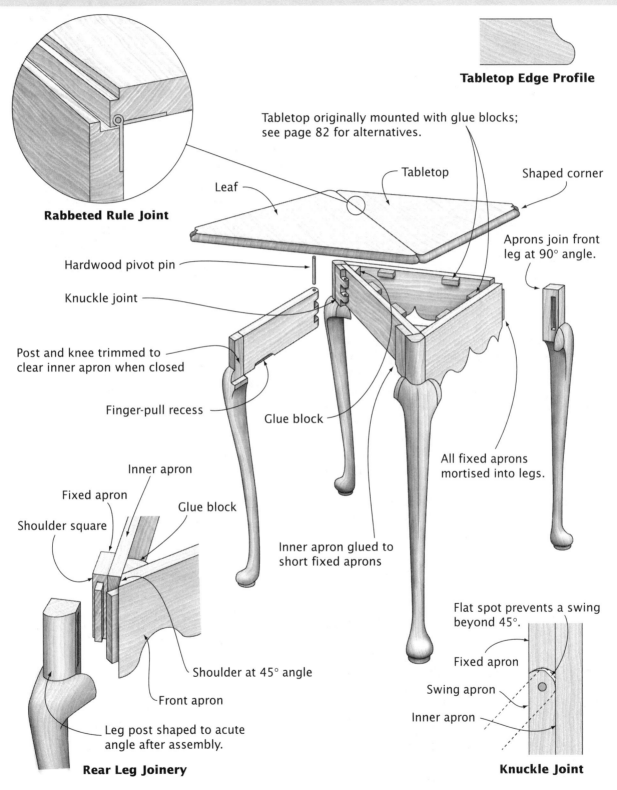

Tabletop Edge Profile

Rabbeted Rule Joint

Tabletop originally mounted with glue blocks; see page 82 for alternatives.

Leaf

Tabletop

Shaped corner

Hardwood pivot pin

Aprons join front leg at 90° angle.

Knuckle joint

Post and knee trimmed to clear inner apron when closed

Finger-pull recess

Glue block

All fixed aprons mortised into legs.

Inner apron

Fixed apron

Glue block

Shoulder square

Inner apron glued to short fixed aprons

Flat spot prevents a swing beyond 45°.

Fixed apron

Swing apron

Shoulder at 45° angle

Inner apron

Front apron

Leg post shaped to acute angle after assembly.

Rear Leg Joinery

Knuckle Joint

SIDE TABLE

Sideboard Table

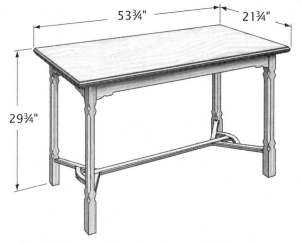

I n the upper-class American and European dining room in the 1700s, one would find an oblong table set at a wall close to the kitchen. It was a side table, intended as a staging area for the servants when they served meals.

The side table gave way, in some households, to the sideboard (see page 284), which provided storage as well as a place to set serving dishes. Few of us have servants today, but we still have use for a side table, be it in the dining room, the kitchen, or a wide hall.

The side table shown here is in the Cotswold style, a regional style of British country furniture. The aprons are decoratively cut along their bottom edges, primarily for visual effect. The interesting pattern of chamfers on the legs lightens them.

But a highlight of the table is what is called a hayrake stretcher. The name derives from the stretcher assembly's resemblance to primitive wooden hayrakes. The curved brace in the design produces a very rigid structure.

PLANS

Lynch, Carlyle. "Sideboard Table," *Classic Furniture Projects from Carlyle Lynch*. Emmaus, PA: Rodale Press, 1991. Lynch's large construction drawing of an antique Chinese Chippendale table, together with step-by-step directions and cutting list.

•

"Side Table in Walnut," *Making Antique Furniture*. Hertfordshire, UK: Argus Books, 1988. Pretty good drawings and construction directions for building a turned-leg side table with 3 drawers.

DESIGN VARIATIONS A contrast in weight is the immediate theme of these side-table variations. Compare the two variations with the archetype. The archetypal table would be the middleweight on this card.

The veneered table, a British design, is clearly the featherweight. Its appearance is airy and elegant, and its thin turned legs exaggerate its height. Although there are no pulls, the bowed front apron is composed of three drawer fronts, a practical feature in a side table. Equally practical is the absence of a front stretcher—there's no conflict with a server's feet.

The heavyweight has stocky legs, a shelf at stretcher level, wide aprons, and a marble top, which contributes more to the table's actual weight than to its visual weight.

Veneered Side Table

Marble-Topped Side Table

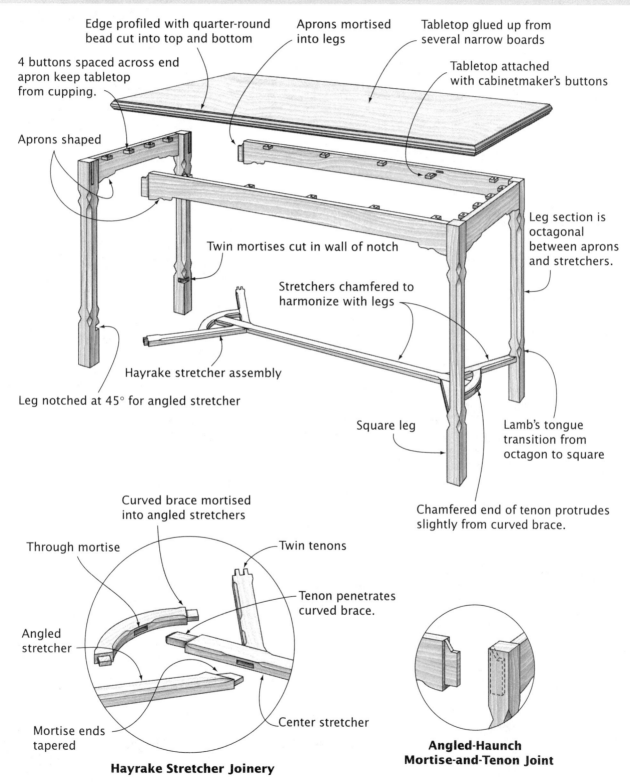

Edge profiled with quarter-round bead cut into top and bottom

Aprons mortised into legs

Tabletop glued up from several narrow boards

4 buttons spaced across end apron keep tabletop from cupping.

Tabletop attached with cabinetmaker's buttons

Aprons shaped

Twin mortises cut in wall of notch

Leg section is octagonal between aprons and stretchers.

Stretchers chamfered to harmonize with legs

Hayrake stretcher assembly

Leg notched at 45° for angled stretcher

Square leg

Lamb's tongue transition from octagon to square

Chamfered end of tenon protrudes slightly from curved brace.

Curved brace mortised into angled stretchers

Through mortise

Twin tenons

Tenon penetrates curved brace.

Angled stretcher

Mortise ends tapered

Center stretcher

Hayrake Stretcher Joinery

Angled-Haunch Mortise-and-Tenon Joint

SOFA
TABLE

Side Table, Hall Table,
Glove Table

64"

13"

28"

PLANS

Mandel, Mitch. "Building Thomas Moser's Bow-Front Table." *American Woodworker*, Vol. IV, No. 3 (July/August 1988), pp. 22–28. In a plan once removed, one woodworker details how to build a sofa table designed by another.

•

McCall, Gene. "Sofa Table Complements Antiques," *Tables and Chairs: The Best of Fine Woodworking.* Newtown, CT: The Taunton Press, 1995. A Chinese Chippendale table with glass inserts in the tabletop.

•

Taylor, V. J. "Regency-Style Sofa Table," *How to Build Period Country Furniture.* New York: Stein and Day, 1978. Plans for a piece that our 19th-century forebears thought of as a sofa table.

Thomas Sheraton, who is credited by furniture historians with the "invention" of the sofa table, wouldn't recognize it today. But a lot has changed since Sheraton's design book was published in the 1790s. The table shown is similar to a side table, though somewhat narrower. It's designed to stand behind a sofa that's in the center of a room, rather than backed up against a wall. The top is about level with the top of the sofa back. A lamp might be on it instead of on a side table.

The table is in what is often called the Chinese Chippendale style. It has Marlborough legs—straight and square—and fairly wide aprons. Intricate fretwork and an applied astragal molding embellish the stand. Rather than stretchers, the table has a shelf.

Sheraton's sofa table, shown in the "Design Variations," was a low occasional table placed in front of the sofa for tea and refreshments, games, reading, or writing.

DESIGN VARIATIONS

The original sofa table had drawers and drop leaves. While it might seem far removed from the contemporary sofa table, it isn't. The essence of the form is the medium-height, oblong tabletop. The contour of the top and the style of stand supporting it are the variables.

Original Sofa Table

Bow-Front Sofa Table

Country-Style Sofa Table

NOTE: Profile is molded directly on the tabletop edge.

Ovulo

Bead

Cove

Tabletop Edge Profile

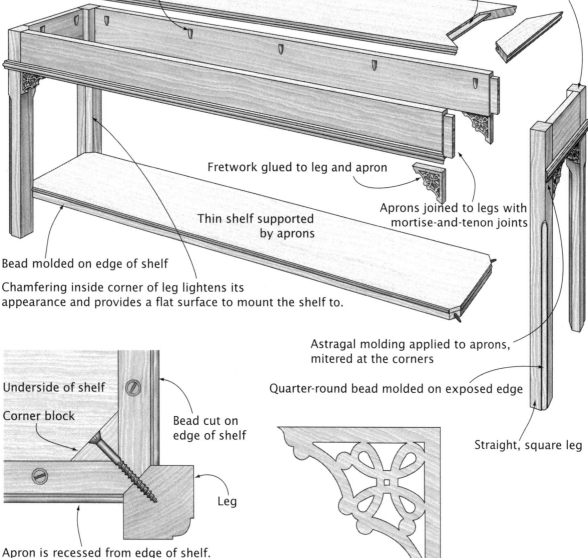

Breadboard ends are mitered.

Top attached with screws driven through pockets in aprons

Tongue-and-groove joins breadboard end to tabletop; see page 80 for alternative constructions.

The aprons and legs are flush.

Fretwork glued to leg and apron

Aprons joined to legs with mortise-and-tenon joints

Thin shelf supported by aprons

Bead molded on edge of shelf

Chamfering inside corner of leg lightens its appearance and provides a flat surface to mount the shelf to.

Astragal molding applied to aprons, mitered at the corners

Quarter-round bead molded on exposed edge

Straight, square leg

Underside of shelf

Corner block

Bead cut on edge of shelf

Leg

Apron is recessed from edge of shelf.

Shelf-Mounting

Fretwork

END
TABLE

18"

18"

18"

Design Variations. But for low seating, a low end table is appropriate.

The decorative details arise from the construction, which is straightforward. The overall appearance is capped by the contrasting wood tones of the top and the leg-and-apron assembly.

The legs are slightly tapered on their inside faces and have a discrete chamfer on the outside corner. The narrow aprons are mortised into the legs. The plywood top is veneered with an exotically figured wood. It is set inside the aprons, rather than resting atop them.

A t the end of many a sofa is an end table. Ideally, it is level with the sofa's arm. Just a slight movement of your arm places your hand on the table...to get your glass, to select a bonbon, to pick up a magazine, to switch on the lamp.

The diminutive end table shown above is a very simple and contemporary example of the form. At 18 inches, it stands somewhat lower than the 22- to 23-inch norm for end tables— lower, for example, than the ones shown as

PLANS

Frid, Tage. "Making an End Table," *The Best of Fine Woodworking: Tables and Chairs.* Newtown, CT: The Taunton Press, 1995. Good plans and procedural photos, excellent directions for building a contemporary version of a traditional form.

●

Shumaker, Karl. "Parsons Table," *American Woodworker,* No. 12 (January/February 1990), pp. 22–27. Extensive, detailed plans and directions for making a low, contemporary end table.

DESIGN VARIATIONS

The varieties of end tables are endless. Just three are shown here.

One is a traditional leg-and-apron table. The legs are constructed by face-gluing contrasting woods, exposing a strip of the darker wood at the outside corner.

A modern interpretation of the Arts-and-Crafts style incorporates a shelf, which is actually common on end tables.

A contemporary design rounds out the trio. It has straight round legs, each with a ball turned on the top. The aprons join the legs just below the balls. A glass top rests on the balls.

Tapered-Leg End Table

Arts-and-Crafts End Table

Glass-Topped End Table

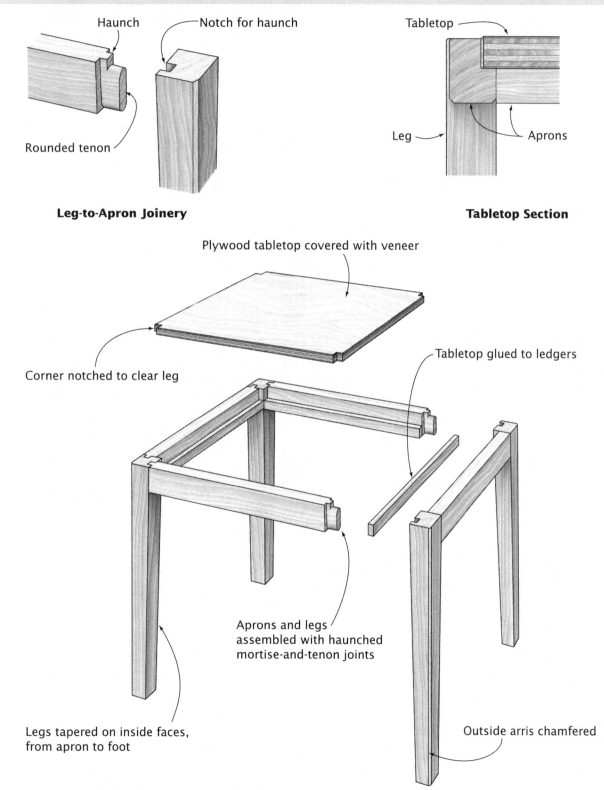

Haunch

Notch for haunch

Rounded tenon

Leg-to-Apron Joinery

Tabletop

Leg

Aprons

Tabletop Section

Plywood tabletop covered with veneer

Corner notched to clear leg

Tabletop glued to ledgers

Aprons and legs assembled with haunched mortise-and-tenon joints

Legs tapered on inside faces, from apron to foot

Outside arris chamfered

SPLAY-LEG
END TABLE

Tavern Table

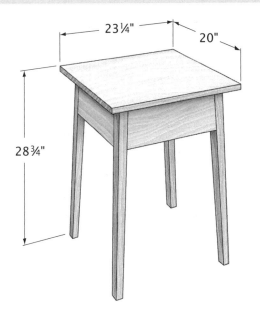

23¼"

20"

28¾"

Although the splayed-leg configuration could result in compound angles between legs and aprons, that isn't the case in the example shown. Here the aprons are angled, too. The builder works strictly with simple angles, but upon assembly, the result is a complex appearance.

I t's small and lightweight. Doesn't take up much room. The splay of the legs makes it stable, resistant to tipping. These qualities make it the ideal occasional table—useful for numerous light-duty, utilitarian tasks.

The design's origins date back to colonial taverns. Such tables were used to serve patrons who couldn't (or wouldn't) sit at the common tables. Its light weight made it easy to carry table and meal to wherever the patron sat, and the splayed legs allowed the table to be set over his legs.

PLANS

Gottshall, Franklin H. "Round-Top Card Table," *Simple Colonial Furniture.* New York: Bonanza Books, 1984. Round table with "country cabriole" legs; nice table but a cryptic presentation.

Hylton, Bill. "Splay-Leg Table," *Country Pine.* Emmaus, PA: Rodale Press, 1995. Construction of a simple table presented in exhaustive detail.

Hylton, William H. "Splay-Legged Table," *The Weekend Woodworker Quick-and-Easy Projects.* Emmaus, PA: Rodale Press, 1992. Drawings, parts list, and step-by-step for building a delicate-looking table.

Salomonsky, Verna Cook. "Maple Table," *Masterpieces of Furniture Design.* New York: Dover Publications, 1953. Measured drawings only of an oval-top, turned-leg table with stretchers.

DESIGN VARIATIONS One thing a woodworker knows is that a small table can be tippy if the legs are too close together. Splaying the legs provides a broader base, making the table more stable without making the table's footprint larger than its top.

This concept applies regardless of the size and style of the table, as the variations displayed here demonstrate.

Table with Sharply Splayed Legs

Round Table

Table with Stretchers

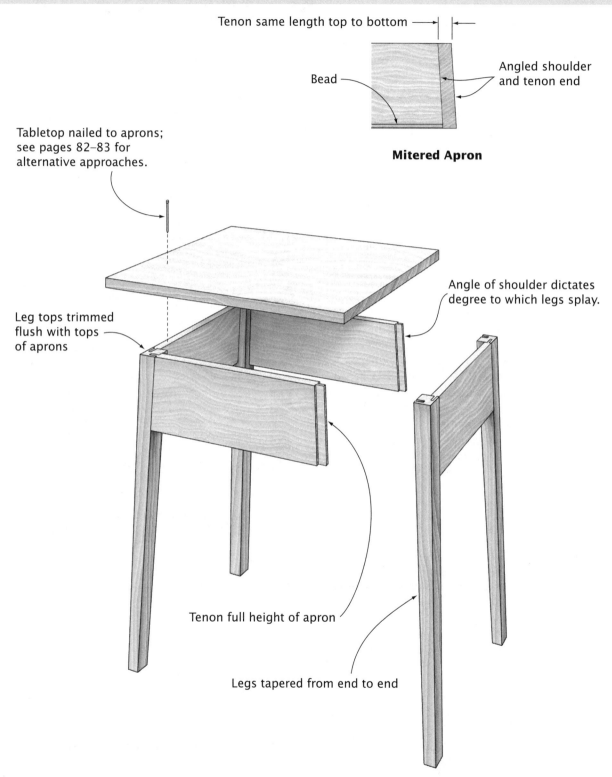

Tenon same length top to bottom

Bead

Angled shoulder and tenon end

Mitered Apron

Tabletop nailed to aprons; see pages 82–83 for alternative approaches.

Angle of shoulder dictates degree to which legs splay.

Leg tops trimmed flush with tops of aprons

Tenon full height of apron

Legs tapered from end to end

END TABLE
WITH DRAWER

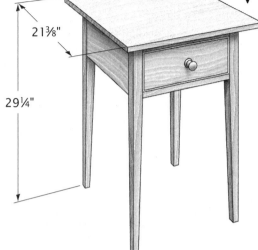

21⅜"

21⅜"

29¼"

End Table, Side Table, Bedside Table, Lamp Table

adapted to the intended use, but the construction need not change. Regardless of the table's size and style, the basic joinery depicted on the opposite page can apply.

PLANS

Hylton, William H. "Bedside Table," *The Weekend Woodworker Quick-and-Easy Projects.* Emmaus, PA: Rodale Press, 1992. Detailed plans and directions for a table with turned legs.
•
Mehler, Kelly. "Cherry Side Table," *American Woodworker,* No. 17 (November/December 1990), pp. 20–25. A Shaker-style table.
•
Moser, Thomas. "Sidestand," *Measured Shop Drawings for American Furniture.* New York: Sterling Publishing Co., 1985. Measured drawings for a delicate table from Moser's furniture line.
•
Wilkinson, R. S. "Maple Side Table," *American Woodworker,* No. 44 (March/April 1995), pp. 54–57. Done in the Hepplewhite style, a small table with a serpentine top.

W ere there an archetype for an occasional table, this might be it.

The basic form—a small, square top, a single drawer—lends itself to all sorts of work around the home or office. It can be a chairside or bedside table, a lamp stand in an otherwise dark hallway, a telephone table (book's in the drawer, close at hand but out of sight), a silent servant beside an entryway.

The dimensions of the table should be

DESIGN VARIATIONS

Many stylistic variations are possible within the basic form of this occasional table, as these three examples demonstrate. The serpentine-top table, though it lacks the characteristic string inlays and ornate banding, is an authentic Hepplewhite piece. Its charm lies in its finely shaped top. The Shaker-style table has a kind of severe grace. Its charm lies in its good proportions and simple lines. It has no ornamentation; few Shaker pieces did. The third table is in the vernacular style, designed around turned legs and an intended use as a bedside table.

Serpentine-Top End Table

Shaker-Style End Table

End Table with Turned Legs

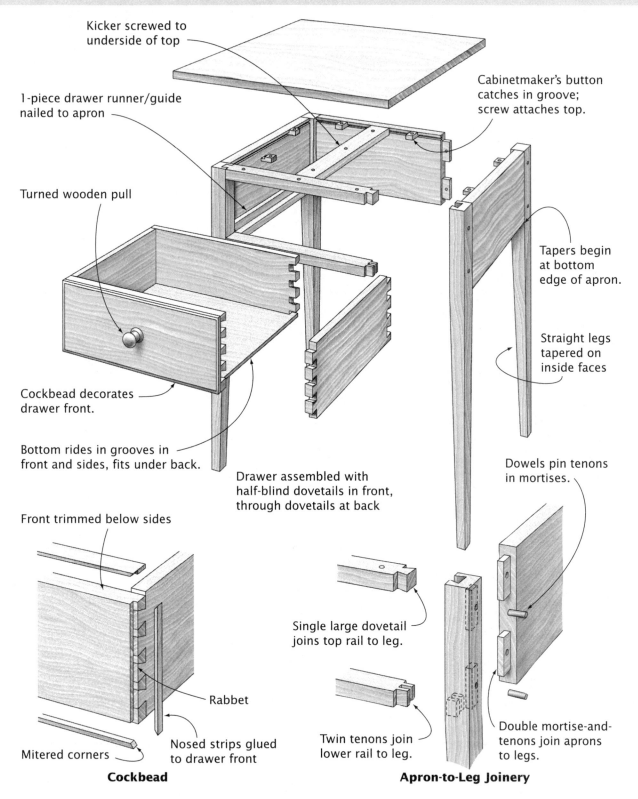

Kicker screwed to underside of top

Cabinetmaker's button catches in groove; screw attaches top.

1-piece drawer runner/guide nailed to apron

Turned wooden pull

Tapers begin at bottom edge of apron.

Straight legs tapered on inside faces

Cockbead decorates drawer front.

Bottom rides in grooves in front and sides, fits under back.

Drawer assembled with half-blind dovetails in front, through dovetails at back

Dowels pin tenons in mortises.

Front trimmed below sides

Single large dovetail joins top rail to leg.

Rabbet

Twin tenons join lower rail to leg.

Double mortise-and-tenons join aprons to legs.

Mitered corners

Nosed strips glued to drawer front

Cockbead

Apron-to-Leg Joinery

BUTLER'S
TABLE

20¾"

32"

17"

PLANS

Abram, Norm, with Tim Snyder. "Butler's Table," *Classics from the New Yankee Workshop*. Boston: Little, Brown & Co., 1990. An archetypal project presented in methodical, "here's how I built it" fashion.

•

"Butler's Tray Table." *Woodsmith*, No. 14 (March 1981), pp. 10–11. A stretcherless stand with a frame-and-panel tray presented as a step-by-step project.

•

Engler, Nick. "Butler's Table," *Finishing*. Emmaus, PA: Rodale Press, 1992. The stand for this butler's tray has a shelf; good plans and step-by-step.

An early, elegant form of tray and stand, the butler's table survives today primarily as a coffee table. But the first such tables were in fact used by butlers to serve tea.

Nothing shabby could find its way into the aristocratic home in 18th-century England, not even a servant's tray. The butler's tray and its stand were elegant and made of rich woods.

The butler's table is essentially a leg-and-apron stand with a removable tabletop. The stand shown has Marlborough legs and crossed stretchers.

The top is a rectangular tray with curved leaves that fold up, rather than down, on special spring-loaded hinges mortised into the top surface. Each leaf has a hand-grip opening cut into it. When the leaves are up, they form a gallery around the tray, and the tray is easy to carry. When folded down, the leaves transform the tray into an oval tabletop.

DESIGN VARIATIONS The stand tends to be the focus of any design variations. The tray doesn't change (except perhaps in size), probably because the essence of the form is the tray. Early versions of the butler's table used a sawbuck stand like those still used as tray stands in restaurants. The more archetypal form is varied by altering the stretcher configuration, by eliminating the stretchers altogether, or by substituting a shelf for the stretchers.

Leg-and-Apron Stand

Stand with Shelf

Folding Sawbuck Stand

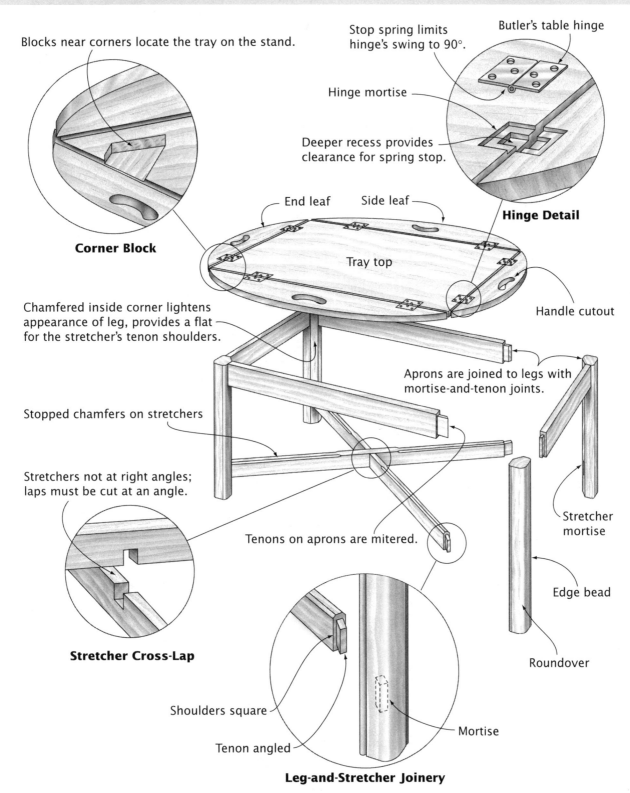

Blocks near corners locate the tray on the stand.

Corner Block

Stop spring limits hinge's swing to 90°.

Butler's table hinge

Hinge mortise

Deeper recess provides clearance for spring stop.

Hinge Detail

End leaf

Side leaf

Tray top

Handle cutout

Chamfered inside corner lightens appearance of leg, provides a flat for the stretcher's tenon shoulders.

Aprons are joined to legs with mortise-and-tenon joints.

Stopped chamfers on stretchers

Stretcher mortise

Stretchers not at right angles; laps must be cut at an angle.

Tenons on aprons are mitered.

Edge bead

Stretcher Cross-Lap

Roundover

Shoulders square

Tenon angled

Mortise

Leg-and-Stretcher Joinery

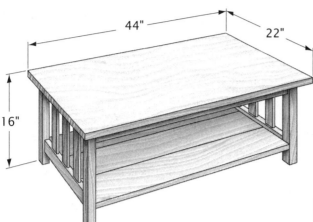

44"

22"

16"

COFFEE
TABLE

Occasional Table, Knee Table

18 to 30 inches wide, and quite variable in length, often nearly as long as the sofa. Coffee tables, which occupy center stage of the showcase room of most homes, are a favorite of both designers and craftsmen.

Coffee tables are a reflection of a fairly recent shift in the way we use our free time and our homes, spending more time relaxing, reading magazines and newspapers, and chatting. A table the size and height of a coffee table in a Queen Anne or Chippendale style may be very well done and quite attractive but is certainly not a reproduction of any original.

A coffee table's size and height presume a willingness to have drinks or desserts while sitting on (or in) a sofa, an impracticality as long as hooped skirts were in vogue. The most common dimensions are 16 to 18 inches high,

PLANS

Erickson, Ben. "Neo-Egyptian Coffee Table," *American Woodworker*, No. 16 (October 1990), pp. 36–39. Contemporary leg-and-apron design with scroll ends to the tabletop; drawings and instructions.

•

Moser, Thomas. "Coffee Table (24 inch)," "Knee Table," and "Coffee Table (30 inch)." *Measured Shop Drawings for American Furniture.* New York: Sterling Publishing Co., 1985. 3 different tables; drawings only.

•

Rae, Andy. "Craftsman-Style," *American Woodworker*, No. 37 (April 1994), pp. 40–41. Simplified Arts-and-Crafts design with shelf. Complete drawings but no instructions.

DESIGN VARIATIONS

Variations in coffee table design boggle the mind. They can be light and airy or solid and heavy, traditional or avant-garde, with or without drawers hung from the underside of the tabletop, with or without a magazine shelf doubling as a stretcher for the legs. Coffee tables with a glass top over a till for small collectibles are popular.

While a traditional table structure consisting of four legs joined with aprons supporting the top is the most common, designs with trestles, slab ends, and pedestals are easily found. Just about the only variable that doesn't change much is the height: 16 to 18 inches is just right.

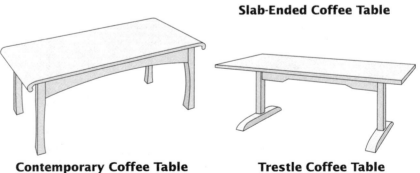

Slab-Ended Coffee Table

Contemporary Coffee Table

Trestle Coffee Table

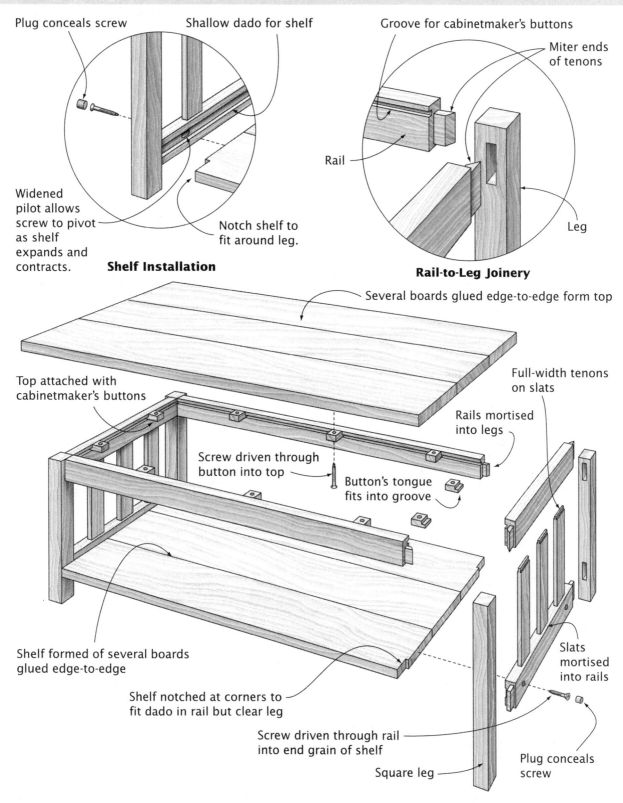

Plug conceals screw

Shallow dado for shelf

Widened pilot allows screw to pivot as shelf expands and contracts.

Notch shelf to fit around leg.

Shelf Installation

Groove for cabinetmaker's buttons

Miter ends of tenons

Rail

Leg

Rail-to-Leg Joinery

Several boards glued edge-to-edge form top

Top attached with cabinetmaker's buttons

Screw driven through button into top

Button's tongue fits into groove

Full-width tenons on slats

Rails mortised into legs

Shelf formed of several boards glued edge-to-edge

Shelf notched at corners to fit dado in rail but clear leg

Screw driven through rail into end grain of shelf

Square leg

Slats mortised into rails

Plug conceals screw

TRIPOD
TABLE

Candle Stand, Tripod Stand, Round Stand, Sewing Stand

20" 18¼"

27"

DESIGN VARIATIONS The Shakers weren't the only makers of tripod tables, as the drawings here demonstrate. Slender, elegant candle stands designed during the Queen Anne period are reproduced widely today. With its small tabletop, the example shown is clearly a candle stand. In the Federal period, more variety was introduced in terms of leg forms and tabletop shapes and styles. Though the pedestal is the same in both Federal styles shown, the change in leg contour and tabletop shape transforms the overall appearance.

Federal Style

Queen Anne Style   **Federal Style**

Tripod tables were particularly popular during the 18th century. They were used to hold everything from candlesticks and wineglasses to teapots and sewing implements.

In the 19th century, the Shakers produced tripod tables in variety and considerable quantity. In fact, next to the slat-backed chair, the round stand is the most recognizable form of Shaker furniture. Yet, as the drawings suggest, the round stand was not the only type of tripod table made. The Shakers made unique sewing stands, having square or rectangular tops with drawers hung from their undersides.

The opposite page presents alternative Shaker-style tops for a single tripod base.

Look at the tripod base first. Because of the splay angle, a great deal of racking stress is put on the legs, pulling them away from the column. To reinforce the joinery, a metal plate called a "spider" is nailed or screwed to the base of the column and legs.

The tabletops are mounted on the pedestal by means of a cleat, or brace, screwed to its underside. A tenon on the pedestal's tip is glued and wedged in a socket in the brace.

PLANS

Kassay, John. "Stands," *The Book of Shaker Furniture.* Amherst, MA: University of Massachusetts Press, 1980. Measured drawings for several different Shaker tripod tables. No construction directions.

•

Treanor, Robert. "Shaker Sewing Stand," *American Woodworker*, No. 27 (July/August 1992), pp. 50–54. Good construction directions for reproducing a Shaker piece.

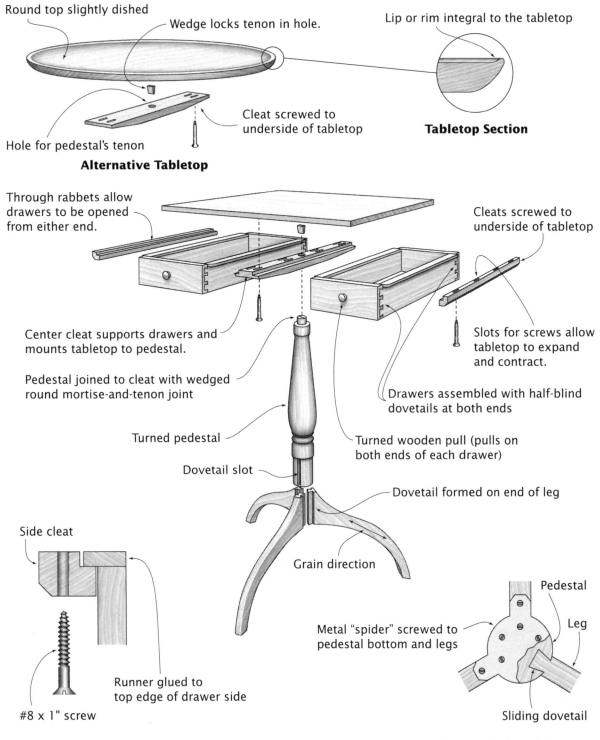

Round top slightly dished

Wedge locks tenon in hole.

Lip or rim integral to the tabletop

Tabletop Section

Cleat screwed to underside of tabletop

Hole for pedestal's tenon

Alternative Tabletop

Through rabbets allow drawers to be opened from either end.

Cleats screwed to underside of tabletop

Center cleat supports drawers and mounts tabletop to pedestal.

Slots for screws allow tabletop to expand and contract.

Pedestal joined to cleat with wedged round mortise-and-tenon joint

Drawers assembled with half-blind dovetails at both ends

Turned pedestal

Turned wooden pull (pulls on both ends of each drawer)

Dovetail slot

Dovetail formed on end of leg

Side cleat

Grain direction

Pedestal

Leg

Metal "spider" screwed to pedestal bottom and legs

Runner glued to top edge of drawer side

Sliding dovetail

#8 x 1" screw

Drawer Runner

Leg-to-Pedestal Joinery

TILT-TOP
TABLE

*Tip-and-Turn Table,
Tip-Top Stand, Candle Stand,
Circular Tripod Table*

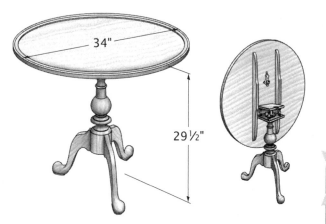

34"

29½"

The tilt-top table entered the furniture mainstream in the Queen Anne period. In those practical days, a table that was not in use was an obstruction. This table's top could be tipped up when not in use, so the table could be set against a wall and take up very little space.

Individual tables were distinguished mainly by their pedestal turnings, the shape of their feet, the design of the tabletop's molded edge, and, of course, the table's size. One with a top smaller than 20 inches in diameter was generally used as a candle stand, while the larger ones served as tea tables and display stands.

Some tilt-tops had tabletops that could turn as well as tip (hence the name tip-and-turn table). The host or hostess could pour a cup of tea, then turn the tabletop to deliver it to the guest, seated opposite. This was accomplished through what was known as a birdcage.

PLANS

Bird, Lonnie. "Queen Anne Tilt-Top Table," *American Woodworker,* No. 29 (November/December 1992), pp. 22–27. A dish-top table.

•

Dunbar, Michael. "Candlestand" and "Tip-Top Table," *Federal Furniture.* Newtown, CT: The Taunton Press, 1986. 2 plans in 1 source: a candle stand with a 15" × 17" oval top, and a table with a serpentine top.

•

Margon, Lester. "18th Century Walnut Tip-Top Table," *Construction of American Furniture Treasures.* New York: Dover Publications, 1975. A dish-top table.

DESIGN VARIATIONS

As with many other types of furniture, the design of tilt-top tables is in the details. Vary the size and shape of the top. A given stand could have a plain round or oval tabletop, a dished top, a piecrust top, or a square top. At the extremes, of course, the pedestal and legs must be rescaled. A top that's too small in relation to the stand looks ridiculous. Too large a top makes the table unstable.

Experiment, too, with the profile of the turned pedestal and the style of the legs. Four options are shown below.

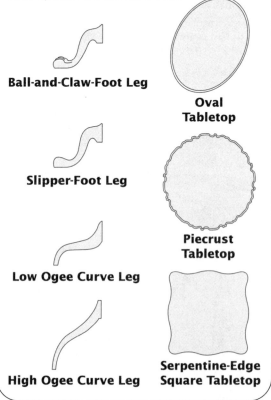

Ball-and-Claw-Foot Leg

Slipper-Foot Leg

Low Ogee Curve Leg

High Ogee Curve Leg

Oval Tabletop

Piecrust Tabletop

Serpentine-Edge Square Tabletop

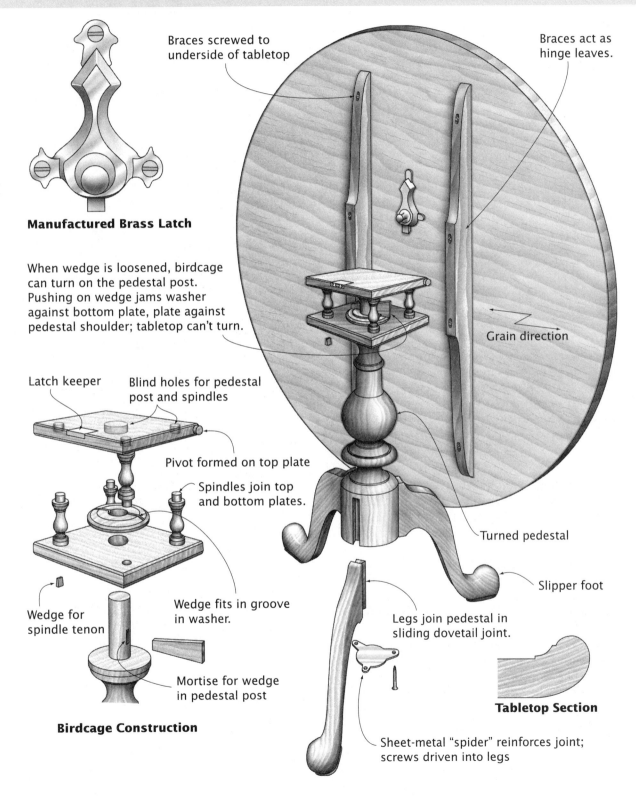

Manufactured Brass Latch

Braces screwed to underside of tabletop

Braces act as hinge leaves.

When wedge is loosened, birdcage can turn on the pedestal post. Pushing on wedge jams washer against bottom plate, plate against pedestal shoulder; tabletop can't turn.

Grain direction

Latch keeper

Blind holes for pedestal post and spindles

Pivot formed on top plate

Spindles join top and bottom plates.

Wedge for spindle tenon

Wedge fits in groove in washer.

Mortise for wedge in pedestal post

Birdcage Construction

Turned pedestal

Slipper foot

Legs join pedestal in sliding dovetail joint.

Sheet-metal "spider" reinforces joint; screws driven into legs

Tabletop Section

BASIN STAND

Washstand, Dry Sink

Abram, Norm, with David Sloan. "Shaker Washstand," *Mostly Shaker From The New Yankee Workshop*. Boston, MA: Little, Brown & Co., 1992. A modern design in traditional style with enclosed lower cabinet. Good drawings, photos, and comprehensive instructions.

•

Lyons, Richard A. "Stand Table," *Making Country Furniture*. Englewood Cliffs, NJ: Prentice-Hall, 1987. Attractive but simple design does not require lathe. Adequate drawings, 1 page of instructions.

PLANS

24⅛" 16½" 34½"

A need as timeless as a place to wash the sleep out of our eyes in the morning inspires a variety of furniture designs. Some form of basin stand filled that need for centuries. The design requirements for the basin stand were two: a place to put the pitcher of water that you carried from the pump and a place to put a basin at a convenient height for washing your face.

The most common survivors of the form are from the last century and the first part of this century. They seldom include more than two features beyond the minimum of a place for pitcher and basin. These two "luxury" features are splashboards for the protection of nearby items and a drawer for keeping a few wash-up–related items.

Washbasins are utilitarian furniture rather than display furniture but nevertheless often show some taste and decoration in their design, most often in the careful shaping of essential parts like the legs and splashboards. When those of us with modern plumbing want to include these simple but often elegant designs in our homes, we usually use them as a home for houseplants, or maybe just as decoration, with pitcher and basin in place.

DESIGN VARIATIONS

Common variations on the washbasin theme include the amount of decoration, the taste and tradition reflected in the decoration, and the space the design was intended to fit into. Turned legs, imaginatively shaped edges on splashboards and aprons, and designs to fit into a corner are all common. Stark, strictly utilitarian basin stands were perhaps most common of all but were less likely to be preserved after seeing heavy use.

2-Tier Stand

Shaker Stand

Corner Stand

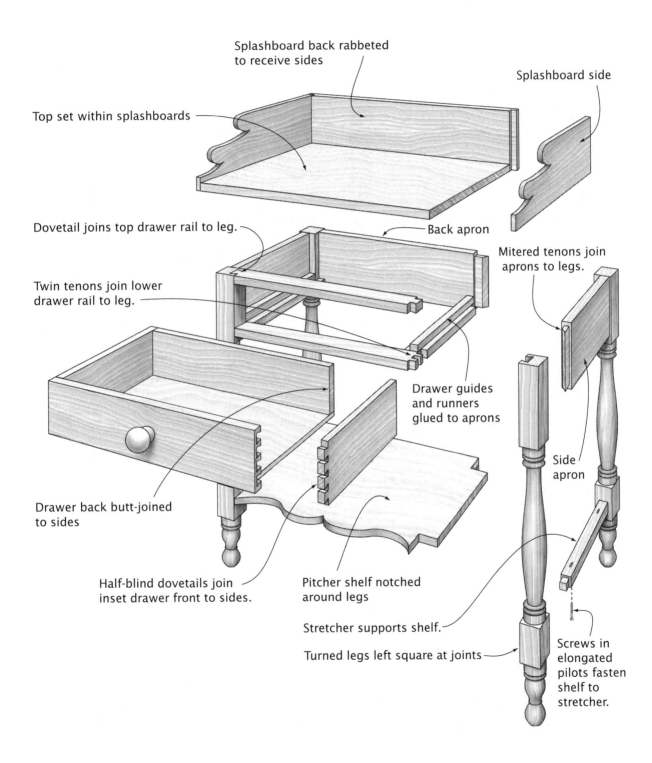

Splashboard back rabbeted to receive sides

Splashboard side

Top set within splashboards

Dovetail joins top drawer rail to leg.

Back apron

Mitered tenons join aprons to legs.

Twin tenons join lower drawer rail to leg.

Drawer guides and runners glued to aprons

Side apron

Drawer back butt-joined to sides

Half-blind dovetails join inset drawer front to sides.

Pitcher shelf notched around legs

Stretcher supports shelf.

Turned legs left square at joints

Screws in elongated pilots fasten shelf to stretcher.

DRESSING STAND

Lowboy, Vanity Table, Dressing Table

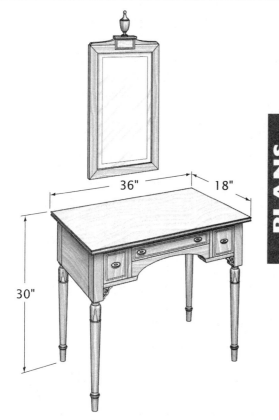

36" 18"

30"

Lynch, Carlyle. "Queen Anne Lowboy," *Classic Furniture Projects from Carlyle Lynch*. Emmaus, PA: Rodale Press, 1992. Drawings and instructions for reproducing a 1713 lowboy. Cabriole legs, no mirror.

•

Schoen, Edward J. "Dressing Table," *Cabinetry*, edited by Robert A. Yoder. Emmaus, PA: Rodale Press, 1992. Comprehensive drawings and step-by-step building procedures. Recent design with traditional appearance. Turned legs, hinged 3-section mirror.

PLANS

DESIGN VARIATIONS

Variations among dressing stands cut across the whole spectrum of furniture design traditions. Examples that lack an attached mirror or mirrors typically have an associated wall-hung mirror. The side mirrors on those with multiple mirrors are usually hinged. The mirror on the Beau Brummell Dressing Table folds down, then the two wings fold over it, greatly reducing the space occupied when not in use. All have multiple drawers sized for cosmetic containers of the period and often a drawer fitted for keeping jewelry.

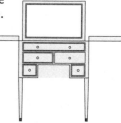

Beau Brummell Dressing Table

U nlike a washstand or bed, a dressing stand does not serve basic human needs. It serves the customs of the middle and upper classes, who have wealth to spend on cosmetics, jewelry, and other finery. Hence, we don't find strictly utilitarian versions of the dressing stand. Nor do we find examples from traditions that frowned on frivolous decoration, such as the Shakers. The most elementary examples are from rural areas where sophisticated furniture makers were not to be found, but even these show an attention to detail indicating that the customer could afford some luxury.

The design nevertheless has a lengthy history, with examples from all of the major furniture design traditions. Typical features include a comfortable height for seated use, adequate legroom, drawers for cosmetics and jewelry, one or more mirrors, fine woods, extensive though sometimes subdued decoration, fine craftsmanship, and delicate, even feminine, lines.

20th-Century Dressing Table

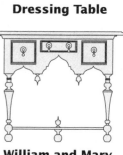

William and Mary Dressing Table

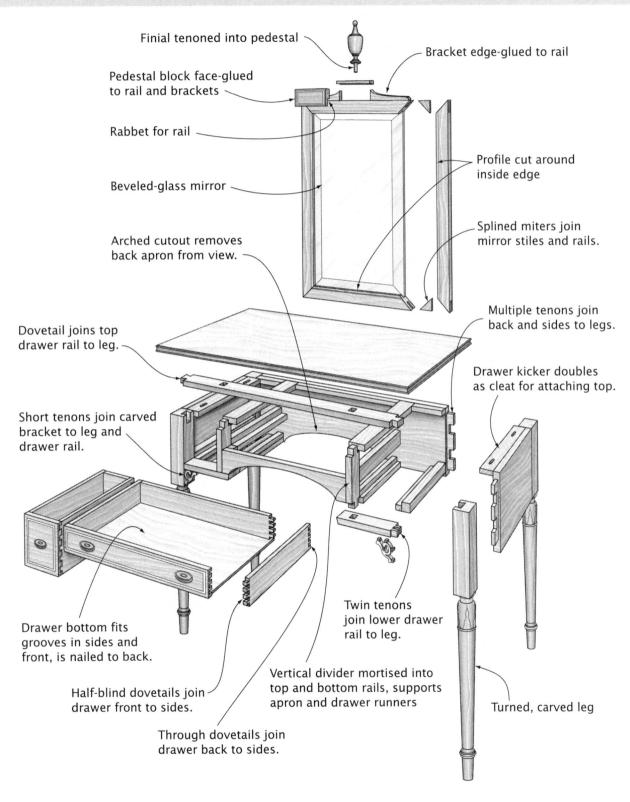

Finial tenoned into pedestal

Bracket edge-glued to rail

Pedestal block face-glued to rail and brackets

Rabbet for rail

Beveled-glass mirror

Profile cut around inside edge

Splined miters join mirror stiles and rails.

Arched cutout removes back apron from view.

Multiple tenons join back and sides to legs.

Dovetail joins top drawer rail to leg.

Drawer kicker doubles as cleat for attaching top.

Short tenons join carved bracket to leg and drawer rail.

Drawer bottom fits grooves in sides and front, is nailed to back.

Twin tenons join lower drawer rail to leg.

Half-blind dovetails join drawer front to sides.

Vertical divider mortised into top and bottom rails, supports apron and drawer runners

Turned, carved leg

Through dovetails join drawer back to sides.

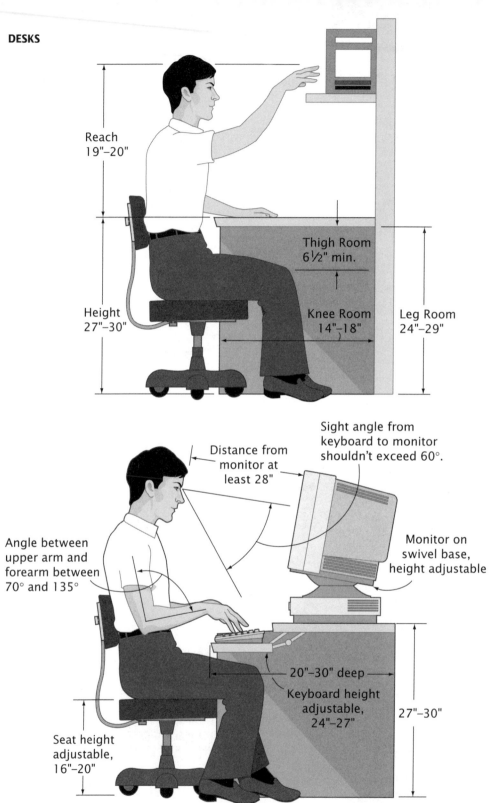

Reach
19"–20"

Height
27"–30"

Thigh Room
6½" min.

Knee Room
14"–18"

Leg Room
24"–29"

Sight angle from
keyboard to monitor
shouldn't exceed 60°.

Distance from
monitor at
least 28"

Angle between
upper arm and
forearm between
70° and 135°

Monitor on
swivel base,
height adjustable

20"–30" deep

Keyboard height
adjustable,
24"–27"

27"–30"

Seat height
adjustable,
16"–20"

DESKS

Whether we like it or not, most of us spend more time sitting at desks than in easy chairs. And the work we do while seated there tends to be repetitive. So, if dimensions are off just a tad, mere inconvenience and discomfort are apt to blossom into a headache or body aches.

To help you design a desk that will help you be comfortable and stay focused on your work, here are basic standards:

DESK HEIGHT: Distance from floor to top surface of the desktop. The average range is 27 to 30 inches.

LEGROOM: Distance from floor to underside of the desktop. Plan on allowing from 24 to 29 inches.

THIGH ROOM: Distance from chair seat to the desktop's underside, with chair drawn up to the desk. The minimum dimension here is 6 1/2 inches.

KNEE ROOM: Vertical distance from desk's edge to an obstruction that would block the sitter's legs with the chair drawn up. (The legs might be blocked by a stretcher, panel, or nothing but the wall behind the desk.) Good design dictates allowing between 14 and 18 inches.

REACH: Vertical distance the sitter can reach without standing up. The standard here is 19 to 20 inches.

A comfortable desk can become a painful-to-use desk when a computer is set on it. Some changes are needed to accommodate a computer. You still need room for your legs, but the keyboard and monitor need to be positioned appropriately or you will get a stiff neck, sore wrists, and tired eyes.

KEYBOARD HEIGHT: Distance from the floor to the top of the computer keyboard. It should be adjustable, ranging from 24 to 27 inches, which is less than desk height.

SIGHT ANGLE: The angle between the sight line to the keyboard and the sight line to the monitor. Angle should not exceed 60 degrees.

WRITING
DESK

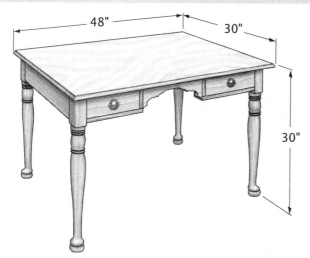

48" · 30"

30"

Desk, Writing Table

popularity boosted by executives, who like its clutter-free appearance and the message it delivers: "No unfinished business here!"

A well-designed writing desk seriously intended for writing, like the one shown here, had a cutout in the front apron for more leg room. Sometimes it was off-center to the left for right-handed customers. It would usually have at least one drawer for pens, ink, and paper.

A writing desk is a table specialized for handwriting. It differs from a pedestal desk by having four table legs for support instead of two narrow chests of drawers.

Its popularity grew along with literacy in a time when the only alternative to face-to-face conversation was the handwritten letter. Typically, it had a leather-covered writing surface because leather was kind to quills. The demand for this desk diminished with the invention of the typewriter and plummeted with the spread of the telephone. Today it is back, its

PLANS

Lyons, Richard A. "Writing Desk," *Making Country Furniture.* Englewood Cliffs, NJ: Prentice-Hall, 1987. A leather-topped writing table with 2 drawers, turned legs; adequate drawings, brief instructions.

Watts, Simon. "Folding Desk," *Building a Houseful of Furniture.* Newtown, CT: The Taunton Press, 1983. A contemporary design with folding top and stationery case; good drawings and instructions.

DESIGN VARIATIONS

Changes in furniture styles have driven obvious design variations in writing desks. But the needs of the user also have prompted variations. Today, as 200 years ago, elegance means the shape is graceful and clutter is absent. But a compulsive correspondent might need a desk with a case of pigeonholes and small drawers on top.

George Washington's hard-working model gave the writing desk definition a firm push toward what we know as a pedestal desk. It has a low gallery along the ends and partway along the back edges of the desktop, ostensibly to prevent work from being pushed onto the floor.

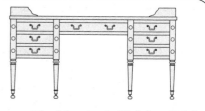

George Washington's Writing Table

Federal Writing Desk

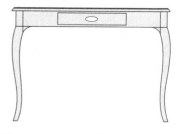

Contemporary Writing Desk

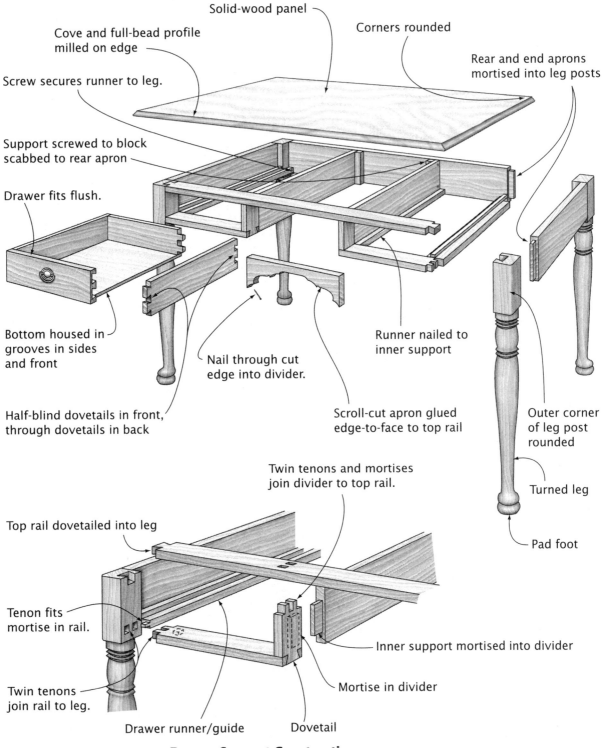

Solid-wood panel

Cove and full-bead profile milled on edge

Corners rounded

Rear and end aprons mortised into leg posts

Screw secures runner to leg.

Support screwed to block scabbed to rear apron

Drawer fits flush.

Bottom housed in grooves in sides and front

Nail through cut edge into divider.

Runner nailed to inner support

Scroll-cut apron glued edge-to-face to top rail

Half-blind dovetails in front, through dovetails in back

Outer corner of leg post rounded

Turned leg

Pad foot

Twin tenons and mortises join divider to top rail.

Top rail dovetailed into leg

Tenon fits mortise in rail.

Twin tenons join rail to leg.

Inner support mortised into divider

Mortise in divider

Drawer runner/guide

Dovetail

Drawer Support Construction

SLANT-TOP
DESK

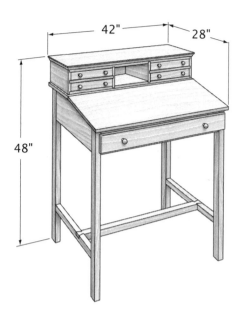

42"   28"

48"

*Schoolmaster's Desk, Stand-Up Desk,
Standing Desk, Writing Desk*

DESIGN VARIATIONS The appearance and utility of this desk are subject to its proportions. While the archetype shown is a standing desk, that might not suit you. To transform it into a writing-style desk, which is to say one at which you work when seated in a chair, you merely have to shorten the legs and perhaps omit the stretchers. Changing the style of leg and the gallery arrangement also alters the desk's appearance.

Another common variant is the storekeeper's desk. This standing style has a deep cabinet with two or more drawers, as well as the well under the lift lid.

Low Desk   **Storekeeper's Desk**

This is an evocative piece of furniture. Visions of Bob Cratchit come to mind. Bartleby the Scrivener. Green eyeshades and account books. Or The Schoolmaster, standing between his stand-up slant-top desk and blackboard, scowling out at schoolchildren seated at their lower slant-top desks, bent over their workbooks.

The slant-top desk is the working person's desk. Its gently sloped working surface is better for writing, drawing, and similar activities than a flat surface. If you spend hours doing these activities, you are better off with a slant-top desk than with a flat writing desk. The work surface slope can be customized, but a good standard is 10 degrees.

The work surface of the typical slant-top desk is hinged to provide access to the oddly shaped well or compartment. The depth of the compartment, and how it is furnished, varies widely. The model shown provides undifferentiated storage beneath the lid. As in the model, a drawer is often incorporated below the well.

Likewise, the superstructure varies. The desk shown has an attractive yet functional case with drawers and compartments for organizing and storing office necessaries.

PLANS

Moser, Thomas. "Standing Desk," "Lectern Desk," and "High Desk," *Measured Shop Drawings for American Furniture*. New York: Sterling Publishing Co., 1985. Measured drawings of 3 different slant-top desks.

Rittenhouse, Nelson. "Slant-Top Writing Desk," *American Woodworker*, No. 23 (November/December 1991), pp. 30–35. A low desk of contemporary design.

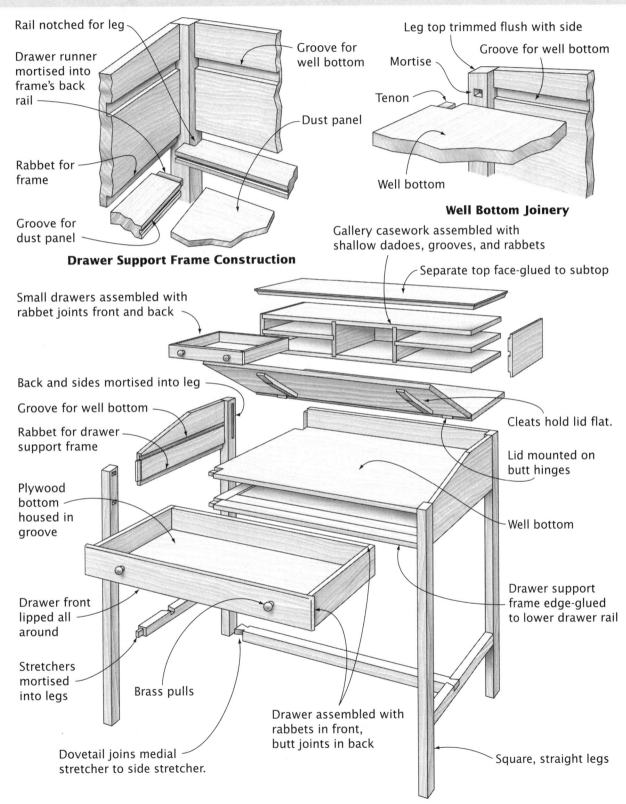

Rail notched for leg

Groove for well bottom

Drawer runner mortised into frame's back rail

Dust panel

Rabbet for frame

Groove for dust panel

Drawer Support Frame Construction

Leg top trimmed flush with side

Groove for well bottom

Mortise

Tenon

Well bottom

Well Bottom Joinery

Gallery casework assembled with shallow dadoes, grooves, and rabbets

Separate top face-glued to subtop

Small drawers assembled with rabbet joints front and back

Back and sides mortised into leg

Groove for well bottom

Rabbet for drawer support frame

Cleats hold lid flat.

Lid mounted on butt hinges

Plywood bottom housed in groove

Well bottom

Drawer support frame edge-glued to lower drawer rail

Drawer front lipped all around

Stretchers mortised into legs

Brass pulls

Drawer assembled with rabbets in front, butt joints in back

Dovetail joins medial stretcher to side stretcher.

Square, straight legs

POST-OFFICE
DESK

Plantation Desk

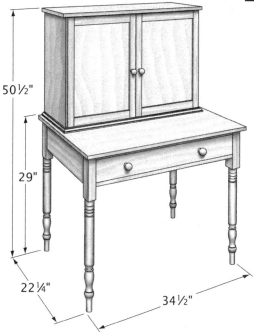

50½"

29"

22¼"

34½"

DESIGN VARIATIONS Imagine how many different table styles you've seen. Then visualize all of the different wall cabinets. Think about all of the possible combinations. Some wouldn't work, but many would. That's exactly how to redesign a post-office desk. The example shown below is just one of the many variations possible.

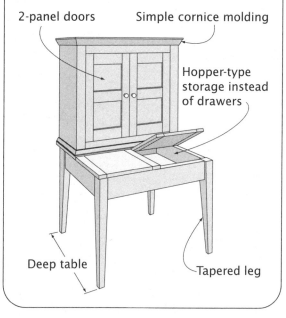

2-panel doors

Simple cornice molding

Hopper-type storage instead of drawers

Deep table

Tapered leg

Rural folk tend to be practical, thrifty, and ingenious. If this desk looks like a table with a cabinet on top, then more likely than not, that's exactly what it is. While the piece shown probably was never anything but this desk, many examples of this style are "marriages" of two different pieces—a table and a cupboard, for example.

A desk, after all, fulfills two needs—it offers a place to do writing or bookkeeping, and it offers a place to organize and file papers, receipts, bills, and letters. A wall cabinet redone with vertical dividers and perhaps small drawers inside isn't at all removed in function from the pigeonhole galleries of slant-front and rolltop desks and secretaries. It's just easier to construct. And a writing desk isn't far removed from a leg-and-apron table.

The name "post-office desk" is surely a contemporary one. In many rural areas, a storekeeper would serve as part-time postmaster. A desk like the one shown, set in a corner of the store, would be the entire post office.

PLANS

Engler, Nick, and Mary Jane Favorite. "Plantation Desk," *American Country Furniture.* Emmaus, PA: Rodale Press, 1990. Plans for a contemporary reproduction of this rural style of desk.

•

Lynch, Carlyle. "Post-Office Desk," *The Best of Fine Woodworking: Traditional Furniture Projects.* Newtown, CT: The Taunton Press, 1991. Lynch's attractive measured drawing, plus some history and construction directions.

Back boards set into rabbets in sides, overlap subtop and bottom; nailed in place.

Top attached with screws driven through subtop

Thin, flat door panel

Door frame joined with mortises and tenons

Sides joined to bottom with through dovetails, to the top with half-blind dovetails; see page 27 for alternatives.

Cabinet

Partitions and dividers glued in shallow dadoes

Molding attached to tabletop holds cabinet in position.

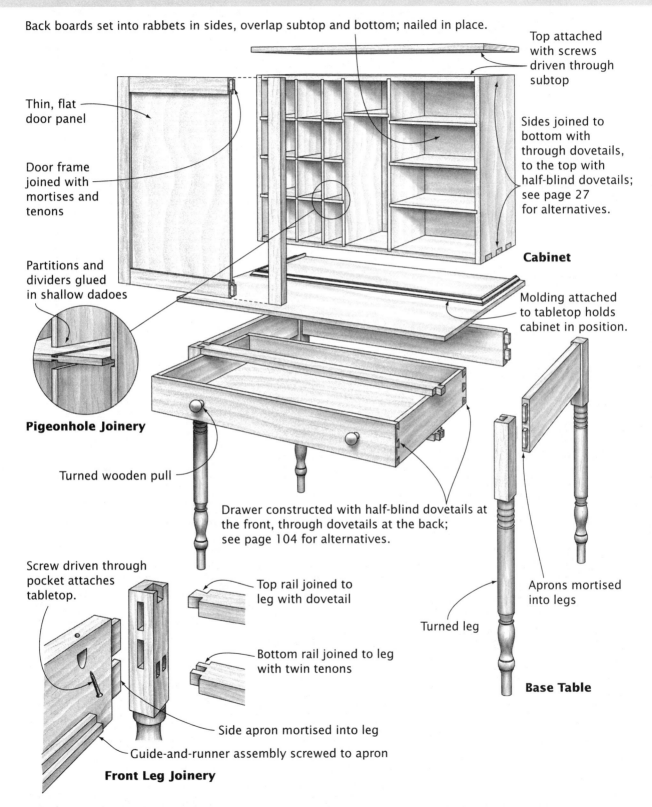

Pigeonhole Joinery

Turned wooden pull

Drawer constructed with half-blind dovetails at the front, through dovetails at the back; see page 104 for alternatives.

Aprons mortised into legs

Turned leg

Base Table

Screw driven through pocket attaches tabletop.

Top rail joined to leg with dovetail

Bottom rail joined to leg with twin tenons

Side apron mortised into leg

Guide-and-runner assembly screwed to apron

Front Leg Joinery

SLANT-FRONT
DESK ON FRAME

Ladies' Desk

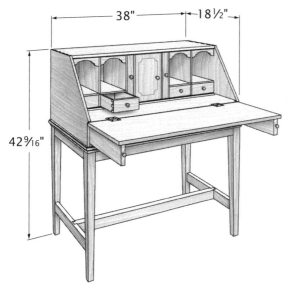

38" 18½"

42⁹⁄₁₆"

DESIGN VARIATIONS The two desks shown below present two levels of variations on the desk-on-frame theme. The so-called ladies' desk displays characteristics of the Federal style. But it also shows the impact of deepening the frame for drawers, and of shortening the desk.

The other example shows off the country Queen Anne style, with its turned cabriole legs and scroll-cut aprons. But this desk has a taller desk box with drawers incorporated below the drop lid.

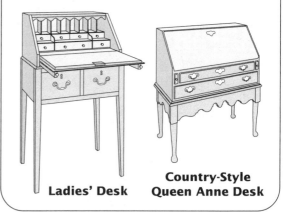

Ladies' Desk

Country-Style Queen Anne Desk

The first desks were boxes with a slanted lid. To write on it, one would balance it on one's knees or set it on a table. During the 18th century, the desk box and the table were united, creating a more substantial piece of furniture, well suited to both writing and storage.

The desk on frame shown is a good example of practicality combined with craftsmanship. The desk takes up very little space; but with the lid open, there's a surprisingly large work surface and an ample storage area for household records and correspondence.

It has a lot in common both with the "Slant-Top Desk" shown on page 200 and the "Slant-Front Desk" shown on page 206. The former is a type of desk-box-on-legs, while the latter is a type of desk-box-on-bureau.

The *slant-top desk* has a lid that's a relatively few degrees off horizontal. It's hinged along its upper edge. You use the lid as a writing surface when it is closed. The *slant-front desk,* on the other hand, has a lid that's a relatively few degrees from vertical. It is hinged along its lower edge. You use the lid as a writing surface when it is open.

PLANS

Abram, Norm, with Tim Snyder. "Slant-Front Desk," *The New Yankee Workshop.* Boston: Little, Brown, & Co., 1989. Plans and directions for building a rather spare, sleek desk.

●

Gottshall, Franklin H. "Sheraton Desk," *Masterpiece Furniture Making.* Harrisburg, PA: Stackpole Books, 1979. Classic desk with lots of inlay; decent drawings and directions.

●

Vandal, Norman. "Desk on Frame," *Queen Anne Furniture.* Newtown, CT: The Taunton Press, 1990. Excellent plans for a country Queen Anne desk.

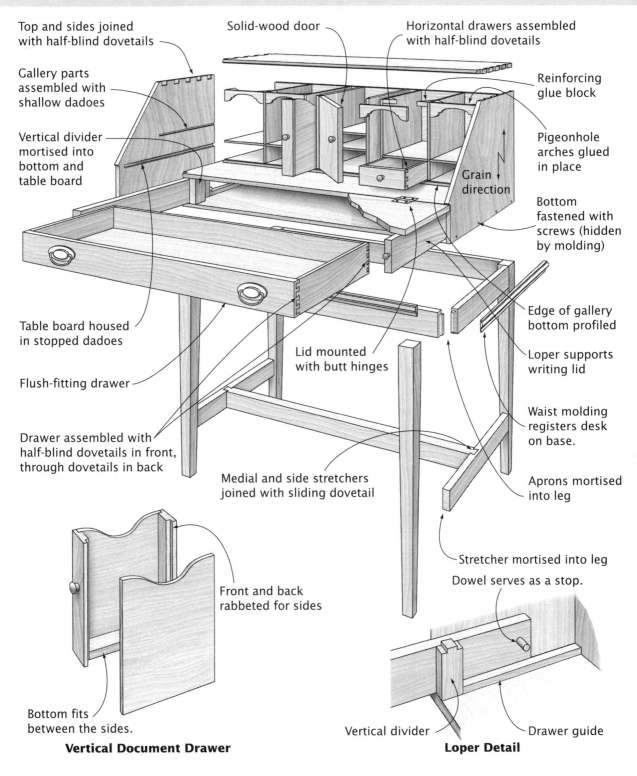

Top and sides joined with half-blind dovetails

Solid-wood door

Horizontal drawers assembled with half-blind dovetails

Gallery parts assembled with shallow dadoes

Reinforcing glue block

Vertical divider mortised into bottom and table board

Pigeonhole arches glued in place

Grain direction

Bottom fastened with screws (hidden by molding)

Table board housed in stopped dadoes

Lid mounted with butt hinges

Edge of gallery bottom profiled

Loper supports writing lid

Flush-fitting drawer

Waist molding registers desk on base.

Drawer assembled with half-blind dovetails in front, through dovetails in back

Aprons mortised into leg

Medial and side stretchers joined with sliding dovetail

Stretcher mortised into leg

Dowel serves as a stop.

Front and back rabbeted for sides

Bottom fits between the sides.

Vertical Document Drawer

Vertical divider

Drawer guide

Loper Detail

SLANT-FRONT
DESK

Slant-Top Desk, Slope-Top Desk, Drop-Front Desk

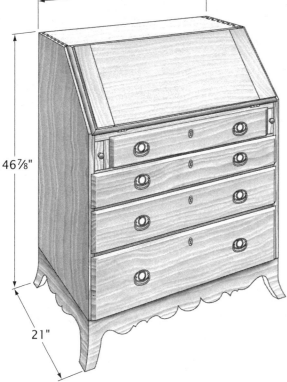

38⅜"

46⅞"

21"

DESIGN VARIATIONS The slant-front desk form emerged during the William and Mary period and has flourished to this day. Style becomes evident primarily in the detailing—moldings, foot forms, and so forth. The William and Mary version shown below has a pronounced base molding, double-bead tack molding outlining the drawers and lid, and bulbous turned feet. A Chippendale desk would have ball-and-claw feet and more than a bit of carving. A contemporary-style piece might be devoid of ornamentation.

William and Mary Slant-Front Desk

For contemporary Americans, this has to be a curious sort of desk. It is at once an attractive piece of furniture and a pretty poor desk.

You can't pull a chair up square to the writing surface; your knees jam against the drawers. It will accommodate only the daintiest laptop computer. The drawer proportions are wrong for files and papers.

Yet it's a desk you'd like to have. It's a showpiece now as it was back in the early 18th century, when the style emerged. A desk like this might have been in a bedchamber, with personal and business papers in the desk compartment and clothing in the drawers.

The basic construction is like that of a chest of drawers, but the upper front edges of the sides angle back to accommodate the closed lid. The lid is hinged along its bottom edge and, when open, is supported by pull-out struts called lopers.

PLANS

Gottshall, Franklin H. "Curly Maple Slant-Top Desk," *Masterpiece Furniture Making.* Harrisburg, PA: Stackpole Books, 1979. Lovely desk, good drawings, quirky write-up.

●

Margon, Lester. "Historic Desk of Drop-Front Design," *Construction of American Furniture Treasures.* New York: Dover Publications, 1975. Reproducing a piece with ball-and-claw feet.

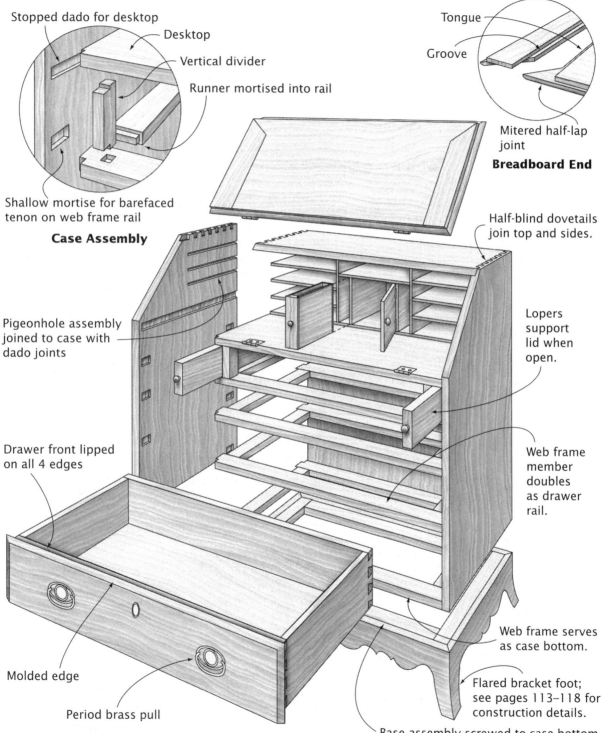

Case Assembly

Stopped dado for desktop

Desktop

Vertical divider

Runner mortised into rail

Shallow mortise for barefaced tenon on web frame rail

Pigeonhole assembly joined to case with dado joints

Drawer front lipped on all 4 edges

Molded edge

Period brass pull

Breadboard End

Tongue

Groove

Mitered half-lap joint

Half-blind dovetails join top and sides.

Lopers support lid when open.

Web frame member doubles as drawer rail.

Web frame serves as case bottom.

Flared bracket foot; see pages 113–118 for construction details.

Base assembly screwed to case bottom

NOTE: Drawer constructed with half-blind dovetails in front, through dovetails in back; see page 104 for alternative constructions.

FALL-FRONT DESK

Breakfront

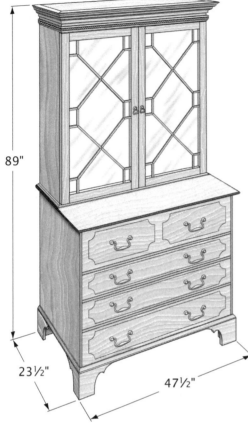

89"

23½"

47½"

A fall-flap is a door that is hinged along its bottom edge. Vertical when closed, it "falls" open, typically to form a horizontal writing surface. It is this flap that distinguishes a fall-front desk.

The example shown here is modeled on several 18th-century pieces. The "desk" is but one drawer. At that time, such a desk was often incorporated into a secretary or chest-bookcase, but also into a breakfront or even a chest-on-chest. You would slide the drawer about halfway out, then open the fall-flap to reveal a stationery case with lots of small drawers and pigeonholes. Hidden compartments were common in such desks.

PLANS

Taylor, V. J. "Building a Secretaire-Bookcase," *Fine Woodworking* on *Making Period Furniture*. Newtown, CT: The Taunton Press, 1985. Very complete drawings, decent text and cutting list for an 18th-century British fall-front desk.

DESIGN VARIATIONS

The fall-front desk isn't limited to a drawer-sized space within a chest or cupboard. Some are single-purpose and very spacious pieces, as shown below.

The Shaker desk, often called a double trustee's desk because it was intended to be used by two people, is a fairly well known piece. In Shaker fashion, it is free of ornament and pretension but is very functional.

The Empire desk, on the other hand, is a showpiece with its columns and other neoclassical design motifs. But it, too, is a functional desk, with stationery drawers and a spacious writing surface. Compare it to the "Slant-Front Desk" on the previous page; though the Empire desk is only a foot taller, it *seems* to offer a lot more working space. That may be because a fall-flap can be large (more so than the writing flap of a slant-front desk) without looking odd, because it is vertical when closed.

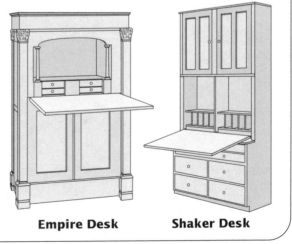

Empire Desk   **Shaker Desk**

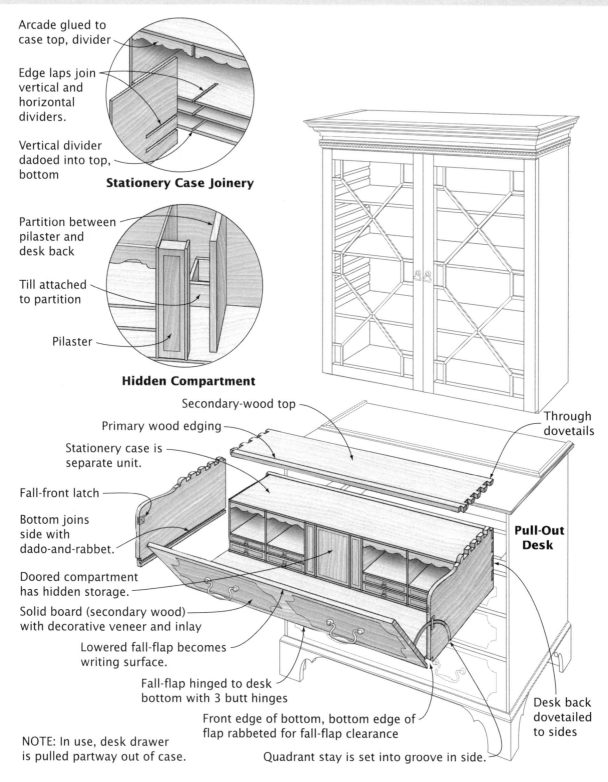

Arcade glued to case top, divider

Edge laps join vertical and horizontal dividers.

Vertical divider dadoed into top, bottom

Stationery Case Joinery

Partition between pilaster and desk back

Till attached to partition

Pilaster

Hidden Compartment

Secondary-wood top

Primary wood edging

Stationery case is separate unit.

Fall-front latch

Bottom joins side with dado-and-rabbet.

Doored compartment has hidden storage.

Solid board (secondary wood) with decorative veneer and inlay

Lowered fall-flap becomes writing surface.

Fall-flap hinged to desk bottom with 3 butt hinges

Front edge of bottom, bottom edge of flap rabbeted for fall-flap clearance

NOTE: In use, desk drawer is pulled partway out of case.

Through dovetails

Pull-Out Desk

Desk back dovetailed to sides

Quadrant stay is set into groove in side.

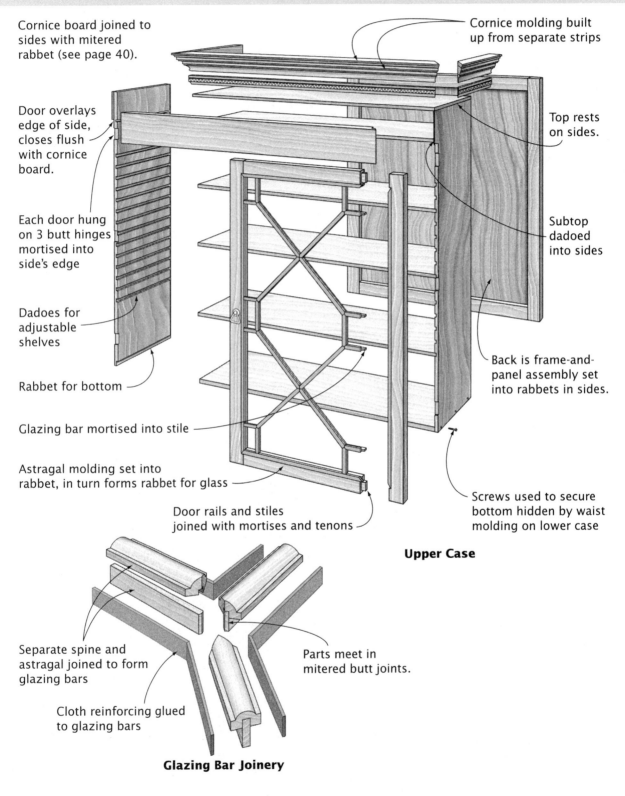

Cornice board joined to sides with mitered rabbet (see page 40).

Cornice molding built up from separate strips

Door overlays edge of side, closes flush with cornice board.

Top rests on sides.

Each door hung on 3 butt hinges mortised into side's edge

Subtop dadoed into sides

Dadoes for adjustable shelves

Rabbet for bottom

Back is frame-and-panel assembly set into rabbets in sides.

Glazing bar mortised into stile

Astragal molding set into rabbet, in turn forms rabbet for glass

Door rails and stiles joined with mortises and tenons

Screws used to secure bottom hidden by waist molding on lower case

Upper Case

Separate spine and astragal joined to form glazing bars

Parts meet in mitered butt joints.

Cloth reinforcing glued to glazing bars

Glazing Bar Joinery

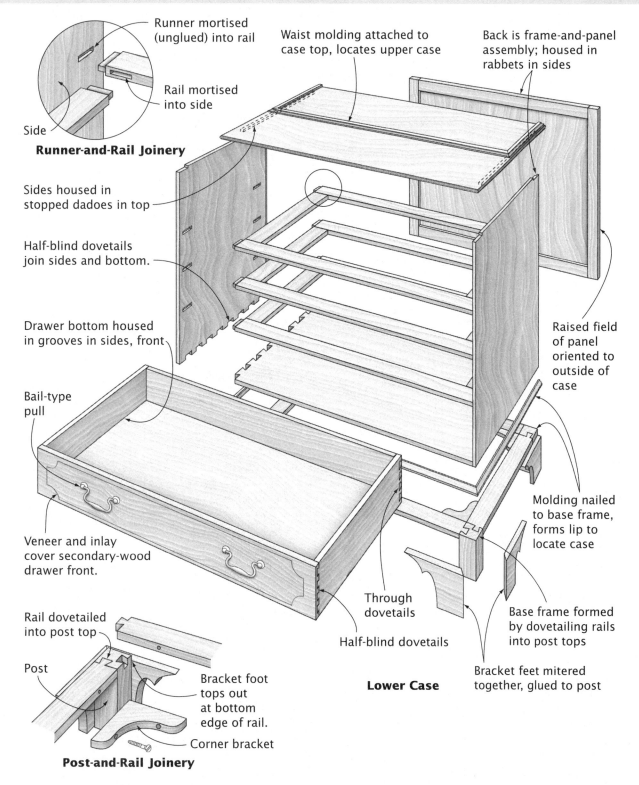

Runner mortised (unglued) into rail

Rail mortised into side

Side

Runner-and-Rail Joinery

Waist molding attached to case top, locates upper case

Back is frame-and-panel assembly; housed in rabbets in sides

Sides housed in stopped dadoes in top

Half-blind dovetails join sides and bottom.

Drawer bottom housed in grooves in sides, front

Raised field of panel oriented to outside of case

Bail-type pull

Veneer and inlay cover secondary-wood drawer front.

Molding nailed to base frame, forms lip to locate case

Through dovetails

Half-blind dovetails

Lower Case

Base frame formed by dovetailing rails into post tops

Bracket feet mitered together, glued to post

Rail dovetailed into post top

Post

Bracket foot tops out at bottom edge of rail.

Corner bracket

Post-and-Rail Joinery

SECRETARY

Desk and Bookcase

93"

18¹¹⁄₁₆"   39⅞"

DESIGN VARIATIONS

Secretaries were built in great variety. The British especially were taken with elaborate pieces, displaying ostentatious pediments and finials, exotic veneers, and intricate inlays.

In contrast is the example shown below, a rural piece. As is often the case, it has a reserve—that rural conservativism—that is sorely missed in many high-style pieces. This secretary has a simple slant-front desk as its base, and a bookcase with solid-wood paneled doors, a flat top, and an unpretentious cornice.

Desks varied more than the bookcases. The writing surface of most was at a slope when closed, flat when open. But the angle varied widely, and some closed to a vertical position. Some revealed elaborate drawers and pigeonholes when opened; others simply provided a writing surface, revealing nothing.

Moravian Desk and Bookcase

In the world of furniture, a chest of drawers with some sort of fold-down writing surface built into it is a desk; and when it supports a cupboard for books, it is known as a secretary. The combination of desk and bookcase was not uncommon as far back as the early 18th century.

The archetype, shown above, portrays well the classic bookcase-on-desk form. In many of its details, however, it is a bit unusual and very appealing.

The desk, for example, has four drawers rather than three. The desk flap does not open to reveal a stationery case; the stationery drawers are incorporated into the bookcase. The writing surface is sloped when the flap is both open and closed.

PLANS

Dunbar, Michael. "Secretary," *Federal Furniture.* Newtown, CT: The Taunton Press, 1986. Nifty Federal-era secretary presented in extensive drawings and some how-to instructions; no step-by-step or materials list.

•

Lynch, Carlyle. "Salem Desk and Bookcase," *Classic Furniture Projects from Carlyle Lynch.* Emmaus, PA: Rodale Press, 1992. Excellent drawings, good how-to instructions, comprehensive materials list.

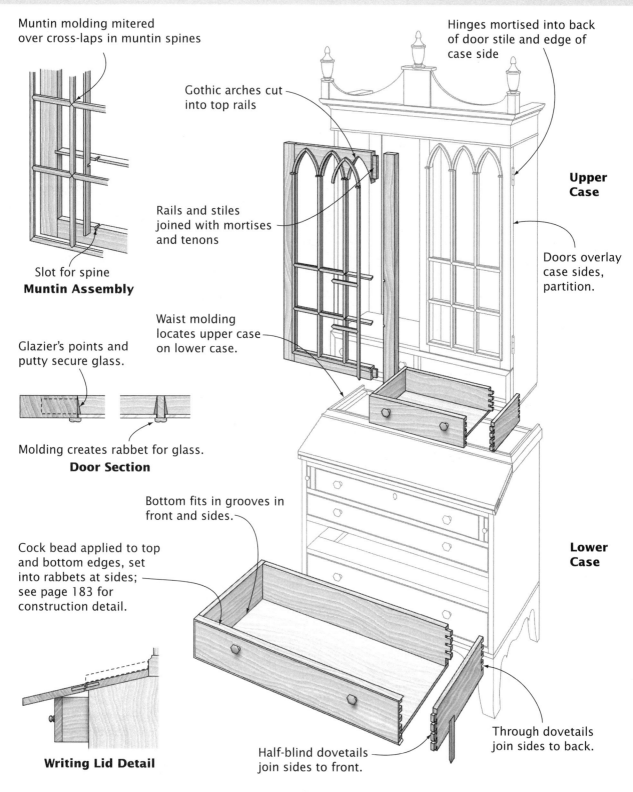

Muntin molding mitered over cross-laps in muntin spines

Slot for spine
Muntin Assembly

Gothic arches cut into top rails

Hinges mortised into back of door stile and edge of case side

Upper Case

Rails and stiles joined with mortises and tenons

Doors overlay case sides, partition.

Glazier's points and putty secure glass.

Molding creates rabbet for glass.
Door Section

Waist molding locates upper case on lower case.

Bottom fits in grooves in front and sides.

Cock bead applied to top and bottom edges, set into rabbets at sides; see page 183 for construction detail.

Lower Case

Writing Lid Detail

Half-blind dovetails join sides to front.

Through dovetails join sides to back.

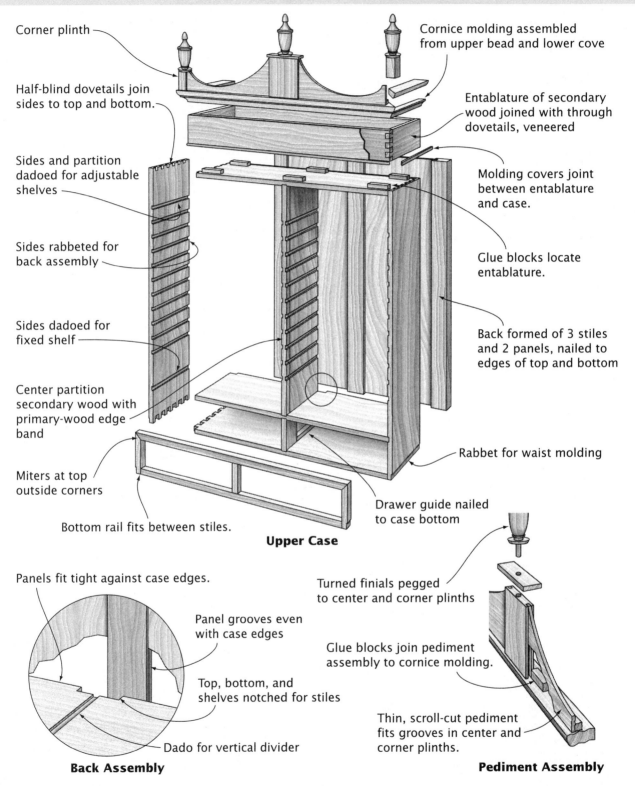

Corner plinth

Half-blind dovetails join sides to top and bottom.

Sides and partition dadoed for adjustable shelves

Sides rabbeted for back assembly

Sides dadoed for fixed shelf

Center partition secondary wood with primary-wood edge band

Miters at top outside corners

Bottom rail fits between stiles.

Cornice molding assembled from upper bead and lower cove

Entablature of secondary wood joined with through dovetails, veneered

Molding covers joint between entablature and case.

Glue blocks locate entablature.

Back formed of 3 stiles and 2 panels, nailed to edges of top and bottom

Rabbet for waist molding

Drawer guide nailed to case bottom

Upper Case

Panels fit tight against case edges.

Panel grooves even with case edges

Top, bottom, and shelves notched for stiles

Dado for vertical divider

Back Assembly

Turned finials pegged to center and corner plinths

Glue blocks join pediment assembly to cornice molding.

Thin, scroll-cut pediment fits grooves in center and corner plinths.

Pediment Assembly

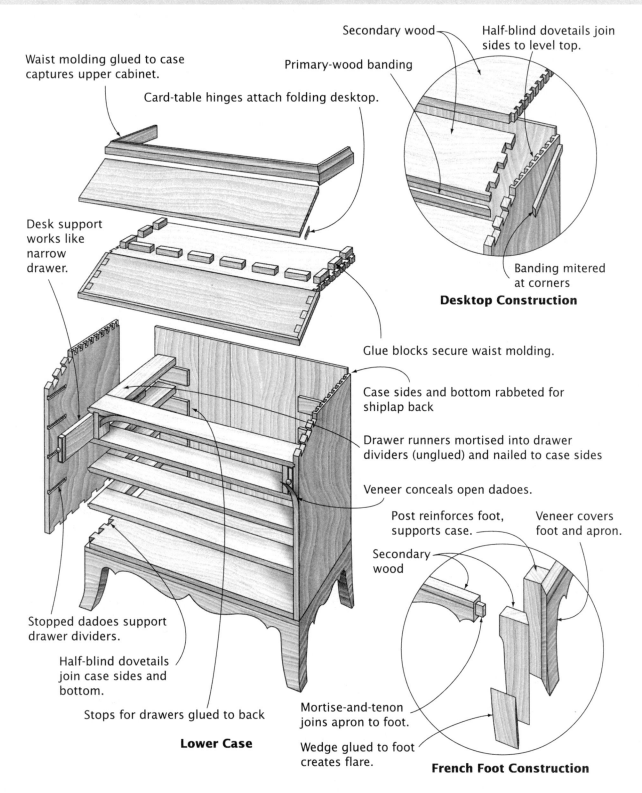

Waist molding glued to case captures upper cabinet.

Card-table hinges attach folding desktop.

Secondary wood

Primary-wood banding

Half-blind dovetails join sides to level top.

Banding mitered at corners

Desktop Construction

Desk support works like narrow drawer.

Glue blocks secure waist molding.

Case sides and bottom rabbeted for shiplap back

Drawer runners mortised into drawer dividers (unglued) and nailed to case sides

Veneer conceals open dadoes.

Post reinforces foot, supports case.

Veneer covers foot and apron.

Secondary wood

Stopped dadoes support drawer dividers.

Half-blind dovetails join case sides and bottom.

Stops for drawers glued to back

Lower Case

Mortise-and-tenon joins apron to foot.

Wedge glued to foot creates flare.

French Foot Construction

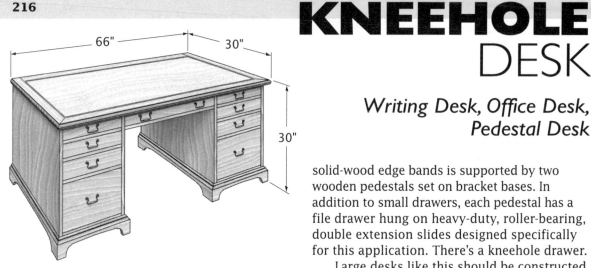

KNEEHOLE DESK

Writing Desk, Office Desk, Pedestal Desk

solid-wood edge bands is supported by two wooden pedestals set on bracket bases. In addition to small drawers, each pedestal has a file drawer hung on heavy-duty, roller-bearing, double extension slides designed specifically for this application. There's a kneehole drawer.

Large desks like this should be constructed so they can be disassembled into their major components for moving.

PLANS

Margon, Lester. "Heirloom Desk of Moderate Dimensions," *Construction of American Furniture Treasures*. New York: Dover Publications, 1975. A small but very fine block-front desk. Complete drawings with details and adequate instructions.

●

Moser, Thomas. "Panel Desk," *Measured Shop Drawings for American Furniture*. New York: Sterling Publishing Co., 1985. A mammoth desk built entirely of solid wood. Complete drawings including details but no instructions.

The kneehole desk is an amalgam of several basic furniture forms. In this case, it consists of two chests of drawers, or pedestals, supporting a tabletop. The pedestals typically are joined by upper and lower drawer rails housing a shallow drawer over the kneehole. Often, a modesty panel closes the kneehole opposite the user.

In its most rudimentary form, a functional, hardworking desk can be cobbled together using two 28-inch-high file cabinets for the pedestals and a flush door for the top. For today's office work, a pull-out keyboard tray should be installed.

The desk shown is clearly not "cobbled together." Its hardwood-plywood top with inlay and

---

DESIGN VARIATIONS

Beyond variations of furniture style, kneehole desks vary widely in size from mammoth, owner-of-the-bank–sized executive desks to diminutive pen-a-thank-you-note–sized desks for the home. Some of the smallest have only a single pedestal, substituting a pair of legs on the other end of the desk. Occasionally, as in the block-front below, the kneehole is representational rather than strictly functional.

The intended purpose of the desk is also reflected in the size of the drawers. Serious, working desks often have a file drawer in at least one of the pedestals. A few executive desks are built with a drawer fitted for liquor bottles and glasses. A desk for writing letters may have a side drawer fitted with shallow trays for a selection of stationery.

Most kneehole desks have a shallow drawer over the kneehole, often with a pen and pencil tray just behind the drawer front.

Executive Desk

Block-Front Kneehole Desk

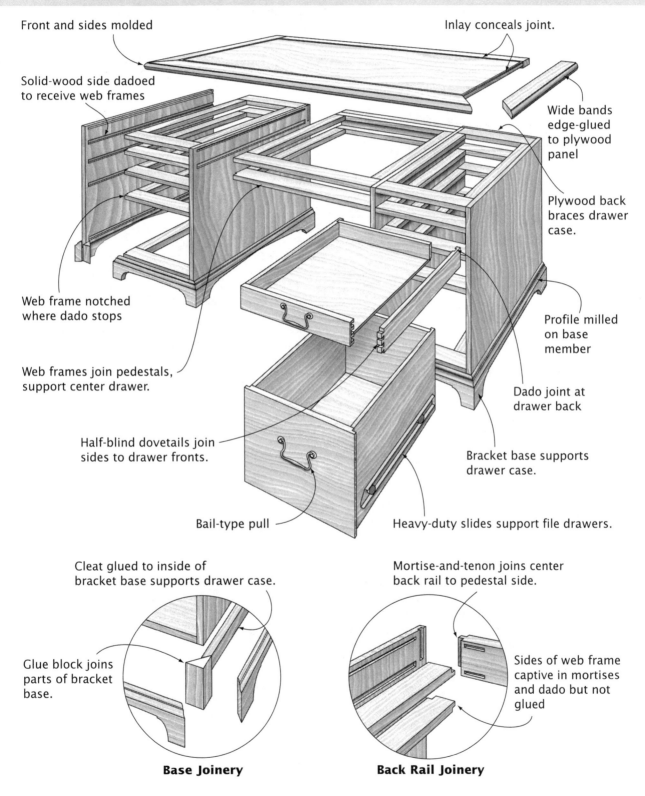

Front and sides molded

Inlay conceals joint.

Solid-wood side dadoed to receive web frames

Wide bands edge-glued to plywood panel

Plywood back braces drawer case.

Web frame notched where dado stops

Web frames join pedestals, support center drawer.

Half-blind dovetails join sides to drawer fronts.

Profile milled on base member

Dado joint at drawer back

Bracket base supports drawer case.

Bail-type pull

Heavy-duty slides support file drawers.

Cleat glued to inside of bracket base supports drawer case.

Mortise-and-tenon joins center back rail to pedestal side.

Glue block joins parts of bracket base.

Sides of web frame captive in mortises and dado but not glued

Base Joinery

Back Rail Joinery

DAVENPORT
DESK

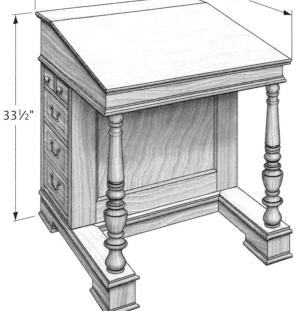

28⅞"

23"

33½"

DESIGN VARIATIONS While the davenport desk form would seem to constrain a designer, such was not the case. Many of the early davenport designs were fiendishly clever, with secret compartments, swing-out drawers, and pigeonholes that rose from the desk at the release of a hidden catch.

The first design shown at left below has a more elaborate desk-box than the archetype. The writing surface slopes quite steeply, and inlaid bands create a frame on it. The top has a gallery, a common feature on davenports. Because the desk-box's overhang is modest, half-columns glued to the case are all that is needed.

The second desk at right below has more going on. The desk-box has a serpentine front, and C-scrolls are used instead of turned or tapered columns. This desk is equipped with casters, which make it easy to move.

The story, possibly apocryphal, is that the very first desk of the sort shown here was built in London in the late 1700s for a Captain Davenport. Ostensibly, he needed a compact desk for his cramped shipboard quarters. He got the desk, and to this day, the desk has his name.

Characteristically, the davenport desk is small, with a slant-top desk-box resting on a case with drawers, and sometimes cupboards, that open to both sides rather than to the front. The desk-box extends well beyond the face of the case and is supported by columns or pillars. The kneehole thus created is really vestigial, providing little room for one's legs.

While the desk is compact, it doesn't seem well suited to cramped quarters. Open space is needed on both sides if the drawers are to be accessible. However, since the back is as finished as the front, the desk could be positioned in the center of a room.

The desk shown is a contemporary copy in the mid-19th-century davenport desk style. These tended to be elaborately decorated with exotic veneers, and this version is no exception.

PLANS

Jones, Thomas H. "Davenport Desk," *Heirloom Furniture You Can Make.* New York: Popular Science Books, 1987. This davenport desk project is one-of-a-kind, but the plans and construction directions leave a lot to the imagination.

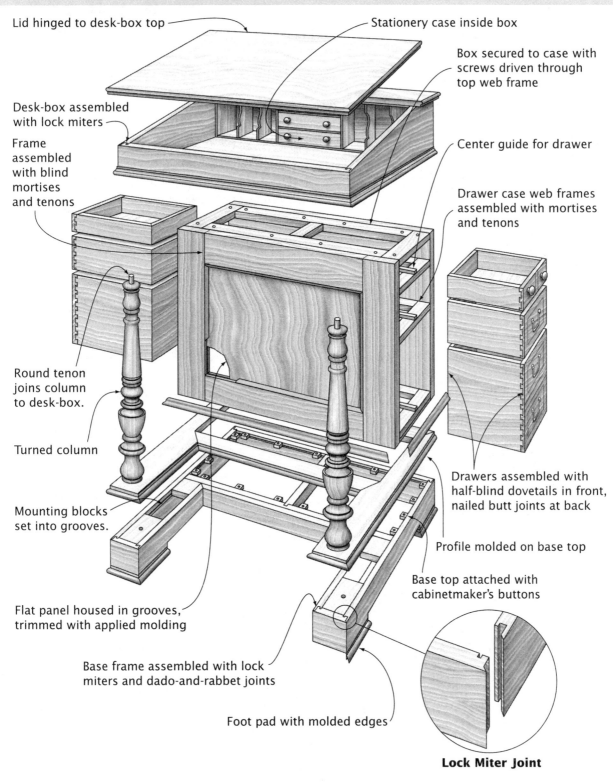

Lid hinged to desk-box top

Stationery case inside box

Box secured to case with screws driven through top web frame

Desk-box assembled with lock miters

Frame assembled with blind mortises and tenons

Center guide for drawer

Drawer case web frames assembled with mortises and tenons

Round tenon joins column to desk-box.

Turned column

Mounting blocks set into grooves.

Drawers assembled with half-blind dovetails in front, nailed butt joints at back

Profile molded on base top

Base top attached with cabinetmaker's buttons

Flat panel housed in grooves, trimmed with applied molding

Base frame assembled with lock miters and dado-and-rabbet joints

Foot pad with molded edges

Lock Miter Joint

ROLLTOP DESK

Tambour Desk

48"

36"

53½"

Concealing paper clutter—without disturbing it—is the forte of the rolltop desk. Unless they have piled up to an unreasonable height, you'll mask your bills and papers, correspondence and coffee cup, calculator and accounts, by tugging the rolltop's tambour curtain closed.

And when next you lift the curtain, all your work will still be as you left it. (Of course, that may be a mixed blessing.)

The archetypal American rolltop desk was the patented brainchild of Abner Cutler. In the 1850s, Cutler combined elements from several existing designs to produce a double-pedestal desk (often called a kneehole desk) with a tambour curtain that pulls down to completely enclose the writing surface and its adjacent bank of pigeonholes.

The tambour curtain consists of strips of flat or molded wood, laid out edge to edge and glued to a strong but flexible backing, usually canvas duck. In a rolltop desk, the ends of the strips are housed in parallel grooves cut in the desk's top case. As the curtain is moved from the closed to the open positions, it moves above and drops down behind the pigeonhole case. While it dealt with clutter, the tambour curtain also offered a measure of security, since it could be fitted with a lock.

DESIGN VARIATIONS

The antecedents of Cutler's rolltop stretched back through the Federal-style tambour desks to the French cylinder desk, which first appeared in the early 1700s. The solid, curved cover—the cylinder—would roll back into a housing to expose the writing surface of this desk. The cumbersome cylinder lid soon gave way to the tambour curtain. The first designs had a tambour that moved horizontally to conceal only the stationery case. Sheraton and Hepplewhite designed tambour desks with curtains that moved vertically but still didn't completely cover the writing surface. The example shown here has a pull-out writing surface.

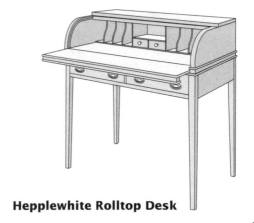

Hepplewhite Rolltop Desk

PLANS

Baumert, Kenneth. "Building a Roll-Top Desk," *The Best of Fine Woodworking: Traditional Furniture Projects.* Newtown, CT: The Taunton Press, 1991. The archetypal oak rolltop desk.

•

Jones, Thomas H. "Hepplewhite Desk," *Heirloom Furniture You Can Make.* New York: Popular Science Books, 1987. A writing-style desk with a tambour curtain and a pull-out writing surface.

Pigeonhole Unit: Constructed as separate assembly, fitted in place

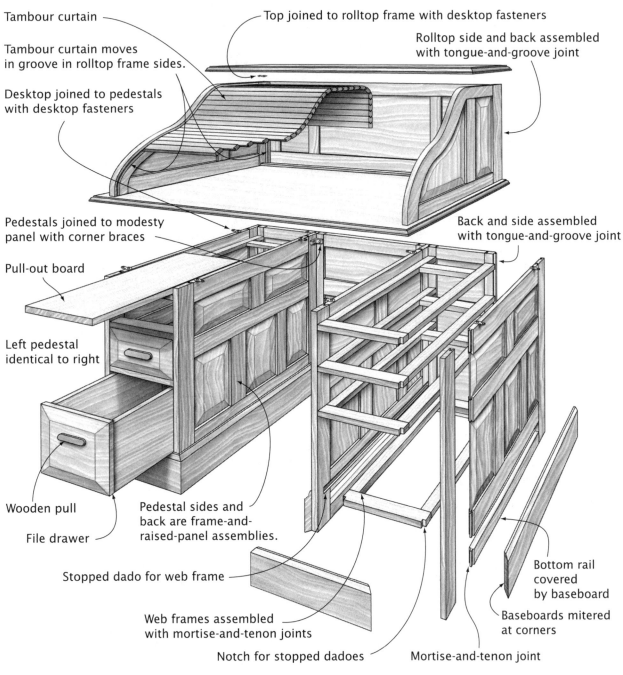

Tambour curtain

Tambour curtain moves in groove in rolltop frame sides.

Desktop joined to pedestals with desktop fasteners

Top joined to rolltop frame with desktop fasteners

Rolltop side and back assembled with tongue-and-groove joint

Pedestals joined to modesty panel with corner braces

Back and side assembled with tongue-and-groove joint

Pull-out board

Left pedestal identical to right

Wooden pull

File drawer

Pedestal sides and back are frame-and-raised-panel assemblies.

Stopped dado for web frame

Web frames assembled with mortise-and-tenon joints

Notch for stopped dadoes

Mortise-and-tenon joint

Bottom rail covered by baseboard

Baseboards mitered at corners

COMPUTER
DESK

76½" 30"

30"

J ust as computers have changed work, they have changed the office and the desk. The need is to accommodate the Digital Dictator, usually while maintaining a traditional desk appearance.

The desk shown conceals the CPU and a small laser printer or fax machine inside the left pedestal. Necessary ventilation and cabling ports are easy to provide using grommets and grilles sold specifically for those purposes. Setting the components in traylike drawers simplifies access, as does incorporating a door into the pedestal back.

PLANS

"Computer Center," *Cabinets and Built-Ins.* Upper Saddle River, NJ: Creative Homeowner Press, 1996. A very simple but effective computer desk; cutting and hardware list, step-by-step, a few simple drawings.

•

Engler, Nick. "Computer Workstation," *Desks and Bookcases.* Emmaus, PA: Rodale Press, 1990. A contemporary desk-and-bookcase design with open shelves and a trestle-table desk; complete plans, cutting list, and construction directions.

•

Storch, William. "Computer Desk," *American Woodworker,* Vol. V, No. 4 (July/August 1989), pp. 34–39. Single-pedestal desk puts the computer on the desktop, a printer in the pedestal.

The right pedestal houses two standard-sized file drawers. The monitor alone stands on the spacious desktop. The keyboard shelf is fixed between the pedestals.

DESIGN VARIATIONS

The archetypal desk (above) suggests that a traditional desk form can be adapted to the computer. The single-pedestal version shown demonstrates that even a small desk can cope with a powerful computer. The CPU and a printer or fax machine can be housed in the single pedestal, while a leg-and-apron hold up the other end of the desktop. A pull-out shelf for the keyboard and mouse is used.

The computer-age desk-and-bookcase uses modern materials and quick-and-easy joinery, and it shows. This desk provides space for notebooks and files but puts the hardware in the open. There is a shelf in the kneehole for the CPU, and a pull-out tray for the keyboard. The monitor goes on the desktop, above the keyboard.

Single-Pedestal Desk

Desk-and-Bookcase

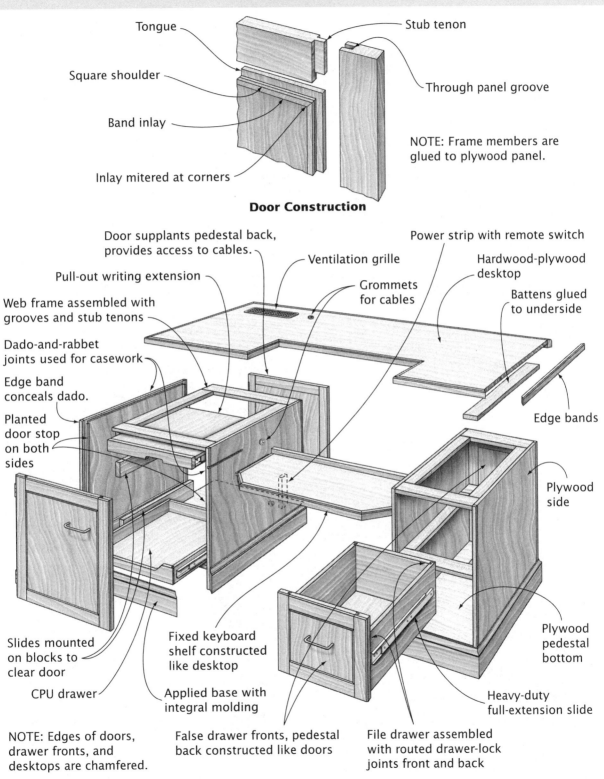

Tongue

Square shoulder

Band inlay

Inlay mitered at corners

Stub tenon

Through panel groove

NOTE: Frame members are glued to plywood panel.

Door Construction

Door supplants pedestal back, provides access to cables.

Pull-out writing extension

Web frame assembled with grooves and stub tenons

Dado-and-rabbet joints used for casework

Edge band conceals dado.

Planted door stop on both sides

Ventilation grille

Grommets for cables

Power strip with remote switch

Hardwood-plywood desktop

Battens glued to underside

Edge bands

Plywood side

Slides mounted on blocks to clear door

CPU drawer

Fixed keyboard shelf constructed like desktop

Applied base with integral molding

Plywood pedestal bottom

Heavy-duty full-extension slide

NOTE: Edges of doors, drawer fronts, and desktops are chamfered.

False drawer fronts, pedestal back constructed like doors

File drawer assembled with routed drawer-lock joints front and back

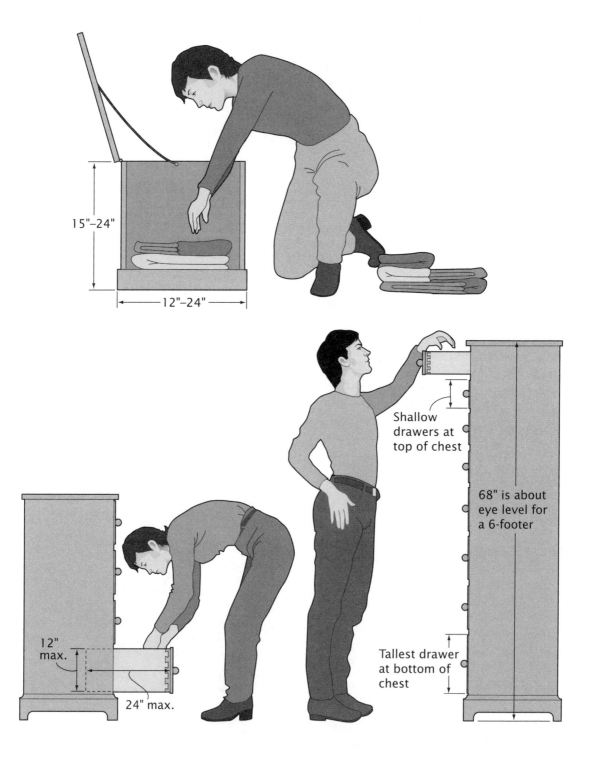

15"–24"

12"–24"

Shallow
drawers at
top of chest

68" is about
eye level for
a 6-footer

Tallest drawer
at bottom of
chest

12"
max.

24" max.

CHESTS

Chests may look handsome, may in fact be works of art, but their function is humble: *storage*.

BLANKET CHEST: The baseline form is the lidded chest, and it provides the lowest level of organization: The belongings either are in the chest or are not. To retrieve a coverlet or a blanket from the bottom, you must settle onto one knee and methodically remove *everything*.

Dimensions for lidded chests vary greatly. Length is seldom a problem, but storage in a chest that's too wide or deep is. Keep the width between 12 and 24 inches, the depth between 15 and 24 inches. Typical lengths range from 30 to 60 inches.

CHEST OF DRAWERS: Drawers resolve many storage access and organization problems. The challenge is to size both the drawers and the chest to provide a workable level of storage organization and at the same time to make the piece physically easy to use.

These are commonsense rules: big drawers at the bottom, small drawers at the top. No drawer too big to open and close (though modern hardware has raised the dimension threshold here). No drawer too high to see into. And not so many drawers in a case that you can't easily remember what—generally speaking, anyway—is stored in each.

To make it manageable for the widest range of people, the largest drawer should not exceed 12 inches in height, 24 inches in depth, and 48 inches in width. But there's a lot of leeway.

CHEST-ON-CHEST: This piece presses the "highest drawer" rule, and its dimensions explain why it generally is considered "the man's chest." Height ranges from 72 to 84 inches, which puts the highest drawer above eye level for all but the tallest people. Width ranges from 36 to 48 inches, which makes a full-width drawer awkward for a small person to deal with. Depth ranges from 18 to 24 inches.

DRESSER: In a bedroom suite, this low, wide chest of drawers is often thought of as being for "the woman." Its overall height of 29 to 34 inches puts all the drawers below adult eye level. Positioning drawers in side-by-side stacks keeps them of a manageable width, even in a piece 72 inches long.

SIX-BOARD
CHEST

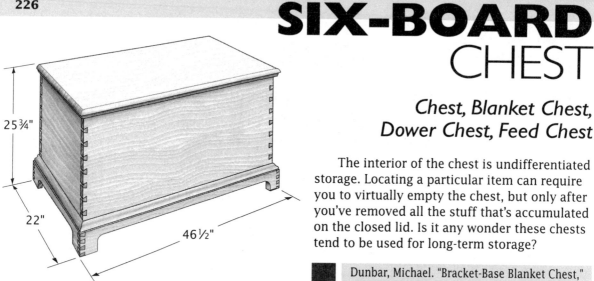

25¾"

22"

46½"

Chest, Blanket Chest, Dower Chest, Feed Chest

The interior of the chest is undifferentiated storage. Locating a particular item can require you to virtually empty the chest, but only after you've removed all the stuff that's accumulated on the closed lid. Is it any wonder these chests tend to be used for long-term storage?

PLANS

Dunbar, Michael. "Bracket-Base Blanket Chest," *Federal Furniture*. Newtown, CT: The Taunton Press, 1986. Very traditional dovetailed chest.

●

Hylton, Bill. "Blanket Chest," *Country Pine*. Emmaus, PA: Rodale Press, 1995. Plans, cutting list, and step-by-step for a "baseless" chest.

●

Lyons, Richard A. "Primitive Blanket Chest" and "Six-Board Blanket Chest," *Making Country Furniture*. Englewood Cliffs, NJ: Prentice-Hall, 1987. Plans for 2 different chests in 1 source; the names tell all.

The six-board chest varies widely in size, construction, appearance, and use, but the form is absolutely fundamental. It's just a box with a lid, and it's for storage. And it just may be the oldest furniture form.

The name, of course, comes from the number of boards needed to construct it. While some chests are built strictly with six boards, they are far more likely to resemble the sophisticated form shown as the archetype.

DESIGN VARIATIONS

Although very plain, the six-board chest is enormously interesting because of the endless varieties you can find. Here are only three. The primitive chest has end panels, set cross-grain to the front and back, that extend below the bottom for form feet. The footed chest is a turnip-footed, crudely dovetailed chest with wooden hinges. The baseless chest is a simple chest with a base molding but no feet.

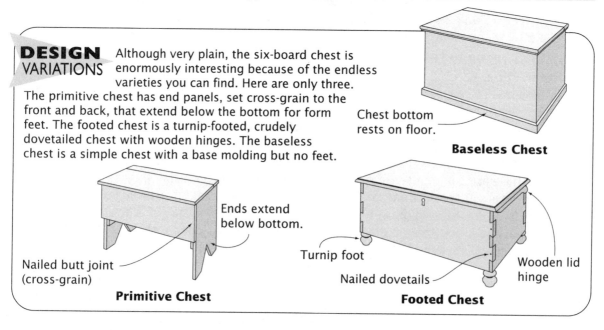

Chest bottom rests on floor.

Baseless Chest

Ends extend below bottom.

Nailed butt joint (cross-grain)

Primitive Chest

Turnip foot

Nailed dovetails

Wooden lid hinge

Footed Chest

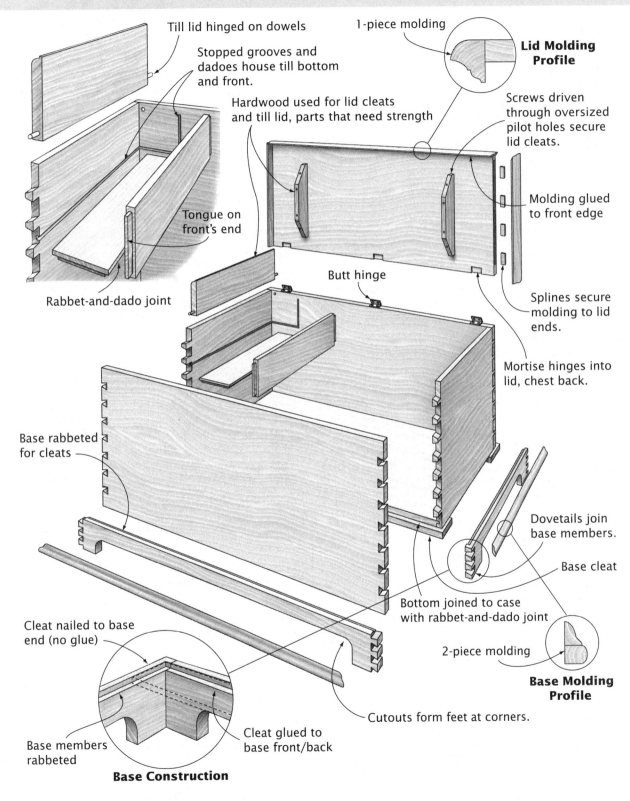

Till lid hinged on dowels

Stopped grooves and dadoes house till bottom and front.

Hardwood used for lid cleats and till lid, parts that need strength

Tongue on front's end

Rabbet-and-dado joint

1-piece molding

Lid Molding Profile

Screws driven through oversized pilot holes secure lid cleats.

Molding glued to front edge

Butt hinge

Splines secure molding to lid ends.

Mortise hinges into lid, chest back.

Base rabbeted for cleats

Dovetails join base members.

Base cleat

Bottom joined to case with rabbet-and-dado joint

2-piece molding

Base Molding Profile

Cutouts form feet at corners.

Cleat nailed to base end (no glue)

Base members rabbeted

Cleat glued to base front/back

Base Construction

MULE CHEST

52"

23½"

28¾"

Dower Chest, Blanket Chest

drawers (just as a mule is a hybrid of a horse and a donkey). The mule chest sometimes was proportioned like a blanket chest, but with only a single drawer. More often it was quite tall, with two or three fairly deep drawers, topped by a lidded compartment. In some examples, molding was applied to the face of the chest, mimicking drawer fronts.

PLANS

Kassay, John. "Chests," *The Book of Shaker Furniture.* Amherst, MA: University of Massachusetts Press, 1980. Measured drawings of a single-drawer Shaker chest.

●

Margon, Lester. "Pennsylvania Provincial Dower Chest," *Construction of American Furniture Treasures.* New York: Dover Publications, 1975. Plans for a "unicorn chest," complete with patterns for painting it.

●

Shea, John G. "Pine Chest with Drawer," *Antique Country Furniture of North America.* New York: Van Nostrand Reinhold, 1975. Measured drawing of a New England mule chest with false drawers and a scrolled skirt.

When drawers are added to a six-board chest, a smorgasbord of design and construction options presents itself. Studying chests from several traditions can better prepare you for designing and building your own original.

The familiar blanket chest, a roughly knee-high lidded chest with two or three shallow drawers incorporated just above the base, is out of the Pennsylvania Dutch tradition. The drawing shows just one example.

Chests in the New England tradition are usually examples of the true mule chest, a hybrid that mates the lidded chest and the chest of

DESIGN VARIATIONS Chests from three traditions display their different approaches to the same furniture form. The sizes and proportions vary, as do the number and scale of the drawers. The Pennsylvania Dutch chest is the antecedent of today's blanket chest, while the New England chest is on its way to being a chest of drawers.

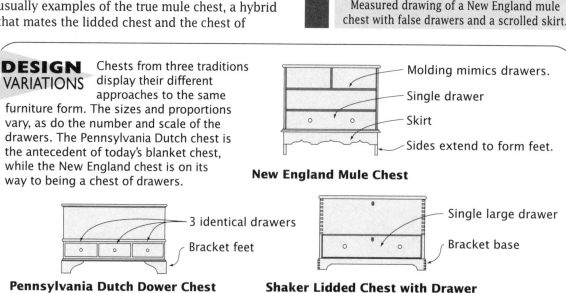

Molding mimics drawers.

Single drawer

Skirt

Sides extend to form feet.

New England Mule Chest

3 identical drawers

Bracket feet

Single large drawer

Bracket base

Pennsylvania Dutch Dower Chest

Shaker Lidded Chest with Drawer

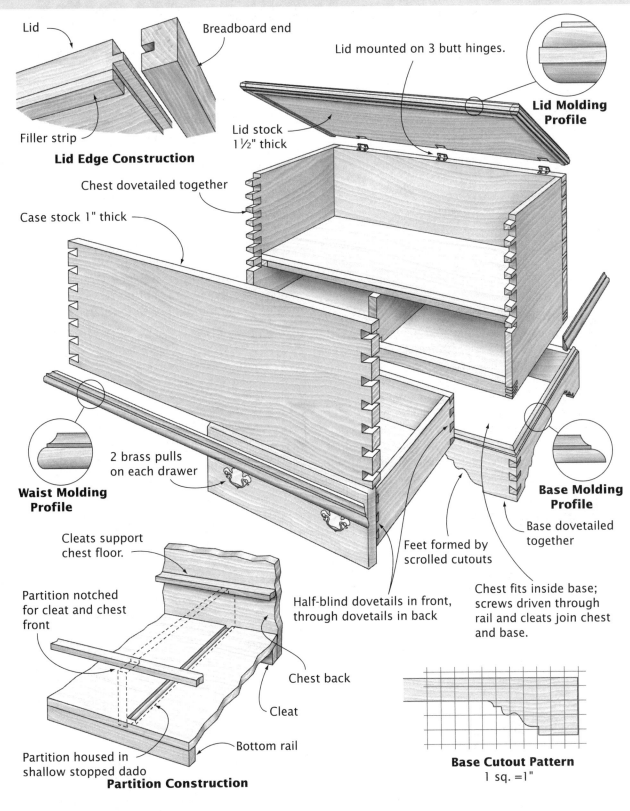

Lid

Breadboard end

Lid mounted on 3 butt hinges.

Lid Molding Profile

Filler strip

Lid Edge Construction

Lid stock 1½" thick

Chest dovetailed together

Case stock 1" thick

Waist Molding Profile

2 brass pulls on each drawer

Waist Molding Profile

Base Molding Profile

Base Molding Profile

Base dovetailed together

Feet formed by scrolled cutouts

Chest fits inside base; screws driven through rail and cleats join chest and base.

Cleats support chest floor.

Partition notched for cleat and chest front

Half-blind dovetails in front, through dovetails in back

Chest back

Cleat

Bottom rail

Partition housed in shallow stopped dado

Partition Construction

Base Cutout Pattern
1 sq. =1"

FRAME-AND-PANEL
CHEST

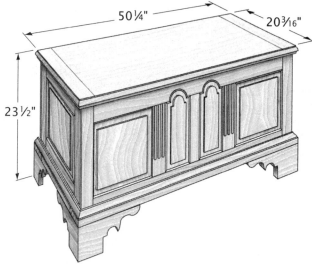

50¼"

20³⁄₁₆"

23½"

So the use of frame-and-panel construction here must be for aesthetics. Certainly, it makes the chest's construction more involved.

The front, back, and end assemblies are joined with rabbet joints. In turn, they are set on the bottom frame, forming an open box or case. This is exactly the way the six-board chest is constructed.

The aesthetic potential of frame-and-panel construction is exploited well here, with the arch-topped panels and the fluted stiles. The inclusion of those special panels dictated the joinery. The panels are set into rabbets, with quarter-round molding used to retain them.

The front, back, and ends of this chest are each a separate frame-and-panel assembly. To spice up the appearance of the chest, the designer incorporated arch-topped accent panels in the front assembly.

In most circumstances, the frame-and-panel construction method is used to minimize the negative impact of wood movement. But if you look at the "Six-Board Chest" on page 226, you'll see that wood movement will have little impact.

PLANS

Hill, Jack. "Chest," *Making Family Heirlooms.* New York: St. Martin's Press, 1985. Construction directions—no plans, per se—for an easy-to-build contemporary chest.

•

Jones, Thomas H. "Blanket Chest," *Heirloom Furniture You Can Make.* New York: Popular Science Books, 1987. Construction directions for a traditional-looking chest with cedar lining.

DESIGN VARIATIONS

Different cabinetmakers exploit the creative potential of frame-and-panel construction in different ways. As these examples show, the style of the panels as well as their proportions and layout can be varied. One chest here is entirely frame-and-panel, while the others use solid panels selectively. The base can be an extension of the case or an entirely separate construction.

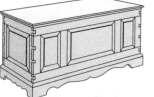

Dovetailed Frame-and-Panel Chest

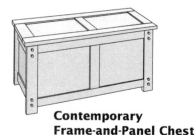

Contemporary Frame-and-Panel Chest

Frame-and-Panel Chest with Solid-Panel Ends

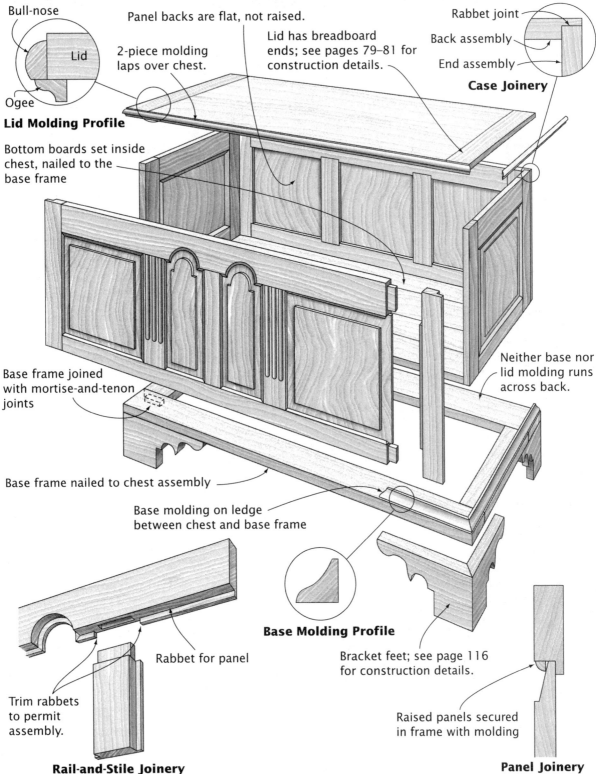

Bull-nose

Lid

Ogee

Lid Molding Profile

2-piece molding laps over chest.

Panel backs are flat, not raised.

Lid has breadboard ends; see pages 79–81 for construction details.

Rabbet joint

Back assembly

End assembly

Case Joinery

Bottom boards set inside chest, nailed to the base frame

Base frame joined with mortise-and-tenon joints

Base frame nailed to chest assembly

Base molding on ledge between chest and base frame

Neither base nor lid molding runs across back.

Base Molding Profile

Bracket feet; see page 116 for construction details.

Rabbet for panel

Trim rabbets to permit assembly.

Rail-and-Stile Joinery

Raised panels secured in frame with molding

Panel Joinery

POST-AND-PANEL
CHEST

41"

21"

25⅞"

PLANS

Gottshall, Franklin H. "Paneled Chest," *Simple Colonial Furniture.* New York: Bonanza Books, 1984. Plans for an archetypal chest.

●

Hass, Ivan. "Blanket Chest," *American Woodworker,* Vol. V, No. 3 (September/October 1989), pp. 52–56. Plans for a contemporary post-and-panel chest.

●

Hylton, Bill. "Post-and-Panel Chest," *Country Pine.* Emmaus, PA: Rodale Press, 1995. First-rate plans for building a traditional chest with raised panels.

I n use, this gothic-looking chest is like most others of the "blanket chest" genre. What makes it different is its construction. Instead of the familiar six-board construction style, it is of the post-and-panel style.

The standard rationale for using post-and-panel construction is to deal with wood movement. Built of wide boards, a chest will shrink and expand considerably, but with little practical effect. The chest would change height slightly during the course of seasons; but in six-board chest construction, there aren't major cross-grain joints to be stressed. It's in a cabinet with drawers and a flush door that this wood movement causes problems.

The builder of this chest surely was less concerned with wood movement than with appearance. While it is more distinctive than a six-board chest, it is loaded with cross-grain joinery, especially in the application of the molding to the panels. The best approach is to nail the triangular blocks and the molding to the panels. Nailed joints tend to be just a little more flexible than glued joints.

As a furniture-making project, this chest might be more challenging than that six-board chest, what with all the mortise-and-tenon joints, the panels, and the moldings. But it doesn't have dovetails.

DESIGN VARIATIONS

Three chests display just a part of the design range possible in the post-and-panel form. The traditional raised-panel chest has a two-panel front and feet turned on the leg posts. The next chest exhibits not only how an unembellished, flat-panel chest looks but also how changing the proportions of a chest alters its appearance. In the contemporary chest, the leg form is altered dramatically, anchoring the piece to the floor. The positioning of the stiles is also a departure from the traditional.

Raised-Panel Chest

Flat-Panel Chest

Contemporary Chest

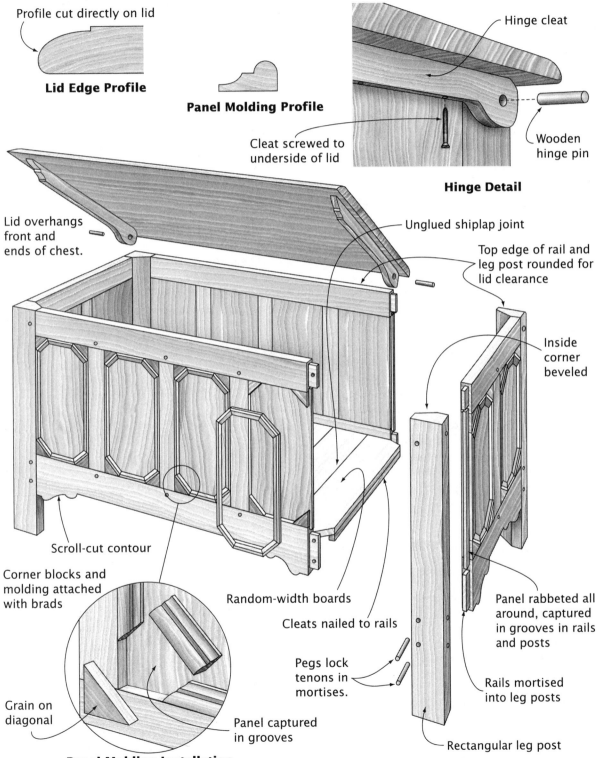

Profile cut directly on lid

Lid Edge Profile

Panel Molding Profile

Hinge cleat

Cleat screwed to
underside of lid

Wooden
hinge pin

Hinge Detail

Lid overhangs
front and
ends of chest.

Unglued shiplap joint

Top edge of rail and
leg post rounded for
lid clearance

Inside
corner
beveled

Scroll-cut contour

Corner blocks and
molding attached
with brads

Random-width boards

Cleats nailed to rails

Panel rabbeted all
around, captured
in grooves in rails
and posts

Rails mortised
into leg posts

Pegs lock
tenons in
mortises.

Grain on
diagonal

Panel captured
in grooves

Rectangular leg post

Panel Molding Installation

CHEST
OF DRAWERS

41½" 18⅞"

41⅞"

the years. Look at the archetype: That's it! About 3½ feet tall, 3 to 3½ feet wide. Three or four drawers, graduated in height, each extending the full width of the case. Often two half-width drawers at the top, in place of that fourth full-width drawer. The top overhangs the front and sides just a little. Some sort of base or feet raise the case a half-foot or so off the floor.

The example shown might be labeled as Shaker-inspired or country. The stylistic embellishments are nil. The attraction lies in the proportions and workmanship.

A case fitted with drawers is the basis for dozens of furniture forms. What it is is a chest of drawers, sure. But that leads to dressers and bureaus, to tall chests and chests-on-chests, to desks and secretaries, to file cabinets and kitchen cabinets, to linen presses and every other piece of furniture that has more than a couple of drawers in it.

Despite there being so many variations, the configuration of what people call a "chest of drawers" has been surprisingly consistent over

PLANS

Abram, Norm. "Chest of Drawers," *American Woodworker,* Vol. IV, No. 2 (March/April 1989), pp. 16–23. Norm lays out the construction of a basic chest of drawers.

•

Lynch, Carlyle. "Hepplewhite Chest of Drawers," *The Best of Fine Woodworking: Traditional Furniture Projects.* Newtown, CT: The Taunton Press, 1991. A Lynch measured drawing, supported by parts list and construction notes.

DESIGN
VARIATIONS

Here are just three of the possible chest-of-drawer style variations. All three of these chests are of the same overall dimensions as the archetype, but the details are different. The Queen Anne chest has bracket feet, period bail pulls and matching keyhole escutcheons, and moldings around the bottom and just under the top. The Federal chest has all full-width drawers, French feet, a profile molded on the top's edge, bail pulls with oval backing plates, and modest escutcheons. The William and Mary chest has post legs, a heavy base molding, molding around the top and around the drawers, and teardrop pulls.

Queen Anne Chest   **Federal Chest**   **William and Mary Chest**

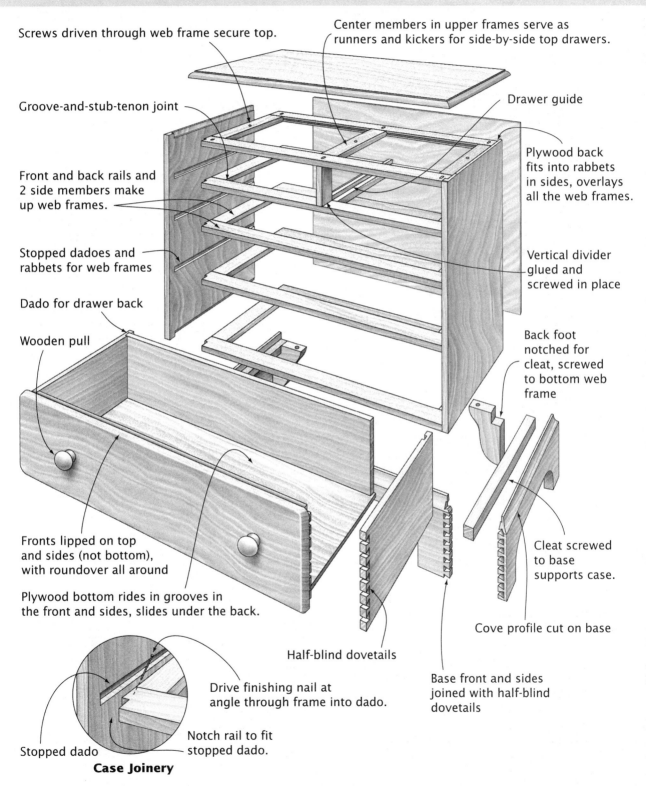

Screws driven through web frame secure top.

Center members in upper frames serve as runners and kickers for side-by-side top drawers.

Groove-and-stub-tenon joint

Drawer guide

Front and back rails and 2 side members make up web frames.

Plywood back fits into rabbets in sides, overlays all the web frames.

Stopped dadoes and rabbets for web frames

Vertical divider glued and screwed in place

Dado for drawer back

Wooden pull

Back foot notched for cleat, screwed to bottom web frame

Cleat screwed to base supports case.

Fronts lipped on top and sides (not bottom), with roundover all around

Plywood bottom rides in grooves in the front and sides, slides under the back.

Cove profile cut on base

Half-blind dovetails

Base front and sides joined with half-blind dovetails

Drive finishing nail at angle through frame into dado.

Stopped dado

Notch rail to fit stopped dado.

Case Joinery

CHEST-ON-FRAME

Highboy, Cellarette

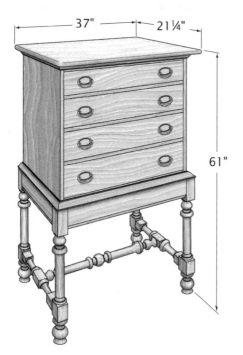

37" 21¼"

61"

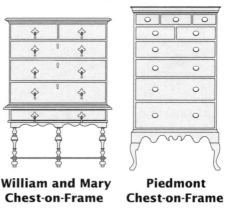

DESIGN VARIATIONS Chests-on-frames vary as widely as the chests that form the top portion and the table-like frames that support them. For balance between the frame and the comparatively heavy appearance of the chest, the frame is usually more robust than that of a comparably sized table. Hence, the Contemporary Silver Chest appears delicate, even though the frame would appear chunky if topped by a tabletop instead of a chest.

Contemporary Silver Chest

William and Mary Chest-on-Frame

Piedmont Chest-on-Frame

Look long and deeply enough, and the lines between furniture types become somewhat fuzzy. When, for example, does a chest with feet become a chest-on-frame? The answer, for our purposes at least, is when the feet or legs are joined to each other with aprons and/or stretchers. In other words, a chest-on-frame is a chest on a topless table.

The chest portion may be a chest of drawers, as in the typical highboy, or a box with a lid, as in the typical cellarette. The topless table may be dining-table height, as in many silver chests on frames, or closer to coffee-table height in many highboy examples. Some, in fact, are so low that it's not easy to tell at a glance whether they meet our "apron" criterion for being a chest-on-frame. Many chests-on-frames include a drawer in the front apron of the "table" portion, just as tables do.

Predictably, construction details for the chest portion are identical to details for chests, and details for the table portion are identical to details for tables.

PLANS

Erickson, Ben. "Silver Chest," *Cabinetry*, edited by Robert A. Yoder. Emmaus, PA: Rodale Press, 1992. Comprehensive drawings and step-by-step building procedures. Dovetailed case with 3 dovetailed drawers, pull-out shelf, tapered legs.

●

Lynch, Carlyle. "Cellaret," *Classic Furniture Projects from Carlyle Lynch*. Emmaus, PA: Rodale Press, 1992. Drawings and instructions for reproducing a 1760 inlaid Hepplewhite cellarette with drawer and partitions for 12 bottles.

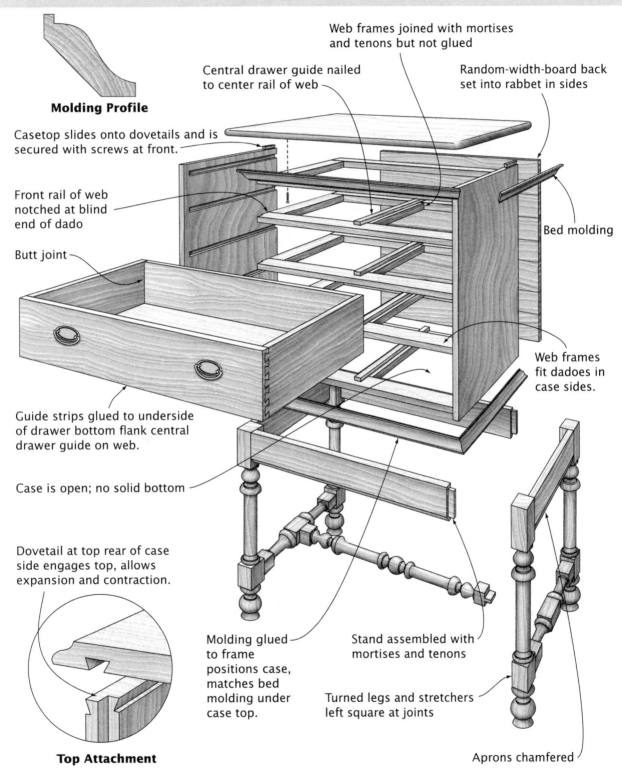

Molding Profile

Web frames joined with mortises and tenons but not glued

Central drawer guide nailed to center rail of web

Random-width-board back set into rabbet in sides

Casetop slides onto dovetails and is secured with screws at front.

Front rail of web notched at blind end of dado

Bed molding

Butt joint

Guide strips glued to underside of drawer bottom flank central drawer guide on web.

Web frames fit dadoes in case sides.

Case is open; no solid bottom

Dovetail at top rear of case side engages top, allows expansion and contraction.

Molding glued to frame positions case, matches bed molding under case top.

Stand assembled with mortises and tenons

Turned legs and stretchers left square at joints

Top Attachment

Aprons chamfered

CHEST-ON-CHEST

Tallboy

73"

19¾"   45"

A relative of the highboy, born at roughly the same time, the chest-on-chest lacks the highboy's graceful legs and skirts; but in turn, it has more room and a sturdier structure. It literally is two chests of drawers, one set atop the other. Typically, the upper case is "captured" by the waist molding attached to the lower case, but seldom are the two cases literally attached.

The example presented here is a contemporary rendition in the "traditional" style. It has ogee bracket feet and base, waist, and cornice moldings, and the lower case has fluted corner posts. Overall, it has six full-width drawers and five smaller ones. The construction, like the design, is traditional.

This chest-on-chest is rather subdued compared to extreme examples produced in the Chippendale and Federal eras. The size of such pieces usually is imposing. Freighting one with block-front or bombé casework, with pilasters, with a heavily carved broken pediment and enormous flame or bouquet finials or even urns and statuary pushes it beyond imposing to monumental (which is only a few synonyms removed from monstrous).

DESIGN VARIATIONS

Empire Chest-on-Chest

Low Traditional Chest-on-Chest

While imposing size and design seem to be hallmarks of the chest-on-chest, these are not requirements. Both chests shown here are subdued in their designs.

The Empire piece represents an interesting challenge to the builder, with its frame-and-panel construction and the turned half-columns applied to the face. The top drawer has a false front suggesting it is three drawers. These design motifs are handsome but hardly flamboyant. The chest is tall, however.

The low chest is in the same "traditional" style as the archetype. But both the upper and lower cases have fewer drawers, reducing their individual and thus combined heights. As is appropriate, the scale of the cornice is reduced along with the chest's height.

PLANS

Abram, Norm. "Chest on Chest," *Classics from The New Yankee Workshop.* Boston: Little, Brown, & Co., 1990. A traditional design of sound construction from America's favorite woodworker.

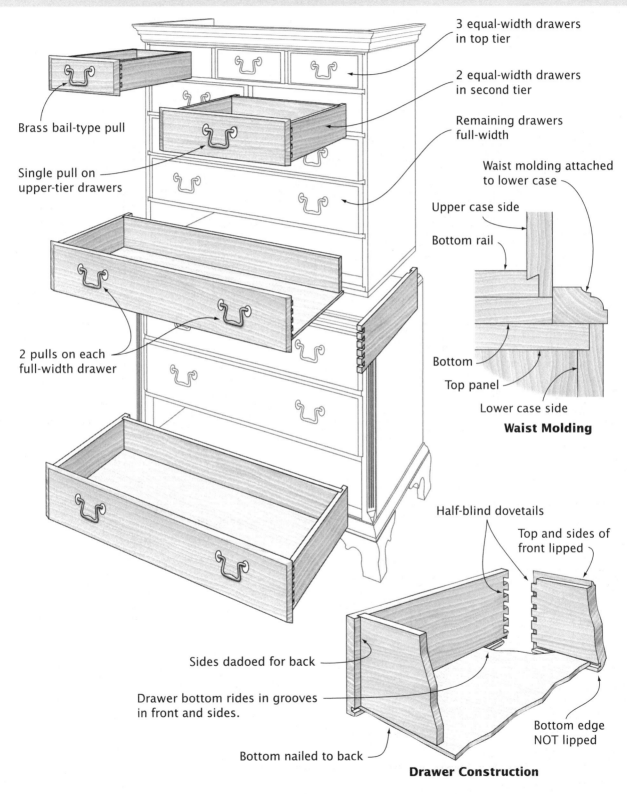

3 equal-width drawers in top tier

2 equal-width drawers in second tier

Remaining drawers full-width

Brass bail-type pull

Single pull on upper-tier drawers

Waist molding attached to lower case

Upper case side

Bottom rail

Bottom

Top panel

Lower case side

Waist Molding

2 pulls on each full-width drawer

Half-blind dovetails

Top and sides of front lipped

Sides dadoed for back

Drawer bottom rides in grooves in front and sides.

Bottom edge NOT lipped

Bottom nailed to back

Drawer Construction

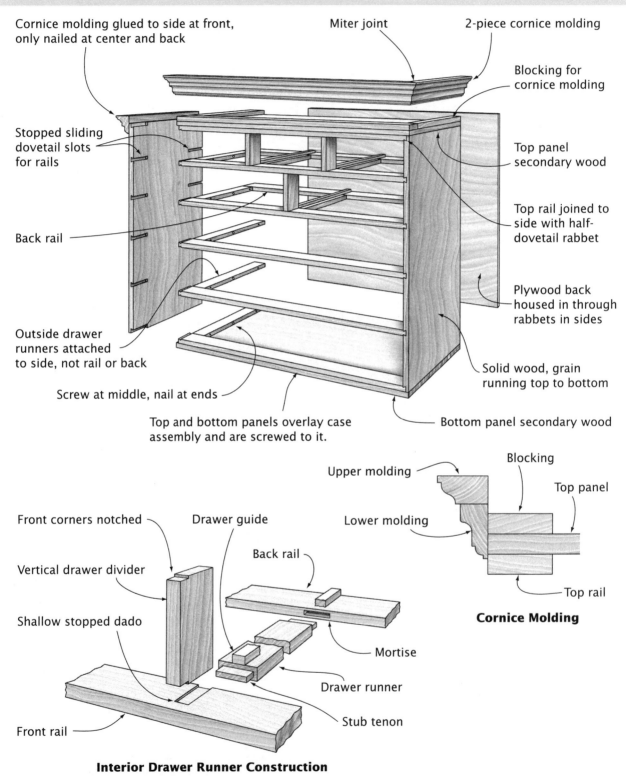

Cornice molding glued to side at front, only nailed at center and back

Miter joint

2-piece cornice molding

Blocking for cornice molding

Stopped sliding dovetail slots for rails

Top panel secondary wood

Top rail joined to side with half-dovetail rabbet

Back rail

Plywood back housed in through rabbets in sides

Outside drawer runners attached to side, not rail or back

Screw at middle, nail at ends

Solid wood, grain running top to bottom

Top and bottom panels overlay case assembly and are screwed to it.

Bottom panel secondary wood

Upper molding

Blocking

Top panel

Lower molding

Top rail

Cornice Molding

Front corners notched

Drawer guide

Vertical drawer divider

Back rail

Shallow stopped dado

Mortise

Drawer runner

Front rail

Stub tenon

Interior Drawer Runner Construction

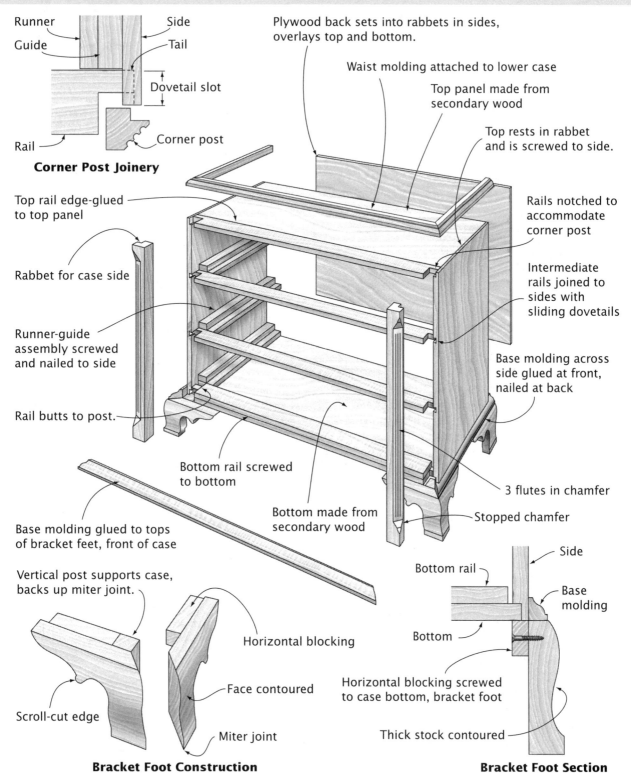

Corner Post Joinery

Runner

Guide

Side

Tail

Dovetail slot

Rail

Corner post

Plywood back sets into rabbets in sides, overlays top and bottom.

Waist molding attached to lower case

Top panel made from secondary wood

Top rests in rabbet and is screwed to side.

Top rail edge-glued to top panel

Rabbet for case side

Runner-guide assembly screwed and nailed to side

Rail butts to post.

Rails notched to accommodate corner post

Intermediate rails joined to sides with sliding dovetails

Base molding across side glued at front, nailed at back

3 flutes in chamfer

Stopped chamfer

Bottom rail screwed to bottom

Bottom made from secondary wood

Base molding glued to tops of bracket feet, front of case

Vertical post supports case, backs up miter joint.

Horizontal blocking

Face contoured

Scroll-cut edge

Miter joint

Bracket Foot Construction

Bottom rail

Side

Base molding

Bottom

Horizontal blocking screwed to case bottom, bracket foot

Thick stock contoured

Bracket Foot Section

TALL
CHEST

69⅝"

19⅞"

45¾"

W hat makes a chest of drawers a "tall chest?" Having the uppermost drawers at eye level. At just under 6 feet, the chest shown here is clearly a *tall* chest for most people.

But also, the tall chest has only a single case. This differentiates it from the "Chest-on-Chest" on page 238 and the "Highboy" on page 256.

The tall chest is not typical of any formal style period. Rather, it seems to be a vernacular piece, built by cabinetmakers working outside the formal style centers—Boston, Newport, New York, Philadelphia, and Charleston. Some creative and attractive tall chests were built in the North Carolina piedmont, for example. The archetype is based on a selection of tall chests built in Chester County, Pennsylvania, early in the 19th century.

Regardless of where they were made, tall chests typically have a stack of four full-width drawers of graduated height, topped by an arrangement of smaller drawers. The three-over-two arrangement shown is the most common. The smaller a drawer is, the easier it is to open and close. Reducing the size of the highest drawers makes the chest easier to use.

DESIGN VARIATIONS

The focus of design variation often is on the basic form, on scale and proportions, and on ornamentation. But more subtle variations can have a significant impact on the appearance of a furniture piece.

The archetype tall chest is constructed with frame-and-panel side assemblies. There's a large panel and a small panel, with the rail separating them positioned flush with the top edge of the uppermost full-width drawer.

What if the side were changed? The drawings below present the archetype chest with three other side designs. The first has one large panel. The second variant has two equal-sized panels. The third variant eliminates the frame-and-panel construction in favor of solid-panel case construction. How does each compare with the archetype to your eye?

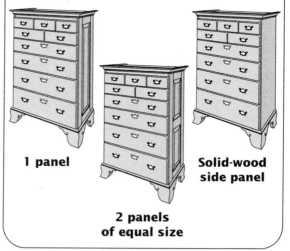

1 panel

2 panels of equal size

Solid-wood side panel

PLANS

Engler, Nick, and Mary Jane Favorite. "Chest of Drawers," *American Country Furniture.* Emmaus, PA: Rodale Press, 1990. Plans, directions, and parts list for Shaker-inspired chest that's just over 5 feet tall, with 6 ungraduated, full-width drawers.

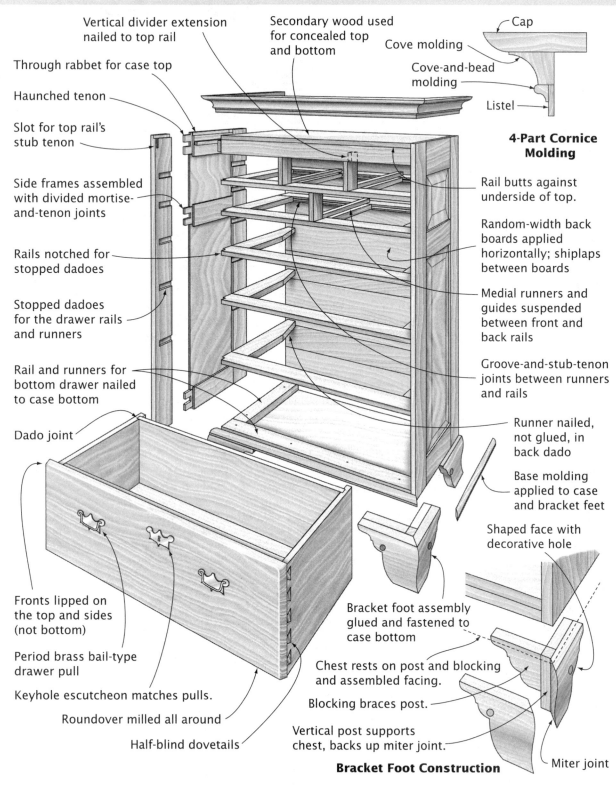

Vertical divider extension nailed to top rail

Through rabbet for case top

Haunched tenon

Slot for top rail's stub tenon

Side frames assembled with divided mortise-and-tenon joints

Rails notched for stopped dadoes

Stopped dadoes for the drawer rails and runners

Rail and runners for bottom drawer nailed to case bottom

Dado joint

Fronts lipped on the top and sides (not bottom)

Period brass bail-type drawer pull

Keyhole escutcheon matches pulls.

Roundover milled all around

Half-blind dovetails

Secondary wood used for concealed top and bottom

Cap

Cove molding

Cove-and-bead molding

Listel

4-Part Cornice Molding

Rail butts against underside of top.

Random-width back boards applied horizontally; shiplaps between boards

Medial runners and guides suspended between front and back rails

Groove-and-stub-tenon joints between runners and rails

Runner nailed, not glued, in back dado

Base molding applied to case and bracket feet

Shaped face with decorative hole

Bracket foot assembly glued and fastened to case bottom

Chest rests on post and blocking and assembled facing.

Blocking braces post.

Vertical post supports chest, backs up miter joint.

Miter joint

Bracket Foot Construction

DRESSER

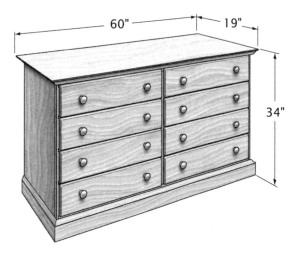

60"   19"

34"

PLANS

"Cherry Dresser," *Woodsmith*, No. 58 (August 1988), pp. 10–15. Small dresser with 2 side-by-side drawers over 2 full-width drawers, frame-and-panel construction, solid base. Presented in exhaustive step-by-step detail.

●

Gottshall, Franklin H. "Salem Chest of Drawers," *Making Antique Furniture Reproductions.* New York: Dover Publications, 1971. This 4-drawer Chippendale piece has fluted quarter columns and bracket feet. Plans and directions are what you should expect from a long-time high school shop teacher.

●

Moser, Thomas. "Eight-Drawer Sidechest" and "Six-Drawer Sidechest," *Measured Shop Drawings for American Furniture.* New York: Sterling Publishing Co., 1985. These dressers have side-by-side banks of drawers. Construction drawings only; no text and cutting lists.

Dresser is a colloquial name for a low chest of drawers, almost always having a mirror. It's likely the name derives from the fact that people dress in front of it. You pull clothing from the drawers, put it on, then check how you look in the mirror.

The dresser shown here would be set against a wall under a large mirror. Its two banks of uniformly sized drawers provide a basic structure for grouping the many clothing items every person owns.

In construction terms, the piece is quite straightforward solid-panel case construction, with sides and a center divider joined with web frames. The case rests on the floor and has a simple applied base molding.

DESIGN VARIATIONS The mirror is important to a dresser, for without one, you can't keep an eye on your appearance as you dress. It need not be attached to the dresser, however. Both the archetype dresser and the example at the right have separate wall-hung mirrors. This makes the dresser easier to construct and allows a big mirror to be used.

Both the cottage and Arts-and-Crafts dressers shown here have attached mirrors supported by brackets. On the cottage dresser, the mirror is fixed, while on the other it can be tipped on pivots located at the midpoint of the mirror sides.

Cottage Dresser   **Arts-and-Crafts Dresser**   **Dresser with Separate Mirror**

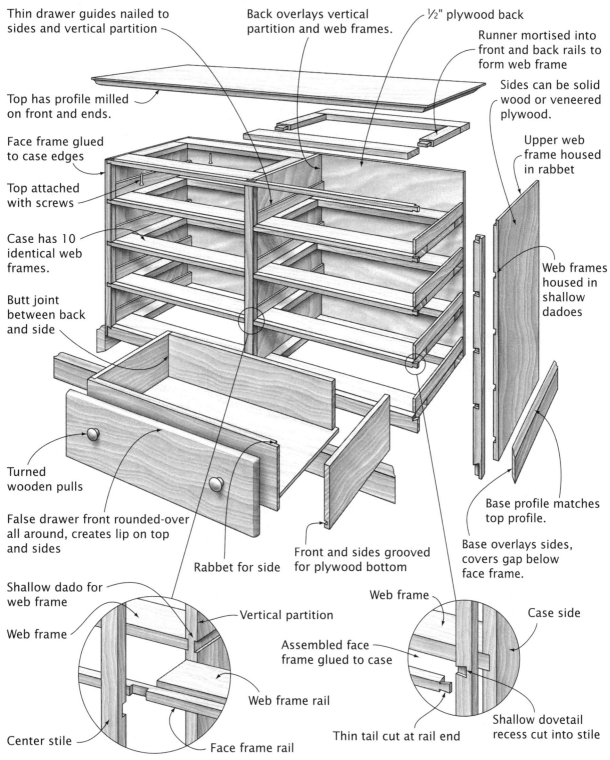

Thin drawer guides nailed to sides and vertical partition

Back overlays vertical partition and web frames.

½" plywood back

Runner mortised into front and back rails to form web frame

Top has profile milled on front and ends.

Sides can be solid wood or veneered plywood.

Face frame glued to case edges

Upper web frame housed in rabbet

Top attached with screws

Case has 10 identical web frames.

Web frames housed in shallow dadoes

Butt joint between back and side

Turned wooden pulls

False drawer front rounded-over all around, creates lip on top and sides

Rabbet for side

Front and sides grooved for plywood bottom

Base profile matches top profile.

Base overlays sides, covers gap below face frame.

Shallow dado for web frame

Web frame

Web frame

Vertical partition

Assembled face frame glued to case

Case side

Center stile

Web frame rail

Face frame rail

Thin tail cut at rail end

Shallow dovetail recess cut into stile

Face Frame Cross-Lap Joint

Dovetail Half-Lap Joint

BUREAU

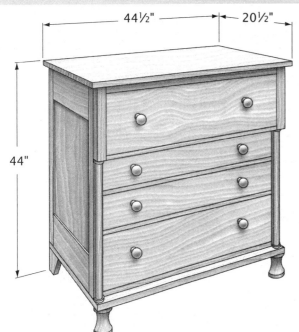

44½" 20½"

44"

PLANS

Richey, Jim. "Post-and-Panel Chests," _Fine Woodworking_ on Making Period Furniture. Newtown, CT: The Taunton Press, 1985. Short article with a good exploded view, sound construction guidelines, but almost no dimensions or other specifics.

●

Shea, John G. "Chest of Drawers," _Making Authentic Pennsylvania Dutch Furniture._ New York: Dover Publications, 1980. Measured drawings of a country bureau; no directions.

"bureau" as a particular form or style, it is fair to define it as a bedroom chest of drawers of low to medium height.

The bureau shown here is typical of those built in the mid-1800s. It's a post-and-panel assembly with no solid bottom. Instead, it sets on an open mitered base frame to which turned front feet and bracket back feet are attached. The drawer dividers and the runner-guide assemblies are mortised into the posts.

Features typical of Empire-style bureaus are the large, protruding top drawer and the turned half-column detail on the front post. In other styles, the top drawers are the smallest.

The bureau as a bedroom chest of drawers is very much an American thing. In France and England, a bureau is what we would call a slant-front desk. The name derived from the French word _bureau,_ for a woolen material used to cover writing desks.

The term was widely adopted in the 19th century. Though it is tough to distinquish

DESIGN VARIATIONS

To further define "bureau," here are three more examples. What they have in common is modest stature, with the tallest topping out at 52+ inches. A bureau is roughly chest high, in other words. To go with their modest stature, the country and the contemporary pieces share a modest appearance. There's no flashy detailing on either one.

In contrast is the flamboyant Empire bureau with, among other details, its awkward C-scroll feet and cross-banded veneer on the lower drawer fronts. It's clumsy but still a bureau.

Country Bureau   **Empire Bureau**   **Contemporary Bureau**

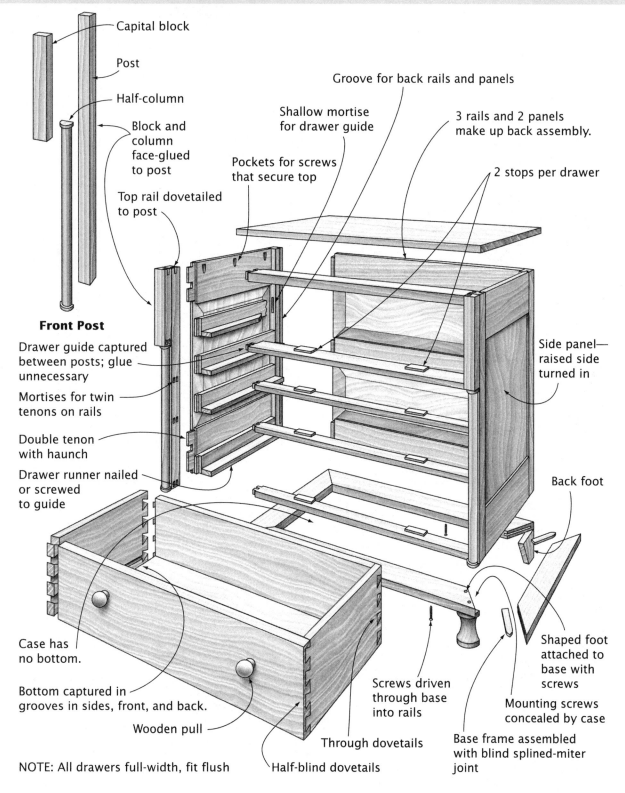

Capital block

Post

Half-column

Block and column face-glued to post

Top rail dovetailed to post

Shallow mortise for drawer guide

Pockets for screws that secure top

Groove for back rails and panels

3 rails and 2 panels make up back assembly.

2 stops per drawer

Side panel— raised side turned in

Front Post

Drawer guide captured between posts; glue unnecessary

Mortises for twin tenons on rails

Double tenon with haunch

Drawer runner nailed or screwed to guide

Back foot

Case has no bottom.

Bottom captured in grooves in sides, front, and back.

Wooden pull

Screws driven through base into rails

Through dovetails

Half-blind dovetails

Shaped foot attached to base with screws

Mounting screws concealed by case

Base frame assembled with blind splined-miter joint

NOTE: All drawers full-width, fit flush

BOMBÉ CHEST

Kettle Chest

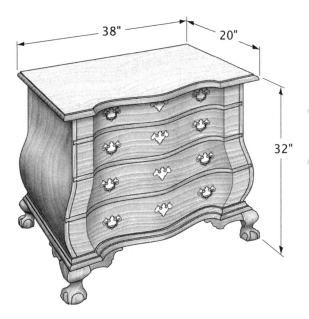

38" 20"

32"

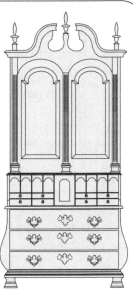

DESIGN VARIATIONS

The bombé form is found on chests of drawers, chests-on-chests, desks with pull-out writing surfaces, and desk-bookcases. In all cases the "bulge" is found only on the lower portion, where it adds visual mass near the floor, and in all cases this bulge portion is fitted with drawers.

Not all bombé furniture combined the bombé shape with serpentine drawer fronts. The compound curves resulting from combining the bombé shape with the serpentine shape mark the pinnacle of the form.

The case sides of earlier examples were shaped only on the outside; the drawers therefore had straight sides, as in the bombé desk shown.

Bombé Desk

N o drawing, or even photograph, can ever do justice to a bombé chest—you must see a fine example in a museum to appreciate fully the spectacular patterns of grain that result from carving these sweeping curves into solid, 3-inch-thick mahogany. This is furniture at its richest, and those who commissioned it were, of necessity, society's richest.

The sides, the drawer fronts, and much of the supporting structure of these 18th-century masterpieces were often shaped from a single, long, thick plank in order to display consistent patterns of grain throughout. Nearly two-thirds of this expensive, imported wood wound up as chips on the shop floor. And the cost of materials was only the beginning of the expense. The labor and skill required for shaping the parts, and then of joining the curved pieces with angled and curved dovetails, went far beyond the requirements of conventional furniture made up of flat surfaces and straight lines. It's fair to say that in skill, cost, and final appearance, a bombé chest compares to a conventional chest much like a fine yacht compares to a dinghy.

Examples with coopered sides, and later examples using veneer, miss the mark.

PLANS

Patterson, Lance. "Boston Bombé Chest," *Fine Woodworking* on *Making Period Furniture*. Newtown, CT: The Taunton Press, 1985. Drawings and overall procedure including bench-top jig for shaping drawers and drawer rails so they match.

Salomonsky, Verna Cook. "Plate 72: Low Chest of Drawers," *Masterpieces of Furniture Design*. New York: Dover Publications, 1953. Critical dimensions only of a museum piece upon which the Patterson plans (above) were partially based.

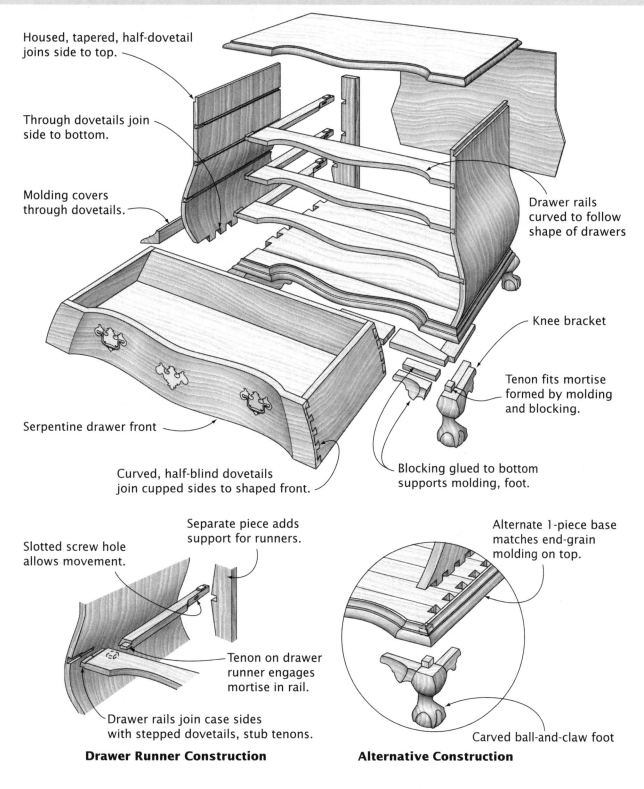

Housed, tapered, half-dovetail joins side to top.

Through dovetails join side to bottom.

Molding covers through dovetails.

Serpentine drawer front

Curved, half-blind dovetails join cupped sides to shaped front.

Drawer rails curved to follow shape of drawers

Knee bracket

Tenon fits mortise formed by molding and blocking.

Blocking glued to bottom supports molding, foot.

Slotted screw hole allows movement.

Separate piece adds support for runners.

Tenon on drawer runner engages mortise in rail.

Drawer rails join case sides with stepped dovetails, stub tenons.

Drawer Runner Construction

Alternate 1-piece base matches end-grain molding on top.

Carved ball-and-claw foot

Alternative Construction

SERPENTINE-FRONT CHEST

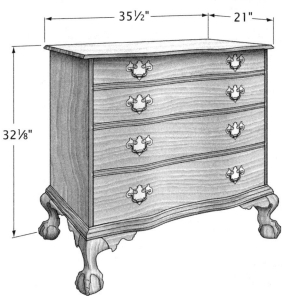

35½" 21"

32⅛"

the block-front and the bombé forms) became signature forms of the style.

When the archetype was built, the chest certainly represented sculpture for the craftsman. Forming the top and each drawer divider, undulating though they were, was straightforward. But each drawer front began as a thick plank. The shape was worked into it with adze and inshave and gouges, then smoothed with compass plane and scraper.

The undulating facade is the first thing about this chest that you see. And that's exactly what the cabinetmaker had in mind.

The curve sculpted into the drawer fronts and base molding and cut into the drawer dividers and top gives extraordinary depth to the chest. The prototype—created during the Chippendale era—produced a paradigm shift of the first order, and chests like this (along with

PLANS

Margon, Lester. "Mahogany and Satinwood Chest of Drawers," *More American Furniture Treasures.* New York: Architectural Book Publishing Co., 1971. Measured drawing of a Hepplewhite reverse-serpentine chest; you provide the engineering.

●

Salomonsky, Verna Cook. "Plate 73: Chest of Drawers," *Masterpieces of Furniture Design.* New York: Dover Publications, 1953. Measured drawing only of a serpentine-front chest from the 1760s.

DESIGN VARIATIONS

Originally, back in the Chippendale era, there were serpentine and reverse-serpentine forms. In the former, the curve is concave at the pulls and convex in the center, as seen in the two outer chests below. The archetype (above) displays the reverse-serpentine curve, with a convex shape at the pulls and a concave shape at the center. Somewhat later, during the Federal period, the simple bowfront form appeared.

An interesting sidelight here is that, unlike the block-front and bombé forms, the serpentine-front form transcended the Chippendale era. It was widely used in Federal chests, as you can see. And even today, it is used in contemporary designs, albeit primarily in simple bowfront and hollow-front configurations only. The serpentine and reverse-serpentine, which would be relatively easy to produce on the band saw, are used primarily in reproductions.

Serpentine-Front Federal Chest

Bow-Front Federal Chest

Serpentine-Front Chippendale Chest

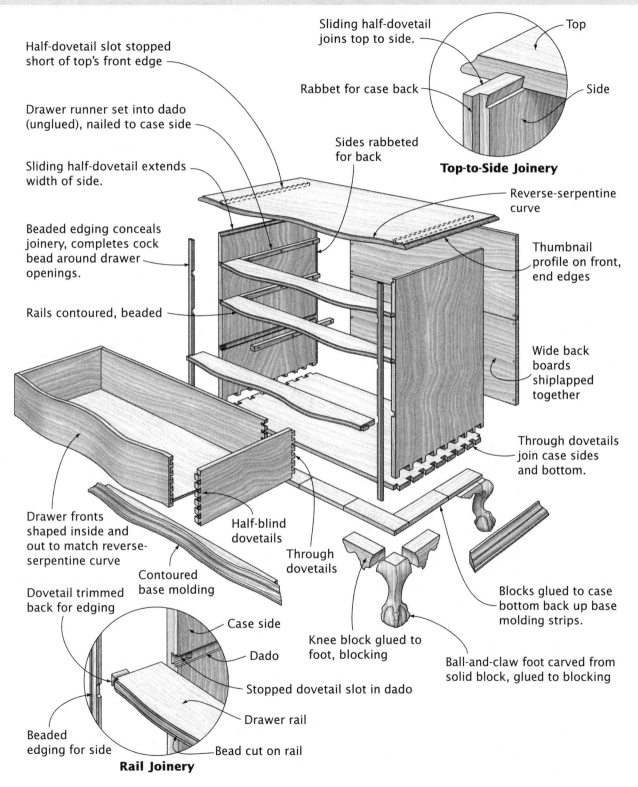

Half-dovetail slot stopped short of top's front edge

Drawer runner set into dado (unglued), nailed to case side

Sliding half-dovetail extends width of side.

Beaded edging conceals joinery, completes cock bead around drawer openings.

Rails contoured, beaded

Drawer fronts shaped inside and out to match reverse-serpentine curve

Dovetail trimmed back for edging

Contoured base molding

Beaded edging for side

Rail Joinery

Case side

Dado

Stopped dovetail slot in dado

Drawer rail

Bead cut on rail

Half-blind dovetails

Through dovetails

Knee block glued to foot, blocking

Sliding half-dovetail joins top to side.

Rabbet for case back

Top-to-Side Joinery

Top

Side

Sides rabbeted for back

Reverse-serpentine curve

Thumbnail profile on front, end edges

Wide back boards shiplapped together

Through dovetails join case sides and bottom.

Blocks glued to case bottom back up base molding strips.

Ball-and-claw foot carved from solid block, glued to blocking

BLOCK-FRONT
CHEST

38½" 23½"

34½"

been traced to specific New England regions; but all block-front pieces exhibit an undulating facade composed of two convex columns, or blocks, flanking a concave column. In some pieces, the contour is exhibited in the base molding and the top. In others, like the chest of drawers shown here, the blocks terminate with exquisite shell or fan carvings.

PLANS

Gottshall, Franklin H. "Blockfront Chest-on-Chest," *Making Antique Furniture Reproductions.* New York: Dover Publications, 1971. Drawings, some text, a cutting list. If you've mastered the skills needed for this demanding level of working, these plans may be enough to go on.

•

Schultz, E. F. "Building Blockfronts," *Fine Woodworking on Making Period Furniture.* Newtown, CT: The Taunton Press, 1985. Measured drawings of 2 different block-fronts accompany a short article with some very useful detail drawings.

Block-front case construction is among the most demanding work a cabinetmaker will ever face. The joinery is difficult, to be sure, but it is the carving that takes the breath away. Each drawer front is carved from one very thick piece of wood—usually mahogany.

The original block-fronts date to the late 18th century, but the form continues to be reproduced. Three well-defined variations have

DESIGN VARIATIONS

Multifaceted variation is found in the block-front design. On the one hand, there is variety in the way characteristic elements were combined. On the other, we see the design applied to different case forms. The chest of drawers may have been the most common and thus the most familiar of the block-front pieces. But there exist 18th-century slant-front desks, desk-and-bookcase pieces, and even more elaborate chests-on-chests that are block-front designs.

The Newport chest-on-chest shown is considered by some to be *the* finest example of American cabinetry. The upper case has five full-width drawers and three small side-by-side top drawers. The blocked sections of the upper case have fan carvings at top and bottom.

In the Connecticut slant-front desk shown, each block terminates in a squared-off carved arch.

Connecticut Slant-Front Desk

Newport Chest-on-Chest

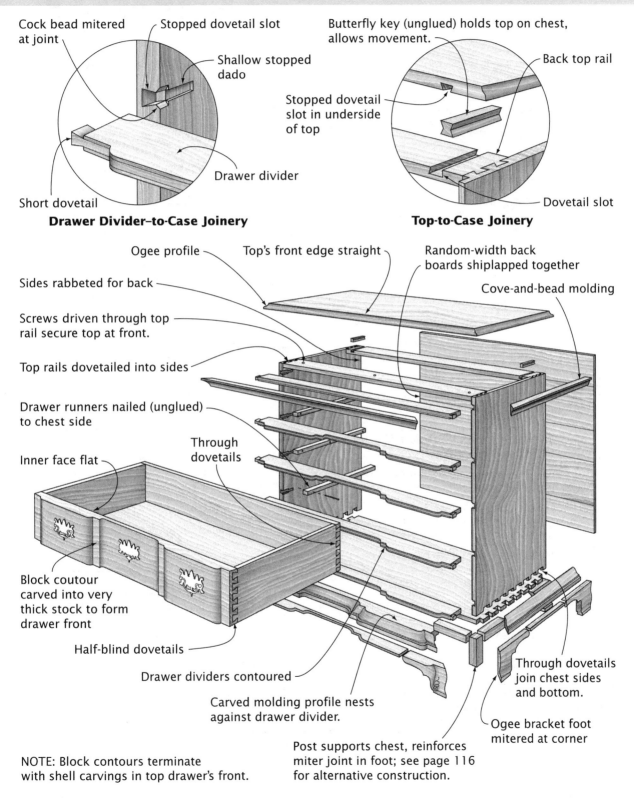

Drawer Divider–to-Case Joinery

Cock bead mitered at joint

Stopped dovetail slot

Shallow stopped dado

Drawer divider

Short dovetail

Top-to-Case Joinery

Butterfly key (unglued) holds top on chest, allows movement.

Back top rail

Stopped dovetail slot in underside of top

Dovetail slot

Ogee profile

Top's front edge straight

Random-width back boards shiplapped together

Sides rabbeted for back

Cove-and-bead molding

Screws driven through top rail secure top at front.

Top rails dovetailed into sides

Drawer runners nailed (unglued) to chest side

Through dovetails

Inner face flat

Block coutour carved into very thick stock to form drawer front

Half-blind dovetails

Drawer dividers contoured

Carved molding profile nests against drawer divider.

Through dovetails join chest sides and bottom.

Ogee bracket foot mitered at corner

Post supports chest, reinforces miter joint in foot; see page 116 for alternative construction.

NOTE: Block contours terminate with shell carvings in top drawer's front.

LOWBOY

Dressing Table, Side Table

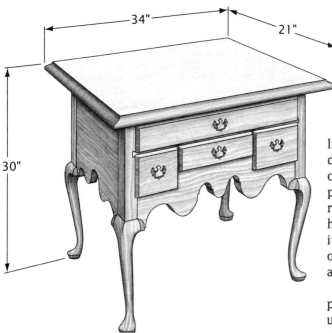

34"
21"
30"

Placed in a bedroom, the highboy held linens and clothes, while the lowboy (or dressing table, as it was likely to have been called in the 18th century) contained personal items such as combs, jewelry, hair ribbons, and cosmetics. Often, a mirror was hung above the lowboy, a chair set in front of it. But the lowboy was attractive and capable of serving as a side table, a serving table, or a writing desk as easily as a dressing table.

Because lowboys were intended to be placed against a wall, their backs were usually made of a secondary wood—pine or chestnut—and the edge profile molded on the front and sides of the top didn't extend across the back.

The lowboy is a very distinctive type of dressing or side table. It is primarily a William and Mary/Queen Anne/Chippendale form and is almost invariably associated with the highboy.

When designed and built as part of a set, back in the 18th century, the lowboy was a scaled-down version of the highboy's base, with the same basic proportions and all the same features. The arrangement of its drawers varied, but one or two tiers was usual. Deep drawers at the sides of the lower tier often extended below a shallow drawer in the center.

PLANS

Bird, Lonnie. "Philadelphia Lowboy," *American Woodworker,* No. 38 (June 1994), pp. 46–51.

•

Lynch, Carlyle. "Queen Anne Lowboy," *Classic Furniture Project from Carlyle Lynch.* Emmaus, PA: Rodale Press, 1992.

•

Vandal, Norman. "Dressing Table," *Queen Anne Furniture.* Newtown, CT: The Taunton Press, 1990.

DESIGN VARIATIONS

The range of lowboy designs is impossible to convey with only a couple of examples. The southern-style lowboy shown at right has a single tier of drawers and a skirt that, compared to that of the archetype, is sedate. The Connecticut lowboy has legs bent only slightly at the knee, a shell carving on the center drawer, acorn drops, and a top with wide overhangs.

Southern-Style Queen Anne Lowboy

Connecticut Lowboy

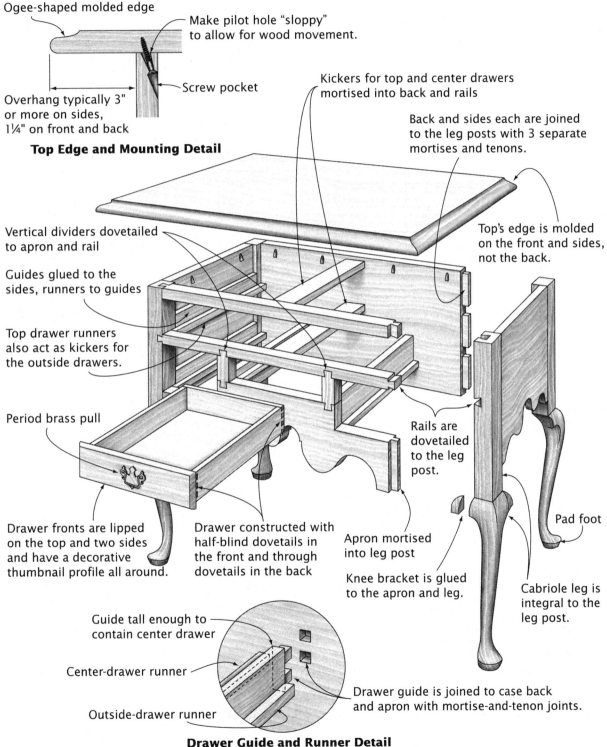

Ogee-shaped molded edge

Make pilot hole "sloppy" to allow for wood movement.

Screw pocket

Overhang typically 3" or more on sides, 1¼" on front and back

Top Edge and Mounting Detail

Kickers for top and center drawers mortised into back and rails

Back and sides each are joined to the leg posts with 3 separate mortises and tenons.

Vertical dividers dovetailed to apron and rail

Guides glued to the sides, runners to guides

Top's edge is molded on the front and sides, not the back.

Top drawer runners also act as kickers for the outside drawers.

Period brass pull

Rails are dovetailed to the leg post.

Drawer fronts are lipped on the top and two sides and have a decorative thumbnail profile all around.

Drawer constructed with half-blind dovetails in the front and through dovetails in the back

Apron mortised into leg post

Pad foot

Knee bracket is glued to the apron and leg.

Cabriole leg is integral to the leg post.

Guide tall enough to contain center drawer

Center-drawer runner

Outside-drawer runner

Drawer guide is joined to case back and apron with mortise-and-tenon joints.

Drawer Guide and Runner Detail
NOTE: See page 109 for alternative drawer constructions.

HIGHBOY

High Chest, High Chest of Drawers, Chest-on-Frame

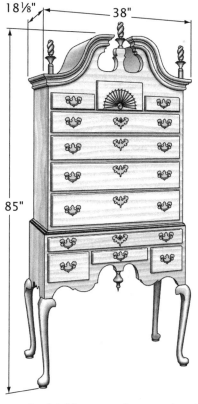

18⅛" 38"

85"

PLANS

Margon, Lester. "Early American Highboy" and "Early Trumpet-Legged Colonial Highboy," *Construction of American Furniture Treasures.* New York: Dover Publications, 1975. 2 different highboys. Good drawings, directions.

Vandal, Norman. "Flat-Top High Chest" and "Bonnet-Top High Chest," *Queen Anne Furniture.* Newtown, CT: The Taunton Press, 1990. Excellent history and plans, essential for anyone interested in building a highboy.

vase-and-trumpet legs joined by scroll-cut stretchers and always a flat-topped chest.

The archetypal highboy is the bonnet-top style with a broken scroll pediment, a Queen Anne innovation. The highboy illustrated has graceful cabriole legs, a high-cut skirt with a single drop, fan carving on the uppermost drawer, and, of course, the bonnet top with a pedestal flame finial and flanking guardian finials. This is high-end furniture making.

The highboy surely must be the single classic piece of American furniture. It is an enormously challenging piece to build and might well be a cabinetmaker's highest achievement.

A form unique to and characteristic of 18th-century America, the earliest examples were in the William and Mary style, with as many as six

DESIGN VARIATIONS From lean and graceful youth to heavy dowager, the highboy traced a familiar evolutionary path. The early forms, which were in the William and Mary style, tended to be stout, ungainly, and not particularly steady. In the form's adolescence, Queen Anne examples displayed carving on drawers and more elegant and sophisticated leg and skirt contours. By the Chippendale era, the highboy had bulked up, displaying a deep lower case perched on short, stout legs, a ponderous bonnet top, and an excess of carving.

Philadelphia Chippendale Highboy

Flat-Topped Highboy

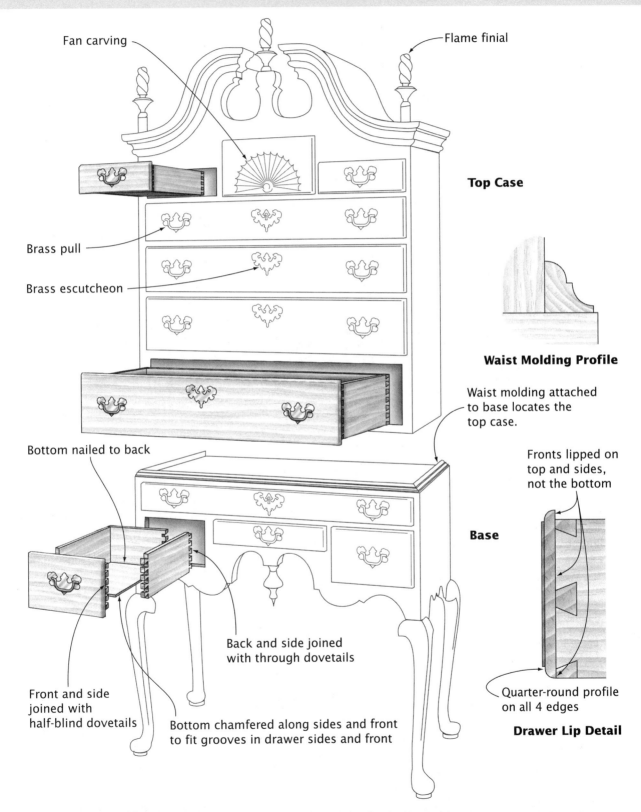

Fan carving

Flame finial

Top Case

Brass pull

Brass escutcheon

Waist Molding Profile

Waist molding attached to base locates the top case.

Bottom nailed to back

Base

Fronts lipped on top and sides, not the bottom

Back and side joined with through dovetails

Front and side joined with half-blind dovetails

Bottom chamfered along sides and front to fit grooves in drawer sides and front

Quarter-round profile on all 4 edges

Drawer Lip Detail

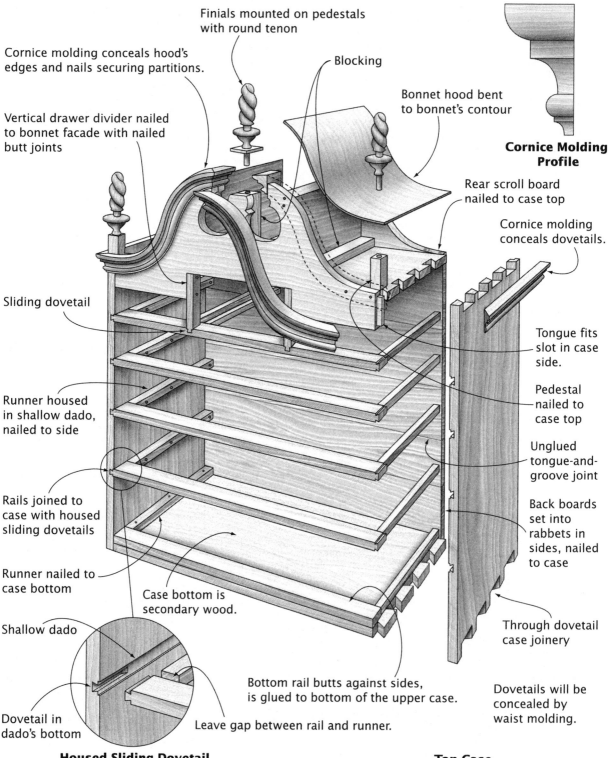

Finials mounted on pedestals with round tenon

Cornice molding conceals hood's edges and nails securing partitions.

Blocking

Bonnet hood bent to bonnet's contour

Cornice Molding Profile

Vertical drawer divider nailed to bonnet facade with nailed butt joints

Rear scroll board nailed to case top

Cornice molding conceals dovetails.

Sliding dovetail

Tongue fits slot in case side.

Pedestal nailed to case top

Runner housed in shallow dado, nailed to side

Unglued tongue-and-groove joint

Rails joined to case with housed sliding dovetails

Back boards set into rabbets in sides, nailed to case

Runner nailed to case bottom

Shallow dado

Case bottom is secondary wood.

Through dovetail case joinery

Dovetail in dado's bottom

Bottom rail butts against sides, is glued to bottom of the upper case.

Leave gap between rail and runner.

Dovetails will be concealed by waist molding.

Housed Sliding Dovetail

Top Case

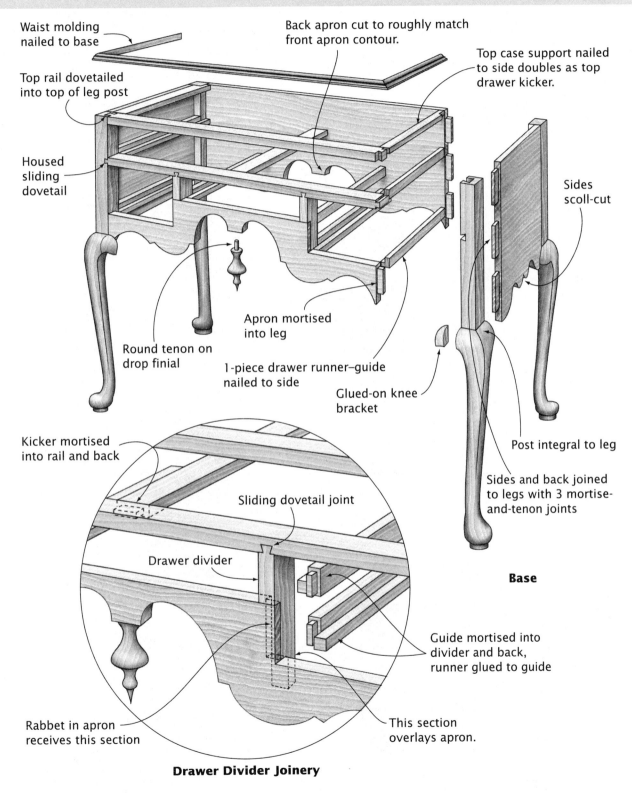

Waist molding nailed to base

Back apron cut to roughly match front apron contour.

Top case support nailed to side doubles as top drawer kicker.

Top rail dovetailed into top of leg post

Housed sliding dovetail

Sides scroll-cut

Round tenon on drop finial

Apron mortised into leg

1-piece drawer runner–guide nailed to side

Glued-on knee bracket

Post integral to leg

Sides and back joined to legs with 3 mortise-and-tenon joints

Base

Kicker mortised into rail and back

Sliding dovetail joint

Drawer divider

Guide mortised into divider and back, runner glued to guide

Rabbet in apron receives this section

This section overlays apron.

Drawer Divider Joinery

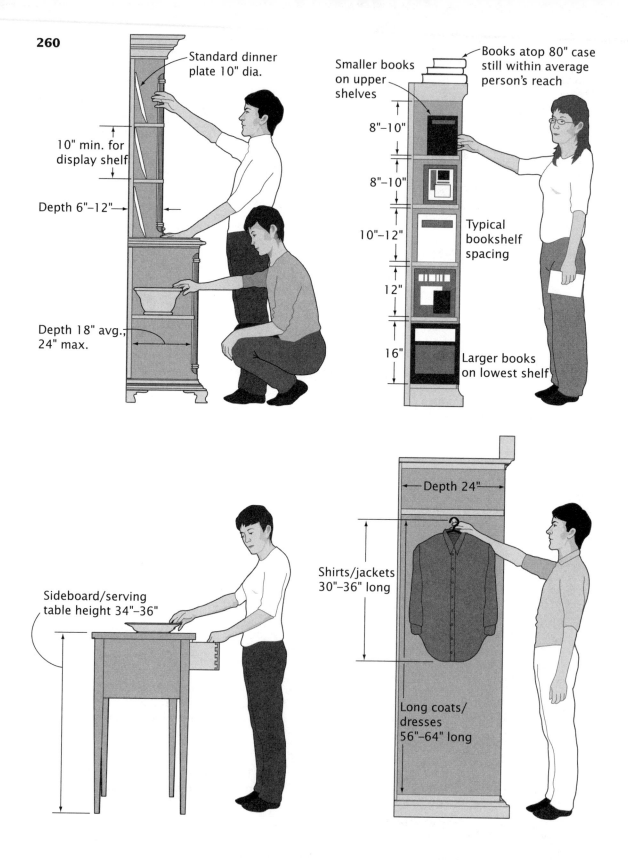

Standard dinner plate 10" dia.

10" min. for display shelf

Depth 6"–12"

Depth 18" avg., 24" max.

Smaller books on upper shelves

Books atop 80" case still within average person's reach

8"–10"

8"–10"

10"–12"

Typical bookshelf spacing

12"

16"

Larger books on lowest shelf

Sideboard/serving table height 34"–36"

Depth 24"

Shirts/jackets 30"–36" long

Long coats/ dresses 56"–64" long

CABINETS

Cabinet is a loose term. It serves as a catchall for an amorphous range of pieces, from simple open shelves to complex breakfronts. The most involved designs incorporate both cupboard space (shelves behind doors, glazed or not) and drawers, and—sometimes—open shelves, too. While there are some size conventions for each type of furniture to guide you, dimensions should be dictated by your particular needs and circumstances. Here are some of the ways in which cabinets are sized to accommodate their use.

WALL-HUNG CUPBOARD: The depth of these cabinets typically is shallow, partly to compensate for having to reach up into them, and partly because large items are seldom stored in them. The maximum depth is 12 inches. For ease of access, the cabinet should be positioned with its highest shelf no more than 80 inches above the floor.

DISPLAY OR CHINA CABINET: Distance between shelves is usually 10 inches or more but should be altered as necessary to accommodate specific items. For ease of access, keep maximum height and depth reasonable—no shelf higher than 80 inches, no shelf deeper than 24 inches.

BOOKCASE: Shelving must fit not only the room but also the books. Generally, shelves are 8 inches deep and 10 inches apart for standard-format books and 12 inches deep and 13 inches apart for larger illustrated books. Keep in mind the average person's reach as you plan the overall height of the bookcase, holding the top shelf at or below 80 inches from the floor.

SIDEBOARD: This is a storage cabinet, but it is also a countertop. The top surface should be at a height convenient for serving food and drink while standing. That means it should be about 36 inches high.

FILE CABINET: Height varies with the number of drawers—28 inches for a two-drawer unit and 52 inches for four drawers. The width is determined by whether the files will be letter-sized or legal-sized. The depth can vary to suit your needs.

WARDROBE: Before houses had closets, people hung their clothes in wardrobes. Because dresses and coats were long, the wardrobe was tall, typically around 6 to 7 feet tall.

WALL SHELF

Hanging Shelf, Display Shelf

25¾"

30"

6⅛"

PLANS

Dunbar, Michael. "Display Shelf," *Federal Furniture.* Newtown, CT: The Taunton Press, 1986. History of and plans for a tiered display shelf from the Federal era.

•

Hylton, Bill. "Hanging Display Shelf," *Country Pine.* Emmaus, PA: Rodale Press, 1995. Detailed plans for a wall-hung shelf with a beaded face frame.

•

Lyons, Richard A. "Wall Shelf," *Making Country Furniture.* Englewood Cliffs, NJ: Prentice-Hall, 1987. Plans for a shelf that can be hung on a wall or set on a counter.

Selecting a single shelf unit to represent all such units is almost painful. If ever a piece of furniture exists in wide variety, it is the lowly wall shelf. The "Design Variations" examples drive this point home.

But they also press upon you the fact that wall shelves are almost always vernacular pieces. Sure, Chippendale's famous pattern book had a "china shelf" or two, but the modest wall shelf is not a hallmark of his or any other style.

The chosen piece meets the criteria for a "model" wall-hung display shelf. It is reasonably typical—no quirky oddball, this shelf. It is utilitarian, it is made with straightforward joinery, but it is also attractive. The shelf sides are shaped in a way that highlights each individual shelf. The overhang of the bottom, stark as it is, adds visual interest. Capping the piece is a simple cornice molding.

Hung on the wall or set on a counter, these shelves can exhibit those small treasures that everyone has and wants to display.

DESIGN VARIATIONS Hallmarks of vernacular pieces include utility, practicality, and entertaining creativity. Scan across the wall shelf variations on display here. Each exudes a flinty practicality, yet none is stark. The baubles or treasures to be set on each shelf will be "framed" for display in some unique way.

Lobed sides carry the eye from the narrow top shelf to the wide bottom shelf. Vestigial feet are integrated into the bottom lobe.

Too shallow for books, this shelf's beaded face frame does frame cherished objects.

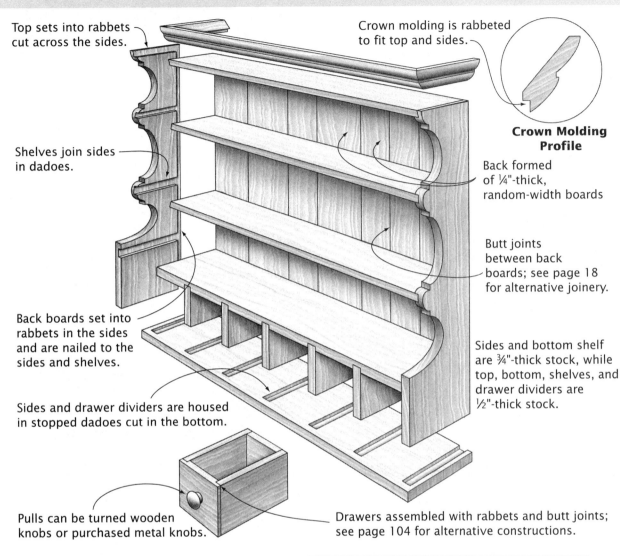

Top sets into rabbets cut across the sides.

Crown molding is rabbeted to fit top and sides.

Crown Molding Profile

Shelves join sides in dadoes.

Back formed of ¼"-thick, random-width boards

Butt joints between back boards; see page 18 for alternative joinery.

Back boards set into rabbets in the sides and are nailed to the sides and shelves.

Sides and bottom shelf are ¾"-thick stock, while top, bottom, shelves, and drawer dividers are ½"-thick stock.

Sides and drawer dividers are housed in stopped dadoes cut in the bottom.

Pulls can be turned wooden knobs or purchased metal knobs.

Drawers assembled with rabbets and butt joints; see page 104 for alternative constructions.

A shallow plate rack parallels hanging display shelves in design and construction.

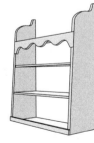

Designed to be positioned at or below eye level, this shelf can be wall-hung or set on a table.

Elaborately scroll-cut edges on the sides and a matching fascia on top embellish this practical shelf.

WALL-HUNG CUPBOARD

16½"   7½"

19"

The piece shown as archetypal is relatively small, done in a country or vernacular style. The case is assembled with through dovetails and has a vertical-board back, a face frame, and a single raised-panel door. Moldings accent the top and bottom edges and conceal the dovetails. It might as easily have been built in the 18th or 19th century as in the 20th.

A century ago, this construction certainly would have been archetypal for all sorts of case pieces. Now it is seen exclusively in handcrafted pieces. More commonplace today are wall-hung pieces like kitchen cabinets (see page 332), usually built with sheet materials and simple machine-cut joinery.

PLANS

Dunbar, Michael. "Hanging Cupboard," *Cabinetry,* edited by Robert A. Yoder. Emmaus, PA: Rodale Press, 1992. Plans for a cupboard strikingly similar to the archetype.

●

Shea, John G. "Pennsylvania German Hanging Cupboard," *Antique Country Furniture of North America.* New York: Van Nostrand Reinhold Co., 1975. Measured drawing for a double-door vernacular cupboard.

The range of sizes, configurations, and styles of wall-hung cupboards is as broad as a prairie horizon. Make a cupboard, hang it on a wall. You've got a wall-hung cupboard.

DESIGN VARIATIONS The wall-hung cupboard is a small pleasure. Since colonial days, multitudes of these practical pieces have been built, but seldom are they showy. They don't dominate a room or call attention to themselves. This is not to say they are invariably plain.

Here is a sampling. While the multidrawer piece was probably built as a spice cabinet, the others are of indeterminate use. Surely they were intended as utilitarian, but not dowdy, pieces. The spice cabinet has a simple broken pediment; the Pennsylvania Dutch cupboards have scroll-cut skirts. The tallest of them has a formal appearance, thanks to its massive cornice. And even the plain cupboard has a Shaker elegance.

Shaker Style

Spice Cabinet with Drawers

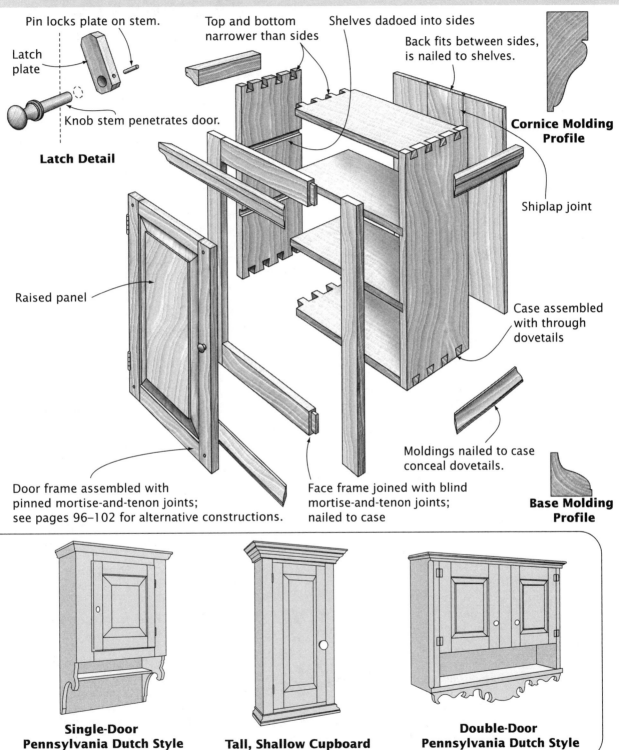

Pin locks plate on stem.

Latch plate

Knob stem penetrates door.

Latch Detail

Top and bottom narrower than sides

Shelves dadoed into sides

Back fits between sides, is nailed to shelves.

Cornice Molding Profile

Shiplap joint

Raised panel

Case assembled with through dovetails

Door frame assembled with pinned mortise-and-tenon joints; see pages 96–102 for alternative constructions.

Face frame joined with blind mortise-and-tenon joints; nailed to case

Moldings nailed to case conceal dovetails.

Base Molding Profile

Single-Door Pennsylvania Dutch Style

Tall, Shallow Cupboard

Double-Door Pennsylvania Dutch Style

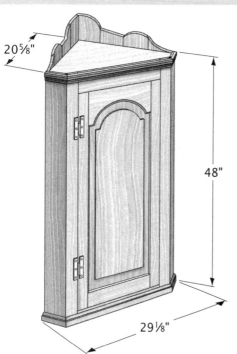

20⅝"

48"

29⅛"

HANGING
CORNER
CUPBOARD

DESIGN VARIATIONS No two cabinetmakers will design even a simple hanging corner cupboard alike. Here, one cabinetmaker made a cabinet with a glass door so the contents would be on display and not simply out of the way. Another combined out-of-sight storage with a couple of open display shelves. The third added embellishments like a scalloped face frame to an otherwise utilitarian storage cupboard.

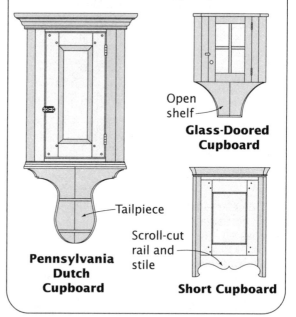

Open shelf

Glass-Doored Cupboard

Tailpiece

Scroll-cut rail and stile

Pennsylvania Dutch Cupboard

Short Cupboard

Designed especially to hang in a corner, this type of cupboard found its place in the rural homes of Europe and North America beginning in the 18th century. Intended for storage, the hanging corner cupboard didn't merit the kind of attention a cabinetmaker might have lavished on its larger kin, the corner cupboard. Nevertheless, attractive examples still exist and are still being built today.

Take the hanging corner cupboard that's shown. There's no fancy joinery in this piece, nor is there fancy veneering or inlay. It is merely endowed with harmonious proportions and sound construction.

The back boards, for example, are ship-lapped without glue, and they're fastened to the sides, top, and bottom with nails. These boards extend above the top, forming a decorative scalloped edge.

The door with its arch-topped panel is the trickiest part to build, if only because raising the panel requires a bit of handwork.

At 48 inches high, this is a tall cupboard to be hung on a wall—taller than those we are used to seeing in our kitchens, for example.

PLANS

Bentzley, Craig. "Pennsylvania Hanging Cupboard," *American Woodworker*, No. 22 (September/October 1991), pp. 18–23. An original design in a traditional style.

•

Lynch, Carlyle. "Hanging Corner Cupboard," *American Woodworker*, Vol. V, No. 3 (May/June 1989), pp. 16–21. Plans and construction directions for a Moravian chest from Old Salem, NC.

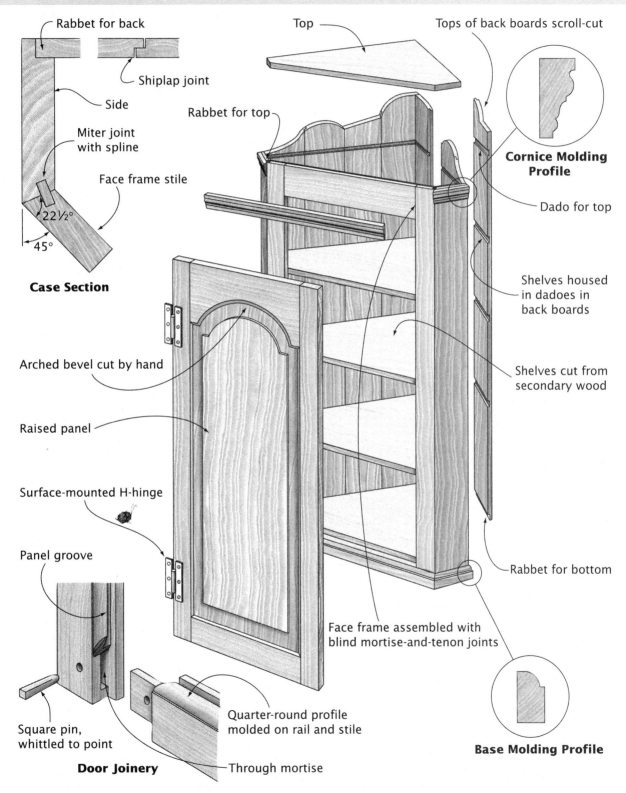

Rabbet for back

Shiplap joint

Side

Miter joint
with spline

Face frame stile

22½°

45°

Case Section

Top

Rabbet for top

Arched bevel cut by hand

Raised panel

Surface-mounted H-hinge

Panel groove

Square pin,
whittled to point

Door Joinery

Quarter-round profile
molded on rail and stile

Through mortise

Face frame assembled with
blind mortise-and-tenon joints

Tops of back boards scroll-cut

**Cornice Molding
Profile**

Dado for top

Shelves housed
in dadoes in
back boards

Shelves cut from
secondary wood

Rabbet for bottom

Base Molding Profile

DRY SINK

Water Bench, Bucket Bench, Washstand

46"

18"   50"

their new forms, they became known as water benches, washstands, and dry sinks.

Today, a reproduction dry sink is more likely to be in the living room or family room than in the kitchen. The cupboard provides useful storage, while the top serves as a display area.

On the whole, dry sinks are practical—pieces without pretense. Very basic joinery was used in the originals.

Two hundred years ago, water for drinking, cooking, and the very occasional washing was brought to the house in buckets, which were set then on the "bucket bench."

Bucket benches eventually sported doors, splash guards around the top, and other embellishments. They became less austere, more stylish. And they became more like today's sinks: a place to do food preparation and washing, more a place of work than a place of storage. In

PLANS

Engler, Nick, and Mary Jane Favorite. "Dry Sink," *American Country Furniture.* Emmaus, PA: Rodale Press, 1990. An archetypical dry sink.

•

Hylton, Bill. "Dry Sink," *Country Pine.* Emmaus, PA: Rodale Press, 1995. Another archetype; excellent plans and directions.

•

Kettell, Russell Hawes. "Water Bench with Drawers and Cupboard," *The Pine Furniture of Early New England.* New York: Dover Publications, 1956. Measured drawing only.

DESIGN VARIATIONS

Dry sinks were built in an eye-popping array of configurations. The style was mainly what we today call "country" but which most accurately might be termed "kitchen utility." The evolution of the piece, depicted in the three variations here, can suggest ways to vary the design.

The bucket bench is a simple set of shelves. The low dry sink is a simple cupboard with the top recessed, while the water bench has a high back and scalloped sides supporting a pair of drawers just below eye level. None of these forms has a base, as the sides and face frame are cut out to form feet.

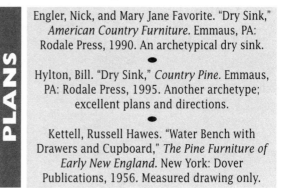

Low Dry Sink   **Bucket Bench**   **Water Bench**

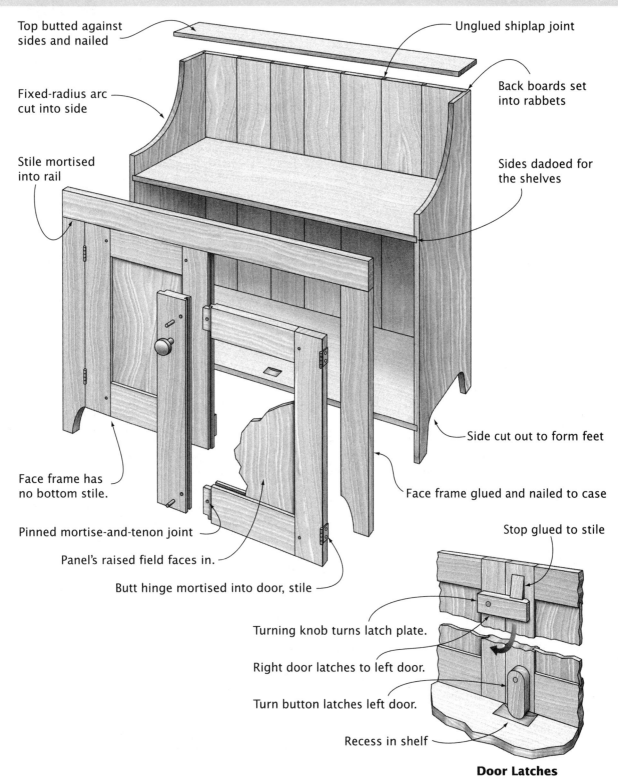

Top butted against sides and nailed

Unglued shiplap joint

Fixed-radius arc cut into side

Back boards set into rabbets

Stile mortised into rail

Sides dadoed for the shelves

Face frame has no bottom stile.

Side cut out to form feet

Pinned mortise-and-tenon joint

Face frame glued and nailed to case

Panel's raised field faces in.

Butt hinge mortised into door, stile

Stop glued to stile

Turning knob turns latch plate.

Right door latches to left door.

Turn button latches left door.

Recess in shelf

Door Latches

PIE
SAFE

42"   18¼"

51¾"

DESIGN
VARIATIONS

Pie safe styles vary widely. The single-door model most clearly—and unapologetically—projects the original utilitarian nature of the form. The jelly cupboard–like piece has a little gallery around the top and a single drawer. The most polished of the three combines general storage below with a pie safe section on top.

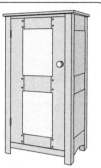

Standing 1-Door Cupboard-Style Pie Safe

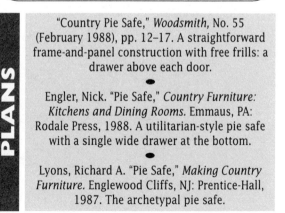

Medium-Height Pie Safe with Drawer

Tall Combination Pie Safe and Cupboard

Kitchen furniture is not country furniture. But a pie safe is often considered a country piece. Decades after the last pie safe saw use as a storage place for perishable foods, we tend to forget that the same unadorned, wholly functional furniture pieces, such as worktables and pie safes, were used in both country and city kitchens.

The pie safe shown is archetypal of the form. Except for the feet turned on the leg posts and the pattern of the tin piercing, it is devoid of the ornamental touches that mark almost all country furniture pieces. It is strictly functional.

Those pierced tin panels represent the apex of pie safe evolution, by the way. While the holes permitted passage of air, they were too small for flies to get through. The metal deterred rodents. As the drawing on the opposite page shows, the panels can be installed in a simple framework in several ways.

As a bonus, the holes can be punched in highly personal patterns. Welcome, ornamentation, to the kitchen!

PLANS

"Country Pie Safe," *Woodsmith*, No. 55 (February 1988), pp. 12–17. A straightforward frame-and-panel construction with free frills: a drawer above each door.

●

Engler, Nick. "Pie Safe," *Country Furniture: Kitchens and Dining Rooms*. Emmaus, PA: Rodale Press, 1988. A utilitarian-style pie safe with a single wide drawer at the bottom.

●

Lyons, Richard A. "Pie Safe," *Making Country Furniture*. Englewood Cliffs, NJ: Prentice-Hall, 1987. The archetypal pie safe.

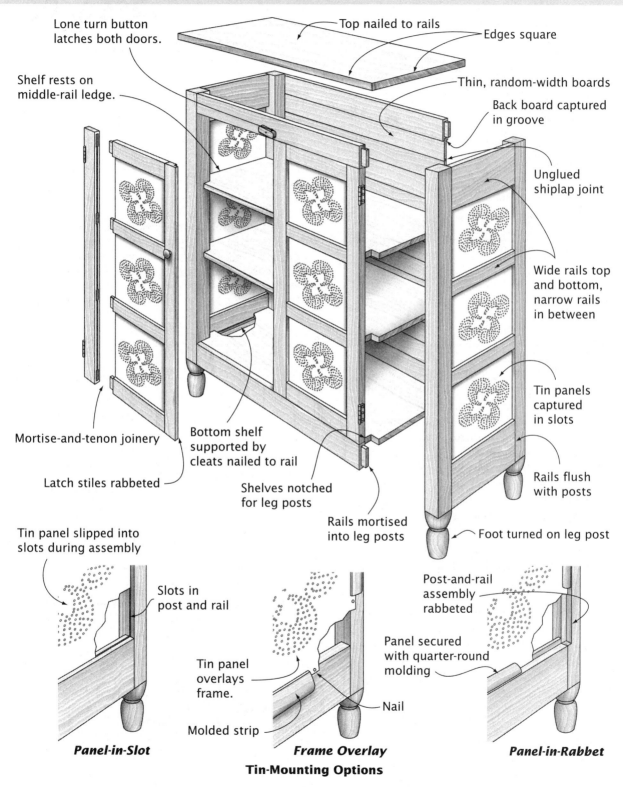

Lone turn button latches both doors.

Shelf rests on middle-rail ledge.

Top nailed to rails

Edges square

Thin, random-width boards

Back board captured in groove

Unglued shiplap joint

Wide rails top and bottom, narrow rails in between

Tin panels captured in slots

Rails flush with posts

Foot turned on leg post

Mortise-and-tenon joinery

Latch stiles rabbeted

Bottom shelf supported by cleats nailed to rail

Shelves notched for leg posts

Rails mortised into leg posts

Tin panel slipped into slots during assembly

Slots in post and rail

Tin panel overlays frame.

Molded strip

Nail

Post-and-rail assembly rabbeted

Panel secured with quarter-round molding

Panel-in-Slot

Frame Overlay
Tin-Mounting Options

Panel-in-Rabbet

SPICE CABINET

Spice Box

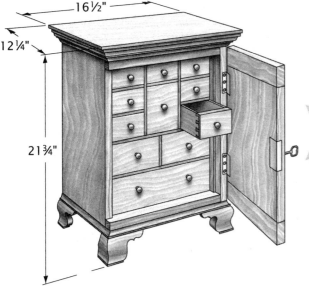

16½"

12¼"

21¾"

DESIGN VARIATIONS Rather than focus on the cosmetics, let's look at variations inside the spice cabinet: hidden drawers. Almost every spice cabinet had one or two. The easiest to construct is the tiny box that's at the back of a drawer space. A shortened drawer is inserted in front of it, concealing it. Harder to build is the drawer hidden in the front of the case. The drawer opens to the back and is concealed behind the back. When a slide beneath the bottom drawer is pulled, the back can be lowered to reveal the hidden drawer.

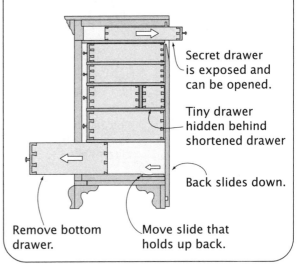

Secret drawer is exposed and can be opened.

Tiny drawer hidden behind shortened drawer

Back slides down.

Remove bottom drawer.

Move slide that holds up back.

Spice cabinets, miniatures of floor-standing cabinets, were originally intended for storing spices. Behind a single door were as many as a dozen small drawers. Because spices were costly in the 17th and 18th centuries, the cabinet door could be locked.

Spice cabinets were made and used in many parts of the country. Some very attractive examples were built in the North Carolina piedmont. Nowhere, however, did the form persevere as long as it did in southeastern Pennsylvania's Chester County.

Beginning with William and Mary examples in the late 17th century, spice cabinets were built throughout the Queen Anne and Chippendale periods and on into the 19th century, when some exhibited Hepplewhite features.

Not simply a small box with a door and some drawers, the spice cabinet was a showpiece, displaying all the refinements and ornaments of larger, high-style cabinetry. (If you couldn't afford a highboy, you'd buy a nice spice cabinet.) Surviving Chester County examples display bowfront and arch-top casework, fairly complex door forms, ornamental feet, stylish moldings, flashy veneers, and intricate inlay.

PLANS

Bentzley, Craig. "Pennsylvania Spice Box," *American Woodworker*, No. 36 (January/February 1994), pp. 28–33. Excellent plans for an archetypal Chester County, Pennsylvania, spice cabinet.

●

Krutsky, Alex. "Spice Boxes," *The Best of Fine Woodworking: Traditional Furniture Projects.* Newtown, CT: The Taunton Press, 1991. Plans for a cabinet with bun feet and hidden drawers.

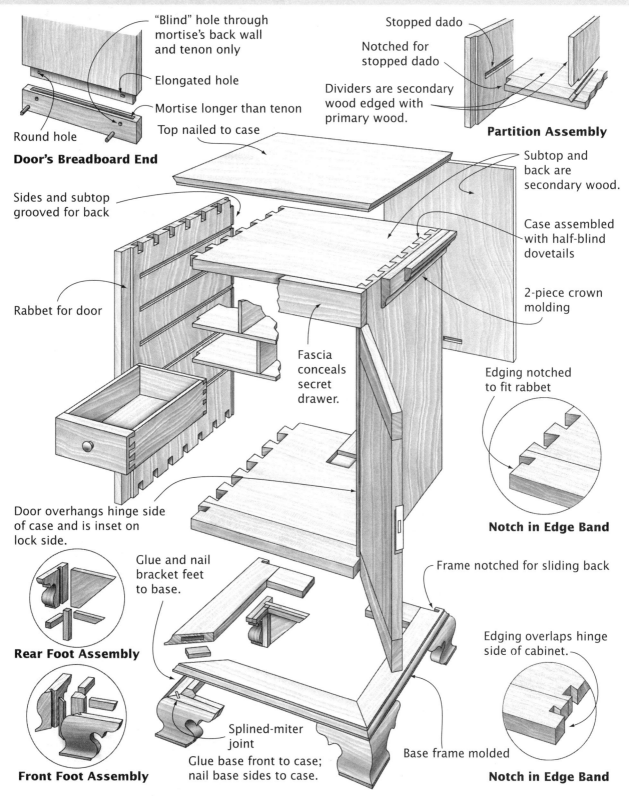

"Blind" hole through mortise's back wall and tenon only

Elongated hole

Mortise longer than tenon

Round hole

Top nailed to case

Door's Breadboard End

Stopped dado

Notched for stopped dado

Dividers are secondary wood edged with primary wood.

Partition Assembly

Subtop and back are secondary wood.

Sides and subtop grooved for back

Rabbet for door

Case assembled with half-blind dovetails

2-piece crown molding

Fascia conceals secret drawer.

Edging notched to fit rabbet

Notch in Edge Band

Door overhangs hinge side of case and is inset on lock side.

Glue and nail bracket feet to base.

Frame notched for sliding back

Rear Foot Assembly

Splined-miter joint

Glue base front to case; nail base sides to case.

Base frame molded

Edging overlaps hinge side of cabinet.

Front Foot Assembly

Notch in Edge Band

CHIMNEY
CUPBOARD

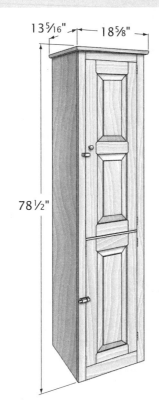

13⁵⁄₁₆"   18⁵⁄₈"

78½"

DESIGN VARIATIONS The variety of chimney cupboard styles and sizes ranges from the fairly sophisticated, with crown moldings and brass hardware, to simpler ones nailed together from a few wide boards.

Because the tall, narrow configuration isn't very flexible, access to the storage must be a prime design focus. The archetype has two doors, with the taller one on top. But the taller door could be on the bottom. The doors could be of equal size. There could be three or more doors.

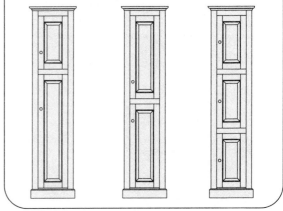

Chimney cupboard projects always reproduce this particular Shaker piece and only this piece. By acclamation, then, this must be the archetype. The original was built in the early 19th century at the New Lebanon, New York, Shaker community; and today, it is in the collection of the Metropolitan Museum of Art in New York City.

Chimney cabinets got their name from their appearance, not from their function. They were tall and slender, like a chimney, and held anything from dishes to jams and jellies.

Though not rare, freestanding, tall, narrow cupboards are somewhat uncommon. That the original chimney cupboard was a Shaker piece comes as no surprise. The Shakers were well known for customizing cabinetry to fit the available space. Thus, presented with an odd corner, the Shaker cabinetmaker would fill it from margin to margin, from floor to ceiling.

This is just your basic cupboard or cabinet, built in a very narrow configuration. Build a tall skinny box with shelves inside, then add doors.

PLANS

"Chimney Cabinet," *The Weekend Woodworker Quick and Easy Country Projects.* Emmaus, PA: Rodale Press, 1994. A simplified and somewhat modernized cabinet project, complete with drawings, cutting list, and directions.

Hylton, Bill. "Narrow Amish Cabinet," *Country Pine.* Emmaus, PA: Rodale Press, 1995. A very different turn on the concept of a tall, skinny cabinet. Excellent construction plans and drawings.

Kassay, John. "Built-ins and Cupboards," *The Book of Shaker Furniture.* Amherst, MA: University of Massachusetts Press, 1980. Measured drawings of the Shaker original.

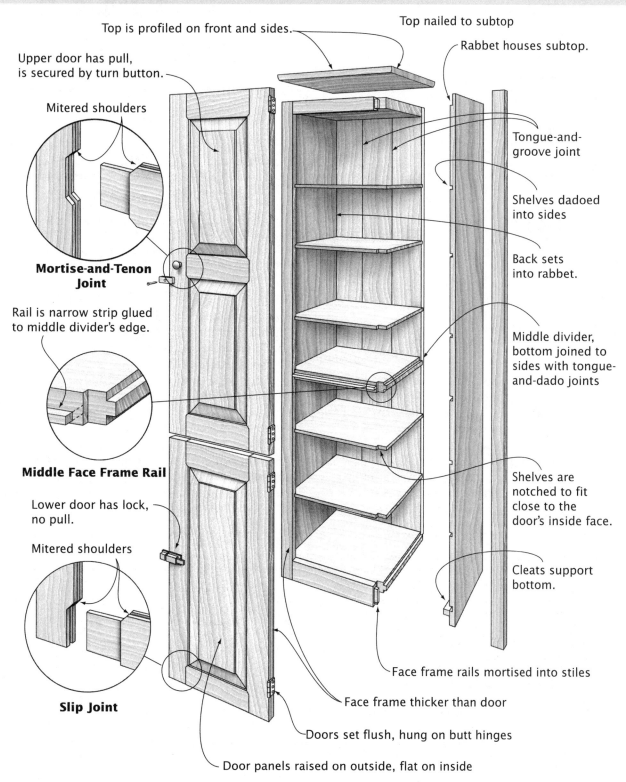

Top is profiled on front and sides.

Top nailed to subtop

Upper door has pull, is secured by turn button.

Rabbet houses subtop.

Mitered shoulders

Tongue-and-groove joint

Mortise-and-Tenon Joint

Shelves dadoed into sides

Back sets into rabbet.

Rail is narrow strip glued to middle divider's edge.

Middle divider, bottom joined to sides with tongue-and-dado joints

Middle Face Frame Rail

Shelves are notched to fit close to the door's inside face.

Lower door has lock, no pull.

Mitered shoulders

Cleats support bottom.

Slip Joint

Face frame rails mortised into stiles

Face frame thicker than door

Doors set flush, hung on butt hinges

Door panels raised on outside, flat on inside

JELLY CUPBOARD

Storage Cupboard, Dish Cupboard, Kitchen Sideboard

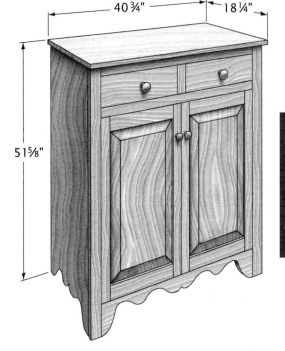

40¾" 18¼"

51⅝"

PLANS

Hylton, William. "New England Pine Cupboard," *The Weekend Woodworker: Quick-and-Easy Projects.* Emmaus, PA: Rodale Press. 1992. A typical 42-inch-high cupboard with no drawer; good drawings and instructions.

●

Lyons, Richard A. "Jelly Cupboard," *Making Country Furniture.* Englewood Cliffs, NJ: Prentice-Hall, 1987. 3 drawers over 2 doors, 5 feet high; adequate drawings, outline of procedure.

The jelly cupboard wasn't just a rural piece, although we think of it as such today. Urbanites, rich and poor alike, had kitchen cupboards for foodstuffs, just as country folk did. And a general-purpose kitchen cupboard is what a jelly cupboard really was.

The earliest jelly cupboards were primitive open shelves. The form's evolution was driven initially by necessity. One was to keep dust, dirt, and vermin out, so the shelves got doors. Then convenience of use introduced drawers—think of them as a stack of boxes that don't have to be unstacked to gain access to any one of them.

With its roots in the average household, the typical jelly cupboard is assembled with simple, robust joints, including nails, mortise-and-tenon, shiplap, tongue-and-groove, and dovetail—joints requiring few tools.

The jelly cupboard shown is a later example of the genre, displaying a modest sense of style, along with greater skill on the part of the maker. It has two drawers above a pair of doors that close over three fixed shelves.

DESIGN VARIATIONS

The evolution of the jelly cupboard is evident in the variations shown here. It's likely the earliest cupboards had primitive batten doors. Less valued, they were less likely to survive. Interestingly, the major difference between the primitive cupboard shown and the dish cupboard is the doors. The raised panels do make a statement about the relative prosperity and sophistication of the dish cupboard's owner. Drawers are found only in the less primitive examples, such as the form called a buffet by the French-Canadians. Decorative touches are seldom more extensive than a scroll cut at the bottom and perhaps a bit of molding.

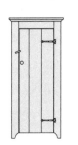

Primitive Jelly Cupboard

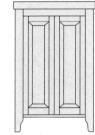

Dish Cupboard

French-Canadian Buffet

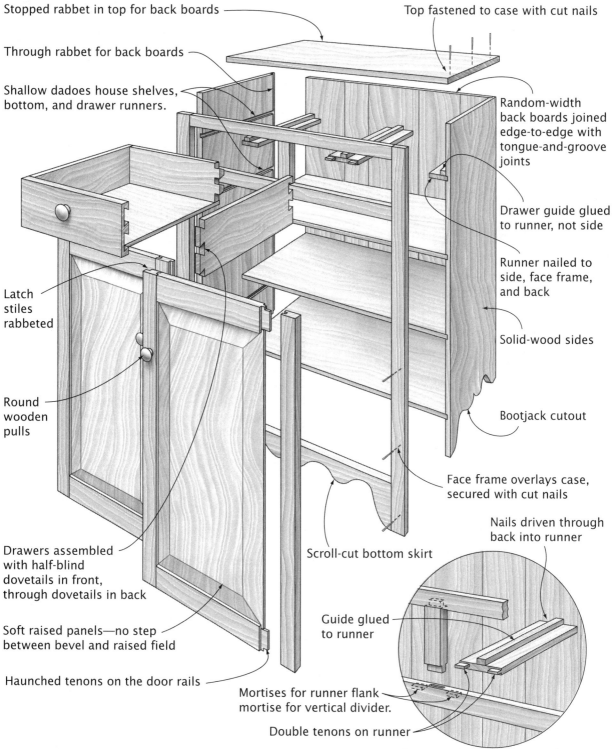

Stopped rabbet in top for back boards

Through rabbet for back boards

Shallow dadoes house shelves, bottom, and drawer runners.

Latch stiles rabbeted

Round wooden pulls

Drawers assembled with half-blind dovetails in front, through dovetails in back

Soft raised panels—no step between bevel and raised field

Haunched tenons on the door rails

Top fastened to case with cut nails

Random-width back boards joined edge-to-edge with tongue-and-groove joints

Drawer guide glued to runner, not side

Runner nailed to side, face frame, and back

Solid-wood sides

Bootjack cutout

Face frame overlays case, secured with cut nails

Scroll-cut bottom skirt

Mortises for runner flank mortise for vertical divider.

Double tenons on runner

Nails driven through back into runner

Guide glued to runner

Center Drawer Runner Joinery

HUTCH

Welsh Dresser, Open Dresser, Hutch Cupboard, Pewter Cupboard, Open Cupboard, Kitchen Cupboard

81⅜"

17"

53¾"

The hutch is a transitional piece between the bucket bench and the step-back cupboard. The example shown is typical of those built in northern New England in the 18th century. Though low-key, it is nonetheless nicely proportioned and trimmed out.

The joinery used is typical for case construction. The sides and shelves are joined with dadoes, the various frames with mortise-and-tenon joints. The drawer frame is glued to the face frame, rather than the case sides, which is an unusual approach.

PLANS

Burak, Matthew. "Colonial Hutch," *American Woodworker*, No. 54 (October 1996), pp. 34–40. A reproduction in the style of the 18th century.

●

Margon, Lester. "Pennsylvania German Cupboard," *Construction of American Furniture Treasures*. New York: Dover Publications, 1975. A Pennsylvania Dutch hutch built in 1765.

DESIGN VARIATIONS The archetype shown displays little of the "primitive" ornamentation and bald utility often associated with hutches. As an alternative, look at the characteristics of the hutches at right. Some of us are drawn more to their odd proportions and flamboyant scroll-cut surfaces than to another piece's refined elegance. Plate bars and spoon notches not only put dishes and utensils close at hand but add them to the exhibition.

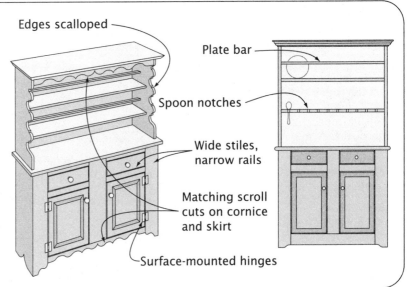

Edges scalloped

Plate bar

Spoon notches

Wide stiles, narrow rails

Matching scroll cuts on cornice and skirt

Surface-mounted hinges

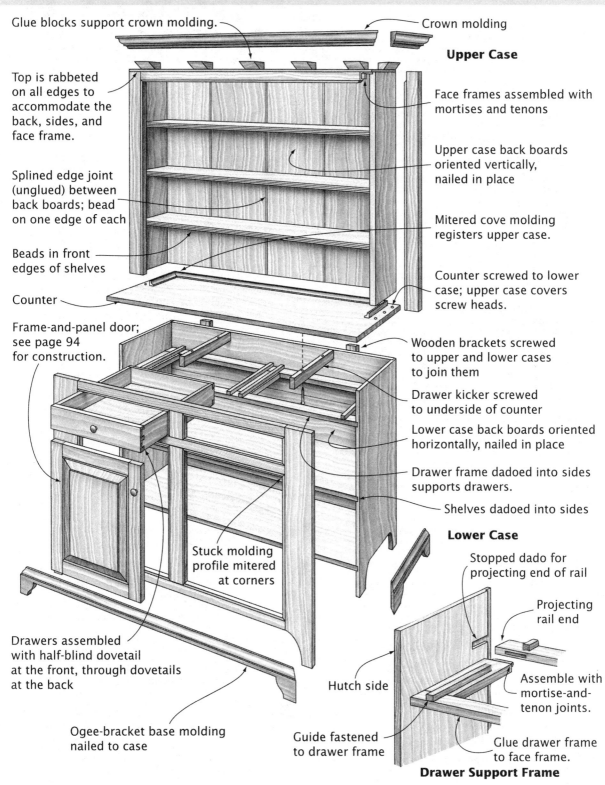

Glue blocks support crown molding.

Crown molding

Upper Case

Top is rabbeted on all edges to accommodate the back, sides, and face frame.

Face frames assembled with mortises and tenons

Splined edge joint (unglued) between back boards; bead on one edge of each

Upper case back boards oriented vertically, nailed in place

Beads in front edges of shelves

Mitered cove molding registers upper case.

Counter

Counter screwed to lower case; upper case covers screw heads.

Frame-and-panel door; see page 94 for construction.

Wooden brackets screwed to upper and lower cases to join them

Drawer kicker screwed to underside of counter

Lower case back boards oriented horizontally, nailed in place

Drawer frame dadoed into sides supports drawers.

Shelves dadoed into sides

Stuck molding profile mitered at corners

Lower Case

Stopped dado for projecting end of rail

Projecting rail end

Drawers assembled with half-blind dovetail at the front, through dovetails at the back

Hutch side

Assemble with mortise-and-tenon joints.

Ogee-bracket base molding nailed to case

Guide fastened to drawer frame

Glue drawer frame to face frame.

Drawer Support Frame

STEP-BACK
CUPBOARD

Dutch Cupboard, China Press,
Dish Dresser

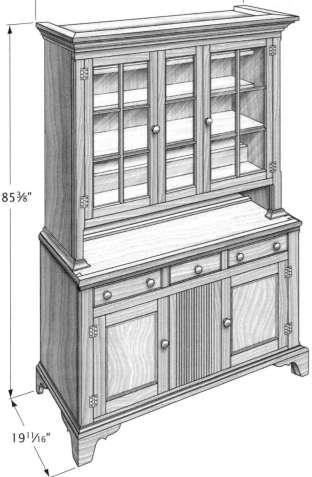

59⅞"

85⅜"

19¹¹⁄₁₆"

DESIGN
VARIATIONS While the Dutch cupboard may be the largest and best-known style of step-backs, it is not the only one.

The primitive cupboard is strictly functional and lacks the ostentatious folk ornamentation typical of the Dutch cupboards. Its construction is as primitive as its appearance. The cases are made of wide boards nailed together. The rails and stiles forming the face frame aren't even joined to each other, only to the case.

The Kentucky cupboard, on the other hand, displays design sophistication in its proportions.

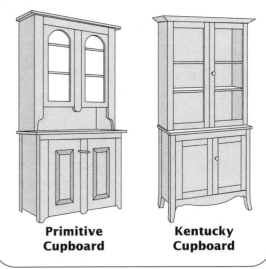

Primitive
Cupboard

Kentucky
Cupboard

The step-back is a large cupboard consisting of a base cupboard with so-called blind doors (those having wooden panels) and an upper cupboard with glazed doors. It is called a step-back because of a difference in depth between the lower and upper sections.

The step-back shown here is a variant of the form known as a Dutch cupboard. It is a kitchen piece that originated with the Germans who settled in North America in the 18th and early 19th centuries. It functioned exactly like a hutch (see page 278). The lower section furnished storage for crocks, pots, and food, while the upper provided a stage for displaying the family's dishes and eating utensils.

PLANS

Gottshall, Franklin H. "Dutch Cupboard of Pine," "Cherry Dutch Cupboard," and "Large Cherry Cutch Cupboard," *Making Early American and Country Furniture.* New York: Dover Publications, 1983. In 1 book, plans and construction directions for 3 different Pennsylvania Dutch step-back cupboards.

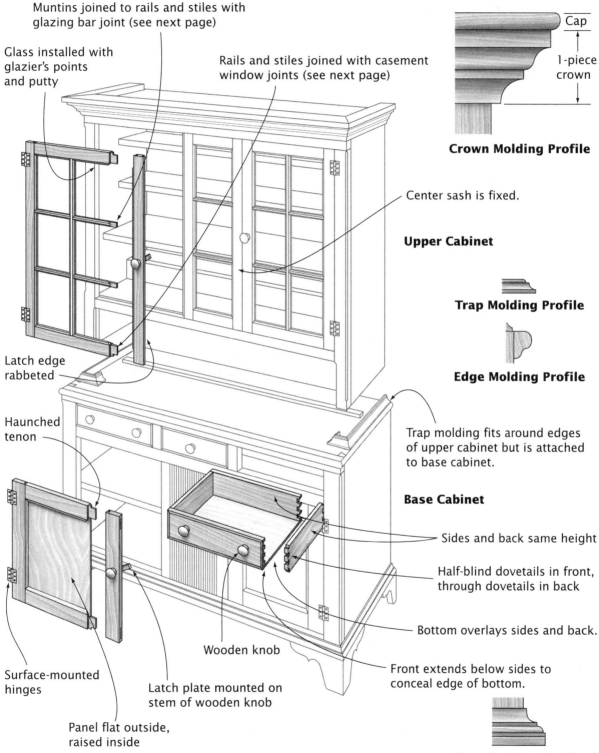

Muntins joined to rails and stiles with glazing bar joint (see next page)

Glass installed with glazier's points and putty

Rails and stiles joined with casement window joints (see next page)

Crown Molding Profile

Cap

1-piece crown

Center sash is fixed.

Upper Cabinet

Trap Molding Profile

Edge Molding Profile

Latch edge rabbeted

Haunched tenon

Trap molding fits around edges of upper cabinet but is attached to base cabinet.

Base Cabinet

Sides and back same height

Half-blind dovetails in front, through dovetails in back

Bottom overlays sides and back.

Wooden knob

Front extends below sides to conceal edge of bottom.

Surface-mounted hinges

Latch plate mounted on stem of wooden knob

Panel flat outside, raised inside

Base Molding Profile

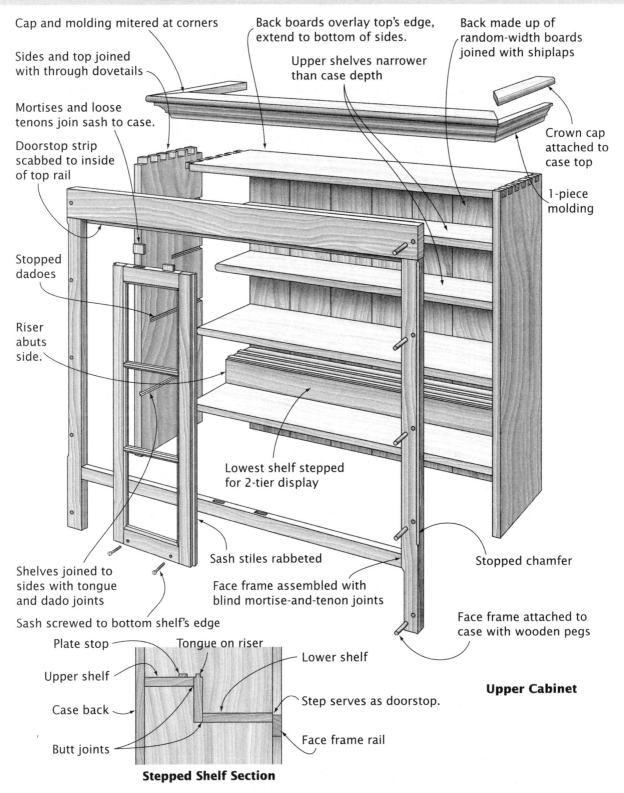

Cap and molding mitered at corners

Sides and top joined with through dovetails

Mortises and loose tenons join sash to case.

Doorstop strip scabbed to inside of top rail

Stopped dadoes

Riser abuts side.

Shelves joined to sides with tongue and dado joints

Sash screwed to bottom shelf's edge

Back boards overlay top's edge, extend to bottom of sides.

Upper shelves narrower than case depth

Lowest shelf stepped for 2-tier display

Sash stiles rabbeted

Face frame assembled with blind mortise-and-tenon joints

Back made up of random-width boards joined with shiplaps

Crown cap attached to case top

1-piece molding

Stopped chamfer

Face frame attached to case with wooden pegs

Upper Cabinet

Plate stop

Tongue on riser

Upper shelf

Case back

Butt joints

Lower shelf

Step serves as doorstop.

Face frame rail

Stepped Shelf Section

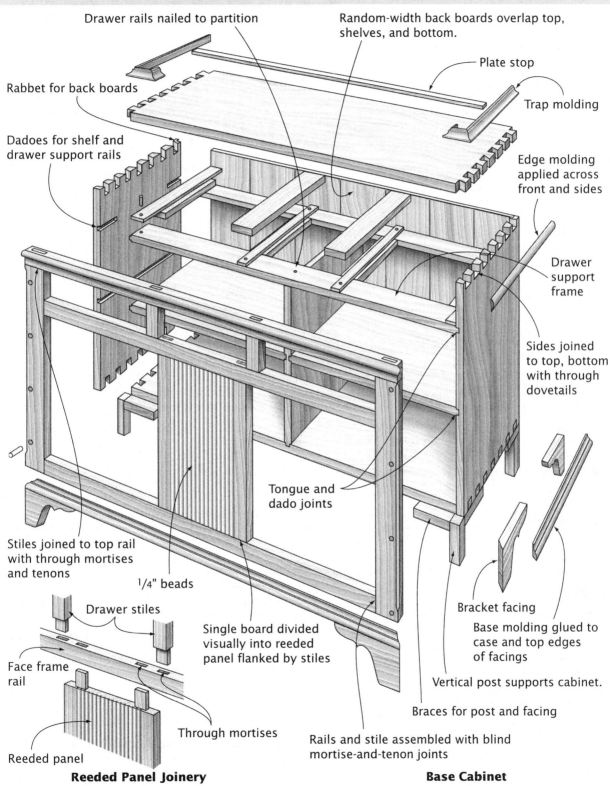

Drawer rails nailed to partition

Random-width back boards overlap top, shelves, and bottom.

Plate stop

Rabbet for back boards

Trap molding

Dadoes for shelf and drawer support rails

Edge molding applied across front and sides

Drawer support frame

Sides joined to top, bottom with through dovetails

Tongue and dado joints

Stiles joined to top rail with through mortises and tenons

1/4" beads

Drawer stiles

Bracket facing

Base molding glued to case and top edges of facings

Single board divided visually into reeded panel flanked by stiles

Face frame rail

Through mortises

Vertical post supports cabinet.

Reeded panel

Braces for post and facing

Rails and stile assembled with blind mortise-and-tenon joints

Reeded Panel Joinery

Base Cabinet

SIDEBOARD

Buffet

57¾"

24¾"

34¾"

PLANS

Rogowski, Gary, "Arts-and-Crafts Sideboard," *Fine Woodworking* (July–December 1997), No. 125, pp. 36–43; No. 126, pp. 78–83; No. 127, pp. 68–75. Construction of an original design in the Arts-and-Crafts style, depicted in 3-part article.

•

Taylor, V. J., "Sideboard with Serpentine Front," *Period Furniture Projects.* Newton Abbot, Devon, UK: David & Charles, 1994. Drawings, cutting list, and construction directions for a reproduction of a late-18th-century design.

The development of the sideboard paralleled that of the dining room as a separate room for eating, especially for entertaining guests with a meal. The name surely was taken from the side table or side board that was used in serving meals in Elizabethan times.

But in the late-18th-century homes of the urban elite of a new nation, serving meals became a more and more elaborate ceremony. The sideboard provided space for the organization, storage, and display of knife boxes, dishes, and glasses. A deep drawer might be fitted with dividers for holding liquor bottles.

Though it originated in England, the reverse-serpentine form shown here, which combines concave end sections with a convex central drawer above an inset pair of doors, was enormously popular in America.

DESIGN VARIATIONS

While the sideboard shown above is representative of the classic form, many built in the same period displayed more restraint. Outside the urban centers especially, sideboards lacked the extra legs, the flamboyant veneers and inlay, and the serpentine contour. They also lacked the storage space.

With time and changes in furniture styles, the sideboard lost its lanky appearance, though it continued to be a showpiece in most homes. By the late 19th century, the oaken sideboard was a case piece offering both a great deal of storage space and ornamentation. An Arts-and-Crafts interpretation from the same time period dispensed with the ornament and gave the case legs without surrendering storage capacity.

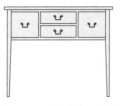

Country Sideboard

Arts-and-Crafts Sideboard

Golden Oak Sideboard

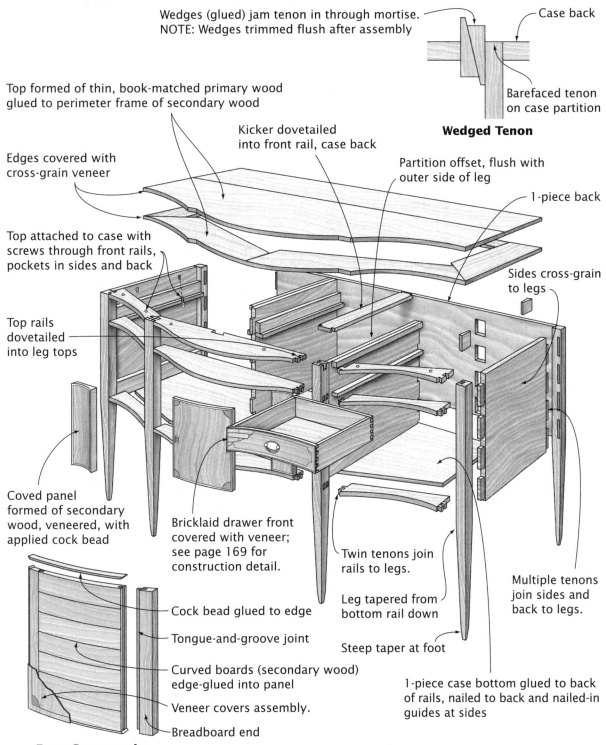

Wedges (glued) jam tenon in through mortise.
NOTE: Wedges trimmed flush after assembly

Case back

Wedged Tenon

Barefaced tenon
on case partition

Top formed of thin, book-matched primary wood
glued to perimeter frame of secondary wood

Kicker dovetailed
into front rail, case back

Partition offset, flush with
outer side of leg

Edges covered with
cross-grain veneer

1-piece back

Top attached to case with
screws through front rails,
pockets in sides and back

Sides cross-grain
to legs

Top rails
dovetailed
into leg tops

Coved panel
formed of secondary
wood, veneered, with
applied cock bead

Bricklaid drawer front
covered with veneer;
see page 169 for
construction detail.

Twin tenons join
rails to legs.

Multiple tenons
join sides and
back to legs.

Leg tapered from
bottom rail down

Cock bead glued to edge

Steep taper at foot

Tongue-and-groove joint

Curved boards (secondary wood)
edge-glued into panel

1-piece case bottom glued to back
of rails, nailed to back and nailed-in
guides at sides

Veneer covers assembly.

Breadboard end

Door Construction

HUNTBOARD

61"

21"

41"

Hunting Board,
Hunt Table, Hunting Table,
Hunt Sideboard

PLANS

Lynch, Carlyle. "A Southern Huntboard," *The Best of Fine Woodworking: Making Period Furniture.* Newtown, CT: The Taunton Press, 1985. An excellent representative of the genre: 4 legs, 2 drawers, 2 cupboards.

●

Smith, David T. "Huntboard," *Cabinetry*, edited by Robert A. Yoder. Emmaus, PA: Rodale Press, 1992. Huntboard with a plate rack.

●

"Southern Huntboard," *Making Antique Furniture.* Hertfordshire, UK: Argus Books, 1988. A 6-legged model.

The huntboard is a form of sideboard developed in the American south in the late 1700s. As its name suggests, it was a sideboard for hunters, especially those who pursued their game on horseback—the storied southern fox hunter. The lore is that saddlesore hunters just in off their horses ate in the hallway, standing up at the huntboard.

The immediate difference between the huntboard and the typical sideboard of the era is the appearance. The sideboard might have been the work of a city cabinetmaker, dressed out in gorgeous veneers, perhaps with carving and elaborate inlay. The huntboard surely would have been a country piece, more simple, more sturdy, befitting its placement in the hallway or out on the porch. Too, huntboards tend to be a few inches taller and perhaps a couple of inches narrower than the sideboard.

The huntboard shown displays traditional appearance but takes advantage of a non-traditional material—plywood. It's practical for the large panels required in the huntboard. Most of the joinery is very traditional, though the approach for mounting the bottom is unusual.

DESIGN VARIATIONS The huntboard form is well defined: a long, narrow table with tall legs and either drawers or cupboards. But within that form, there's room for variation.

The archetype has six legs to support it. The drawers are flanked by compartments with doors. But all you really need are four legs. Use deep drawers instead of compartments. Change the number and configuration of the drawers. Add shelves or a plate rack to the piece. Substitute a scroll-cut apron for the bottom rail.

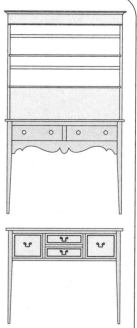

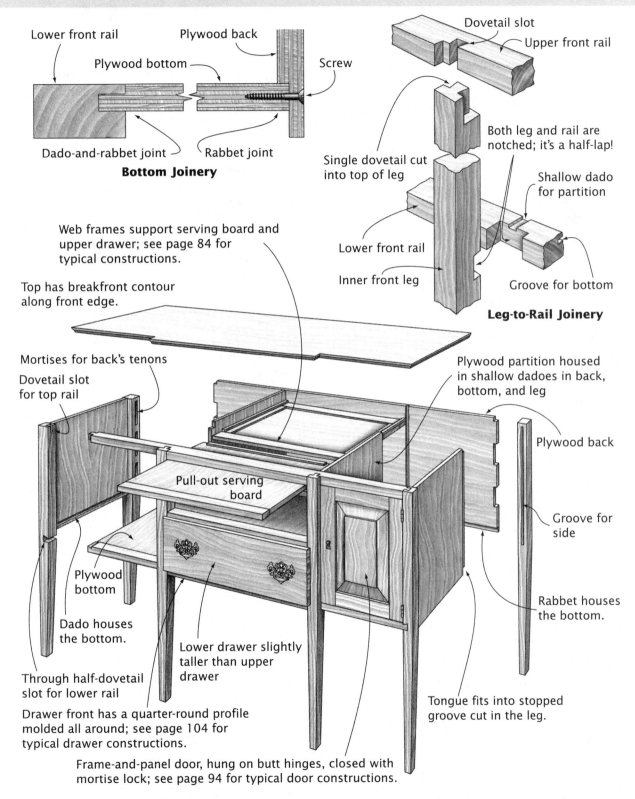

Bottom Joinery

Lower front rail

Plywood back

Plywood bottom

Screw

Dado-and-rabbet joint

Rabbet joint

Dovetail slot

Upper front rail

Single dovetail cut into top of leg

Both leg and rail are notched; it's a half-lap!

Shallow dado for partition

Lower front rail

Inner front leg

Groove for bottom

Leg-to-Rail Joinery

Web frames support serving board and upper drawer; see page 84 for typical constructions.

Top has breakfront contour along front edge.

Mortises for back's tenons

Dovetail slot for top rail

Plywood partition housed in shallow dadoes in back, bottom, and leg

Plywood back

Pull-out serving board

Groove for side

Plywood bottom

Dado houses the bottom.

Lower drawer slightly taller than upper drawer

Through half-dovetail slot for lower rail

Rabbet houses the bottom.

Drawer front has a quarter-round profile molded all around; see page 104 for typical drawer constructions.

Tongue fits into stopped groove cut in the leg.

Frame-and-panel door, hung on butt hinges, closed with mortise lock; see page 94 for typical door constructions.

BUFFET

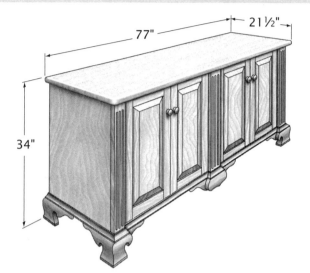

77"

21½"

34"

Originally an Italian form, the buffet was highly developed in England and in France, where there were the *buffet-à-deux-corps,* which was a two-piece cupboard, and the *buffet bas,* a low sideboardlike piece. Nowadays, the buffet is usually a case piece used as a sideboard or a side table.

Part of the beauty of the buffet shown here is its simple construction. At its heart, it is a simple plywood box. Although the trim is quite elegant, it's simple to make. The left-hand doors open to adjustable shelves; the right-hand doors open to drawers. The construction could be simplified even more by putting shelves behind both sets of doors.

The case is built of hardwood plywood, veneered with the primary wood. This eliminates the need to edge-glue boards. Except for the sides, the case could be inexpensive birch plywood, stained to match the primary wood. The rest of the cabinet, including the top, facings, moldings, feet, drawer faces, and doors, is made of the primary wood.

PLANS

Bostock, Glenn, "Cherry Buffet," *Cabinetry,* edited by Robert A. Yoder. Emmaus, PA: Rodale Press, 1992. The full gamut of drawings, cutting list, and step-by-step construction directions for the archetypal buffet.

DESIGN VARIATIONS Each buffet here has both drawers and doors, and they have a significant influence on the piece's overall appearance. In each, the way they look and the way they are arranged is different.

Compare the country buffet's three small drawers with the prominence of the breakfront's drawers. Consider the possible uses. Only the breakfront's drawers seem suited for storing table linens.

Look at the doors. On the traditional buffet their top rails are shaped, lending the piece a more relaxed appearance than the severity of the breakfront's doors.

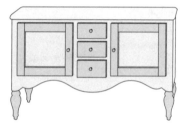

Country Post-and-Panel Buffet

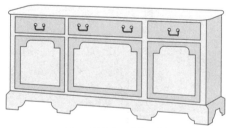

Traditional Buffet

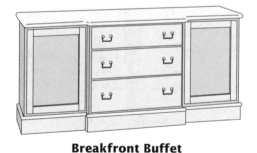

Breakfront Buffet

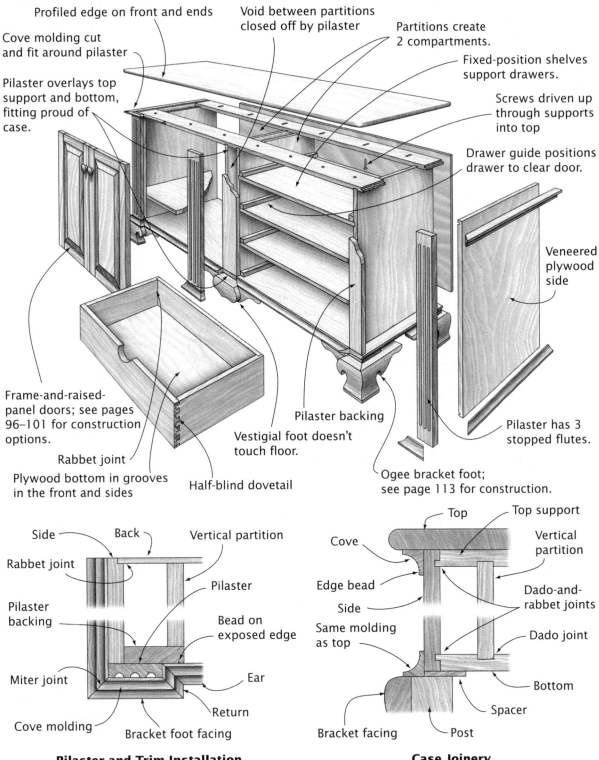

Profiled edge on front and ends

Cove molding cut and fit around pilaster

Pilaster overlays top support and bottom, fitting proud of case.

Void between partitions closed off by pilaster

Partitions create 2 compartments.

Fixed-position shelves support drawers.

Screws driven up through supports into top

Drawer guide positions drawer to clear door.

Veneered plywood side

Frame-and-raised-panel doors; see pages 96–101 for construction options.

Rabbet joint

Plywood bottom in grooves in the front and sides

Half-blind dovetail

Vestigial foot doesn't touch floor.

Pilaster backing

Ogee bracket foot; see page 113 for construction.

Pilaster has 3 stopped flutes.

Side

Back

Vertical partition

Rabbet joint

Pilaster

Pilaster backing

Bead on exposed edge

Miter joint

Ear

Cove molding

Return

Bracket foot facing

Pilaster and Trim Installation

Top

Top support

Cove

Vertical partition

Edge bead

Side

Dado-and-rabbet joints

Same molding as top

Dado joint

Bottom

Spacer

Bracket facing

Post

Case Joinery

40"

68½"

20"

DISPLAY
CABINET

China Cabinet, China Closet, Curio Cabinet, Showcase, Gun Cabinet

280), and breakfronts (see page 298). As the interests of collectors changed, so did the styles of display cabinets.

The Golden Oak style of display cabinet shown here is a product of manufacture. Only the availability of large, curved panes of glass makes its design possible. And it wasn't until the late 19th century that such glass panes could be manufactured at reasonable cost.

PLANS

"Display Cabinet," *Woodsmith*, No. 78, pp. 6–13. Construction directions and drawings for a low-waisted traditional-style display cabinet that can be converted into a gun cabinet.

•

Donnelly, David. "China Cabinet," *American Woodworker*, No. 24 (January/February 1992), pp. 28–33. Plans for a Golden Oak–style display cabinet with curved-glass panels.

•

Kinsman, J. Gregory. "Arts and Crafts Cabinet," *American Woodworker*, No. 32 (May/June 1993), pp. 43–47. Concise plans.

The story of the display cabinet parallels that of collecting. Anything worth collecting is something worth showing off. How better to do it than in a glass-doored cabinet that allows a viewer to see without touching?

The first display cabinets appeared in the 17th century, when nothing was prized as much as an exquisite Chinese porcelain. As domestic potteries were established, "china" became more common, and with it, china cupboards, corner cupboards (see page 296), step-backs (see page

DESIGN VARIATIONS

Contemporary display cabinets may exhibit many traditional design motifs and are, of course, built using traditional joinery, yet they are throughly modern. The traditional cupboard here is scaled perfectly for a collection of rifles or shotguns, though it can easily be fitted with shelves to display other collectibles. The narrow cabinet, often called a curio cabinet or showcase, has doors with a single, large pane rather than divided lights. Even the sides are glass panes. Moreover, the cabinet is fitted with glass shelves, lights, and even a mirrored back, all designed to enhance the way the collection is displayed.

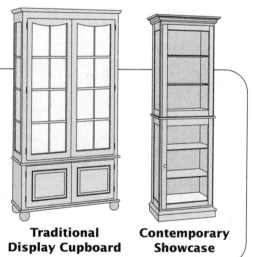

Traditional Display Cupboard

Contemporary Showcase

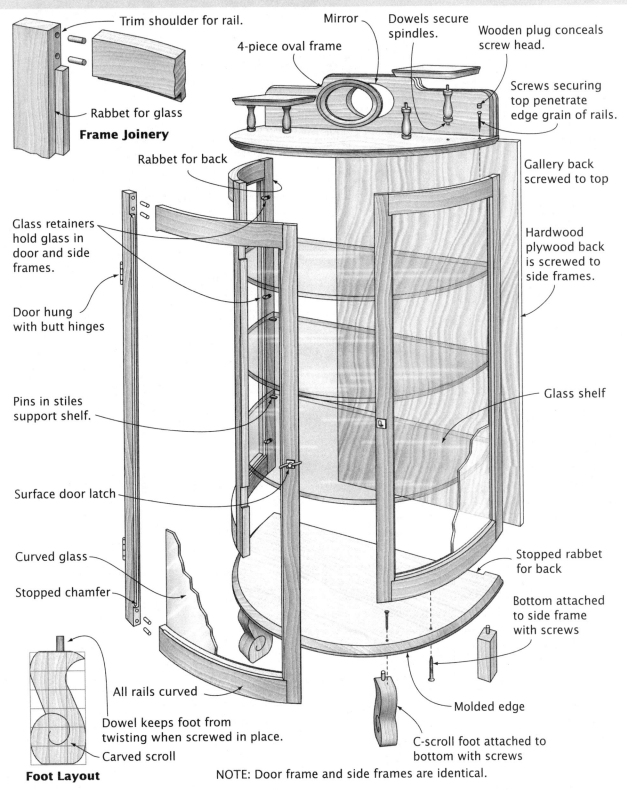

Frame Joinery

Trim shoulder for rail.

Rabbet for glass

Mirror

4-piece oval frame

Dowels secure spindles.

Wooden plug conceals screw head.

Screws securing top penetrate edge grain of rails.

Rabbet for back

Gallery back screwed to top

Glass retainers hold glass in door and side frames.

Door hung with butt hinges

Hardwood plywood back is screwed to side frames.

Pins in stiles support shelf.

Glass shelf

Surface door latch

Curved glass

Stopped chamfer

Stopped rabbet for back

Bottom attached to side frame with screws

All rails curved

Dowel keeps foot from twisting when screwed in place.

Carved scroll

Molded edge

C-scroll foot attached to bottom with screws

Foot Layout

NOTE: Door frame and side frames are identical.

BOOKCASE

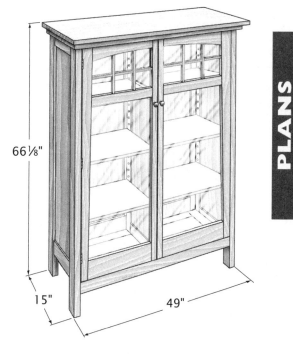

66⅛"

15"   49"

PLANS

"Barrister's Bookcase," *Woodsmith*, No. 29, pp. 16–21. Good step-by-step directions for building a modular, stackable bookcase with awning-type glass doors.

•

"Georgian-Style Bookcase," *Making Antique Furniture.* Hertfordshire, UK: Argus Books, 1988. Plans for a bookcase atop a cupboard, done in a subdued Chippendale style.

•

Tolpin, Jim. "Stickley Bookcase," *Cabinetry,* edited by Robert A. Yoder. Emmaus, PA: Rodale Press, 1992. Plans, cutting list, and step-by-step for building an Arts and Crafts–style bookcase, just like the archetype presented here.

T he bookcase originated as a closet, an integral part of a building. Books were rare, treasured possessions, partly because few folks could read and partly because books *were* handmade. So they were closeted for protection.

In the 17th century, cabinetmakers began building freestanding bookcases, though these generally were huge built-ins. Late in the 18th century, the scale of bookcases began to diminish. The example shown is in the Arts and Crafts style of the late 19th century, for the form is quintessentially Arts and Crafts.

Many frame-and-panel elements—the sides and vertical divider, the bottom, the back—are featured in it. There's even a frame underneath the solid-wood top. But this reproduction makes good use of modern materials—all the panels are hardwood plywood. Too, the shelves are adjustable, thanks to a modern support design.

The doors are somewhat unusual, in that the hinge stiles are tapered, the top rails arched. Using the mortise-and-loose-tenon to assemble the doors makes them somewhat easier to construct. Also interesting is the

DESIGN VARIATIONS

Many interesting forms appeared during the evolution from a closet to an open case of shelves. Some remain of interest to the contemporary cabinetmaker.

The Chippendale bookcase is a result of the marriage of a bookcase and a cupboard. Another such marriage, between a bookcase and a desk, resulted in what sometimes was called a secretary (see page 212).

Later in the evolution came the barrister's bookcase, which featured a lift-up door, glazed with a single pane, for each shelf.

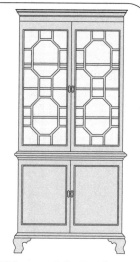

Chippendale Bookcase

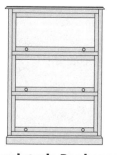

Barrister's Bookcase

construction of the muntins. As the drawing shows, two separate sashes are constructed using half-lap joints, then face-glued together.

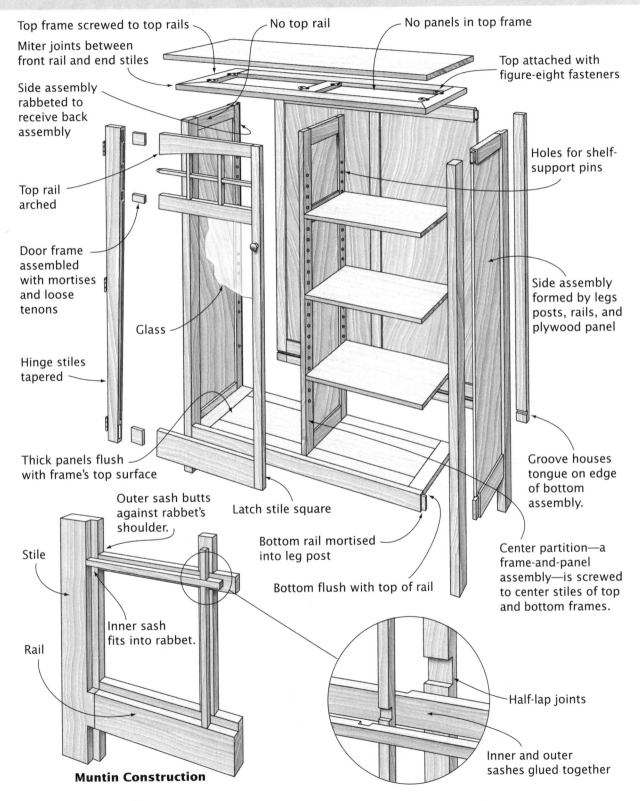

Top frame screwed to top rails

Miter joints between front rail and end stiles

Side assembly rabbeted to receive back assembly

Top rail arched

Door frame assembled with mortises and loose tenons

Glass

Hinge stiles tapered

Thick panels flush with frame's top surface

No top rail

No panels in top frame

Top attached with figure-eight fasteners

Holes for shelf-support pins

Side assembly formed by legs posts, rails, and plywood panel

Groove houses tongue on edge of bottom assembly.

Outer sash butts against rabbet's shoulder.

Latch stile square

Bottom rail mortised into leg post

Bottom flush with top of rail

Center partition—a frame-and-panel assembly—is screwed to center stiles of top and bottom frames.

Stile

Inner sash fits into rabbet.

Rail

Half-lap joints

Inner and outer sashes glued together

Muntin Construction

BOOKSHELVES

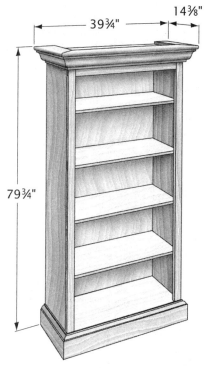

39¾" 14⅜"

79¾"

> ◤ **DESIGN VARIATIONS** Bookshelves don't necessarily need to be imposing constructions reminiscent of a paneled library. Reduce the height, reduce the width. The joinery can be the same, but the resulting bookshelf will be suitable for a chairside or bedside location. The examples shown here present divergent styles. The smaller shelf is a pleasant, traditional frame-and-panel design, while the larger unit displays an elegant utilitarianism. The larger shelf lacks a full back, but the kickboards and back board (extending between the sides above the top shelf) provide triangulation to prevent racking.

Traditional Bookshelf

Contemporary Bookshelf

Very often, when we think of a bookshelf, we think of a board laid across metal brackets snapped into metal standards screwed to a wall. But to a cabinetmaker, a bookshelf is a piece of case furniture: a case, open in front (and even in back), with one or more shelves.

The furniture piece presented here is, to most people today, a *bookcase.* Traditionally, however, a bookcase is a case piece with doors (see "Bookcase" on page 292), while bookshelves are the open shelves found in a library.

The archetype presented here has some major details—the base and cornice—calculated to lend a built-in feel to it. Indeed, the unit could be screwed to a wall, then trimmed out. Two or more units could be ganged together to create a real library. The base could borrow from the room's baseboard, and the cornice molding could be carried around the room.

Materials and construction options abound. For a large unit, plywood is a good choice. You can easily produce the large boards needed, and

you don't have to be nearly as concerned about accommodating wood movement. The edges can be concealed by a face frame.

The unit can have fixed shelves; assemble sides and shelves with some variety of dado joint. Or make the shelves adjustable. Use dowels or pins to support the shelves, or use manufactured standards and clips, as shown.

PLANS

Abram, Norm, with Tim Snyder. "Bookcase," *The New Yankee Workshop.* Boston: Little, Brown, & Co., 1989. Plans and how-I-built-it text for a tall, freestanding unit with adjustable shelves.

•

"Bookcase," *Woodsmith,* No. 49, pp. 12–17. Medium-height bookshelf presented in step-by-step plans.

•

Bostock, Glenn. "Traditional Bookshelves," *Cabinetry,* edited by Robert A. Yoder. Emmaus, PA: Rodale Press, 1992. Plans and construction directions for modular, built-in bookshelves.

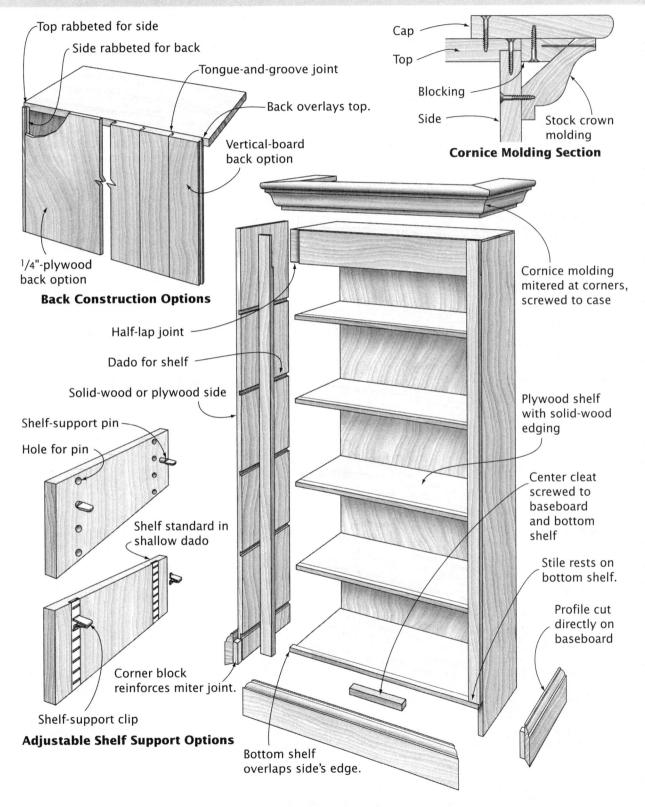

Top rabbeted for side

Side rabbeted for back

Tongue-and-groove joint

Back overlays top.

Vertical-board back option

1/4"-plywood back option

Back Construction Options

Cap

Top

Blocking

Side

Stock crown molding

Cornice Molding Section

Half-lap joint

Dado for shelf

Solid-wood or plywood side

Shelf-support pin

Hole for pin

Shelf standard in shallow dado

Corner block reinforces miter joint.

Shelf-support clip

Adjustable Shelf Support Options

Cornice molding mitered at corners, screwed to case

Plywood shelf with solid-wood edging

Center cleat screwed to baseboard and bottom shelf

Stile rests on bottom shelf.

Profile cut directly on baseboard

Bottom shelf overlaps side's edge.

CORNER
CUPBOARD

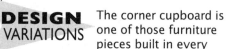

84"

20⅜"

40"

I s the corner cupboard just a practical way of using wasted space? Or is it really a clever way of displaying one's prized china?

Clearly, it is both. It's most often seen in the dining room, which often is a room where windows or doors break up every wall and the large table and many chairs crowd the floor. Because the back of such a cabinet ends up so close to the face, it is the perfect showcase.

The example shown here is a pretty fair representative of the form. The upper part of the cupboard with its single glazed door is larger than the closed-in lower section. There's a drawer for utensils. The wood is fine, the ornamentation restrained.

PLANS

Gottshall, Franklin H. "Shell-Top Corner Cupboard," *Masterpiece Furniture Making.* Harrisburg, PA: Stackpole Books, 1979. Extensive drawings, a cutting list, and some construction notes on an elaborate corner cupboard with broken pediment, flame finials, and a huge shell-carved interior.

Hylton, Bill. "Corner Cupboard," *Country Pine.* Emmaus, PA: Rodale Press, 1995. Almost the antithesis of the previous cupboard; a smaller, simpler piece presented in clear drawings, cutting list, and detailed step-by-step.

DESIGN VARIATIONS

The corner cupboard is one of those furniture pieces built in every size, shape, and style imaginable. There's one for every home, as these three examples suggest.

The shell-top cupboard, which exhibits hundreds of hours' worth of carving, represents the upper crust of the form. At the opposite end of the spectrum is the open-shelved contemporary piece, which is stripped of molded edges, ornamentation, and even a semblance of a base. The country cupboard strikes a balance. It's a bit utilitarian with its solid-panel doors, but the style will harmonize with many decors.

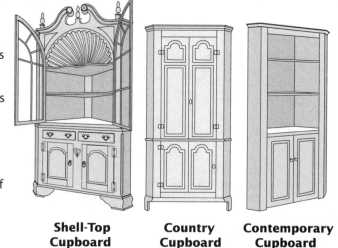

Shell-Top Cupboard   **Country Cupboard**   **Contemporary Cupboard**

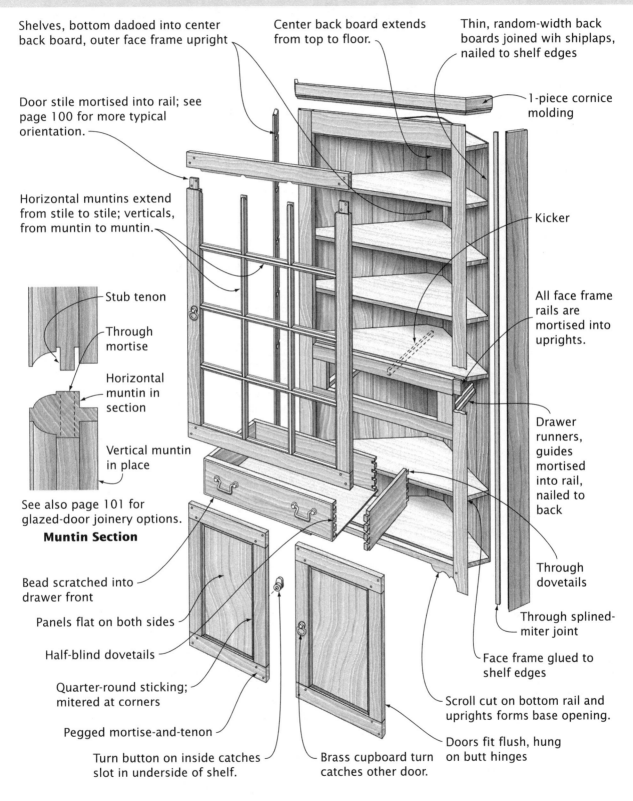

Shelves, bottom dadoed into center back board, outer face frame upright

Center back board extends from top to floor.

Thin, random-width back boards joined wih shiplaps, nailed to shelf edges

Door stile mortised into rail; see page 100 for more typical orientation.

1-piece cornice molding

Horizontal muntins extend from stile to stile; verticals, from muntin to muntin.

Kicker

Stub tenon

Through mortise

Horizontal muntin in section

Vertical muntin in place

All face frame rails are mortised into uprights.

See also page 101 for glazed-door joinery options.

Muntin Section

Bead scratched into drawer front

Panels flat on both sides

Half-blind dovetails

Quarter-round sticking; mitered at corners

Pegged mortise-and-tenon

Turn button on inside catches slot in underside of shelf.

Drawer runners, guides mortised into rail, nailed to back

Through dovetails

Through splined-miter joint

Face frame glued to shelf edges

Scroll cut on bottom rail and uprights forms base opening.

Brass cupboard turn catches other door.

Doors fit flush, hung on butt hinges

BREAKFRONT

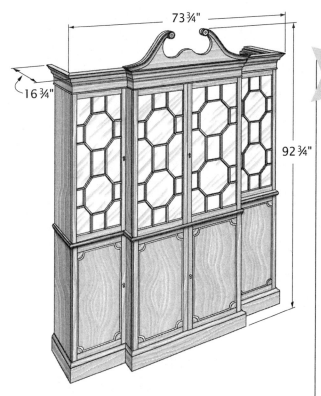

73¾"

16¾"

92¾"

DESIGN VARIATIONS

The breakfront design concept can be put to good use for a variety of purposes. Traditional breakfronts housed books or china. Identical furniture in today's home might also house collections of anything from teacups to kachina dolls.

Modern breakfronts are often designed as entertainment centers, housing audio and video equipment. The design is well suited for this, since the shallower flanking units disguise the depth required in the center unit for a TV set.

While traditional breakfronts are divided into upper and lower sections, some modern breakfronts are divided into center and side sections, allowing a manufacturer to offer a choice of widths and specialized functions.

Though kitchen cabinets are seldom thought of as breakfronts, some makers apply the breakfront concept to them by varying the depths of long stretches of wall cabinets.

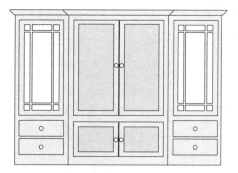

Breakfront Entertainment Center

A large, flat expanse of cabinetry can be very boring and overwhelming. So when a customer required large storage capacity, furniture designers broke up the front of the cabinet into different depths. The result, a breakfront, is still a cabinet with large capacity but a much more pleasing one.

Breakfronts are always big, so big that moving them from shop to customer could be difficult. Since early breakfronts were often over 8 feet tall, even moving them from room to room could be impossible. To solve this problem, they were built in sections to be assembled, usually with screws, after they were in the intended room. The division into sections was made between the upper and lower parts. This allowed the craftsman to assemble the miter joints in the extensive horizontal moldings in the shop, and to apply the finish over the assembled miters.

PLANS

Margon, Lester. "Mahogany Break Front," *Construction of American Furniture Treasures.* New York: Dover Publications, 1975. Drawings including extensive details and instructions for the archetypal breakfront shown.

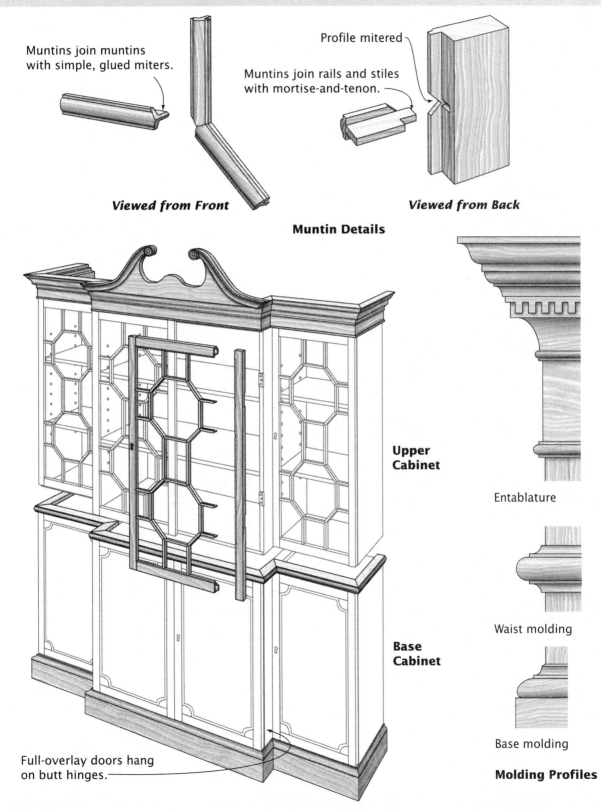

Muntins join muntins with simple, glued miters.

Muntins join rails and stiles with mortise-and-tenon.

Profile mitered

Viewed from Front

Viewed from Back

Muntin Details

Upper Cabinet

Base Cabinet

Full-overlay doors hang on butt hinges.

Entablature

Waist molding

Base molding

Molding Profiles

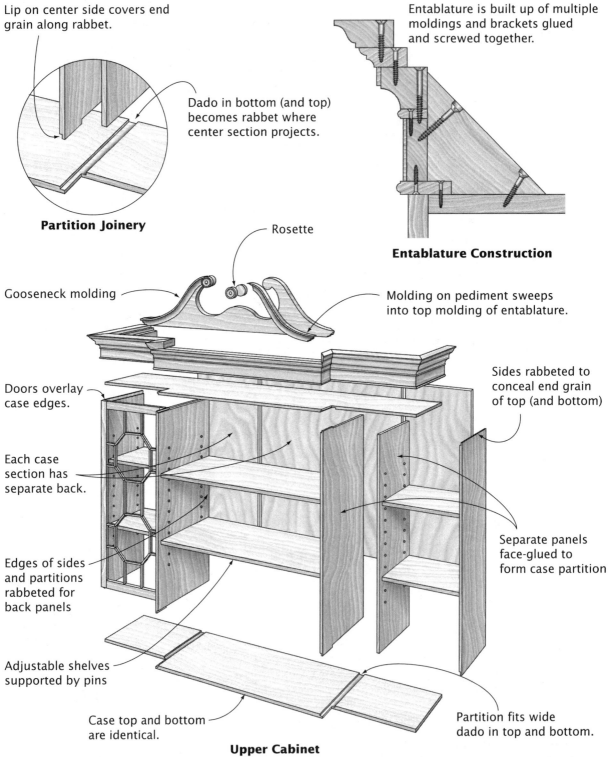

Lip on center side covers end grain along rabbet.

Dado in bottom (and top) becomes rabbet where center section projects.

Partition Joinery

Entablature is built up of multiple moldings and brackets glued and screwed together.

Entablature Construction

Rosette

Gooseneck molding

Molding on pediment sweeps into top molding of entablature.

Doors overlay case edges.

Sides rabbeted to conceal end grain of top (and bottom)

Each case section has separate back.

Edges of sides and partitions rabbeted for back panels

Separate panels face-glued to form case partition

Adjustable shelves supported by pins

Case top and bottom are identical.

Partition fits wide dado in top and bottom.

Upper Cabinet

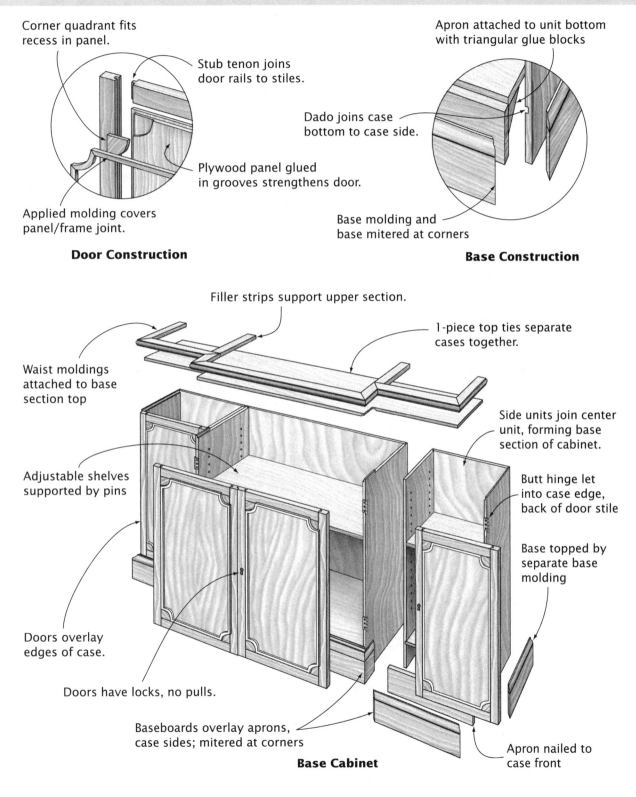

Corner quadrant fits
recess in panel.

Stub tenon joins
door rails to stiles.

Applied molding covers
panel/frame joint.

Plywood panel glued
in grooves strengthens door.

Door Construction

Apron attached to unit bottom
with triangular glue blocks

Dado joins case
bottom to case side.

Base molding and
base mitered at corners

Base Construction

Filler strips support upper section.

1-piece top ties separate
cases together.

Waist moldings
attached to base
section top

Side units join center
unit, forming base
section of cabinet.

Adjustable shelves
supported by pins

Butt hinge let
into case edge,
back of door stile

Base topped by
separate base
molding

Doors overlay
edges of case.

Doors have locks, no pulls.

Baseboards overlay aprons,
case sides; mitered at corners

Base Cabinet

Apron nailed to
case front

TALL-CASE
CLOCK

Tall Clock, Grandfather Clock

90"

21¾"

11"

days, the scale of the case stemmed from the nature of the clockwork. Powered by a weight and chain system, its steady interval was governed by the back-and-forth movement of a pendulum. These appendages dictated that the clockwork be placed high off the floor, and it seemed natural to enclose it in a case.

The casework's evolution from functional to decorative followed naturally from the fact that clocks were owned primarily by the wealthy, who wanted to show off this cutting-edge technology. Why not combine that with cutting-edge cabinetmaking?

DESIGN VARIATIONS

Not all tall clocks share the elaborateness of the archetype. The Shakers, for example, designed and built plain and relatively unembellished tall-case clocks. Only a quarter-round molding at the floor and hood's top break up the plainness of the case shown below. An equally simple cove molding supports the hood. A contemporary clock design flexes the lines of the tall case.

Shaker-Style Tall-Case Clock

Contemporary Tall-Case Clock

Clocks are so common these days—and so miniaturized—that it's hard to imagine it wasn't always so. The grandest of clocks is the tall-case clock, with its painted dial and ornate casework. When tall clocks originated, in colonial

PLANS

Frid, Tage. "Grandmother Clock," in "Casework." *Tage Frid Teaches Woodworking, Book 3: Furnituremaking.* Newtown, CT: The Taunton Press, 1985. Excellent drawings and construction notes for an under-6-foot sculpted-case contemporary clock.

●

Gehret, Phil. "Pennsylvania Tall Clock," *American Woodworker,* No. 25 (March/April 1992), pp. 36–43, and No. 26 (May/June 1992), pp. 36–41. Spread over 2 issues, detailed plans for building the archetypal clock.

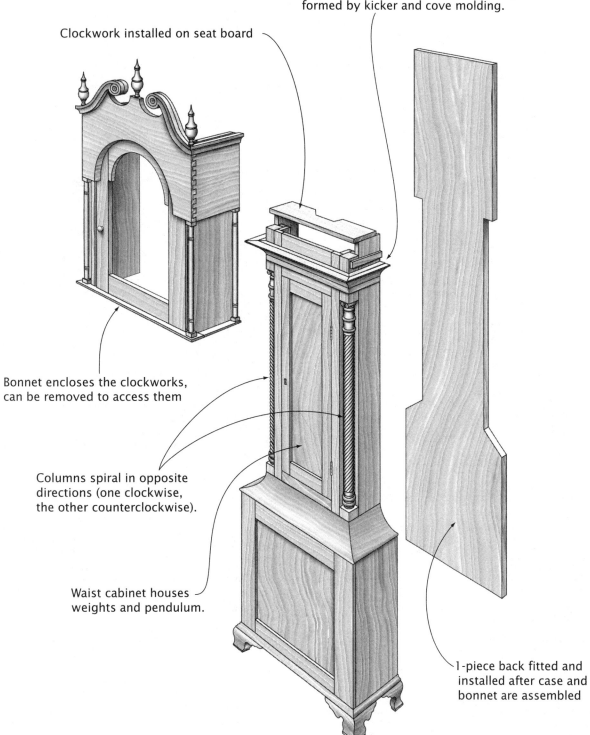

Clockwork installed on seat board

Edge of bonnet's base frame fits into groove formed by kicker and cove molding.

Bonnet encloses the clockworks, can be removed to access them

Columns spiral in opposite directions (one clockwise, the other counterclockwise).

Waist cabinet houses weights and pendulum.

1-piece back fitted and installed after case and bonnet are assembled

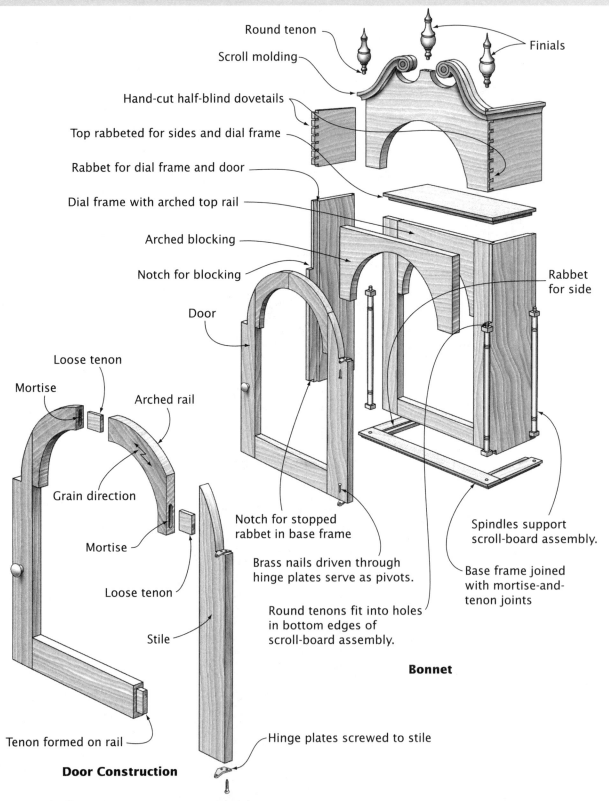

Round tenon

Scroll molding

Finials

Hand-cut half-blind dovetails

Top rabbeted for sides and dial frame

Rabbet for dial frame and door

Dial frame with arched top rail

Arched blocking

Notch for blocking

Rabbet for side

Door

Loose tenon

Mortise

Arched rail

Grain direction

Mortise

Loose tenon

Stile

Notch for stopped rabbet in base frame

Brass nails driven through hinge plates serve as pivots.

Round tenons fit into holes in bottom edges of scroll-board assembly.

Spindles support scroll-board assembly.

Base frame joined with mortise-and-tenon joints

Bonnet

Tenon formed on rail

Hinge plates screwed to stile

Door Construction

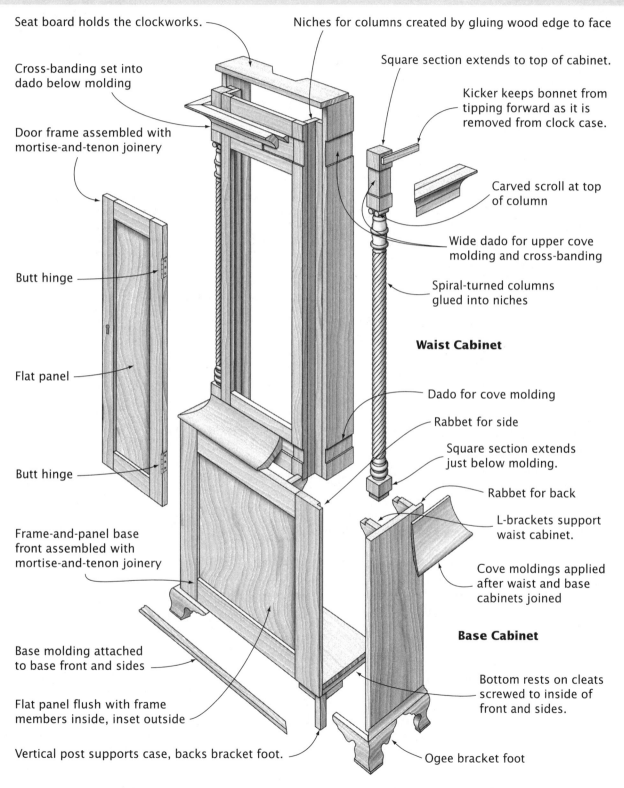

Seat board holds the clockworks.

Cross-banding set into dado below molding

Door frame assembled with mortise-and-tenon joinery

Butt hinge

Flat panel

Butt hinge

Frame-and-panel base front assembled with mortise-and-tenon joinery

Base molding attached to base front and sides

Flat panel flush with frame members inside, inset outside

Vertical post supports case, backs bracket foot.

Niches for columns created by gluing wood edge to face

Square section extends to top of cabinet.

Kicker keeps bonnet from tipping forward as it is removed from clock case.

Carved scroll at top of column

Wide dado for upper cove molding and cross-banding

Spiral-turned columns glued into niches

Waist Cabinet

Dado for cove molding

Rabbet for side

Square section extends just below molding.

Rabbet for back

L-brackets support waist cabinet.

Cove moldings applied after waist and base cabinets joined

Base Cabinet

Bottom rests on cleats screwed to inside of front and sides.

Ogee bracket foot

FILE
CABINET

Filing Cabinet

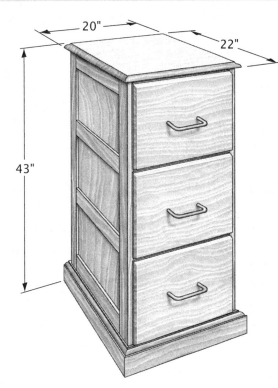

DESIGN VARIATIONS The appearance of a file cabinet can be altered through changes in construction, as well as through cabinet and drawer configuration. It is still a tall, deep cabinet, but the slab-sided case with exposed dovetail joinery does present a different appearance. The hardware-free drawer fronts (*below right*) have a sleek, contemporary look. To change the footprint of the cabinet, change the drawer orientation. A cabinet in which the files are arrayed from side to side (*below left*), rather than front to back, isn't deep, but it is wide.

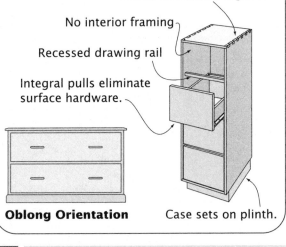

Panels dovetailed together

No interior framing

Recessed drawing rail

Integral pulls eliminate surface hardware.

Oblong Orientation

Case sets on plinth.

Hard as it may be to believe today, the file cabinet revolutionized business when it was introduced at the beginning of the 20th century. What it did was provide a logical and accessible means of organizing business correspondence and records. It is far superior to the pigeonholes of a desk, for example.

Even in this digital era, a stand-alone file cabinet is useful, even in a home office. A desk drawer sized for file folders is only a start.

Typically, file cabinets are all metal, built in factories; but a cabinetmaker can make an equally smooth-operating and far more attractive one of wood. Special file-cabinet hardware—full-extension slides, hanging file racks, pulls—is widely available.

In a file cabinet, all drawers are the same size, scaled to accommodate folders for 8 1/2 × 11 or 8 1/2 × 14 documents. File cabinets are generally deeper than the typical cabinet, running 28 to 30 inches front to back. Regardless of the proportion and depth of the drawers, the cabinet's construction is the same.

PLANS

"File Cabinet: Old Fashioned Organization," *Woodsmith*, No. 29 (September/October 1983), pp. 10–15.

•

Mandel, Mitch. "Oak Filing Cabinet," *American Woodworker*, Vol. V, No. 3 (May/June 1989), pp. 28–35.

•

Moser, Thomas. "File Cabinet (Four Drawer)," *Measured Shop Drawings for American Furniture*. New York: Sterling Publishing, 1985.

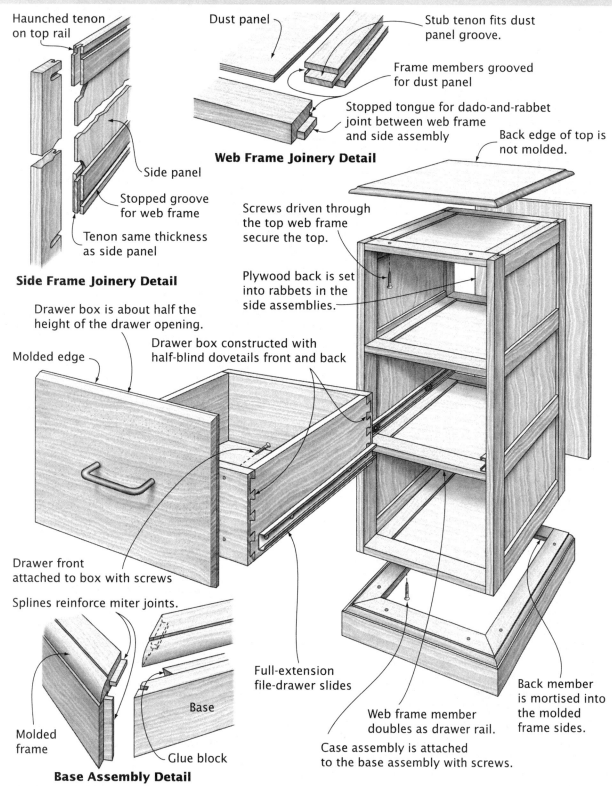

Haunched tenon on top rail

Side panel

Stopped groove for web frame

Tenon same thickness as side panel

Side Frame Joinery Detail

Dust panel

Stub tenon fits dust panel groove.

Frame members grooved for dust panel

Stopped tongue for dado-and-rabbet joint between web frame and side assembly

Web Frame Joinery Detail

Back edge of top is not molded.

Screws driven through the top web frame secure the top.

Plywood back is set into rabbets in the side assemblies.

Drawer box is about half the height of the drawer opening.

Drawer box constructed with half-blind dovetails front and back

Molded edge

Drawer front attached to box with screws

Splines reinforce miter joints.

Base

Molded frame

Glue block

Base Assembly Detail

Full-extension file-drawer slides

Web frame member doubles as drawer rail.

Case assembly is attached to the base assembly with screws.

Back member is mortised into the molded frame sides.

CREDENZA

70¾"

21⅜"

34¼"

Credenza! It sounds Italian. And Italian it once was. During the Renaissance, the Italians built heavily decorated, sideboard-like credenzas to hold valuables. It's probably natural that Americans would adopt the name for an executive's office sideboard, where he or she stows business valuables.

The credenza shown here, for example, has two shallow drawers and a file drawer in its center section. Flanking these drawers are two compartments with doors. Behind the doors are adjustable shelves. It is a commodious piece.

In appearance, this bowfront credenza is sleek and contemporary, just the ticket for a modern executive office. Instead of hardware pulls that would clutter its clean lines, this credenza has grooves in the edges of the doors and drawer fronts that serve as pulls. Its construction is also contemporary, with plywood being used for many of its components.

PLANS

Moser, Thomas. "Bowfront Credenza," *Measured Shop Drawings for American Furniture.* New York: Sterling Publishing Co., 1985. Extensive drawings of a drawer-filled credenza; no additional construction guidance provided, however.

DESIGN VARIATIONS Different office decors demand different styles of credenzas. A paneled office with traditional mahogany furnishings needs a matching credenza. This one has bracket feet, period brass pulls, and traditional moldings. It also has 3 of its 9 drawers set up for files. An office done up in the fumed oak of the Arts-and-Crafts style needs a credenza done in that style. The piece shown provides a generous amount of storage.

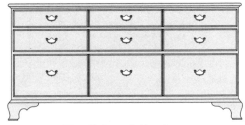

Traditional Credenza

Arts-and-Crafts Credenza

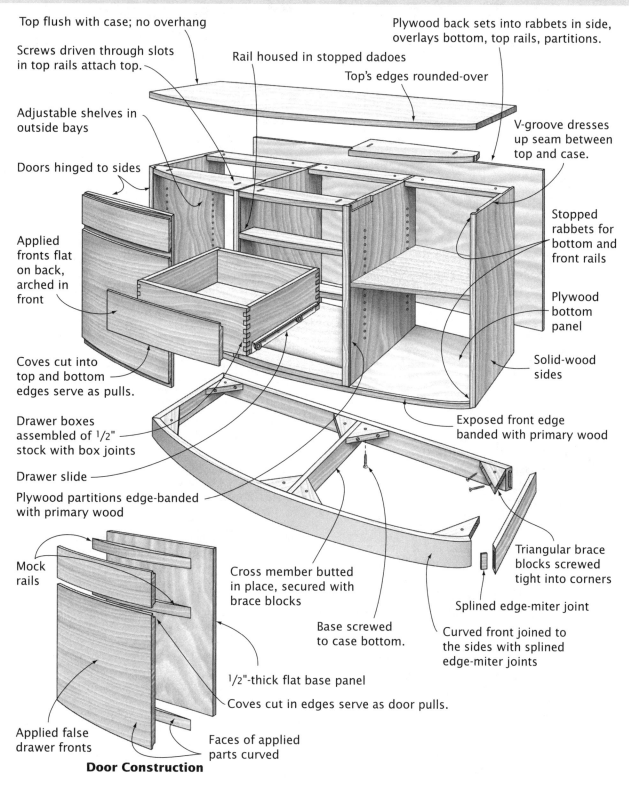

Top flush with case; no overhang

Screws driven through slots in top rails attach top.

Adjustable shelves in outside bays

Doors hinged to sides

Applied fronts flat on back, arched in front

Coves cut into top and bottom edges serve as pulls.

Drawer boxes assembled of 1/2" stock with box joints

Drawer slide

Plywood partitions edge-banded with primary wood

Mock rails

Applied false drawer fronts

Door Construction

Faces of applied parts curved

1/2"-thick flat base panel

Coves cut in edges serve as door pulls.

Base screwed to case bottom.

Cross member butted in place, secured with brace blocks

Plywood back sets into rabbets in side, overlays bottom, top rails, partitions.

Rail housed in stopped dadoes

Top's edges rounded-over

V-groove dresses up seam between top and case.

Stopped rabbets for bottom and front rails

Plywood bottom panel

Solid-wood sides

Exposed front edge banded with primary wood

Triangular brace blocks screwed tight into corners

Splined edge-miter joint

Curved front joined to the sides with splined edge-miter joints

ENTERTAINMENT
CENTER

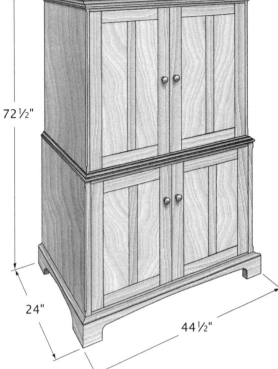

72½"

24"

44½"

DESIGN VARIATIONS Two basic entertainment-center forms predominate. One, seemingly a bedroom breakaway, houses a stack of components behind wooden doors in what appears to be a traditional armoire or linen press. The give-away is its depth. To accommodate even a moderate-sized TV, the case must be considerably deeper than the typical linen press.

The second form is a contemporary, modular-appearing cabinet. This style will will accommodate a mammoth TV a bit more gracefully and will house a greater number of individual components as well.

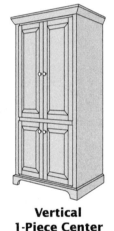

Horizontal Center

Vertical 1-Piece Center

Twenty years ago, the "entertainment center" didn't exist. The manufacturer packaged the television in its own wooden console. Stereo components were set on bookshelves. But as the array of consumer electronics burgeoned, demand mounted for a centralized place to put it all.

The resulting cabinetry is the most recent example we have of the evolution of furniture. The entertainment center shown is similar to the "Linen Press" on page 318, which held linens and clothing. The new center, however, holds a television and VCR in the upper case, and audio and game components in the lower case.

Although it looks traditional, modern hardware equips the center with pocket doors and a pull-out swivel mount for the TV, allowing virtually unobstructed viewing. A chase built into the back of the piece keeps all the wiring out of sight, while providing an escape for the heat generated by all the electronics.

PLANS

"Entertainment Center," *Woodsmith*, No. 81 (June 1992), pp. 6–15. Directions for building a contemporary, side-by-side center presented in step-by-illustrated-step detail.

•

Erickson, Ben. "Entertainment Center," *Cabinetry*, edited by Robert A. Yoder. Emmaus, PA: Rodale Press, 1992. A linen press–style center for a modest assortment of components.

•

Schoen, Edward. "Entertainment Center," *American Woodworker*, No. 57 (February 1997), pp. 47–55. Good article provides design guidelines, basic construction drawings, construction tips, but no project-specific lists or step-by-step.

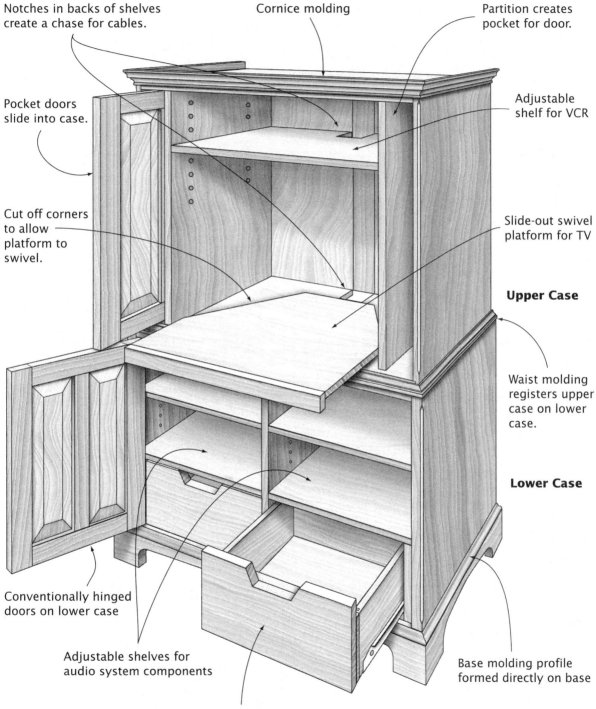

Notches in backs of shelves create a chase for cables.

Cornice molding

Partition creates pocket for door.

Pocket doors slide into case.

Adjustable shelf for VCR

Cut off corners to allow platform to swivel.

Slide-out swivel platform for TV

Upper Case

Waist molding registers upper case on lower case.

Lower Case

Conventionally hinged doors on lower case

Adjustable shelves for audio system components

Base molding profile formed directly on base

Drawers for video and CD storage

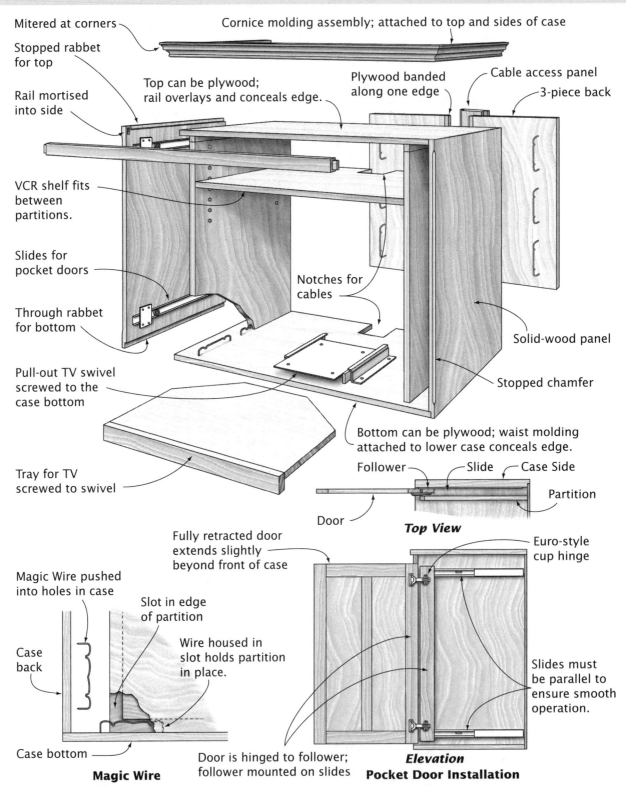

Mitered at corners

Stopped rabbet for top

Rail mortised into side

Top can be plywood; rail overlays and conceals edge.

Cornice molding assembly; attached to top and sides of case

Plywood banded along one edge

Cable access panel

3-piece back

VCR shelf fits between partitions.

Slides for pocket doors

Through rabbet for bottom

Pull-out TV swivel screwed to the case bottom

Tray for TV screwed to swivel

Notches for cables

Solid-wood panel

Stopped chamfer

Bottom can be plywood; waist molding attached to lower case conceals edge.

Follower   Slide   Case Side

Partition

Door

Top View

Fully retracted door extends slightly beyond front of case

Magic Wire pushed into holes in case

Slot in edge of partition

Wire housed in slot holds partition in place.

Case back

Case bottom

Magic Wire

Door is hinged to follower; follower mounted on slides

Euro-style cup hinge

Slides must be parallel to ensure smooth operation.

Elevation
Pocket Door Installation

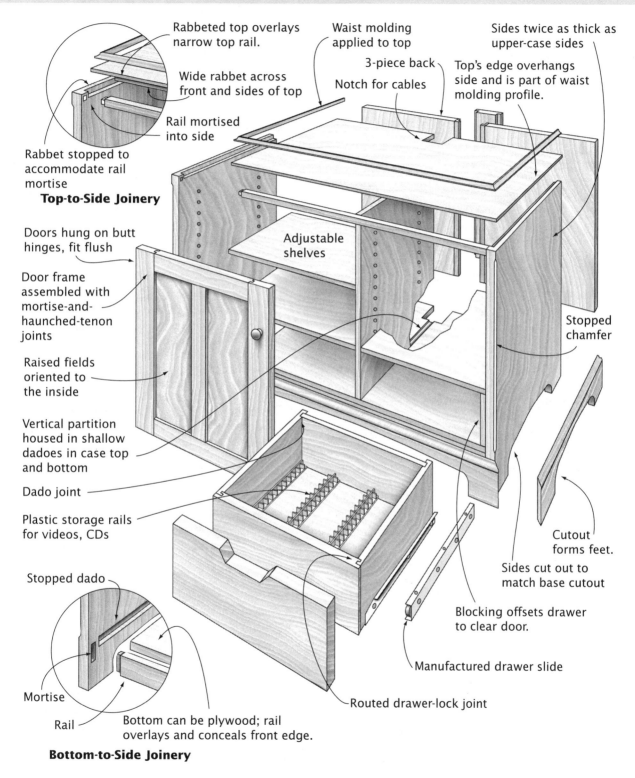

Rabbeted top overlays narrow top rail.

Waist molding applied to top

Sides twice as thick as upper-case sides

Wide rabbet across front and sides of top

3-piece back

Top's edge overhangs side and is part of waist molding profile.

Notch for cables

Rail mortised into side

Rabbet stopped to accommodate rail mortise

Top-to-Side Joinery

Doors hung on butt hinges, fit flush

Adjustable shelves

Door frame assembled with mortise-and-haunched-tenon joints

Stopped chamfer

Raised fields oriented to the inside

Vertical partition housed in shallow dadoes in case top and bottom

Dado joint

Plastic storage rails for videos, CDs

Stopped dado

Cutout forms feet.

Sides cut out to match base cutout

Blocking offsets drawer to clear door.

Mortise

Manufactured drawer slide

Rail

Routed drawer-lock joint

Bottom can be plywood; rail overlays and conceals front edge.

Bottom-to-Side Joinery

WASHSTAND

Commode, Nightstand

47¼"

17¼"

31"

At one time, the washstand was the bathroom. You didn't have running water, so you had no bathroom. But in your bedroom, you had a washstand. It was the stand where you washed.

On top would be a large wash basin and pitcher. Washcloth and towels hung behind them on the towel rack. Shaving mug and brush, razor, soap, and other toilet articles would be in the top drawer. The lower drawers would hold fresh towels and linens. And behind the little door would be the chamberpot.

Nowadays, of course, washstands are splendid occasional cabinets. The washstand shown is the sort of piece factory-made by the thousands in the late 19th and early 20th centuries—The Age of Golden Oak. For the

woodworker, it is an interesting and educational cabinetmaking project.

The archetype piece is "frame-and-panel madness!" The back is a frame-and-panel unit, as are the two sides. These are joined with three virtually identical web frame units to form the case. There's even a web frame that underlies the top. In addition, the little door is a frame-and-panel assembly.

DESIGN VARIATIONS While many washstands surely were built by individual craftsmen, the most familiar examples were factory-made. And variety abounded. In the two variations shown below, the builders departed from the rectilinear by introducing curves in the front edge of the top and repeating that contour in the front of the upper drawer and the rail immediately below it.

Probably the most apparent difference between the archetype and the variants shown below is the drawer arrangement. Also, the bottom rail and the towel rack rail and uprights are scroll-cut.

In addition, the serpentine-front version features post-and-panel construction.

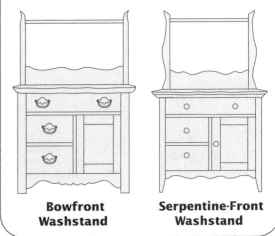

Bowfront Washstand   **Serpentine-Front Washstand**

PLANS

Yoder, Milford, "Bedside Chest," in *Cabinetry*, edited by Robert A. Yoder. Emmaus, PA: Rodale Press, 1992. Detailed drawings, cutting and hardware lists, and step-by-step directions for building the archetypal washstand.

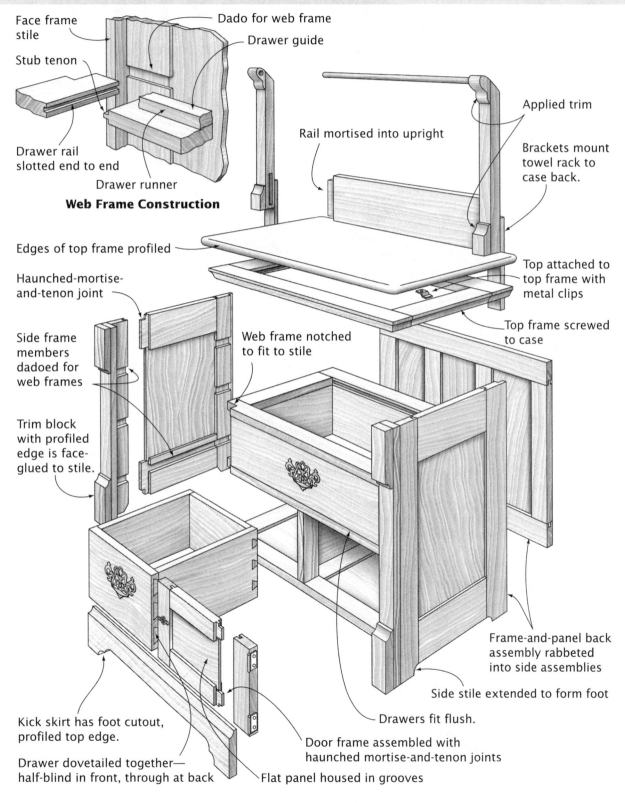

Face frame stile

Dado for web frame

Drawer guide

Stub tenon

Drawer rail slotted end to end

Drawer runner

Web Frame Construction

Rail mortised into upright

Applied trim

Brackets mount towel rack to case back.

Edges of top frame profiled

Haunched-mortise-and-tenon joint

Top attached to top frame with metal clips

Top frame screwed to case

Side frame members dadoed for web frames

Web frame notched to fit to stile

Trim block with profiled edge is face-glued to stile.

Frame-and-panel back assembly rabbeted into side assemblies

Side stile extended to form foot

Kick skirt has foot cutout, profiled top edge.

Drawers fit flush.

Door frame assembled with haunched mortise-and-tenon joints

Drawer dovetailed together—half-blind in front, through at back

Flat panel housed in grooves

NIGHTSTAND

Night Table, Bedside Stand

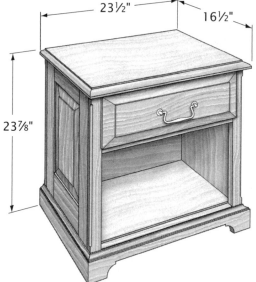

23½"

16½"

23⅞"

N ightstands likely evolved from candle stands that were once set next to the bed to hold a candle. Eventually, the candle stand was expanded to provide space for storing reading material and reading glasses and other related items. And so, the nightstand was born.

A stand—or small table—it was. Nowadays, a nightstand is likely to be a small cabinet or cupboard, as is the example shown above.

In this case, it is a frame-and-panel assembly with a drawer and an open compartment. The joinery, shown clearly in the drawing on the opposite page, is simple and strong, and the decoration is restrained.

Out of context, a nightstand may seem to be a small, odd cabinet; but in context, next to a bed with a lamp and alarm clock, it seems right at home.

PLANS

"Traditional Oak Night Stand," *Woodworker's Journal*, September/October 1997, pp. 32–37. Article provides dimensioned drawings, cutting list, and brief construction directions for a 1-drawer cabinet with an open shelf.

●

"Cherry Night Stand," *Woodsmith*, No. 76, pp. 6–11. A 3-drawer nightstand presented in well-illustrated, step-by-step detail.

DESIGN VARIATIONS

Everyone has a different bedtime routine, but almost always it involves a little bedside table or cabinet. You need a lamp that can be switched off after you are safely under the covers. You need a drawer for those glasses and, perhaps, the TV remote. You need a place for bedtime reading.

The nightstands shown here have basic similarities of size. In general, the tabletop should be positioned just above the mattress. The top should accommodate a lamp, perhaps an alarm clock and a telephone. All will do this.

In appearance, the examples shown range from a table to a cupboard to a chest of drawers. So what do you want the nightstand next to your bed to look like? What sort of bedside storage do you need? The open stand is traditional, certainly, but it's an invitation to clutter. The cupboard will hide the clutter but make it difficult to find the one item you want. The chest of drawers provides the means to sort the clutter.

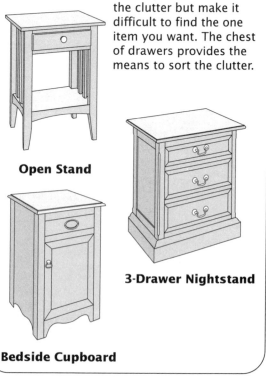

Open Stand

3-Drawer Nightstand

Bedside Cupboard

Thumbnail Profile

Web frames assembled with (unglued) mortise-and-loose-tenon joints

Plywood panel

Back and face frame overlap the sides.

Screws driven through web frame secure top.

Thumbnail profile on front, end edges

Panel recessed on inside, raised on outside

Drawer-lock joint

Through dado for bottom

Stopped rabbet on front, back rails; through rabbet on sides

False front has raised field.

Plywood bottom with hardwood edge band

Stopped chamfers soften corners of face frame.

Extended stiles support case.

Separate base molding glued to base and case

Applied baseboards mitered at front corners

Base Molding Profile

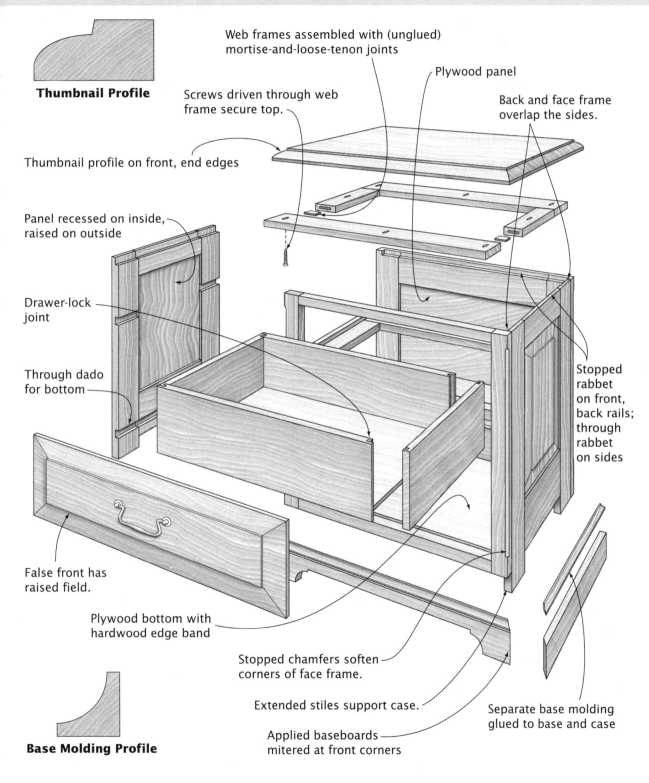

LINEN PRESS

Press, Clothes Press, Press Cupboard

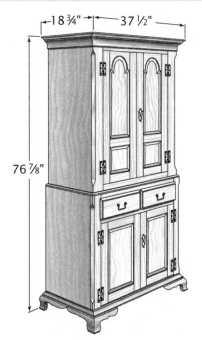

─18¾"─→ ├─ 37½" ─┤

76⅞"

T he linen press is a case piece intended for storing clothes and linens. Its use and, to some extent, its construction make it a relative of the wardrobe.

The American model shown is a rural piece whose maker was willing to stray from the strict form that confined his big-city counterparts. The upper case is the taller of the two. The fluted columns are an interesting embellishment, as are the upper case's arch-topped doors.

It is a straightforward case piece with largely traditional joinery. The drawer support setup is somewhat crude, since the two drawers simply rest on a shelf and have no guides to prevent them from getting cocked as they are opened and closed.

Handberg, Ejner. *Measured Drawings of Shaker Furniture & Woodenware.* Stockbridge, MA: The Berkshire Traveller Press, 1991. Measured drawing but no construction directions.

●

Lynch, Carlyle. "Linen Press," *Classic Furniture Projects from Carlyle Lynch.* Emmaus, PA: Rodale Press, 1990. Measured drawing of a museum piece, along with construction directions.

▷ **DESIGN VARIATIONS** Changing the style of doors, tops, and bases transforms the linen press. So, too, do changes in height-to-width proportion, top-case-to-bottom-case proportion, and the number and size of drawers.

Flat crown molding

2-panel doors

Full-width drawers

Turned feet

Edge of top molded

No face frame

Short lower case

Simplified base

Shaker style

Flush-paneled doors

Drawers graduated in height

1-piece case

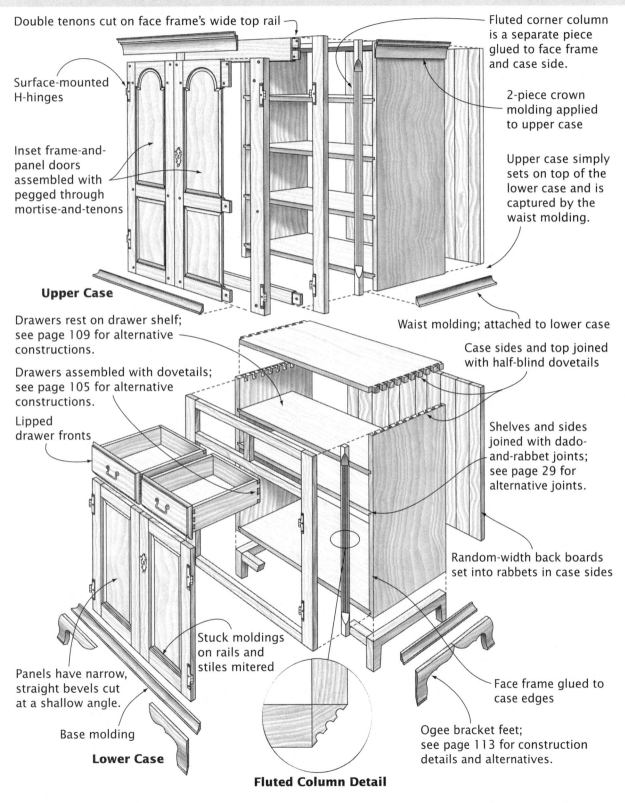

Double tenons cut on face frame's wide top rail

Fluted corner column is a separate piece glued to face frame and case side.

Surface-mounted H-hinges

2-piece crown molding applied to upper case

Inset frame-and-panel doors assembled with pegged through mortise-and-tenons

Upper case simply sets on top of the lower case and is captured by the waist molding.

Upper Case

Drawers rest on drawer shelf; see page 109 for alternative constructions.

Waist molding; attached to lower case

Case sides and top joined with half-blind dovetails

Drawers assembled with dovetails; see page 105 for alternative constructions.

Lipped drawer fronts

Shelves and sides joined with dado-and-rabbet joints; see page 29 for alternative joints.

Random-width back boards set into rabbets in case sides

Panels have narrow, straight bevels cut at a shallow angle.

Stuck moldings on rails and stiles mitered

Face frame glued to case edges

Base molding

Ogee bracket feet; see page 113 for construction details and alternatives.

Lower Case

Fluted Column Detail

BONNET
CUPBOARD

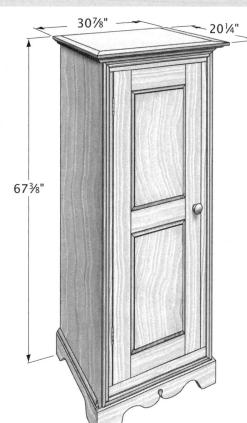

30⅞" 20¼"

67⅜"

DESIGN VARIATIONS French-Canadian furniture built in Montreal and Quebec City in the 18th and 19th centuries is a subset of French provincial furniture, the style produced in Normandy, Brittany, and other provinces of France remote from Paris. While the archetype bonnet cupboard shows the influences introduced after the ouster of the French by the British, the alternative below is clearly of French lineage. Its provincial origins are evident in the relatively low-key nature of the carving.

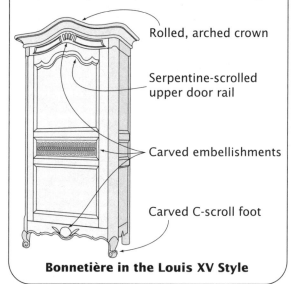

Rolled, arched crown

Serpentine-scrolled upper door rail

Carved embellishments

Carved C-scroll foot

Bonnetière in the Louis XV Style

Ever heard of a *bonnetière?* It's a "bonnet cupboard," a French provincial furniture form that emerged in the late 17th century and continued to be built through the 19th century.

It is a fairly tall, narrow cupboard with a single door that was for storing the elaborate high bonnets worn by women in Normandy and Brittany. In French Canada, this type of cupboard was nearly always used as a general wardrobe rather than as a bonnet cupboard exclusively. The cupboard shown may have been used as a washstand as well as a wardrobe. A basin, soap, and other toilet articles would have been placed on a shelf, and a mirror would have hung on the inside of the door.

Though this cupboard lacks the diamond-point panels and scrolled rails and panels typical of French provincial cupboards and armoires, that's simply a result of its being built in the mid- or late 19th century, well after the

French influence had waned. It does have the prominent cornice characteristic of French-Canadian furniture. As is typical, the three-piece cornice is attached using long nails.

PLANS

Hylton, Bill. "Quebec Bonnet Cupboard," *Country Pine.* Emmaus, PA: Rodale Press, 1995. These plans for the archetype cupboard include extensive drawings, cutting and hardware lists, and thorough step-by-step construction directions.

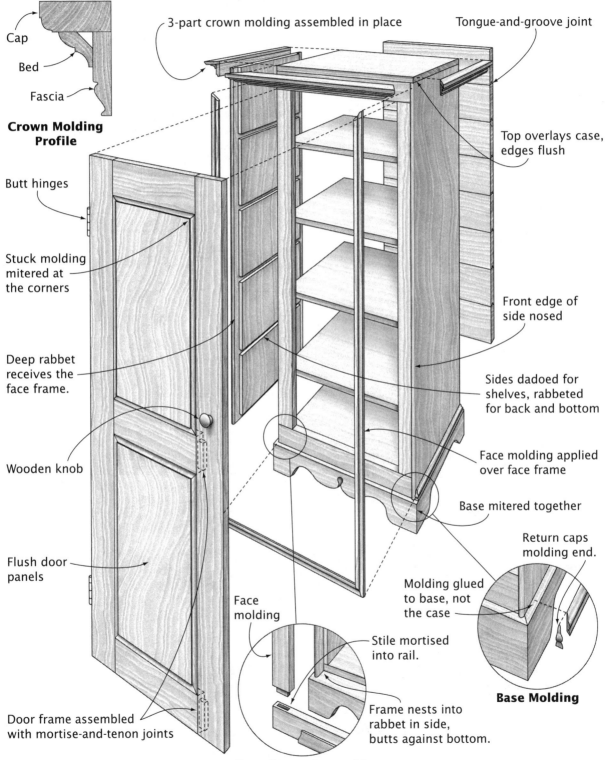

Cap

Bed

Fascia

**Crown Molding
Profile**

3-part crown molding assembled in place

Tongue-and-groove joint

Top overlays case,
edges flush

Butt hinges

Stuck molding
mitered at
the corners

Front edge of
side nosed

Deep rabbet
receives the
face frame.

Sides dadoed for
shelves, rabbeted
for back and bottom

Wooden knob

Face molding applied
over face frame

Flush door
panels

Base mitered together

Return caps
molding end.

Molding glued
to base, not
the case

Face
molding

Stile mortised
into rail.

Door frame assembled
with mortise-and-tenon joints

Frame nests into
rabbet in side,
butts against bottom.

Base Molding

Face Frame Assembly

ARMOIRE

Wardrobe, Linen Press, Schrank

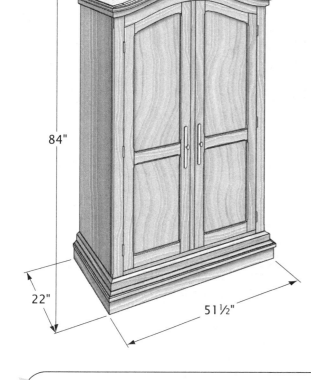

84"

22"

51½"

Built-in clothes closets were rarely seen in homes before 1900. Among the cupboards created for storing clothes and linens was the large, freestanding closet, which originated in Europe. The French term for such a closet, *armoire,* has stuck in the American lexicon.

The modern interpretation shown has the requisite features—tall doors closing over a section with shelves and a section with a rod for hanging dresses, trousers, and suits.

PLANS

"Armoire," *Woodsmith,* No. 67, pp. 18–25. A contemporary interpretation of the armoire, built using modern materials and joinery; construction presented in well-illustrated, step-by-step detail.

Lohr, Jeffry, "Arts & Crafts Armoire," *American Woodworker,* No. 46 (August 1995), pp. 26–32. Drawings and construction notes for an armoire with attractive Arts-and-Crafts detailing.

DESIGN VARIATIONS

Armoires vary greatly in style, appearance, and construction. But one feature all share is imposing size. This is a closet, after all. (And ofttimes in the past it was a chest of drawers, too.) Consequently, the armoire typically embraces a system of storage, as the examples shown here suggest. Most have shelves for folded linens, sweaters, or assorted clothing. Most also provide space for hanging clothes and have a hanger rod, pegs, or hooks for that purpose.

Almost universally, armoires have two tall doors. A wardrobe will often have drawers below the doors; but in the armoire, the drawers are hidden behind the doors. Today, the armoire form is being adapted to house TVs, stereos, and other electronic gear.

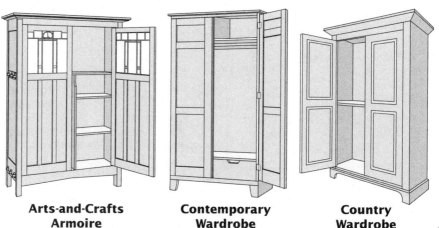

Arts-and-Crafts Armoire

Contemporary Wardrobe

Country Wardrobe

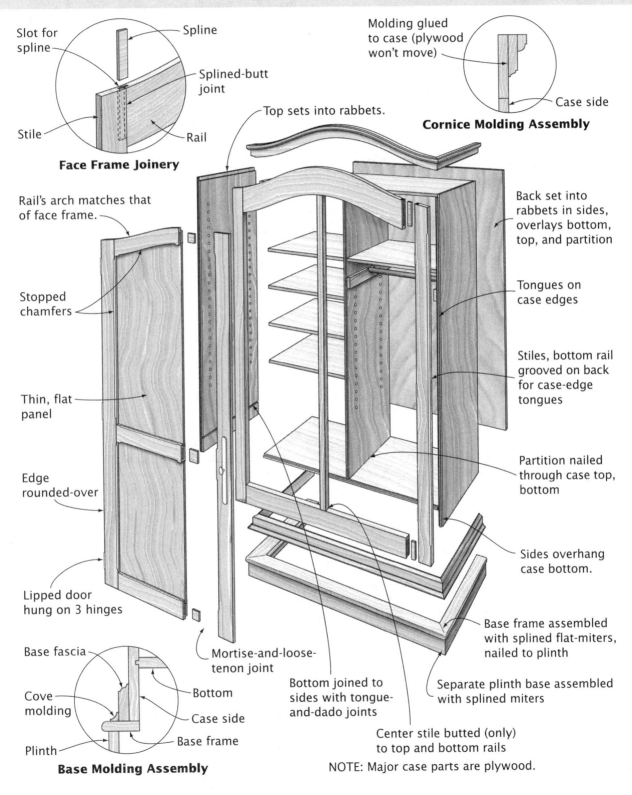

Face Frame Joinery

Slot for spline

Spline

Splined-butt joint

Stile

Rail

Cornice Molding Assembly

Molding glued to case (plywood won't move)

Case side

Top sets into rabbets.

Rail's arch matches that of face frame.

Stopped chamfers

Thin, flat panel

Edge rounded-over

Lipped door hung on 3 hinges

Back set into rabbets in sides, overlays bottom, top, and partition

Tongues on case edges

Stiles, bottom rail grooved on back for case-edge tongues

Partition nailed through case top, bottom

Sides overhang case bottom.

Base Molding Assembly

Base fascia

Cove molding

Plinth

Bottom

Case side

Base frame

Mortise-and-loose-tenon joint

Bottom joined to sides with tongue-and-dado joints

Center stile butted (only) to top and bottom rails

Base frame assembled with splined flat-miters, nailed to plinth

Separate plinth base assembled with splined miters

NOTE: Major case parts are plywood.

SCHRANK

71" 23½" 83⁵⁄₁₆"

A base section had two or more drawers, usually side by side. The piece stood on bun feet or bracket feet, and it was topped with a heavy, overhanging architectural cornice.

Brought to America by immigrants from the German Palatinate beginning in the 1680s, it remained a popular form amongst Germanic groups until the end of the 18th century. The earliest schranks made in America often were ornamented with paint and inlay, depicting names and initials surrounded by hearts, tulips, birds, and flowers.

Because of its massive size, the schrank was usually a knockdown piece. The doors would be removed first. Next, as the drawing opposite depicts, the top would be freed from the case by removing pins from 6 to 10 mortise-and-tenon joints, then carefully lifted off. Finally, more pins would be removed, and the various case components would be lifted out of mortises and grooves in the base.

The archetype is a Pennsylvania Dutch piece on display at the Conrad Weiser Homestead in Womelsdorf, Pennsylvania. Built in about 1790, it exhibits all the characteristic "schrank" features.

First appearing in 17th-century Germany, the schrank—pronounced *shronk*—is an enormous wardrobe. Typically, a schrank had a generous upright case with two doors. Clothes might be hung on hooks in one half, while folded items filled shelves in the other.

DESIGN VARIATIONS

By its massive size and ostentatious ornament, the schrank originally was a very singular sort of wardrobe. But by the end of the 19th century, it had become difficult to distinquish from the more ordinary armoire or wardrobe (see previous page).

The 18th-century schrank (at near right) is noteworthy because of the scale and layout of the base section. Considerably higher than the base of the archetype shown above, this one has two tiers of drawers. The fairly involved frame-and-panel components and the prominent cornice are typical of the 18th-century Germanic schranks.

The second variation, shown at far right, was built in a German community in East Texas in the late 19th century. While the basic *schrank* form is still there, the scale and the prominence of the moldings (especially the cornice) and feet are much diminished.

18th-Century Schrank **19th-Century Schrank**

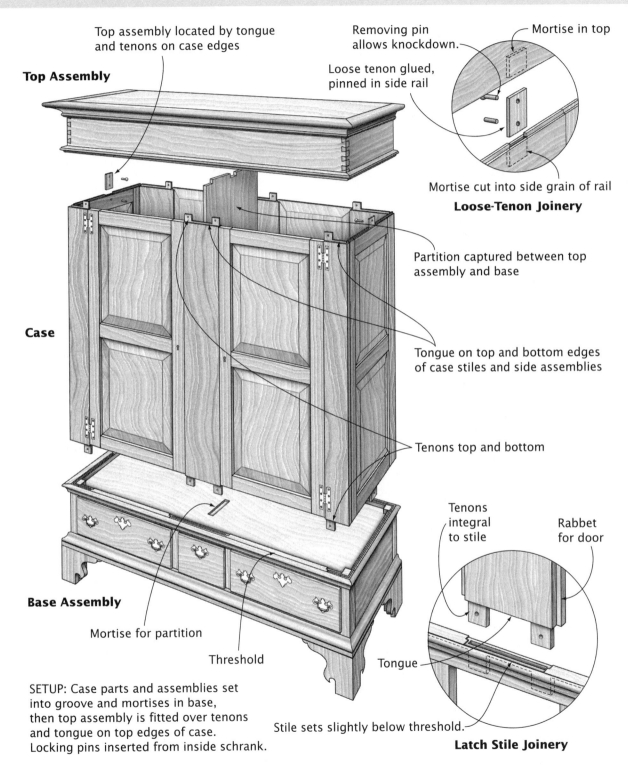

Top Assembly

Top assembly located by tongue
and tenons on case edges

Removing pin
allows knockdown.

Mortise in top

Loose tenon glued,
pinned in side rail

Mortise cut into side grain of rail

Loose-Tenon Joinery

Case

Partition captured between top
assembly and base

Tongue on top and bottom edges
of case stiles and side assemblies

Tenons top and bottom

Base Assembly

Mortise for partition

Threshold

Tenons
integral
to stile

Rabbet
for door

Tongue

Stile sets slightly below threshold.

Latch Stile Joinery

SETUP: Case parts and assemblies set
into groove and mortises in base,
then top assembly is fitted over tenons
and tongue on top edges of case.
Locking pins inserted from inside schrank.

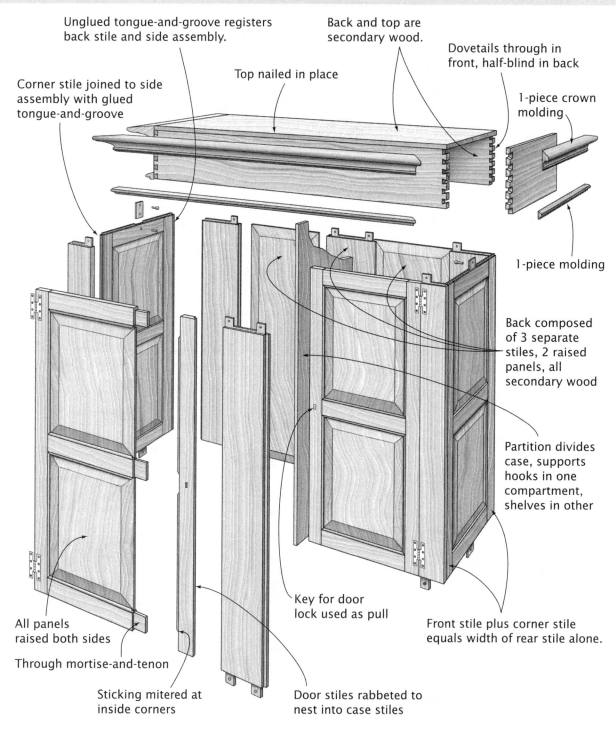

Unglued tongue-and-groove registers back stile and side assembly.

Back and top are secondary wood.

Dovetails through in front, half-blind in back

Top nailed in place

1-piece crown molding

Corner stile joined to side assembly with glued tongue-and-groove

1-piece molding

Back composed of 3 separate stiles, 2 raised panels, all secondary wood

Partition divides case, supports hooks in one compartment, shelves in other

All panels raised both sides

Through mortise-and-tenon

Key for door lock used as pull

Front stile plus corner stile equals width of rear stile alone.

Sticking mitered at inside corners

Door stiles rabbeted to nest into case stiles

NOTE: Side assemblies are constructed like the doors.

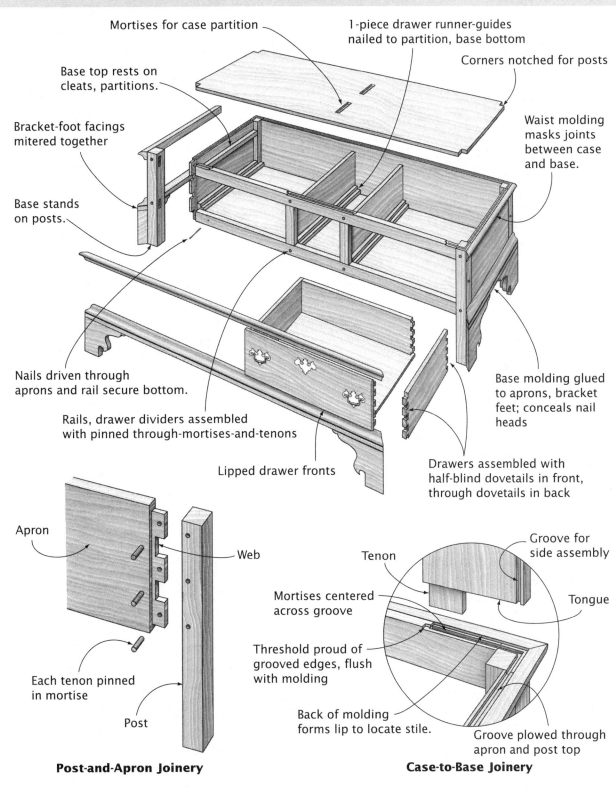

Mortises for case partition

1-piece drawer runner-guides nailed to partition, base bottom

Corners notched for posts

Base top rests on cleats, partitions.

Bracket-foot facings mitered together

Waist molding masks joints between case and base.

Base stands on posts.

Nails driven through aprons and rail secure bottom.

Rails, drawer dividers assembled with pinned through-mortises-and-tenons

Lipped drawer fronts

Base molding glued to aprons, bracket feet; conceals nail heads

Drawers assembled with half-blind dovetails in front, through dovetails in back

Apron

Web

Each tenon pinned in mortise

Post

Groove for side assembly

Tenon

Tongue

Mortises centered across groove

Threshold proud of grooved edges, flush with molding

Back of molding forms lip to locate stile.

Groove plowed through apron and post top

Post-and-Apron Joinery

Case-to-Base Joinery

SEWING DESK

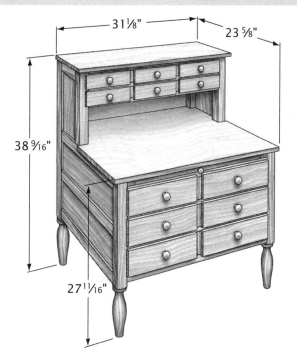

31⅛"
23⅝"
38⁹⁄₁₆"
27¹¹⁄₁₆"

Sewing Table, Sewing Cabinet, Work Stand, Worktable

DESIGN VARIATIONS Surviving Shaker sewing desks range from those more simple than the archetype to those more complex. Shown below is a well-known example of the latter. The upper gallery has six drawers and a small cupboard. With drawers on the side of the lower case as well as its front, this particular desk could be used efficiently by two Sisters, even in a relatively small area.

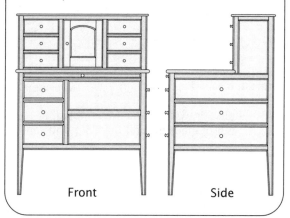

Front   Side

This and similar sewing desks are quintessential Shaker pieces. They are a form of furniture not made by anyone else. At the time they were built, sewing desks were used by the Shaker Sisters as work stations. In a contemporary setting, a sewing desk can serve as a chair-side or bedside table. The standard form features a lower case with drawers, a broad work surface, and an upper gallery with small drawers and, occasionally, a small cupboard.

The Shakers generally were very skillful cabinetmakers. They knew how to combine attractive and utilitarian woods with precise joinery, producing very practical pieces of timelessly attractive design. Nevertheless, they didn't waste their precision.

On this particular desk, the pine tops were simply nailed to the desk's frame. There are no stop blocks to prevent a drawer lip from breaking if the drawer is slammed shut. The desk has a sturdy maple frame but uses pine for the panels. This case was painted red, but the butternut drawer fronts and the walnut knobs were left unpainted. The maker knew his stuff.

PLANS

Kassay, John. "Desks," *The Book of Shaker Furniture.* Amherst, MA: The University of Massachusetts Press, 1980. Measured drawings and a cutting list for a simple sewing desk.

•

Lamb, David. "Shaker Casework," *The Best of Fine Woodworking: Traditional Furniture Projects.* Newtown, CT: The Taunton Press, 1993. A sewing desk with drawers opening to the front and side.

•

Leeke, John. "Shaker Sewing Desk," *American Woodworker*, Vol. IV, No. 4 (September/October 1988), pp. 16–23. Reproduce the sewing table shown here from these plans.

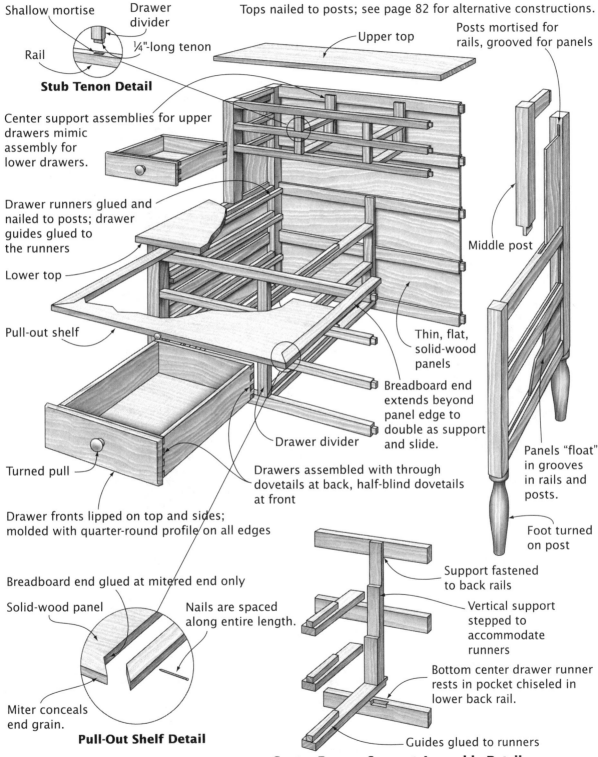

Shallow mortise

Drawer divider

Rail

¼"-long tenon

Stub Tenon Detail

Tops nailed to posts; see page 82 for alternative constructions.

Upper top

Posts mortised for rails, grooved for panels

Center support assemblies for upper drawers mimic assembly for lower drawers.

Middle post

Drawer runners glued and nailed to posts; drawer guides glued to the runners

Lower top

Pull-out shelf

Thin, flat, solid-wood panels

Breadboard end extends beyond panel edge to double as support and slide.

Drawer divider

Turned pull

Drawers assembled with through dovetails at back, half-blind dovetails at front

Panels "float" in grooves in rails and posts.

Foot turned on post

Drawer fronts lipped on top and sides; molded with quarter-round profile on all edges

Breadboard end glued at mitered end only

Solid-wood panel

Nails are spaced along entire length.

Support fastened to back rails

Vertical support stepped to accommodate runners

Bottom center drawer runner rests in pocket chiseled in lower back rail.

Miter conceals end grain.

Pull-Out Shelf Detail

Guides glued to runners

Center Drawer Support Assembly Detail

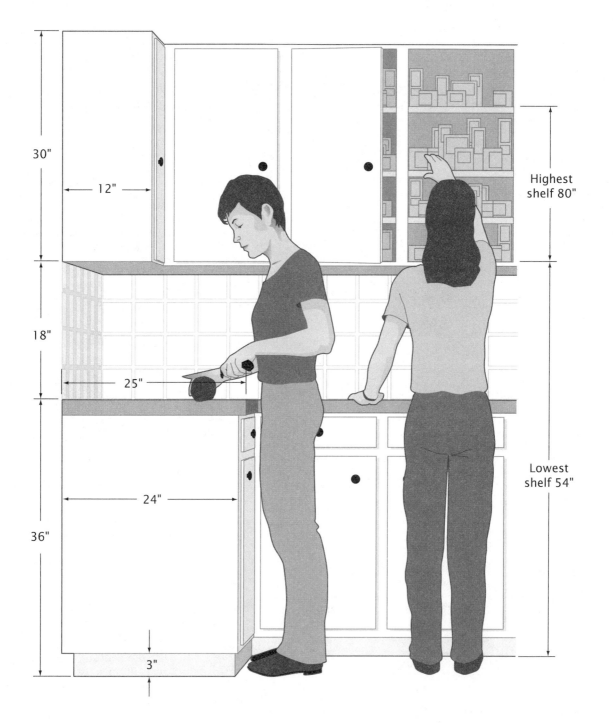

BUILT-IN CABINETS

More than any other furniture, built-in cabinets—primarily kitchen cabinets—have standardized dimensions.

These standards grew out of average human proportions and have been uniformly adopted by manufacturers. So while it might seem sensible to customize a piece's dimensions to fit the dimensions of the people who will own it, when it comes to built-in cabinetry, you deviate from the norms at your own considerable risk.

KITCHEN BASE CABINET: The standard height of a kitchen cabinet is 34 1/2 inches, the standard depth 24 inches. Countertop height is 36 inches, countertop depth 25 inches.

All these dimensions can be customized. But appliances such as dishwashers are designed to fit under countertops of normal height; kitchen sinks, to fit in countertops of normal depth.

Typically, base cabinets have a recess at the floor called the kick-space, about 3 inches deep and 3 to 4 inches high, to accommodate the toes of a person working at the counter.

KITCHEN WALL CABINET: The standards are: 12 inches deep and either 30 inches high or 42 inches high. The depth accommodates the typical dinner plate (10 inches in diameter). The 30-inch height accommodates the reach of the average person (78 to 80 inches). The 42-inch height runs the wall cabinet to the now-typical 8-foot ceiling, even though the top shelf is out of reach for most people.

The wall cabinets should be 16 to 18 inches above the counter. This vertical space accommodates the typical countertop appliances and provides the average person with a clear sight line to the back edge of the counter.

BATHROOM VANITY: Standard height is about 34 inches; but as with kitchen cabinets, this can be varied to suit the user— kids, in particular, who otherwise may have trouble reaching the faucets. Standard depth is 20 inches or somewhat more.

KITCHEN WALL CABINET

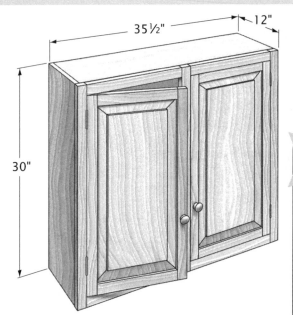

35½"   12"

30"

The modern kitchen is filled, wall to wall and floor to ceiling, with cabinetry. On the walls hang runs of cabinets, almost exactly like the one shown here.

The typical kitchen wall cabinet is a very simple box fitted with adjustable shelves and a door. Use of plywood or other sheet materials expedites construction. The cabinet's appearance is driven by the design and setting of the doors and by whether or not there is a face frame. Details—the wood used for the face, for example, and whether or not sticking embellishes the door and face frames—set an expensive cabinet apart from a cheap one.

PLANS

Draper, William, and Robert Schultz. "Basic Kitchen Wall Cabinet," *Cabinetry,* edited by Robert A. Yoder. Emmaus, PA: Rodale Press, 1992. Plans and directions for building well-detailed, traditional-style wall cabinets with glazed doors.

•

Engler, Nick. "Putting It All Together: A Cabinetry Project," *Making Built-In Cabinets.* Emmaus, PA: Rodale Press, 1992. A section of this chapter provides dimensioned drawings, cutting lists, and directions for framed wall cabinets.

DESIGN VARIATIONS

The obvious way to vary the appearance of a wall cabinet is to change the doors. But there are at least three fundamental either-or choices that impact the appearance of your kitchen wall cabinets.

First, you can choose between the common 30-inch cabinet, which ends a foot shy of the standard 8-foot ceiling, and the 42-inch cabinet, which fills that dead space with extra cabinet space.

Second, you can add a traditional touch by installing a cornice molding on the cabinet.

Finally, you should decide whether or not you want face frames. While this ostensibly is a structural choice, it has an effect on appearance as well.

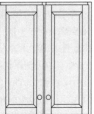

30" Cabinet vs. 42" Cabinet

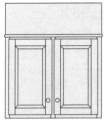

Cabinet with Soffit vs. Cabinet with Cornice

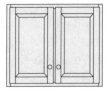

Cabinet with Face Frame vs. Frameless Cabinet

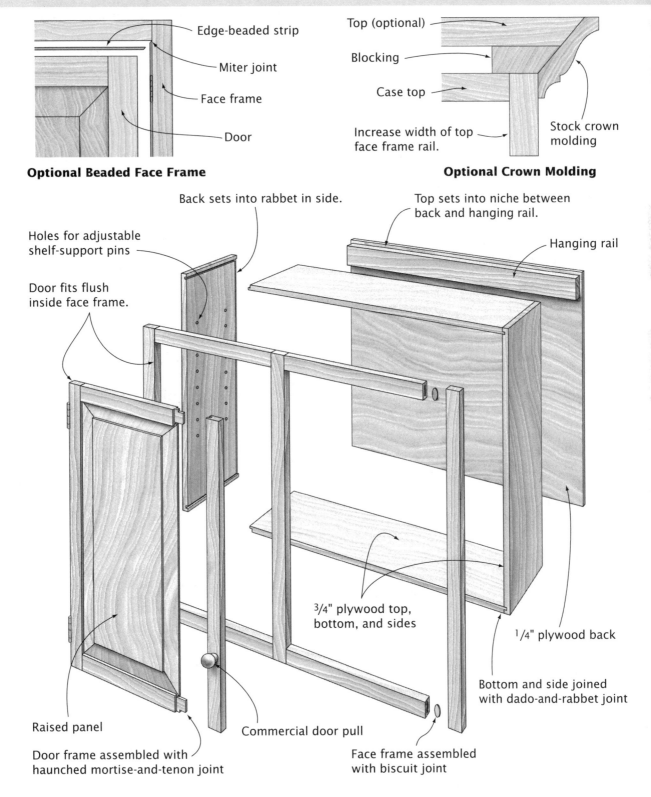

Optional Beaded Face Frame

Edge-beaded strip

Miter joint

Face frame

Door

Optional Crown Molding

Top (optional)

Blocking

Case top

Increase width of top face frame rail.

Stock crown molding

Back sets into rabbet in side.

Top sets into niche between back and hanging rail.

Holes for adjustable shelf-support pins

Hanging rail

Door fits flush inside face frame.

3/4" plywood top, bottom, and sides

1/4" plywood back

Raised panel

Commercial door pull

Bottom and side joined with dado-and-rabbet joint

Door frame assembled with haunched mortise-and-tenon joint

Face frame assembled with biscuit joint

KITCHEN BASE CABINET

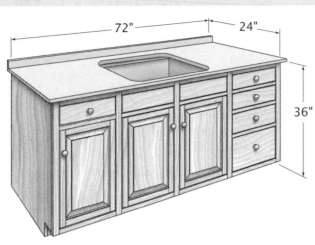

72" 24" 36"

This just may be the newest cabinet form in this book. While other cupboards and cabinets often date back hundreds of years, the sort of kitchen cabinet shown here is a 20th-century concept.

It was during the postwar building boom of the late 1940s that many cabinetmakers began to specialize in building kitchen and bath cabinets to supplant hutches, worktables, and pantry closets. Today, runs of these cabinets fill almost every kitchen built in America. They share three fundamental characteristics.

First, they're usually made from plywood and similar sheet materials. Because these manufactured materials are more stable than wood, construction can be simplified.

Second, the cabinets are modular, with each unit being a standardized box equipped with shelves and drawers and doors. Modules of different configurations are installed side-by-side to create a cabinet system, tied together with a single countertop.

Finally, the cabinets are built-in; they're screwed to the walls, floor, or ceiling. Some cabinets derive much of their structural strength from this.

The archetypal base cabinet shown here has a bank of drawers, a cupboard with adjustable shelves, and a double-doored bay for the kitchen sink and its plumbing, all in a single case.

PLANS

Draper, William, and Robert Schultz. "Drawer Base and Sink Base Cabinets," *Cabinetry*, edited by Robert A. Yoder. Emmaus, PA: Rodale Press, 1992. Plans and directions for building well-detailed, traditional-style base cabinets.

Engler, Nick. "Putting It All Together: A Cabinetry Project," *Making Built-In Cabinets*. Emmaus, PA: Rodale Press, 1992. A section of this chapter provides dimensioned drawings, cutting lists, and directions for several base cabinets.

DESIGN VARIATIONS

The modularity of modern kitchen cabinets makes it relatively easy to configure a run of cabinets, to incorporate the mix of drawers and shelves you want, and to have them fit the available space. Basic cabinet configurations—two drawers over two doors, for example, or a bank of four drawers—can be built in a variety of widths to fit particular spaces. Shown are a few of the possibilities.

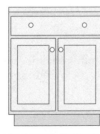

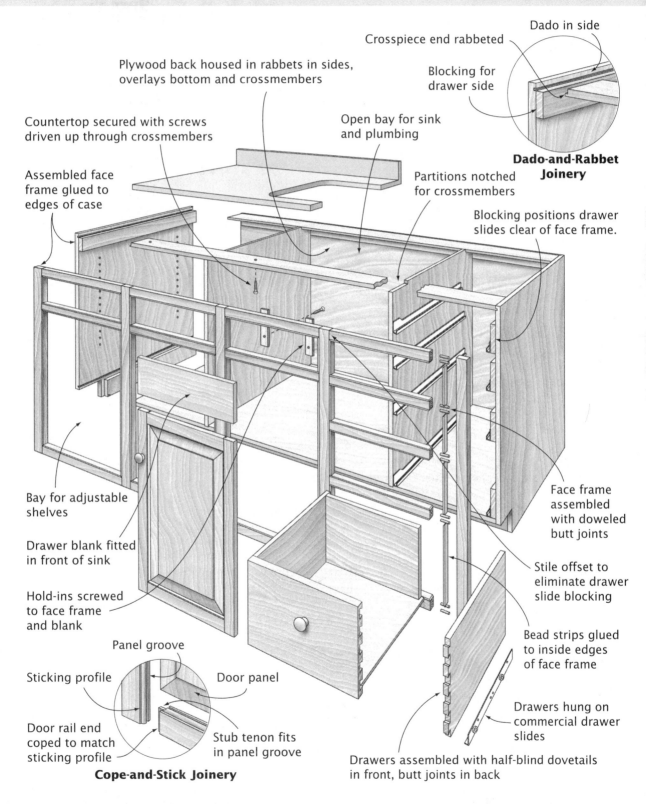

Dado in side

Crosspiece end rabbeted

Blocking for drawer side

Plywood back housed in rabbets in sides, overlays bottom and crossmembers

Dado-and-Rabbet Joinery

Countertop secured with screws driven up through crossmembers

Open bay for sink and plumbing

Partitions notched for crossmembers

Assembled face frame glued to edges of case

Blocking positions drawer slides clear of face frame.

Face frame assembled with doweled butt joints

Bay for adjustable shelves

Drawer blank fitted in front of sink

Stile offset to eliminate drawer slide blocking

Hold-ins screwed to face frame and blank

Bead strips glued to inside edges of face frame

Panel groove

Sticking profile

Door panel

Drawers hung on commercial drawer slides

Door rail end coped to match sticking profile

Stub tenon fits in panel groove

Cope-and-Stick Joinery

Drawers assembled with half-blind dovetails in front, butt joints in back

KITCHEN
CORNER
CABINET

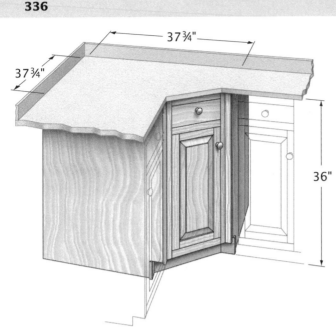

37¾"

37¾"

36"

I n a kitchen filled with cabinets, a corner presents an almost intractable problem. With 2-foot-deep cabinets converging in the corner, a considerable volume of space ends up being neither convenient nor easy to access.

The best solution (best almost by default) is the arrangement shown here. It takes a foot of space away from the base cabinets on both sides to make room for a door set diagonally across the corner. The cabinet shown incorporates a drawer above the door, a common feature in straight base cabinets but seldom in corner cabinets.

With revolving shelves installed, you gain access to the nether reaches, though a great deal of the cabinet's space—in the three far corners—is wasted. The revolving shelves can be somewhat complex, and not every kitchen item will behave itself on a revolving shelf.

PLANS

Engler, Nick. "Putting It All Together: A Cabinetry Project," *Making Built-In Cabinets*. Emmaus, PA: Rodale Press, 1992. Drawings, cutting lists, and directions for a corner cabinet included in this chapter.

●

Jones, Peter. *Shelves, Closets and Cabinets*. New York: Popular Science Books, 1987. A chapter in this book on "Cabinets" includes 2 pages with drawings devoted to the kitchen corner cabinet.

DESIGN VARIATIONS Corner cabinets employ one of two door arrangements: a single door on a diagonal or two doors in line with the faces of the adjoining cabinets. Taken solely on its own merits, the single diagonal door is generally preferred. It allows full-circle, independently revolving, lazy Susan shelves. Unfortunately, it is not compatible with post-formed (molded) one-piece laminated countertops.

Corner cabinets that do not cut the corner diagonally are sometimes fitted with revolving shelves and sometimes with fixed shelves. When revolving shelves are used, they have a pie-shaped cutout where the doors attach. When the cabinet is opened by pushing or pulling on a door, the stored items swing into the room for easy access. To close the cabinet, the whole assembly must be revolved to the closed position.

Lazy Susan Cabinet

Revolving-Door Lazy Susan

Double-Hinged Door

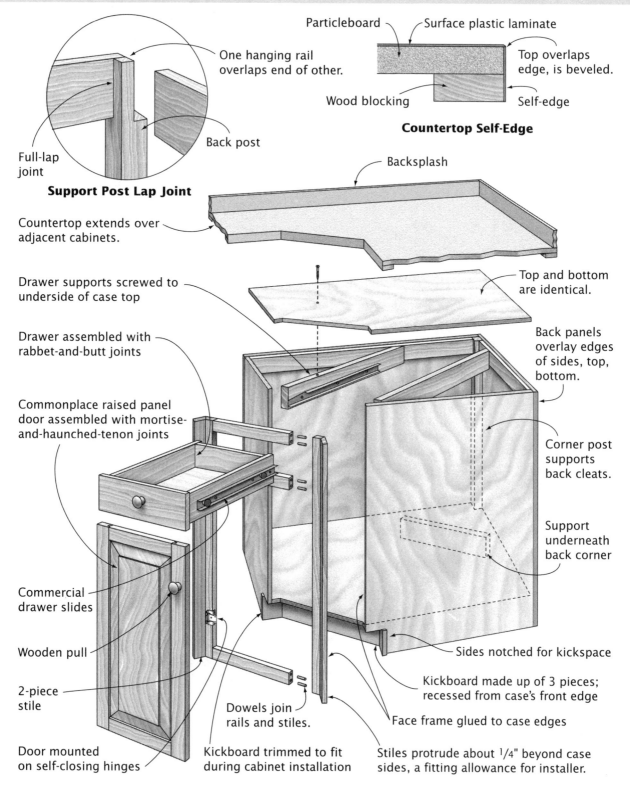

One hanging rail overlaps end of other.

Particleboard

Surface plastic laminate

Top overlaps edge, is beveled.

Wood blocking

Self-edge

Countertop Self-Edge

Back post

Full-lap joint

Support Post Lap Joint

Countertop extends over adjacent cabinets.

Backsplash

Top and bottom are identical.

Drawer supports screwed to underside of case top

Drawer assembled with rabbet-and-butt joints

Back panels overlay edges of sides, top, bottom.

Commonplace raised panel door assembled with mortise-and-haunched-tenon joints

Corner post supports back cleats.

Support underneath back corner

Commercial drawer slides

Wooden pull

2-piece stile

Dowels join rails and stiles.

Sides notched for kickspace

Kickboard made up of 3 pieces; recessed from case's front edge

Face frame glued to case edges

Door mounted on self-closing hinges

Kickboard trimmed to fit during cabinet installation

Stiles protrude about 1/4" beyond case sides, a fitting allowance for installer.

PANTRY
CABINET

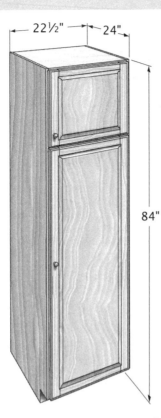

22½"   24"

84"

This pantry's dominating feature is flexible storage. Retrieving a can or jar from the rear of the 2-foot-deep case is easy; shallow drawers are used instead of shelves.

The pantry's appearance, as with other kitchen cabinets, is determined by the wood selected for the exposed components, by the construction style (frameless or framed), and finally by the door style. The particular pantry shown has a frameless case, so the doors overlay the case edges. The flat panels are secured in the rabbeted door frames with bolection molding, which stands proud of both the panel and the frame.

DESIGN VARIATIONS

The pantry's design has two aspects: its outward appearance and its fundamental concept. You can make changes to either aspect.

The appearance can be altered by changing the style of the doors (see page 94 for a gallery of basic door constructions) or by using a face-frame construction. The proportions of the cabinet can be changed; this will also alter the capacity of the pantry. Use a double-doored configuration.

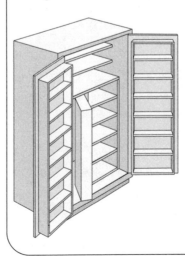

A different storage concept is depicted at left. This pantry has shelves on the doors and swinging as well as fixed shelf units inside the case. This setup is beguiling in concept but can be tiresome to use.

The pantry cabinet has pretty much supplanted the old pantry closet. While it provided lots of food storage space, the pantry closet was architectural and thus costlier than a compact pantry cabinet.

The pantry cabinet is just another form of kitchen cabinet. It's a tall box built using slab construction. Using sheet materials ensures that wood movement won't be a problem. The joinery is simple but sure, and the case is further braced by the wall to which it is screwed.

PLANS

Hylton, William H., ed. "Pantry," *Build Your Harvest Kitchen.* Emmaus, PA: Rodale Press, 1980. The book may be hard to find, and the plans are somewhat rudimentary, but the pantry is well designed and simple to make.

●

"Pantry Cabinet," *Cabinets and Built-Ins: 26 Custom Storage Projects.* Upper Saddle River, NJ: Creative Homeowner Press, 1996. Concise, nicely illustrated plans for a simple double-doored pantry.

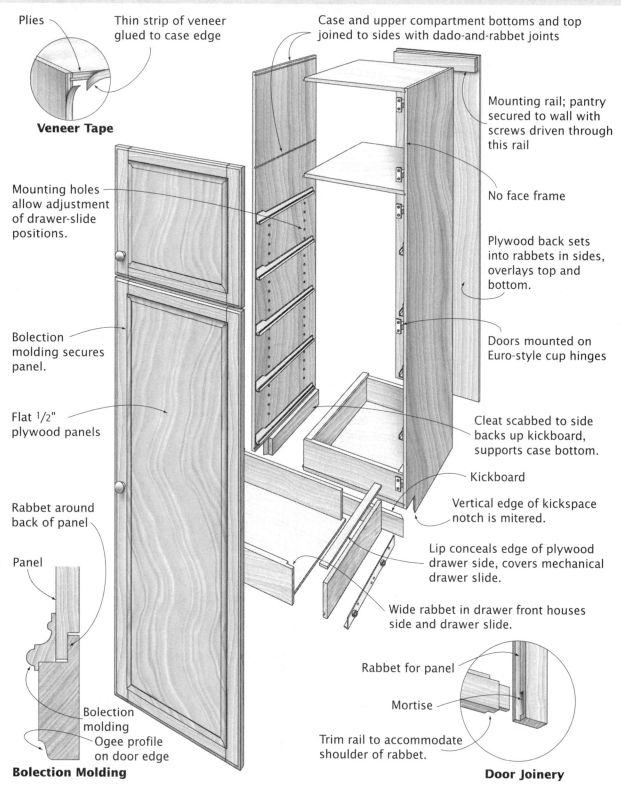

Plies

Thin strip of veneer glued to case edge

Veneer Tape

Case and upper compartment bottoms and top joined to sides with dado-and-rabbet joints

Mounting rail; pantry secured to wall with screws driven through this rail

No face frame

Plywood back sets into rabbets in sides, overlays top and bottom.

Doors mounted on Euro-style cup hinges

Mounting holes allow adjustment of drawer-slide positions.

Bolection molding secures panel.

Flat 1/2" plywood panels

Cleat scabbed to side backs up kickboard, supports case bottom.

Kickboard

Vertical edge of kickspace notch is mitered.

Lip conceals edge of plywood drawer side, covers mechanical drawer slide.

Wide rabbet in drawer front houses side and drawer slide.

Rabbet around back of panel

Panel

Bolection molding

Ogee profile on door edge

Bolection Molding

Rabbet for panel

Mortise

Trim rail to accommodate shoulder of rabbet.

Door Joinery

BATHROOM
VANITY

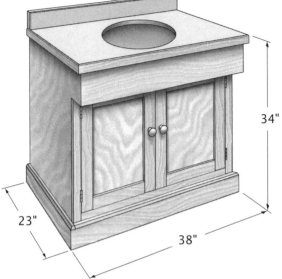

34"

23"

38"

O ne dictionary definition says that vanity is an inflated pride in one's appearance. It's just the sort of pride that got the name vanity to be given to the cabinet that holds the bathroom sink. Like the dressing table—called a vanity by many—the bathroom sink is a place where men and women primp and preen, making themselves "beautiful."

Of course, the bathroom vanity has a practical side. It provides counter space around the sink—a place for the toothbrushes, a cup, toiletries, and sundry bathroom knickknacks. It conceals the plumbing the sink requires. It offers storage for extra soaps and toilet tissue and cleaning supplies. Some vanities even have drawers for toiletries and cosmetics, towels and washcloths, hair dryers, curling irons, and other beautification apparatuses.

Most vanities are the kin of kitchen cabinets, plywood or MDF boxes screwed to the wall and fitted with doors and a countertop. (Typically, a vanity is a couple of inches lower than a kitchen cabinet.) The archetype is just such a cabinet. One difference: Instead of a kickspace at the bottom, it has a protruding waist, which forces the user back and eliminates the need for a kickspace.

PLANS

Bostock, Glenn. "Bathroom Vanity" and "Corner Vanity," *Cabinetry,* edited by Robert A. Yoder. Emmaus, PA: Rodale Press, 1992. Plans, cutting and hardware lists, and step-by-step construction directions for 2 different vanities.

●

Levine, Paul. "Cherry/Maple Vanity," "Ash Vanity with a Teak Top," and "Cherry Vanity with Beaded-Inset Doors," *Cabinets and Built-Ins.* Emmaus, PA: Rodale Press, 1994. Plans for 3 different vanities in 1 volume.

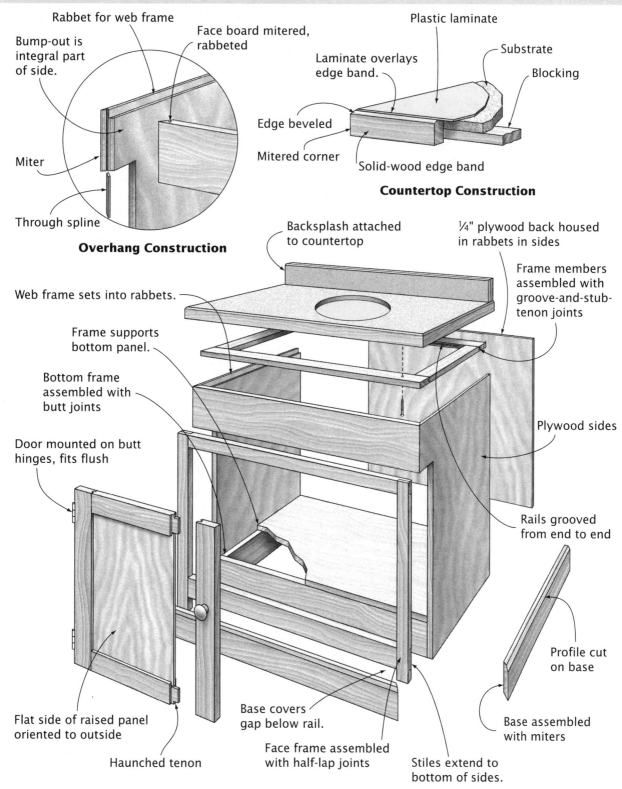

Rabbet for web frame

Bump-out is integral part of side.

Face board mitered, rabbeted

Miter

Through spline

Overhang Construction

Plastic laminate

Laminate overlays edge band.

Substrate

Blocking

Edge beveled

Mitered corner

Solid-wood edge band

Countertop Construction

Backsplash attached to countertop

¼" plywood back housed in rabbets in sides

Web frame sets into rabbets.

Frame members assembled with groove-and-stub-tenon joints

Frame supports bottom panel.

Bottom frame assembled with butt joints

Door mounted on butt hinges, fits flush

Plywood sides

Rails grooved from end to end

Flat side of raised panel oriented to outside

Haunched tenon

Base covers gap below rail.

Face frame assembled with half-lap joints

Stiles extend to bottom of sides.

Profile cut on base

Base assembled with miters

MODULAR
SHELVING
AND STORAGE

106¾"

96"

24"

I t *sounds* like kitchen cabinets—shelving... storage...modular. But think in terms of high-end architectural cabinetry. Think of an opulent study with a fireplace and leather-covered chairs, exquisite carpets, and shelf after shelf of leather-bound books. Think of warm-colored woods and rich detailing.

Modular shelving and storage can embrace that full spectrum. The concept that works in the kitchen works, too, in the family room or living room or study or bedroom. It works wherever you want shelves and cabinets and cupboards built into the room.

The example shown above consists of plywood boxes with handsomely detailed face frames and doors. The various modules are screwed to the walls and to each other, then trimmed with the same baseboard and crown molding used throughout the room.

PLANS

Levine, Paul. "Pine Shelving System," "Entertainment Center in Ash and Ash Burl Veneer," "Dining Room Cabinets," "Cherry Window Seat and Shelves," "Oak Breakfront," "Poplar Closet," and "Bookshelves in Stained Oak," *Cabinets and Built-Ins.* Emmaus, Pa: Rodale Press, 1994. A selection of contemporary-style, modular built-in projects, all in 1 volume. Plans, cutting and hardware lists, step-by-step.

DESIGN VARIATIONS Endless combinations of modules represent only the first level of design variation that is possible with modular shelving and storage. Shown below are just three of the variations possible if you use only the modules depicted in the construction drawings.

Style and detailing, materials and finishing choices take you to higher and higher levels of variation. Here, contemporary styles diverge from the traditional. The richness of walnut or mahogany branch away from the homeyness of pine and maple and from the bald functionality of the Formica-clad. These aren't necessarily cabinets from your kitchen.

Wall of bookshelves

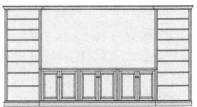

Shelves and cabinets to surround a large window

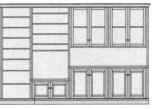

Mixed shelving, display, and storage

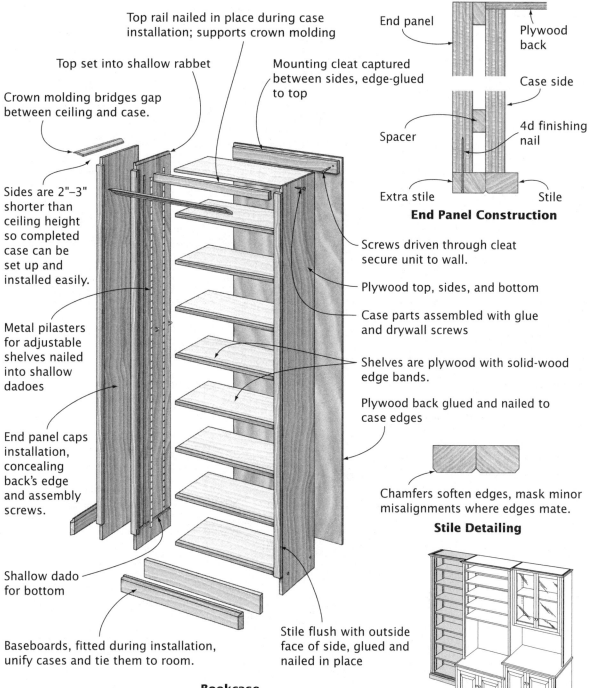

Top rail nailed in place during case installation; supports crown molding

Top set into shallow rabbet

Crown molding bridges gap between ceiling and case.

Mounting cleat captured between sides, edge-glued to top

End panel

Plywood back

Case side

Spacer

4d finishing nail

Sides are 2"–3" shorter than ceiling height so completed case can be set up and installed easily.

Extra stile

Stile

End Panel Construction

Screws driven through cleat secure unit to wall.

Plywood top, sides, and bottom

Case parts assembled with glue and drywall screws

Metal pilasters for adjustable shelves nailed into shallow dadoes

Shelves are plywood with solid-wood edge bands.

Plywood back glued and nailed to case edges

End panel caps installation, concealing back's edge and assembly screws.

Chamfers soften edges, mask minor misalignments where edges mate.

Stile Detailing

Shallow dado for bottom

Baseboards, fitted during installation, unify cases and tie them to room.

Stile flush with outside face of side, glued and nailed in place

Bookcase

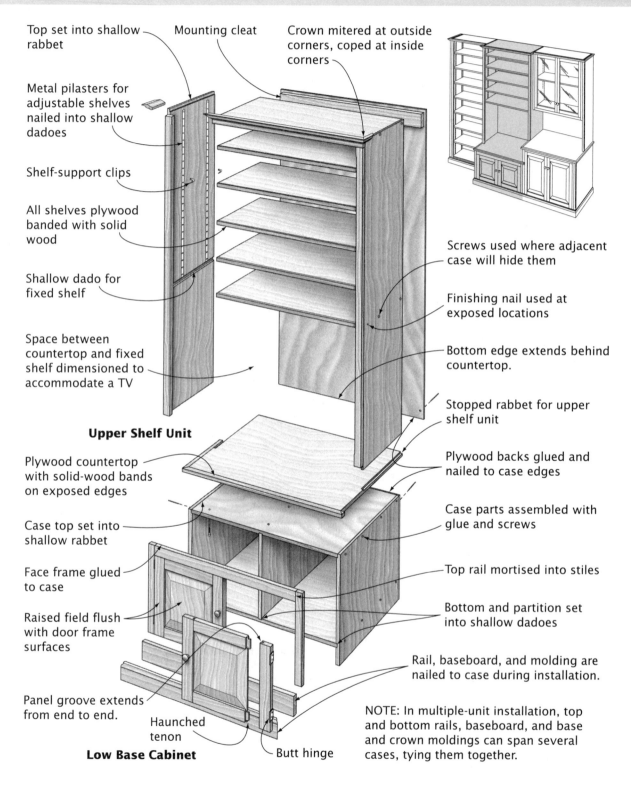

Top set into shallow rabbet

Mounting cleat

Crown mitered at outside corners, coped at inside corners

Metal pilasters for adjustable shelves nailed into shallow dadoes

Shelf-support clips

All shelves plywood banded with solid wood

Shallow dado for fixed shelf

Space between countertop and fixed shelf dimensioned to accommodate a TV

Upper Shelf Unit

Plywood countertop with solid-wood bands on exposed edges

Case top set into shallow rabbet

Face frame glued to case

Raised field flush with door frame surfaces

Panel groove extends from end to end.

Haunched tenon

Low Base Cabinet

Butt hinge

Screws used where adjacent case will hide them

Finishing nail used at exposed locations

Bottom edge extends behind countertop.

Stopped rabbet for upper shelf unit

Plywood backs glued and nailed to case edges

Case parts assembled with glue and screws

Top rail mortised into stiles

Bottom and partition set into shallow dadoes

Rail, baseboard, and molding are nailed to case during installation.

NOTE: In multiple-unit installation, top and bottom rails, baseboard, and base and crown moldings can span several cases, tying them together.

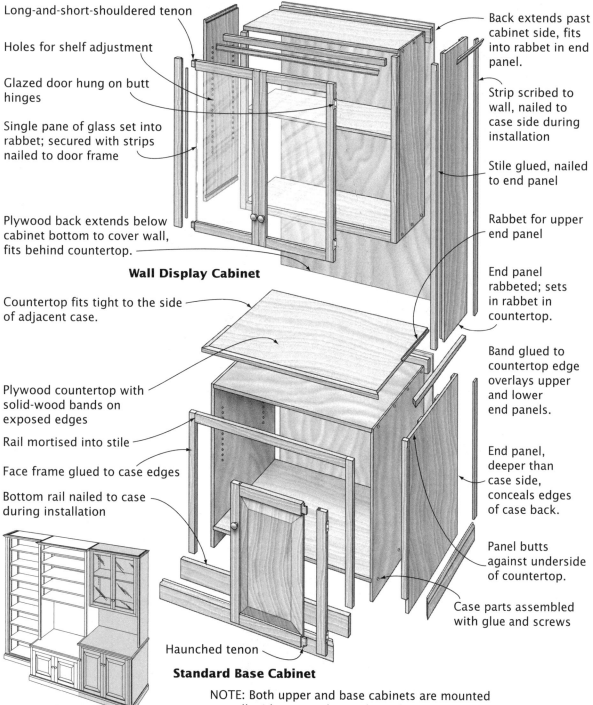

Long-and-short-shouldered tenon

Holes for shelf adjustment

Glazed door hung on butt hinges

Single pane of glass set into rabbet; secured with strips nailed to door frame

Plywood back extends below cabinet bottom to cover wall, fits behind countertop.

Wall Display Cabinet

Countertop fits tight to the side of adjacent case.

Plywood countertop with solid-wood bands on exposed edges

Rail mortised into stile

Face frame glued to case edges

Bottom rail nailed to case during installation

Back extends past cabinet side, fits into rabbet in end panel.

Strip scribed to wall, nailed to case side during installation

Stile glued, nailed to end panel

Rabbet for upper end panel

End panel rabbeted; sets in rabbet in countertop.

Band glued to countertop edge overlays upper and lower end panels.

End panel, deeper than case side, conceals edges of case back.

Panel butts against underside of countertop.

Case parts assembled with glue and screws

Haunched tenon

Standard Base Cabinet

NOTE: Both upper and base cabinets are mounted to wall with screws driven through mounting cleat.

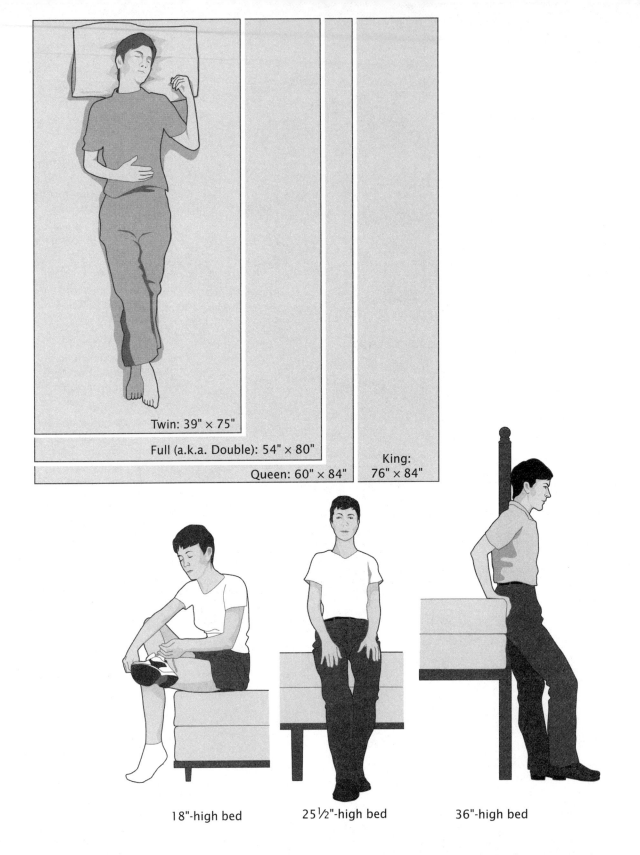

Twin: 39" × 75"

Full (a.k.a. Double): 54" × 80"

Queen: 60" × 84"

King: 76" × 84"

18"-high bed

25½"-high bed

36"-high bed

BEDS

Any bed, even a custom-made bed, begins with the mattress. Unless you travel the (expensive) route of custom-made bedding, you will have to work with the commonly available standard mattress sizes. And having settled on a mattress size, the bed designer must deal with its thickness and with how high it will lie.

TWIN: This is the smallest mattress for an adult that is commonly available. The name derives, of course, from the custom of using a pair of these beds in one bedroom.

FULL: For two adults, the smallest practical mattress size is the full or double. This size is not only wider, it is slightly longer than the twin. Some furniture designers regard this as the mattress with the best proportions.

QUEEN: Longer and wider than the full is the queen. For the big and tall, the queen-size mattress provides space for a full night's sleep.

KING: A full 16 inches wider (though no longer) than the queen, the king nearly doubles the twin's width.

Having dealt with the bed's footprint, we must next address its stature. Typically, a mattress–box spring combination is 14 to 16 inches thick. A lower profile can be had using a special mattress that needs no box spring. The lowest profile of all is offered by a futon.

The thickness of the mattress impacts the width of the side rails and the height of the headboard. The height of the mattress above the floor is a design choice, informed by the style of the bed—a formal four-poster would look odd if its mattress were too close to the floor—and the convenience of the occupants:

18-INCH-HIGH BED: This puts the mattress at about the height of a chair seat, making the bed a convenient station for tying your shoes. Children and people with limited mobility may find this level more to their liking.

24- TO-27-INCH-HIGH BED: Beds generally fall within this range and will feel familiar to most people.

36-INCH-HIGH BED: Colonial beds typically put the mattress at nose-bleed heights. That suits the look of formal rooms with tall furniture and high ceilings but may not suit you.

LOW-POST
BED

33⅝"

86½"

47½"

H ere is your basic bed. The fundamental form is here: four stout posts, one at each corner, supporting and joined by rails that support a mattress in some way. The design dictates the posts' girth and length and contour, the rails' thickness and depth, and whether or not there is any form of headboard and/or footboard incorporated into the structure.

The bed shown is based on an early-18th-century rope bed. The stresses on a rope bed's rails are different than those on rails supporting a modern boxspring and mattress, so they are very thick, as is the case here. To accommodate a modern box spring, L-shaped "bed irons" are screwed to the inner faces of the side rails. Where the side rails are thinner but deeper, slats may be used to support a box spring and mattress.

The height of the headboard varies. In this instance, the headboard is not very high; it wouldn't provide much support for someone who wanted to sit up to read in bed.

Another variable is whether or not the bed has a footboard. This bed does; and while it is lower than the headboard, it repeats the head-board's contour. The footboard keeps the bedclothes from sliding off the end, and it can provide a sense of enclosure. But it also prevents anyone from sitting on the bed's end.

DESIGN VARIATIONS The height of the bedposts and the positioning of the rails impact the form of the posts. In the case of the archetype bed, the posts are relatively short and the rails are relatively high off the floor, so the bedposts have as many turned features below the rails as above.

In the case of the colonial-style bed shown here, the posts are relatively high and the rails low. The bedpost profile thus focuses the eye on the section above the rails. (Low-post is a relative term, clearly. These posts are low in comparison to those on high-post beds; see pages 350–351.) The contemporary bed has simple, functional posts that make no particular statements either above or blow the rails.

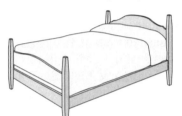

Contemporary-Style Bed

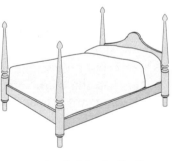

Colonial-Style Bed

PLANS

Day, Jeff. "Pennsylvania Low-Post Bed," *American Woodworker,* Vol. V, No. 1 (January/February 1989), pp. 16–22. Plans, including a detailed leg profile layout, for building the archetypal bed.

•

Warde, John, ed. "Double Bed," *Make It! Don't Buy It!* Emmaus, PA: Rodale Press, 1983. Hard-to-find book has plans for simple bed that uses an unusual half-dovetail mortise-and-tenon with a wedge to join side rails and end assemblies.

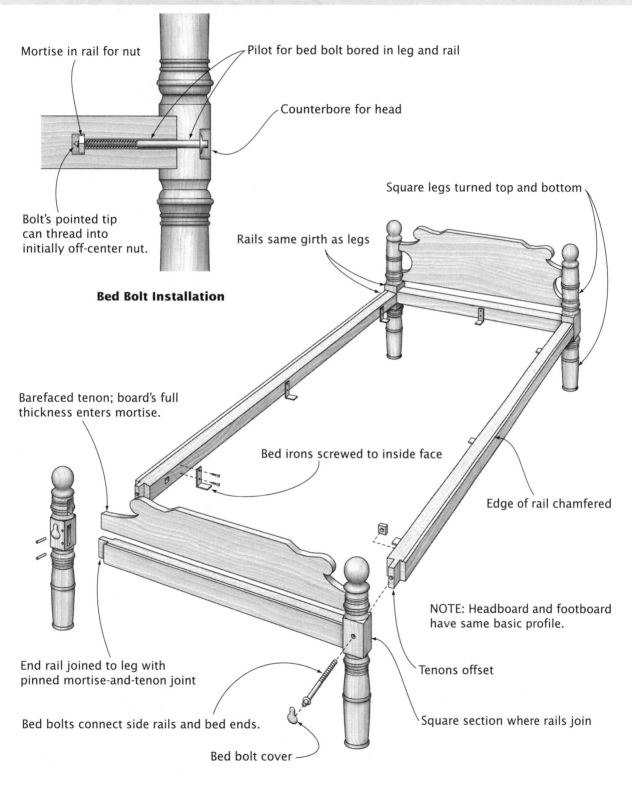

Mortise in rail for nut

Pilot for bed bolt bored in leg and rail

Counterbore for head

Bolt's pointed tip can thread into initially off-center nut.

Bed Bolt Installation

Square legs turned top and bottom

Rails same girth as legs

Barefaced tenon; board's full thickness enters mortise.

Bed irons screwed to inside face

Edge of rail chamfered

NOTE: Headboard and footboard have same basic profile.

End rail joined to leg with pinned mortise-and-tenon joint

Tenons offset

Bed bolts connect side rails and bed ends.

Square section where rails join

Bed bolt cover

HIGH-POST
BED

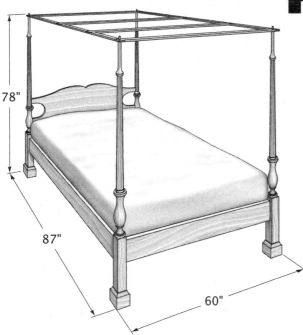

78"

87"

60"

Four-Post Bed, Poster Bed, Canopy Bed

> **DESIGN VARIATIONS** High-post beds followed the design preferences of the day. The Philadelphia High-Post Bedstead of the late 18th century had cabriole legs with ball-and-claw feet. The lack of ornamentation on the posts and headboard is a reflection less of taste than of the reality that they were covered up with fabric and bedding and would not be seen.
>
> Bedsteads for the less affluent were less covered with drapery and so more decorative in the woodwork itself, often including shapely urns, fluting, and carved spirals.

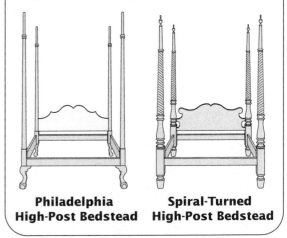

Philadelphia High-Post Bedstead   **Spiral-Turned High-Post Bedstead**

B ed basics have changed substantially in the last 200 years, yet the high-post bed still has a place in the bedroom (so long as the room isn't too small). Whether the decor is early-American or contemporary, the high-post bed fits.

To grasp how remarkable this is, consider that the reason for the 6- to 7-foot-tall posts and the canopy frame that topped them was to support tent-like draperies—heavy ones in winter to contain body heat, light ones in summer to allow air circulation but keep out the flies and mosquitoes. What the posts looked like was largely irrelevant, since they were shrouded in cloth. Consider, too, that the ropes that supported the mattress also held the bedstead together.

Nowadays, a high-post bed is held together with bolted joints. Remove the bolts, and the entire bed can be dismantled, right down to the component posts, rails, and headboard.

The rope that held the mattress high off the cold floors has given way to a box spring supported by deep but slender rails. And the rails usually are lowered so the mattress isn't 2 to 3 feet off the floor.

Best of all, the strong and graceful bedstead has come from behind the curtains.

PLANS

Dunbar, Michael. "High-Post Bed," *Federal Furniture*. Newtown, CT: The Taunton Press, 1986. Measured drawings of and construction notes for a Federal era bed and arched canopy, along with details on "roping a frame."

Gottshall, Franklin H. "Four-Poster Walnut Bed," *Masterpiece Furniture Making*. Harrisburg, PA: Stackpole Books, 1979. Spiral-turned, finial-topped 6-foot posts highlight this bed; good drawings, sketchy directions.

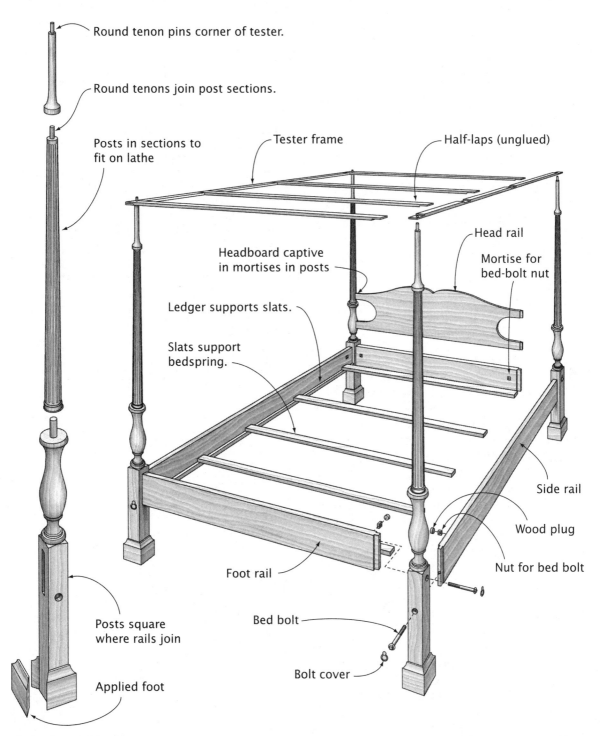

Round tenon pins corner of tester.

Round tenons join post sections.

Posts in sections to fit on lathe

Tester frame

Half-laps (unglued)

Headboard captive in mortises in posts

Head rail

Mortise for bed-bolt nut

Ledger supports slats.

Slats support bedspring.

Side rail

Wood plug

Nut for bed bolt

Foot rail

Posts square where rails join

Bed bolt

Applied foot

Bolt cover

Post Assembly

PENCIL-POST
BED

High-Post Bed, Field Bed

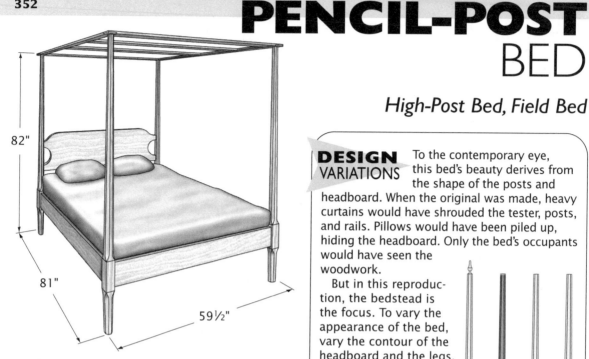

82"

81"

59½"

◢ **DESIGN**
VARIATIONS

To the contemporary eye, this bed's beauty derives from the shape of the posts and headboard. When the original was made, heavy curtains would have shrouded the tester, posts, and rails. Pillows would have been piled up, hiding the headboard. Only the bed's occupants would have seen the woodwork.

But in this reproduction, the bedstead is the focus. To vary the appearance of the bed, vary the contour of the headboard and the legs. Just a few of the many possibilities are shown.

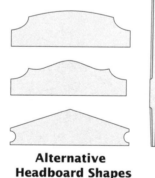

**Alternative
Headboard Shapes**

**Alternative
Post Shapes**

The pencil-post bed is a country version of the high-post bed. It had all the basic features of the high-post bed—mattress raised high above the cold, drafty floor, high posts to support a tester festooned with draperies. But the posts were simplified so they could be produced quickly, without the services of a turner and a long-bed lathe.

Pencil-post is a modern term, and the bed shown here is a contemporary reproduction that has been adapted for modern bedding and modern culture. To accept a box spring and mattress, the side and end rails have been reduced in thickness but increased in depth. They've also been lowered so that the top of the mattress isn't too far off the floor. The headboard has been raised so it will support pillows for someone sitting up and reading in bed (or watching TV).

The structure of the bed has been modified as well. The bed still comes completely apart, but the original would have been held together by the ropes used to support the mattress. In this version, bed bolts are used to join the rails to the posts. (You can imagine the difficulty of moving the assembled head end down a hallway.)

PLANS

Abram, Norm, with Tim Snyder. "Pencil-Post Bed," *Classics from The New Yankee Workshop.* Boston: Little, Brown, & Co., 1990. Thorough, well-illustrated how-I-built-it presentation. The bed is elegant; no tester.

●

Becksvoort, Christian H. "The Pencil-Post Bed," *The Best of Fine Woodworking: Traditional Furniture Projects.* Newtown, CT: The Taunton Press, 1991. Another elegant bed. Bed-building project includes plans for post-tapering jig.

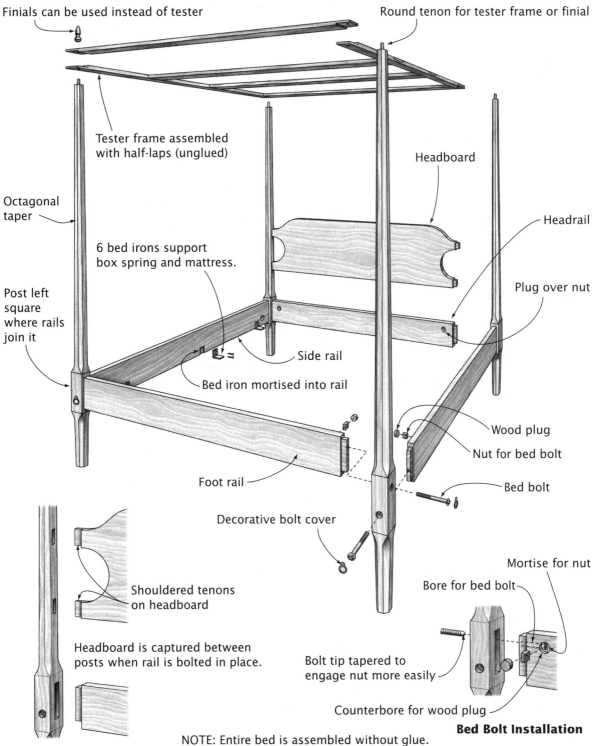

Finials can be used instead of tester

Round tenon for tester frame or finial

Tester frame assembled with half-laps (unglued)

Headboard

Octagonal taper

Headrail

6 bed irons support box spring and mattress.

Plug over nut

Post left square where rails join it

Side rail

Bed iron mortised into rail

Wood plug

Nut for bed bolt

Foot rail

Bed bolt

Decorative bolt cover

Mortise for nut

Bore for bed bolt

Shouldered tenons on headboard

Bolt tip tapered to engage nut more easily

Headboard is captured between posts when rail is bolted in place.

Counterbore for wood plug

Bed Bolt Installation

Headboard Joinery

NOTE: Entire bed is assembled without glue. Rails are bolted to posts. Tester is set in place.

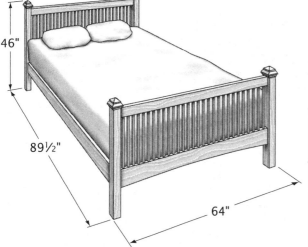

46"

89½"

64"

BANISTER
BED

Baluster Bed

Banister is a synonym for "baluster," meaning an upright support, such as for a handrail. When used as a term for a type of bed, it refers to beds that have balustrade-like structures in place of headboards and footboards.

The short posts, horizontal rails, and balusters that characterize the banister bed are pure style and decoration. Style and decoration have always been important in furniture design. As central heating, electric fans, window screens, and private bedrooms made heavily draped, tall-post beds unnecessary for privacy and warmth and insect-free sleep, furniture design could break off in new directions, and the banister bed was one of the results. The banister headboard won't deflect a draft; it will support pillows.

The style is handsome and well suited to modern homes. As the archetypal bed demonstrates, plain square balusters can do as much for a design as heavy ornamentation and sinuous curves, however graceful.

PLANS

"Contemporary Maple Bed," *Today's Woodworker,* August 1991. Middle-of-the-road, very rectilinear design, presented in plans with good drawings and how-to directions.

●

Cooper, Scott. "Making a Bedroom Suite," *American Woodworker.* August, 1993. Drawings and construction directions for a bed that is a handsome blend of banister and head/foot board.

DESIGN VARIATIONS The visible wood parts of a banister bed are all either vertical or horizontal lines— there are no broad surfaces. From a design point of view, these lines are potent elements for creating visual effect. For example, the very minor rearrangement of having the horizontal rail extend past the post instead of vice versa gives the second bed below a distinctly different appearance than the third.

Similarly, the curve in the outside edges of the posts of the first bed, while slight, give the bed a modern flair that makes the floating top rail quite at home. Grouping the balusters has a similarly high impact.

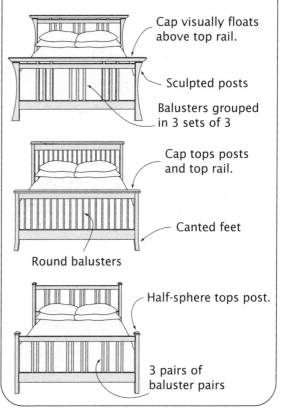

Cap visually floats above top rail.

Sculpted posts

Balusters grouped in 3 sets of 3

Cap tops posts and top rail.

Canted feet

Round balusters

Half-sphere tops post.

3 pairs of baluster pairs

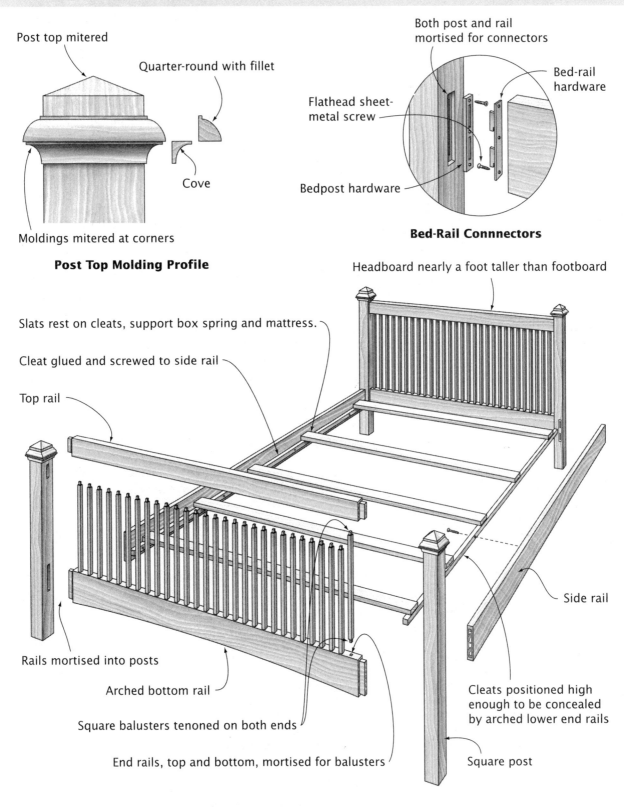

Post top mitered

Quarter-round with fillet

Moldings mitered at corners

Cove

Post Top Molding Profile

Both post and rail
mortised for connectors

Flathead sheet-
metal screw

Bedpost hardware

Bed-rail
hardware

Bed-Rail Connnectors

Headboard nearly a foot taller than footboard

Slats rest on cleats, support box spring and mattress.

Cleat glued and screwed to side rail

Top rail

Rails mortised into posts

Arched bottom rail

Square balusters tenoned on both ends

End rails, top and bottom, mortised for balusters

Side rail

Cleats positioned high
enough to be concealed
by arched lower end rails

Square post

SLEIGH
BED

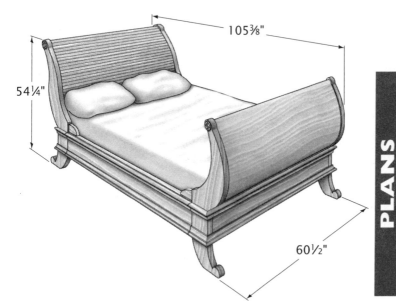

105⅜"

54¼"

60½"

PLANS

Sorenson, Randy. "Sleigh Bed," *American Woodworker*, No. 64 (February 1998), pp. 44-49. With slatted head and foot assemblies, a contemporary turn on the traditional form; good drawings and construction information.

•

Turner, William. "Building a Sleigh Bed," *Beds, and Bedroom Furniture: The Best of Fine Wookworking.* Newtown, CT: The Taunton Press, 1997. Building an extraordinary sleigh bed, with some excellent construction detail drawings but few dimensions; good jumping off point for an experienced woodworker.

The name sleigh bed should tell us a lot about these beds. At the time they first appeared, in the early 19th century, the archetypal horse-drawn sleigh was the transport of choice in snowy weather. With its curved dash and enveloping seat, the sleigh presented a dashing, modern appearance while at the same time providing practical protection and comfort.

The archetypal bed shown here has a curved-dash-like foot assembly, and an S-shaped head assembly that pretty closely resembles the contour of a sleigh's seat (and, as made, can serve as a seat-back for reading in bed).

Though a nearly 200-year-old form, this bed is made using some late-20th-century materials, such as bendable plywood. An early 19th-century woodworker would have coopered the cowls, then veneered them. Today's woodworker can build forms and glue-laminate several thicknesses of bendable plywood over them, perhaps using vacuum equipment to apply the necessary clamping pressure.

DESIGN VARIATIONS

The earliest sleigh beds were box-frame affairs, made very much like sleighs, with a "chassis" for the bedding set on feet. The head and foot assemblies were mounted onto this chassis, much like the box-frame bed at right. That example lacks the imposing presence of the best box-frame sleigh beds but like them is difficult to knock down for moving. (The archetype bed is designed to exhibit a box-frame appearance but have the relative portability of a post-and-rail bed construction.)

Eventually, cabinetmakers sought ways to exploit the form without investing as much work as curved panels required. A common shortcut was to capture flat frame-and-panel assemblies between sinuous posts. A modern device is the use of band-sawed curved slats instead of solid curved panels.

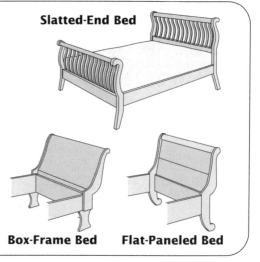

Slatted-End Bed

Box-Frame Bed   **Flat-Paneled Bed**

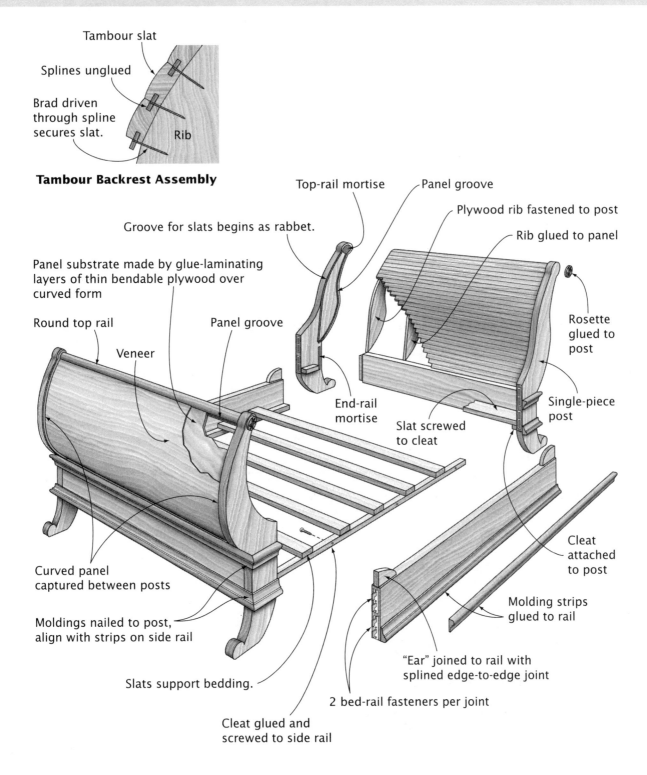

Tambour slat

Splines unglued

Brad driven through spline secures slat.

Rib

Tambour Backrest Assembly

Top-rail mortise

Panel groove

Plywood rib fastened to post

Rib glued to panel

Groove for slats begins as rabbet.

Panel substrate made by glue-laminating layers of thin bendable plywood over curved form

Round top rail

Panel groove

Veneer

Rosette glued to post

End-rail mortise

Slat screwed to cleat

Single-piece post

Curved panel captured between posts

Moldings nailed to post, align with strips on side rail

Cleat attached to post

Molding strips glued to rail

Slats support bedding.

"Ear" joined to rail with splined edge-to-edge joint

2 bed-rail fasteners per joint

Cleat glued and screwed to side rail

DAYBED

42"

44"

82½"

The daybed is a furniture form that has had its original use turned around in the latter half of the 20th century.

Historically, any piece of furniture that you would stretch out on during the day to rest or nap was a daybed. In other words, it was a chair or couch used as a bed. Today, however, it is a bed used as a couch.

The daybed shown here is typical of the contemporary form. In construction terms, it is very much a bed. The end assemblies are connected by side rails. Slats suspended between the side rails support a standard twin-size mattress and box spring. Standard bed-rail hardware allows the bed to be knocked down quickly and easily.

To transform this ordinary bed into a daybed, the backrest assembly is added. It is set on the appropriate side rail, then screwed to the posts and rail.

Festooned with pillows across the ends and back side, this piece can now serve comfortably as a couch. At night, with the extra pillows set aside, it is still a bed.

DESIGN VARIATIONS

The earliest daybed, back in medieval times, was simply a platform with a slanted headrest at one end.

By the beginning of the 18th century, the daybed had evolved into an 8-legged chair with a wildly elongated seat. The Queen Anne daybed shown is representative. More often than not, these daybeds were upholstered or had upholstered cushions. Today, this form is usually called a chaise longue or a chaise lounge.

In the Federal era, the daybed became more couchlike, but with a clear differentiation between the head and foot ends. As the Duncan Phyfe–designed example shows, these daybeds were upholstered furniture.

At around the same time, the French were building alcove beds, which served the same purpose but more closely resembled true beds. The ends were of equal height, and the bed was set against a wall. It is this form that survives today as the daybed.

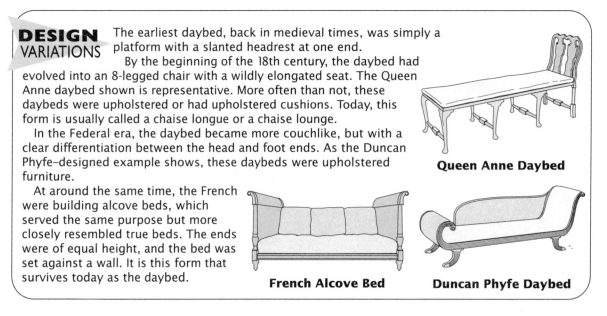

Queen Anne Daybed

French Alcove Bed

Duncan Phyfe Daybed

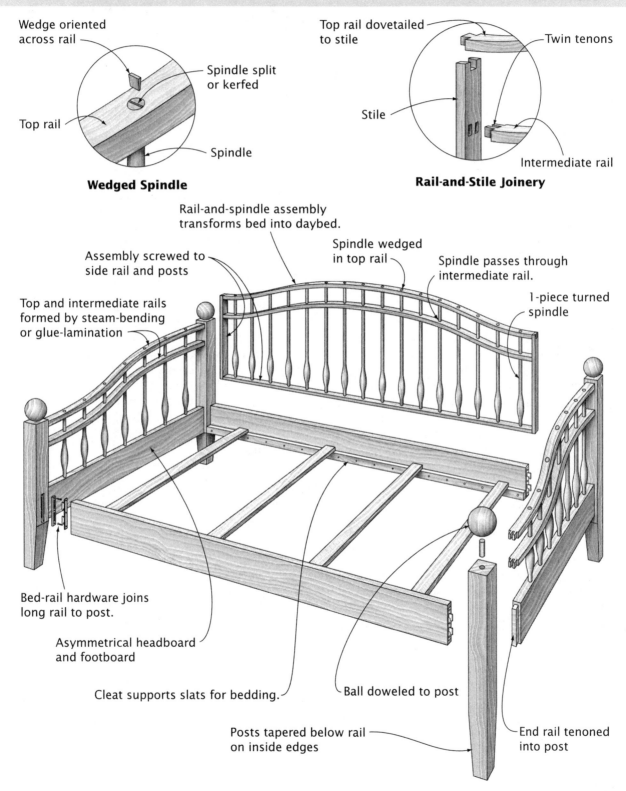

Wedged Spindle

Wedge oriented across rail

Spindle split or kerfed

Top rail

Spindle

Rail-and-Stile Joinery

Top rail dovetailed to stile

Twin tenons

Stile

Intermediate rail

Rail-and-spindle assembly transforms bed into daybed.

Spindle wedged in top rail

Spindle passes through intermediate rail.

1-piece turned spindle

Assembly screwed to side rail and posts

Top and intermediate rails formed by steam-bending or glue-lamination

Bed-rail hardware joins long rail to post.

Asymmetrical headboard and footboard

Cleat supports slats for bedding.

Ball doweled to post

End rail tenoned into post

Posts tapered below rail on inside edges

CAPTAIN'S
BED

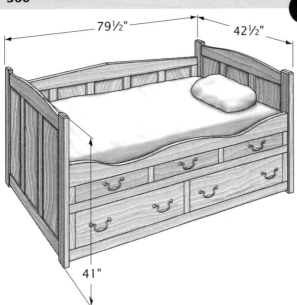

79½"   42½"

41"

PLANS

d'Epagnier, Arnold. "Designing a Captain's Bed," in *Beds and Bedroom Furniture: The Best of Fine Woodworking*. Newtown, CT: The Taunton Press, 1997. General design and construction guidelines for a queen-size captain's bed, but no project-specific dimensions or directions.

•

Watts, Simon. "Bed with Drawers," *Building a Houseful of Furniture*. Newtown, CT: The Taunton, Press, 1983. Good construction drawings of a very basic bed with 2 drawers.

To make use of every square inch of space on board ship, a captain's bed had drawers built in. For most landlubbers, drawers below the mattress equal a captain's bed.

But there's more to it. The true captain's bed was small (not queen-sized), created to fit tight to a bulkhead in a tiny cabin. Another nautical element was the bit of a lip along the front side, intended to keep the cap'n from

being tossed to the deck as his ship rolled and pitched on heavy seas.

The version shown meets all the criteria. It has a high back side, reminiscent of a daybed, and high ends, thereby creating its own alcove. Beneath the mattress are two huge drawers suspended on strong and easy-to-open ball-bearing slides. The apron along the front probably won't keep a slumberer from being tumbled out by an unexpected swell, but the wavelike contour of its top edge is nicely nautical.

DESIGN VARIATIONS Captain's bed designs have ranged from the spartan to the spiffy. The spartan model shown here is low, functional, and relatively easy to build. Its end panels can be basic frame-and-panel or even edge-banded plywood.

The chestlike bed is made with solid-wood or plywood panels. Arched cutouts form virtual posts in the assembled bed. Of course there are drawers below the bedding, a pair on each side.

If a high bed is acceptable, as it might be in a child's small bedroom, two or more tiers of drawers can be built into it, as shown. A step stool makes the bed accessible to even a youngster, while a bunklike guardrail prevents nocturnal tumbles to the floor.

Spartan Bed   **Chestlike Bed**   **High Child's Bed**

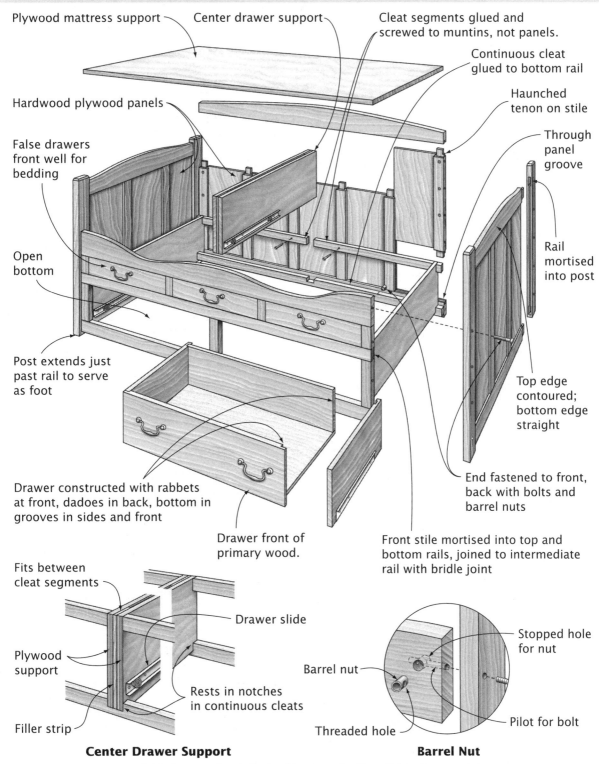

Plywood mattress support

Center drawer support

Cleat segments glued and screwed to muntins, not panels.

Continuous cleat glued to bottom rail

Hardwood plywood panels

Haunched tenon on stile

Through panel groove

False drawers front well for bedding

Rail mortised into post

Open bottom

Post extends just past rail to serve as foot

Top edge contoured; bottom edge straight

Drawer constructed with rabbets at front, dadoes in back, bottom in grooves in sides and front

End fastened to front, back with bolts and barrel nuts

Drawer front of primary wood.

Front stile mortised into top and bottom rails, joined to intermediate rail with bridle joint

Fits between cleat segments

Drawer slide

Stopped hole for nut

Plywood support

Barrel nut

Rests in notches in continuous cleats

Filler strip

Threaded hole

Pilot for bolt

Center Drawer Support

Barrel Nut

NOTE: Drawer depth limited by length of available drawer slides.

PLATFORM
BED

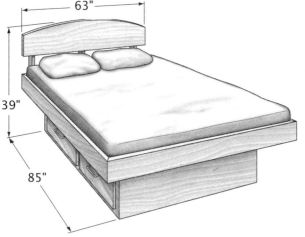

63"

39"

85"

A platform bed is just that, a horizontal flat surface, usually higher than the surrounding area, upon which to lay a mattress. In its baseline form, it is but a shallow step above a mattress on the floor.

The form that probably springs to mind is the platform supported on a slightly smaller frame or pedestal. The bed is raised above floor level, and a kickspace is provided so you don't jam your toes against the platform frame getting into or making up the bed. This is a big advantage over a low metal bed frame, because there aren't legs at the corners to stub your toes on.

A well designed platform can make it appear that the mattress and platform are floating several inches above the floor. A low profile is easy to achieve; when the mattress is 18 inches or so above the floor—about chair-seat height, in other words—it is a good seat when putting on stockings or shoes.

In the form shown here, storage is provided by housing drawers in the pedestal supporting the platform. This can be a practical approach in a small bedroom, where the use of every square inch of floor space must be maximized. It generally requires a compromise between the mattress height that's acceptable and the capaciousness of the drawers. The deeper the drawers, the higher the bed must be. In addition, the overhang can limit your access to the drawers.

DESIGN VARIATIONS

Bedding has particular significance for platform bed design. Shown below are platform beds—sans drawer space—designed for a mattress only and for a mattress and box spring. The bed frames are dramatically different in depth.

The mattress-only bed has the sleek, low profile that one associates with platform beds, while the other looks bloated. The trade-offs are more than visual. A box spring functions as the mattress's shock absorber, giving it a little more bounce and lengthening its life. Without a box spring, the mattress can compress and wear out faster.

Single Bed

Bed with Mattress and Box Spring

PLANS

"Platform Bed," *Cabinets and Built-Ins: 26 Custom Storage Projects.* Upper Saddle River, NJ: Creative Homeowner Press, 1996. Concise, nicely illustrated plans for a platform bed with storage drawers.

•

Watts, Simon. "Platform Bed," *Building a Houseful of Furniture.* Newtown, CT: The Taunton Press, 1983. Plans for the quintessential platform bed; good plan and elevation drawings, helpful text, but no specific step-by-step.

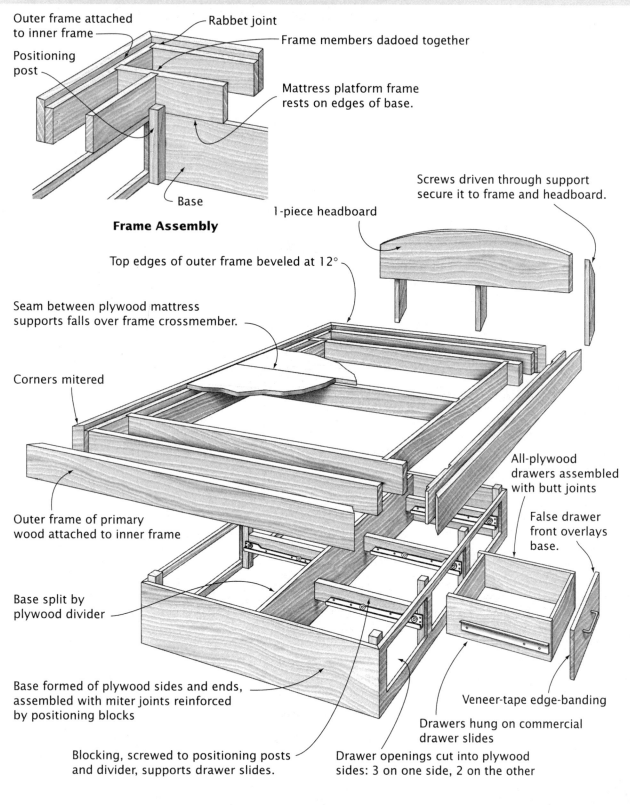

Outer frame attached to inner frame

Positioning post

Rabbet joint

Frame members dadoed together

Mattress platform frame rests on edges of base.

Base

Frame Assembly

1-piece headboard

Screws driven through support secure it to frame and headboard.

Top edges of outer frame beveled at 12°

Seam between plywood mattress supports falls over frame crossmember.

Corners mitered

All-plywood drawers assembled with butt joints

Outer frame of primary wood attached to inner frame

False drawer front overlays base.

Base split by plywood divider

Base formed of plywood sides and ends, assembled with miter joints reinforced by positioning blocks

Veneer-tape edge-banding

Blocking, screwed to positioning posts and divider, supports drawer slides.

Drawers hung on commercial drawer slides

Drawer openings cut into plywood sides: 3 on one side, 2 on the other

HEADBOARD

Dimensions shown on illustration: 102", 19¾", 14", 18", 16"

Tradition says a mattress supported by a post-and-rail bedstead constitutes "a bed." The contemporary reality is that, as often as not, a bed is no more than a mattress and box spring set 6 to 8 inches off the floor on a skimpy metal bed frame.

Clinging to tradition, many a contemporary bed on a metal frame is equipped with a vestigial headboard. It's either perched on posts bolted to the frame or attached to the wall against which the mattress and frame are pushed. The version presented here as archetypal is wall-mounted. It incorporates small night tables. The design is clean and contemporary-looking.

Such a headboard, of course, is more than merely a bow to tradition; the practical reasons that favor having a headboard transcend fashion. Wall-mounting the headboard and night stands adds to the unit's function: It expedites room cleanup. When the bed is pulled away from the wall, it is clear of the headboard, so you have unobstructed access to make up the bed. The night tables are up off the floor, so it's easy to vacuum the floor.

DESIGN VARIATIONS

The tradition of the metal bed-frame headboard is neither long nor storied. Since the form itself is strictly contemporary, that style is certainly more appropriate for the headboard than any other. As a practical matter, the headboard cannot be too elaborate if it is to be secured by a mounting point 8 inches off the floor. Here the archetype headboard has been adapted by extending its stiles into posts.

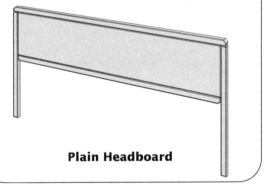

Plain Headboard

PLANS

Watts, Simon. "Headboard with Night Tables," *Building a Houseful of Furniture.* Newtown, CT: The Taunton Press, 1983. Construction drawings and construction guidelines for a "Danish modern"–looking (very '50s) wall-mounted headboard.

"Headboard: A Head Above the Rest," *Woodsmith,* No. 34 (July/August 1984), pp. 10–12. Detailed drawings and construction directions for a contemporary-looking headboard on posts.

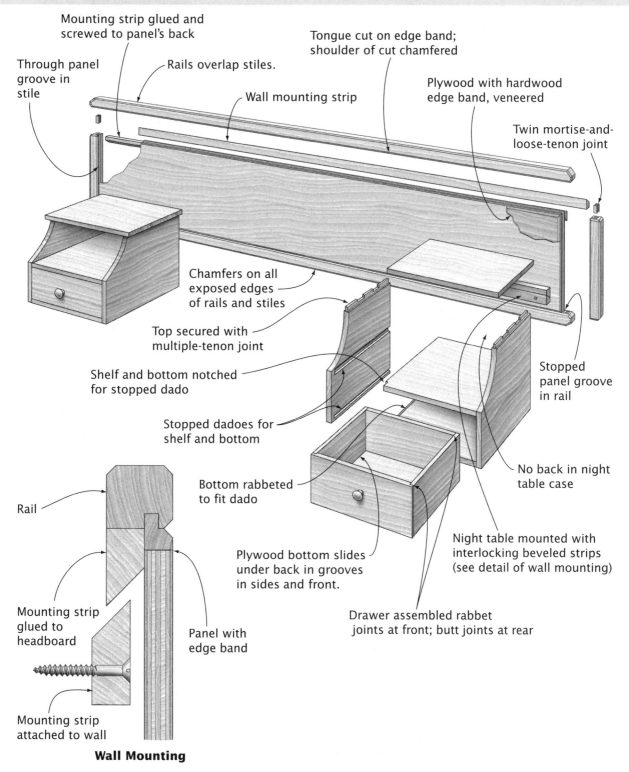

Mounting strip glued and screwed to panel's back

Through panel groove in stile

Rails overlap stiles.

Tongue cut on edge band; shoulder of cut chamfered

Wall mounting strip

Plywood with hardwood edge band, veneered

Twin mortise-and-loose-tenon joint

Chamfers on all exposed edges of rails and stiles

Top secured with multiple-tenon joint

Shelf and bottom notched for stopped dado

Stopped dadoes for shelf and bottom

Bottom rabbeted to fit dado

Stopped panel groove in rail

No back in night table case

Night table mounted with interlocking beveled strips (see detail of wall mounting)

Plywood bottom slides under back in grooves in sides and front.

Drawer assembled rabbet joints at front; butt joints at rear

Rail

Mounting strip glued to headboard

Panel with edge band

Mounting strip attached to wall

Wall Mounting

BUNK
BEDS

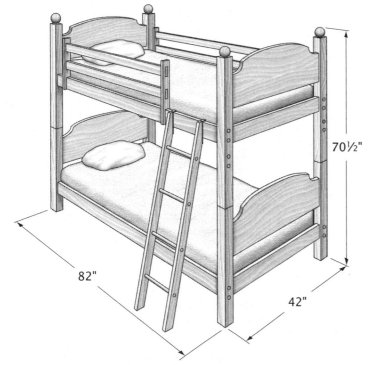

70½"

82"

42"

B unk beds conjure up memories of summer camp or Army boot camp. To pack more kids (or shaved-headed trainees) into a given space, the beds were stacked two high, doubling the sleeping space without having increased the room (or tent) size.

In the small house, too, bunk beds can be a boon. How else would you house two kids in a small bedroom? But the metal cots we slept on in camp are pretty tacky for the home environment.

The bunks shown here are both attractive and flexible. They can be set up side-by-side as a pair of twin beds, or one atop the other as a set of bunks.

Many bunk beds are scaled for the "single" mattress, which is not a standard size. The bunks shown are scaled for standard twin-size mattresses and box springs.

PLANS

"Kid's Single Bed" and "Bunk Bed," *Woodsmith*, No. 38, pp. 12–19. Illustrated construction directions for contemporary bunk beds, including storage drawers under the lower bunk.

•

Watts, Simon. "Bunk Beds," *Building a Houseful of Furniture*. Newtown, CT: The Taunton Press, 1983. Plans for bunks designed and built for a boarding school; thus, a tested, durable design.

DESIGN VARIATIONS There's more than one way to build bunk beds. Shown below are two alternative designs. Both use only a mattress, supporting it on a plywood platform.

In one, the bunks are just that. They can't be configured as twin beds. The joinery is direct—the rails overlay the posts and are screwed in place—but the construction is sturdy.

In the other, the upper and lower bunks are identical and can used as individual beds. To transform one of the beds into the upper bunk, you turn it over.

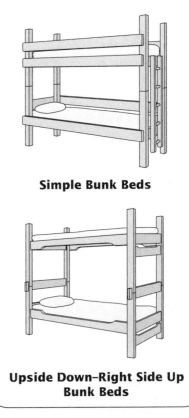

Simple Bunk Beds

Upside Down–Right Side Up Bunk Beds

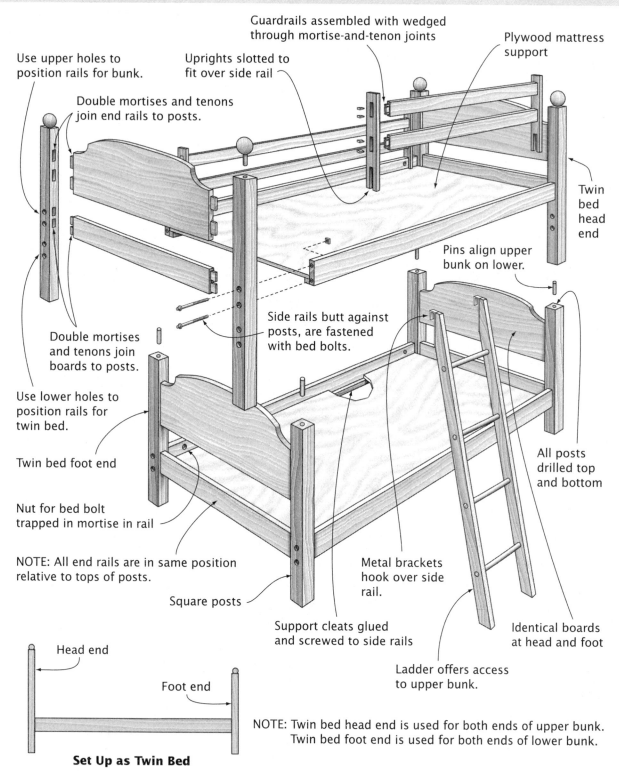

Guardrails assembled with wedged through mortise-and-tenon joints

Uprights slotted to fit over side rail

Plywood mattress support

Use upper holes to position rails for bunk.

Double mortises and tenons join end rails to posts.

Twin bed head end

Pins align upper bunk on lower.

Double mortises and tenons join boards to posts.

Side rails butt against posts, are fastened with bed bolts.

Use lower holes to position rails for twin bed.

Twin bed foot end

All posts drilled top and bottom

Nut for bed bolt trapped in mortise in rail

NOTE: All end rails are in same position relative to tops of posts.

Square posts

Metal brackets hook over side rail.

Identical boards at head and foot

Support cleats glued and screwed to side rails

Ladder offers access to upper bunk.

Head end

Foot end

NOTE: Twin bed head end is used for both ends of upper bunk. Twin bed foot end is used for both ends of lower bunk.

Set Up as Twin Bed